THE SEVENTEENTH CENTURY

THE SEVENTEENTH CENTURY

Sir George Clark

SECOND EDITION

OXFORD UNIVERSITY PRESS

LONDON OXFORD NEW YORK

OXFORD UNIVERSITY PRESS

Oxford London New York
Glasgow Toronto Melbourne Wellington
Cape Town Salisbury Ibadan Nairobi Lusaka Addis Ababa
Bombay Calcutta Madras Karachi Lahore Dacca
Kuala Lumpur Hong Kong Tokyo

First published by the Clarendon Press, 1929
Second edition published, 1947
First issued as an Oxford University Press paperback, 1961
This reprint, 1969

Printed in the United States of America

PREFACE TO THE SECOND EDITION

In this edition I have corrected a number of mistakes and added a good deal of new matter. In several places I have materially changed the argument and its conclusions.

G. N. C.

Cambridge
3 September 1945

FROM THE PREFACE TO THE FIRST EDITION

The foot-notes in this book have been kept down to a minimum. . . . It has not been possible to refer to all the evidence which has been used. . . . Some of the books to which a general reference is given have been drawn upon for other pages where they are not specifically mentioned.

Had it not been for the restriction of foot-notes, I should have wished in many places to acknowledge the gifts of ideas and information which have been made me by my friends, and especially by my colleagues at Oriel and the Fellows and former Fellows of my other colleges of Balliol and All Souls. Several of these have also done me the great kindness of reading portions of the book at different stages of its growth. Mr. W. D. Ross has given me valuable advice on chapters xiii–xv, Mr. Keith Feiling on chapters v–xii, the Rev. J. W. C. Wand on chapter xviii, and Mr. A. L. Rowse on chapters i–iv. Mr. B. H. Sumner generously undertook the labour of reading the whole book in proof. To all these I offer my very sincere thanks, and most of all to my wife, who has helped me with the book constantly and in all manner of ways.

G. N. C.

Oxford
14 January 1929

CONTENTS

MAPS

I
INTRODUCTORY

SOMEWHERE about the middle of the seventeenth century European life was so completely transformed in many of its aspects that we commonly think of this as one of the great watersheds of modern history, comparable with the Renaissance or the Reformation or the French Revolution. For this transition, indeed, we have no single name that we can write with capital letters, but we recognize a change of atmosphere between the earlier part of the century and the later, a change accompanied by storms. The Puritan Revolution and the Civil War made the sharpest break there has ever been in the continuity of English history. Almost simultaneously half a dozen European countries passed through a revolutionary period, and by no mere coincidence.[1] These revolutions differed as much in their results as in their circumstances and causes; in some countries they left behind them absolute monarchies, in others capable republican or parliamentary governments; but everywhere the change from the old world to the new was somehow the same. Everywhere it resembled, more or less, the movement in France from the sanguinary, if romantic, days of Henri Quatre and Richelieu and the Three Musketeers to the sober reign of enlightenment, when fallen ministers no longer perished on the scaffold but retired to their country houses, when violence was at least disguised by polished manners, and when the sun-king Louis XIV shone over the arts and letters of a new Augustan age. About the same time there were changes in almost every sphere. Within a few years of the execution of Charles I and the Peace of Westphalia, the long economic process of the price-revolution, through which the wealth of Europe had expanded, came to an end, to be followed by a new phase of restriction and new commercial conflicts between states. After two centuries of advance there was a pause in geographical discovery and in colonization. In the realm of

[1] See the comparative study of the late R. B. Merriman, *Six Contemporaneous Revolutions* (1938).

thought Galileo was censured at the beginning of the century, and Newton idolized at the end.

It is not difficult to heap these things together and to treat them all as manifestations of some governing principle of history, such as the growth of the spirit of rationalism, or the rise of capitalism. It may even be illuminating to use such startling phrases as 'baroque mathematics' or 'Cartesian economics'. To say that the mercantile system, the rise of standing armies, the discovery of the differential calculus, and the architecture of Sir Christopher Wren were all connected is true, and it is a warning against the narrowness of the specialist who treats economic history or military history, or the history of science or architecture as a self-contained whole, intelligible by itself. But a historian who wishes to carve the meat of reality at the joints will not be satisfied with a vague perception that all these things are connected: he will investigate how they are connected, and how closely. The purpose of this book is to examine some of the more important activities of the seventeenth century, distinguishing their mutual relations and their places in the great transition. It does not aim at covering the whole ground. For one reason or another it omits some subjects no less important than those that it includes, such as agriculture, the family and the position of women, music, much of the history of law. The arrangement is not rigidly systematic; for instance, the subjects overlap at many points. Nor, needless to say, does the book keep strictly to the limits of the chronological century. For some subjects it goes back into the sixteenth century or earlier and for others forward into the eighteenth, farther for some and less far for others, trying to characterize real movements without smudging the points of time.

It would not be misleading to say that the book is about European civilization in the seventeenth century, but it would be an anachronism. No one who was living then would have understood exactly what was meant by this statement or by its equivalent in any other language. No one talked then about European civilization, and few about the seventeenth century: these phrases came into common use later and in consequence of changes in ideas. For us it is an everyday matter to think of the past as divided into lengths of a hundred years, perhaps each with a character of its own. In England this habit was already coming in, and in the year 1700 Dryden's *Secular Masque* was performed, with its disillusioned lines:

All, all of a piece throughout:
(to *Diana*) Thy chase had a beast in view;
(to *Mars*) Thy wars brought nothing about;
(to *Venus*) Thy lovers were all untrue.
'Tis well an old age is out
And time to begin a new.

But even in England this way of thinking was still exceptional, and in other countries it does not seem to have progressed as far as it had done here.

If people did not think of the seventeenth century as we think of the twentieth, or as some of the contemporaries of Dr. Johnson thought of the eighteenth, they had at any rate a clear conception of European civilization. The English word 'civilization' had indeed not yet been coined, nor had its nearest equivalents in other languages; but the process of 'civilizing' was so described; its product was sometimes called 'civility', and 'civilized' men were contrasted with savages and barbarians. The idea had its root in this contrast, and it had long been a part of the common stock of thought. The European conquerors of America not only carried with them the crusading tradition of true religion opposed to idolatry, but were conscious of their superiority in the warlike and industrial arts, and believed that they had a mission to impose law and peace. Throughout the seventeenth century there were men, as there are still, who never doubted that their own civilization was the only civilization. This belief did not always take a militant form. There is a pacific version of it in a fragmentary letter written in 1696 by an English business man:

'To suppose the trade of the world can be driven by any one nation how great so ever is a very great piece of ignorance, all monopolies, restraints on trade to companies exclusive of all others are narrow thoughts that spring up in narrow souls and

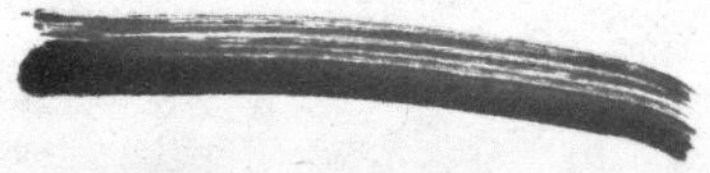

contradict the great design of God Almighty which is to civilize the whole race of mankind, to spread, trade, commerce, arts and manufactures and by them Christianity from Pole to Pole round the whole globe of earth, and therefore I am sure God will blast all those designs that are contrary to his, and ruine those nations and companys that would ingross his blessings, and joyne with the Devil to prevent or at least retard the civilising the. . . .'[1]

At this point the manuscript breaks off, and the remainder of the breathless sentence has disappeared.

Even when it was written it would have seemed to many people old-fashioned and provincial, for the idea of civilization, on the one hand Christian and on the other hand material, was giving way before the idea of a European civilization, one among others in the succession of time and one among others on the surface of the earth. One strand in the traditional idea of civilization had been that which linked it with ancient Greece and Rome, and one way in which the men of the period expressed their sense of superiority was to copy the language and the sentiments of the ancients.

A Roman Soul is bent on higher Views:
To civilize the rude unpolish'd World
And lay it under the Restraint of Laws;
To make Man mild and sociable to Man;
To cultivate the wild, licentious Savage
With Wisdom, Discipline and lib'ral Arts,
Th' Embellishments of Life: Virtues like these
Make Human Nature shine, reform the Soul,
And break our fierce Barbarians into Men.[2]

But the Roman character is assumed the more confidently in these lines because by this time it was generally allowed that the new age had a greatness of its own, comparable with that of the ancient world but different. A long literary controversy on the rival merits of the ancients and the moderns had ended with a complacent estimate at least of the modern sciences and arts.[3] And the current attitude to civilization had changed in many other things besides this diminished reverence for its

[1] Edmund Bohun of Ipswich in a letter to John Cary of Bristol, 2/12 January 1695/6 in Brit. Mus. Add. MS. 5540, fos. 56 ff.

[2] Addison, *Cato* (1713), Act I, sc. iv.

[3] See below, pp. 285–6.

predecessors. From the first serious studies of the American Indians by Franciscan and Jesuit missionaries there had gradually developed a respect for what was good in their ways of life, until in the late seventeenth century primitive men as such seemed to have virtues of their own. Political theorists took a favourable view of the state of nature, 'when wild in the woods the noble savage ran'.[1] Even Addison, after the lines we have quoted, allowed an impenitent barbarian to retort:

> What are these wondrous civilizing Arts,
> This *Roman* Polish, and this smooth Behaviour,
> That render Man thus tractable and tame?
> Are they not only to disguise our Passions . . .
> In short, to change us into other Creatures
> Than what our Nature and the Gods designed us?

There was a nascent scepticism about the claims of civilization, and at the same time those claims were stated more moderately and more maturely.

That civilization itself was differently viewed resulted partly from a changed geographical perspective. Although at the beginning of the century political writers often wrote of the Christian world as the unity to which they belonged, they had little to do with the old Christian communities of Asia and Africa, and they began to speak of their distinctive institutions, principles, and habits as European. Grotius, for instance, wrote that rules like that against poisoned arrows were not universal but were observed by the European nations.[2] In the time of Louis XIV all parties wrote officially of Europe as a political entity: his opponents gave battle in the name of the liberties of Europe, and Louis from time to time 'jugea à propos de donner la paix à l'Europe'.[3] This Europe was neither a definite nor even an unvarying area. The geographers drew its boundary not, as we do, at the Urals but, as the ancient Greeks did, at the River Don; but

[1] See Sir John Myres's valuable article, 'The Influence of Anthropology on the Course of Political Science', in *University of California Studies in History*, vol. iv, no. 1 (1916).

[2] *De Jure Belli et Pacis* (1625), III. IV. xvi. 1; III. VI. iii. 1.

[3] Duguay-Trouin, *Mémoires* (1730), 'Année 1697'.

wherever the geographical continent was supposed to end, two great states, the Russian and the Turkish, were both European and Asiatic. Turkey and its North African dependencies were nominally outside the European political system, but in practice they participated in it, and more fully as time went on. One of the most momentous changes of the century was the effacement of differences between Russia and the countries of the West, culminating in the earthquake of Peter the Great; and the line separating Russia from the West had never been so sharp as the line between Christendom and Islam. Nevertheless, though its extent was never fixed, western and central Europe was the territory of a common tradition of religion, government, and culture. Within it intercourse of all kinds was comparatively easy: the structure of classes, legal relations, economic organization, the arts and sciences were sufficiently alike to mark off this region from the rest of the world.

Its intercourse with the East had never been completely interrupted since the crusading days, and in the seventeenth century it entered on one of its most stimulating periods. The china-makers of Delft took their patterns from Oriental porcelain. Indian printed calicoes were imitated on the banks of the Wandle and the Seine. The names of china and calico themselves are reminders of this. So are other names like 'chintz' which is Indian, 'tea' from the Chinese, 'gingham' and 'gong' from the Malay, all of which came in at this time. When he was at war with France, King Charles II tried to introduce Persian costume in place of French fashions at his court:[1] the attempt was a failure, but it was a sign of the times. Not long afterwards artificers in France and England were imitating Chinese and Japanese lacquer, dyeing, colour-schemes.[2] In the fine arts it was not so easy to graft Eastern on to Western ways; but the curiosity of the West was aroused. There were Chinese portraits in Holland in the fifteen-nineties; Rembrandt copied Mogul drawings.

In literature curiosity was not only aroused: it was richly gratified. In the seventeenth century Oriental studies in the

[1] Evelyn, *Diary*, 18 October 1666.

[2] See A. Reichwein, *Europe and China* (1925).

spheres of language and history began to flourish in England, France, and Holland. In 1704 Galland's French translation of the *Arabian Nights* suddenly enriched the imagination of the West with a new treasury of magic and humour. The East became romantic. But before this there had been a deeper change among the leaders of thought. Among various impulses to Oriental studies in the universities the strongest was the relevance of the Semitic languages to Biblical studies. Some of the leading Arabic texts were printed. The framework of Islamic history began to be known, and more than the framework. At the same time Chinese thought and Chinese society were held up to veneration. Here again the change, long prepared, became noticeable about the middle of the century. Catholic missionaries had long since recognized in many parts of the world that the rites of the heathen were at any rate religious, and Catholicism was better able than Protestantism to appreciate the positive value either of primitive or of Oriental religions.[1] The great English scientist Robert Boyle, who was in many ways typical of the transitional period, knew what a studious man who was also a director of the East India Company could learn, and he found much to admire in the arts and skill of the East. He wrote about 'the most civilized nations of the world (such as anciently the Greeks and Romans and now the Chineses and East Indians)'.[2] But he was a zealous supporter of Protestant missions and he did not include either Islam or Confucianism in the civilization that he praised. Within a very short time both of them were influencing the thought of Englishmen even more than of continental Catholics.

In Oxford in the last thirty years of the seventeenth century two editions were published of a medieval Arabic fable which became famous under the name of *Philosophus Autodidactus*. It is the story of a man who was brought up from babyhood on an island where there was no other human being. He discovered for himself everything of importance in science

[1] For the catholic and protestant views of the natural man, and for some other aspects of religious thought, see Sir Herbert Grierson, *Cross-Currents in Seventeenth Century Literature* (1929).

[2] *Works*, ed. Birch, iii (1744), 409.

and philosophy and theology. Nowadays this intellectual jungle-book is interesting as an example of the influence of Greek thought among the mystics of Mohammedan Spain; but in the seventeenth century it aroused disturbing reflections. In spite of the disparaging comments of its Anglican translator,[1] it impressed some people with the genuineness of non-Christian 'enthusiasm', and others with the agreement of unrevealed religion in East and West. This latter conclusion was drawn about the same time even from the less likely source of the Chinese classics. In 1687 a Latin translation of the *Analects* of Confucius was published: together with the works of travellers and some other translations it enabled many people to judge the Chinese doctrines for themselves. Thus in diverse ways the study of Oriental literature encouraged the tendency, to which science and many other factors had contributed, to seek for a generalized natural religion behind the diversity of creeds.

When religion was still thought of as an element in civilization, it was not uncommonly a rational and ethical rather than a 'mysterious' religion; but the belief was still prevalent that western civilization was Christian, in the sense that 'no Community ever was or can be maintain'd, but upon a Basis of Religion' the 'Cement of Society'.[2] There were new secular philosophies of public and private morality, as indeed there had for a long time past been codes of honour, which were either independent of Christianity or only loosely attached to it. Nevertheless it was obvious that, as a mere matter of fact, society was based on religion in a narrower sense. If we ask how it was that European society not merely survived through the shameless dishonesty, greed, ambition, hatred, cruelty, and hypocrisy of that age, but actually produced so much that was generous and noble, it is not enough to answer that there were 'operative ideals' of justice, truth and humanity. There were few who could justify such principles

[1] Simon Ockley. He rendered the author's name (Abū Bakr ibn al Tufail, al Ishbīlī) as Abu Jaafar, and gave the book the title *The Improvement of Human Reason*: it was published in 1708.

[2] Richard Bentley, *The Folly and Unreasonableness of Atheism* (Boyle Lectures of 1692), 4th ed. (1699), p. 31.

by speculating on morality in the abstract, or by rationally calculating social advantages, and they lived among millions for whom there was no effective morality except the precepts of a religion ruling by supernatural sanctions through elaborately systematized beliefs and powerful institutions. At every point where men were likely to revert to savagery and barbarism, and at many of the points where the natural man was likely to fall short of his best, religion, successfully or unsuccessfully, came to the rescue. The witness in the law-courts took an oath. So did the soldier, the statesman, the judge, the king. Parliaments, armies, and fleets, trading-posts, hospitals and colleges had their chaplains and their prayers. These were not mere survivals; it was impossible to carry on the world's work without them.

There had never been a unity of Christendom secure against heresies and schisms, and since the Reformation sceptics or sectaries had questioned or rejected every article of belief. Every ecclesiastical revolution had reacted on the affairs of states. The relations of the ecclesiastical and the secular authorities had altered everywhere, but very differently in different places. The international authority of the Papacy was receding at a time when the separate states themselves were growing less and less alike. For a thousand years there had been a multitude of them, of various shapes and sizes and characters; all the time they had been coalescing or dividing, each succeeding or failing in the struggle to perpetuate its individual existence. They were not indeed isolated and self-contained; their multiplicity itself made it impossible for them to be so. Statesmen, ecclesiastics, soldiers, and scholars transferred their allegiance from one state to another. The smaller a state was, the more cosmopolitan it had to be. A German duke could not govern his petty principality without engaging officials from the other side of his frontier, and the knights of St. John had to recruit the garrison of Malta from the Catholic gentry of all Europe. Small states, either attracted by the success and efficiency of their greater neighbours or intimidated into compliance with their demands, were more often imitative than eccentric. Thus there were broad differences of type, as for instance between the parliamentary or republican states and the absolute monarchies. But every state exerted itself to maintain some character of its own.

Compared with the states of the present day those of the seventeenth century had far less effective means at their disposal for moulding a community; but they all used such resources as they had. They banished or excluded persons whom they thought undesirable: much of the history of the century revolved, as we shall see, round the opening and shutting of doors to alien merchants or refugees, as policy in economic or other matters swung between liberalism and exclusion. Sometimes a state drove out or repressed some group of its own citizens who sympathized with an enemy or criticized an 'ideology' that served the ends of defence or aggression. They all 'conditioned' their citizens by education, by their control of information, by propaganda, as well as by the regular discipline of law. Their intelligence services and their police were rudimentary, but they were ruthless. Even the most tolerant governments printed news-sheets, subsidized pamphleteers, and tuned the pulpits.

Their immediate aims in doing all this were very complex and varied from state to state. They were all territorial states, claiming authority over the inhabitants of a geographical area. This meant that each community had an economic and 'cultural' basis, and had to use one or more of the local languages for common purposes. Each had as a substratum more or less of the historic and 'racial' elements which together make up nationality.[1] Racialism, linguistic policy, national pride and animosities played a part in history, but nowhere so great a part as they have since come to play. They were complicated and obscured by the personal character of feudal loyalties and by monarchies which were often dynastic and not identified with national feelings. Above all they were confusingly interpenetrated by religion. Languages and nationalities were seldom oppressed unless they were those of religious dissidents. The extreme case of racial persecution was that of Spain, from which the Jews and the

[1] For some observations on races and languages see the Appendix p. 365, and also p. 189 below.

Moriscoes were expelled. It was due to many factors, such as the recent conquest of alien elements, in which Spain was unlike any other country, and the real danger that hostile states might work on their discontent; but the religious motive was decisive in it, and at the heart of the system of censorship and absolute government was the Inquisition. At the other extreme, at the end of the seventeenth century, were England and Holland, where no European man was excluded on account of his race, where speech and worship were free and where government was constitutional. But even these states, though they admitted dissidents and aliens to live in their borders, drew a narrower line round the *pays légal* of the fully privileged who alone were allowed to share, even indirectly, in government. They discriminated between the active and the passive citizens on various grounds, not least according to standards of property; but the line was partly religious. Here too the Jews were excluded from political functions and from some kinds of economic activity and educational opportunity. So were Catholics and some Protestant sectaries.

Even the diversity of the states did not destroy the underlying unity of the civilization. It was like a language which a people inherits from remote antiquity, akin to some other languages, enriched by borrowings, polished by intentional reforms, but full of irregularities and idioms, of the relics of successful and unsuccessful experiments. Like a language it was a link between individual men and women; it had its standards of usage, and it had a 'genius', a quality and expressiveness of its own which made people proud of it and happy to conform to it. A language may be set out in books, such as grammars and dictionaries and histories. No one uses all the words in the dictionary and all the forms in the grammar, let alone uses them all correctly, and the language lives not in these books but in the minds of men, women, and children, in their prose and poetry, their oratory, their conversation, and their song, in dialect and jargon and slang. So the civilization of the seventeenth century was alive in the thoughts and acts of human beings, but we may reasonably attempt to analyse its vocabulary and its grammar.

FRONTIERS OF WESTERN AND CENTRAL EUROPE IN 1601

FRONTIERS OF EASTERN AND NORTHERN EUROPE IN 1601

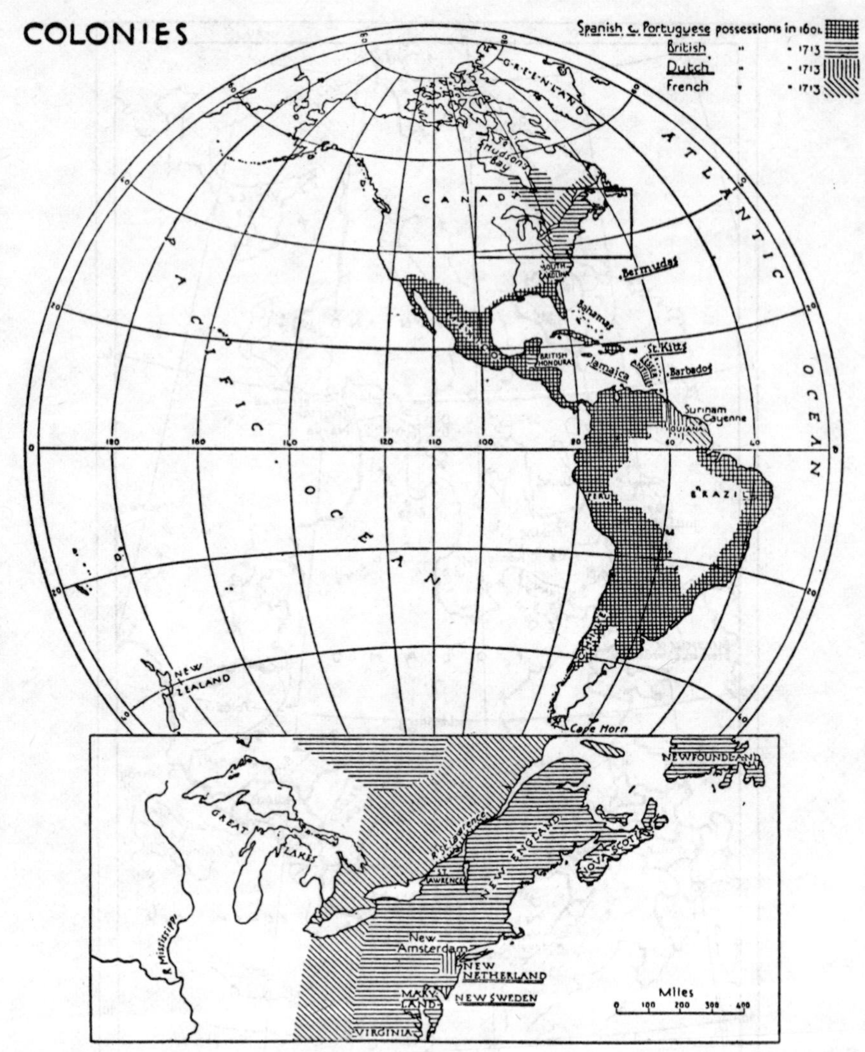
COLONIES
Spanish & Portuguese possessions in 1601
British " " 1713
Dutch " " 1713
French " " 1713
GREENLAND
Hudson's Bay
CANADA
ATLANTIC OCEAN
PACIFIC OCEAN
SOUTH CAROLINA
Bermudas
Bahamas
St. Kitts
BRITISH HONDURAS
Jamaica
Barbados
Surinam
Cayenne
GUIANA
BRAZIL
PERU
CHILE
NEW ZEALAND
Cape Horn
NEWFOUNDLAND
GREAT LAKES
R. St. Lawrence
ST. LAWRENCE
NEW ENGLAND
NOVA SCOTIA
R. Mississippi
New Amsterdam
NEW NETHERLAND
MARYLAND
NEW SWEDEN
VIRGINIA
Miles
0 100 200 300 400

II
POPULATION

ONE of the clearest differences between the seventeenth century and the twentieth is that nowadays government is conducted on the basis of statistics, but then there were scarcely any statistics to be had, and such as existed were very little used. Sir Robert Walpole, who was born in that century, said that in the British House of Commons a man could do more with figures of arithmetic than with figures of rhetoric. That may well have been the temper of the British politician even before his time; but, if it was so, the material for gratifying it was very meagre. It was only towards the end of the seventeenth century that useful statistics began to be compiled and published in the more bustling countries.

While this is quite generally the case, it is nowhere more clear than in the matter of what are now called 'vital statistics', the figures relating to births, deaths, marriages, and population. No country in modern Europe had a regular, periodical, national census before the French Revolution. England and France set the fashion and took the first year of the nineteenth century as their starting-point. No author of the seventeenth made an attempt of any serious scientific value to discover the numbers of the inhabitants of European countries in general. It was still a novel and even a paradoxical idea that these numbers were the beginning of a really methodical understanding of politics and history. The notion seems to have spread outwards from the narrow studies of John Graunt on London Bills of Mortality which he published in 1661. Several English economic writers began to see what might be done by 'political arithmetic'; but they made little real use of such methods, and Graunt's friend, Sir William Petty, who has the best reputation of them all, could only write very vaguely about the comparative populations of England and other countries.[1] The first man who

[1] Both Graunt's work and Petty's have several times been reprinted: the most convenient place to find them is in C. H. Hull's edition of *The Economic Writings of Sir William Petty*, 2 vols., 1899.

both grasped the value of such figures and had tolerably sound figures at his disposal was the great Marshal Vauban in France.[1] Nor, on the whole, are the authors of the seventeenth century at all fertile in the comments and observations which sometimes compensate for the lack of exact information and serve as a guide to such information as there is. If they had made a deep study of these matters they might, even without an elaborate numerical groundwork, have detected the chief causes and results of the facts of population; but what they have to say about these things does not rise above the level of plain common sense. Most of them in all countries held, as was suitable to an age which devoted a great deal of attention to military and naval recruiting, suitable also to the ways of thinking of the 'mercantile system', that a multitude of men meant prosperity to a state Some saw that no state could do with an unlimited multiplication of mouths, and a few, especially Englishmen like Bacon and Raleigh early in the century, feared the vagabondage and disorders that excessive populousness might bring. Opinions like these throw little light on the facts of European society in that age.[2]

Historians, therefore, when they try to put together the available information about these matters cannot expect to get results nearly so accurate or full or useful as those which can be had for the nineteenth century or even the eighteenth. They are tempted to treat with undue respect the few estimates which writers of that age made—mostly each for his own country only—of the numbers of inhabitants. To check or correct these it is necessary to resort to the treacherous method of using collections of figures for a purpose other than that for which they were brought together.

[1] His chief works were written in the last twenty years of Louis XIV. His *Dîme Royale* was reprinted with other important works of the period by E. Daire in his *Économistes financiers du XVIIIe siècle*, 1851.

[2] Raleigh wished to encourage emigration to colonies. The principal contemporary authors who dealt with the subject are mentioned in Stangeland, *Pre-Malthusian Doctrines of Population* (Columbia University Studies in History, &c., xxi, No. 3), 1901. Some additional references are given by J. Bonar, *Theories of Population from Adam Smith to Arthur Young* (1931) and C. R. Gonnard, *Histoire des doctrines de la population* (1923).

By means of certain rules of thumb or certain presumptions about the structure of society, it is possible to infer what was the population of a country from the known, if not always very trustworthy, figures of its taxation returns or religious sects or military levies. But the total amount of such indirect information is far greater than any modern historian has yet succeeded in surveying for any one country, let alone for Europe as a whole, and it is not possible to feel much confidence in inductions which are based on nothing more than a selection from this whole. Moreover, few of the available classes of material are free from the suspicion of inaccuracy, ambiguity, or wilful distortion. Consequently, whatever is said about this question must be said with great reserve.

There is, indeed, no doubt at all that the population of Europe, taken all together, and of almost every part of it, as long as the unit taken is not so small as a single town or village, was very much smaller than it is now. There are villages and towns which have shrunk since then; there are even a few fair-sized districts, such as the Scottish Highlands, which have become less populous because their industries have decayed; but these are exceptions. No place in Europe is far from some countryside which is much more thickly inhabited than it was then. Roughly speaking, this change has been brought about in the last century and a half. It is connected with the great modern changes in sanitation, and in the technique and organization of industry and commerce. It has been greatest in those countries which have been most completely 'industrialized', though exactly how or why it came about we do not yet understand. One thing is clear about this change and *a fortiori* about previous variations in population, whatever they may have been, namely that, compared with the changes which occur in civilized countries now, they were much more spontaneous and unregulated. Governments did indeed sometimes try to encourage the multiplication of hands; but there is no reason to think that their efforts had any considerable effect. So far as individuals were concerned, there was little attempt at control. At present there are several more or less effective devices for 'birth control'. One of the most common of these was known in England in the time of Charles II;

but certainly none was widely used until the nineteenth century. Abortionists, or quacks who claimed to be abortionists, were then, as now, everywhere far from rare, but the effect of their operations was not great. The 'prudential check' did little to keep families down. High birth-rates were everywhere counteracted mainly by high death-rates. Not only bad sanitation and medical ignorance, with the consequent ravages of disease, but even quite important famines were necessary to strike a balance between the number of human beings bred and the number required for the world's business and able to find support. In France, for instance, 1662, 1693, and 1709 were all years of famine. In no department of life were the relations of supply and demand finely or smoothly adjusted, but in none were they at such chaotic variance as in the output of men.

The first thing one would like to know about the results is whether, or where and when, population was rising or falling. About this we know little. Modern authors very commonly repeat the statements of contemporaries that in this or that country, as a result of this or that calamity (usually a war) population fell in alarming proportions. The wars of religion are said to have reduced the population of France.[1] The same is said about the War of the Spanish Succession. In Ireland between 1640 and 1660 war, emigration, and the resettlement of the inhabitants probably caused a heavy fall in numbers.[2] The Great Northern War is thought to have reduced the population of Sweden.[3] The most distressing statements are those made about the Thirty Years' War in Germany. The numbers of Germany are sometimes said to have fallen by half or two-thirds or from more than sixteen millions to less than six.[4] The authority

[1] No authority is given for the statement of Fagniez, *L'économie sociale de la France sous Henri IV* (1890), p. 331, that they reduced the rural population by three millions.

[2] Gardiner, *Commonwealth and Protectorate*, iii (1901), 297, 307, is wisely reluctant to accept any figures.

[3] Axelson, as quoted by other writers without reference, estimates the decrease as from 1,376,000 in 1697 to 1,247,000 in 1718.

[4] This 'appears credible' to K. T. von Inama-Sternegg, whose study 'Die volkswirthschaftlichen Folgen des Dreissigjährigen Kriegs für

of some of the data for these estimates is, however, very dubious, and some of the estimates were made by writers who supposed that a population which has heavy casualties must suffer a corresponding decline of its total numbers, a view which we now know to be mistaken. Even supposing that the reductions were as great as is alleged, it does not follow that they seriously checked a tendency to multiplication if such a tendency was there. There was no lack of births, and there was no irremediable damage to the means of subsistence. In all probability most of these losses were soon and easily made good; and from two independent lines of inquiry it seems to result that in most European countries the population remained fairly stationary or underwent a moderate increase.

The first set of facts which seems to prove this is the body of estimates, such as they are, of populations of different countries at about the beginning and about the end of the century. Possibly the quickest growth was in England, which is known to have been much behind its neighbours in commerce and manufactures at the beginning of the century and at the end of it at least abreast of them. At all events, Dr. Beloch, who has made the best general survey of this subject,[1] suggests four and half millions for the earlier date for England and Wales, while the famous old estimate of Gregory King,[2] still the best we have for the last part of the century, goes as high as five and a half. For France Dr. Beloch puts, at about 1600, no less than sixteen millions; but about 1700 the estimates based by Vauban and others on the *Mémoires des Intendants*, the nearest approach to a real enumeration which had ever been made till then, mostly run at about nineteen millions.[3] General inferences from the quantities of commodities made or transported, from the

Deutschland' in *Hist. Taschenbuch* (Leipzig), 1864, is the basis of the statements of subsequent writers.

[1] 'Die Bevölkerung Europas zur Zeit der Renaissance', in *Zeitschrift für Socialwissenschaft*, iii (1900), 765–86.

[2] In Chalmers, *Estimate of the Comparative Strength of Great Britain*, 1802, and other editions.

[3] See especially Levasseur, *La population francaise*, 3 vols., 1889–92, and G. d'Avenel, *Histoire économique de la propriété, des salaires, etc.*, iii. 424 ff.

figures of the revenues of different states, from the general aspect of civilization, point the same way. The changes in the organization of industry clearly arose from a general increase in the demand for commodities, and, though a number of other causes contributed to it, it seems safe to say that one cause of this increase was a growth of the population of Europe and of most western countries taken separately. We may conclude that the seventeenth century in most of Europe saw, like the sixteenth, a moderate increase of population.[1]

Some exceptions must be named. One is in Hungary. After the battle of Mohacs in 1526 this country had split into three parts, the kingdom of Hungary proper in the west, the part occupied by the Turks in the central lowlands, the tributary principality of Transylvania in the east. By ingenious arguments from the state of the country after it was recovered from the Turks at the end of the seventeenth century it has been inferred, apparently with good reason, that the fertile lowlands were abnormally denuded of men during the Turkish occupation.[2] If this instance is known to us from modern inquiries, there was in the seventeenth century a stock example of a depopulated country, namely Spain. There does not seem to be any critical treatment of the question,[3] but it was accepted as a commonplace that the country was short of hands. Early in the century, in the time of Olivares, efforts were made to increase the population by encouraging agricultural settlements, and in 1625 there was a plan for bringing in Flemish settlers for this purpose.[4] By the end of the seventeenth century the statements about deserted villages were so numerous and striking that there can be no doubt that the population had greatly fallen.

[1] M. Pirenne, *Histoire de Belgique*, iii. 438–9, holds that this was the case in the southern Netherlands, especially among the rural population.

[2] Teleki, *The Evolution of Hungary and its Place in European History*, 1923. This, however, is a propagandist work and must be used with caution.

[3] K. Haebler, *Die wirtschaftliche Blüte Spaniens* (1888), pp. 151, 158, gives for the whole Peninsula 8·4 millions in 1594 and less than 6 millions in 1723; see also Altamira, *Historia de España*, iii. 487–90, iv. 254, where 5,700,000 is suggested for 1700. Some further data are given by E. J. Hamilton in *Economic History Review*, viii (1938), 168–77.

[4] *Correspondence de la cour d'Espagne sur les affaires des Pays-Bas*, vol. ii, No. 690.

Contemporaries ascribed the decline to emigration, which was thought to have had the same effect in Portugal. Modern writers lay stress on the general economic decline of Spain. The expulsion of the Moriscoes, the descendants of the Moors, from southern Spain early in the century was probably more important as a cause of the general decline than for its immediate effect on numbers. The same may be said of a similar event in a neighbouring country at the end of the century, the emigration of Huguenots from France.

The next question which suggests itself is how population was distributed about the Continent, and this has two sides: one economic and the other political. About the economic question, however, the question of how the denser aggregations of people were caused by their economic activities, little need be said. Where certain trades or manufactures flourished, towns grew up and increased. Although some of the great towns of former days, Lisbon, Antwerp, Milan, Venice, were dwindling, others such as London, Paris, Vienna, Amsterdam, and many lesser places multiplied exceedingly.[1] Where towns prosper the country is apt to prosper and employ more hands. The population of Europe was still predominantly rural, and although the growth of towns was a characteristic of the period, this balance was nowhere seriously disturbed. But it is unlikely that we shall ever be able to estimate at all closely the density of population except in a few particular cases, or to decide how it was affected by differences of geography, social custom, and law, and how districts became congested or relieved themselves of an excessive population. The estimates that exist of the density of population in different regions follow in the main political boundaries. They show a great variation from Italy, which besides its great cities had rich country resources, to the bare north of Sweden, Norway, and Finland. The order given by Dr. Beloch is this (the numbers standing

[1] Both at the beginning and at the end of the century there were probably not more than 13 or 14 towns with more than 100,000 inhabitants. The largest cities of Europe, Paris and London, by 1700 far exceeded a quarter of a million: see Sombart, *Der moderne Kapitalismus*, 6th ed., i. 769–70.

for souls to the square kilometre): Italy, 44; Netherlands, 40; France, 34;[1] England and Wales, 30; Germany, 28; Spain and Portugal, 17; Denmark (with its frontiers of 1918), 15; Poland with Prussia, 14; Scotland and Ireland, 12½; Sweden, Norway, and Finland, 1·3, the average for all these countries being less than 20.

These regions mostly correspond to political units or groups of units, and a comparison of their populations is, of course, a good starting-point for a study of their political relations. Here not only the density is interesting, but also the total number, which is a matter of density multiplied by area, so that the order is not at all the same. Germany comes first with about 20 millions, but Germany, by which the Empire is here meant, is rather an aggregate than a single unit. Its strongest unit during most of the century was the Habsburg power, and this appears to have had in the middle of the sixteenth century about 5½ millions, 2 millions in the 'old' dominions (Austria, Styria, Carinthia, Carniola, and the Tyrol), the rest in Bohemia, Moravia, Silesia. Switzerland, still nominally a part of the Empire, though not reckoned in with it here, had about a third of a million. After the Empire in population came France, with 16 millions. Spain and Portugal together had about 10, perhaps 8 or more of these being in Spain.[2] England and Wales had about 4½, Scotland and Ireland 2 million between them, or perhaps a million each. The Dutch republic was well under 3 millions. Poland, with Prussia, which was still nominally under its suzerainty, had in all its enormous area perhaps 11 million people: as late as 1713 East Prussia had still less than half a million. In 1600 Sweden, Norway, and Finland together had less than a million and a half; Denmark, as its frontiers were before 1919, about 600,000. Politically divided as they were in 1600 these countries had, Sweden about 1½ millions, Denmark rather more than a million. Sweden proper had only about three-quarters of a million in the second half of the century. No less than 13 million people,

[1] Levasseur's figure for the end of the century is 40.

[2] For Portugal see W. H. Moreland, *From Akbar to Aurungzeb* (1923), p. 10.

more than there were in any unitary state except France, were divided among the petty principalities and republics of Italy. Venice had nearer two millions than one, Milan more than one, Florence more than three-quarters of a million, Naples nearly as much; but the main point about them is that they were all comparatively small, so that the history of Italy in this century is passive rather than active, and yet taken together they formed a considerable part of Europe, and therefore made a very tempting bait for invaders who wanted money and men. For Russia and Turkey no plausible estimate is possible.

The figures which have just been given show the state of things at the beginning of the period. At the end they were very different, but the changes seem to have been mainly due to the fluctuations of frontiers, not to the multiplication or diminution of the peoples. It might be said that the shortest way of summarizing the political history of the century is to put the two sets of figures for the great powers in parallel rows. Here they are given approximately in millions:

	1600	*1700*
France . . .	16	19
Austrian Habsburgs .	5½	7½
Spain . . .	8	6
England with Ireland .	5½	
Scotland . . .	1	
Great Britain with Ireland		7½

If it were possible to give not the number of subjects in each state but the number of inhabitants of each geographical region at the beginning and the end of the century, there would be no such great advances as those shown in this table by France and Austria. The English advance, on the other hand, is due to natural multiplication and not to the annexation of any new provinces. But the whole is little better than guess-work.

III

ECONOMIC POLICY AND IDEAS

THE growth of population, if and where it came about, was part of the larger fact that this was a time of economic progress. Europe was growing richer; the scale of economic life was becoming greater. This change of scale was not yet so rapid as it became in the next age, but it was not slow, and it was gathering momentum. At the end of the century there were far more ships and looms and houses than at the beginning. There were more rich men and there were richer men. Station for station the standard of life seems to have been generally rising. In every grade of society there was a growing abundance, or at least a diminishing lack, of the material products of labour. This fact, as we shall see, had far more than merely economic importance: it influenced the development of armies, of political institutions, of the fine arts, for a continent cannot grow in riches, any more than a family can, without changing its whole way of life. On the economic side also it was more than a change of scale. As markets, businesses, transactions became larger, they necessarily came to be different in kind. In all organization a change of size means a change of system, and economic progress in the sense of advancing wealth had its counterpart in changing organization.

Business success with other forces was impelling Europe in the direction of capitalism. The seventeenth century does not coincide even roughly with any one distinct phase of economic development, but historians are now agreed that it should be regarded as a part of the time of that 'early capitalism' which first shows itself in the later Middle Ages and lasts until the rise of the fully developed capitalism of the nineteenth century. The limits of this phase may be variously defined according to the aspect of social life which is regarded, but they may be indicated by saying that it is the stretch of time from Machiavelli to Burke, from Columbus to Warren

Hastings, from the Fuggers to the decline of Amsterdam, from Giotto to Tiepolo.[1] It stops short of Adam Smith, James Watt, the Rothschilds, Napoleon, Robert Owen.

The use of the word 'capitalism' as a name for the modern economic system was, I believe, invented in the middle of the nineteenth century by socialists, and it meant a state of society in which the predominant power is that of the owners of capital. It was used to distinguish the modern system from two other types of society, the one ideal, the co-operative commonwealth, the other historical, the pre-capitalistic world of the Middle Ages. The convenience of the latter contrast has led to its being adopted by all kinds of writers whether they are socialists or not. It does not mean that in the earlier time there was no such thing as capital, no business with any capital; though it is true that for a great part medieval business was carried on without capital in the usual sense. Some of the builders of the cathedrals, for instance, built out of income and neither raised loans as modern deans and chapters do, nor kept an account at a bank, nor had any means of keeping their masons at work when the pay-chest was temporarily empty. On the other hand, when this contrast is drawn it does not mean that modern society is uniformly and universally regulated according to a 'system' in which capital or the capitalist must always stand in the same relation to the other elements of society. It is a commonplace that at the present time there is not one economic system, but several systems running alongside of one another, and that every old and superseded system has left some more or less important relics in the interstices of the new. But the broad fact, the contrast of phenomena taken in the mass, remains. In our days the conformation of agricultural, industrial, and commercial life is mainly decided by the application and management of capital. Accumulations of

[1] The last pair of names is suggested with characteristic boldness by Werner Sombart, whose book *Der moderne Kapitalismus*, 6th ed. (reprint of 2nd), 2 vols. in 4 parts, 1924, gives the best general account of the economic history of the seventeenth century, with a valuable survey of the literature of the subject.

money-power, very variously owned and constituted, are available for the carrying on of work, and it is impossible to explain what is the function of an individual, or of a particular kind of work, or of a particular kind of employment or remuneration, in modern society without showing it in relation to these accumulations of money-power.

In the seventeenth century the process of accumulation was going on. Many different types of men by various means were becoming capitalists. Some of the great territorial landlords began to develop the resources of their properties in a new way, not in the old feudal style but, especially where there were minerals under the land, as money-making enterprises. Circumstances which seem at first quite remote from economic life brought into existence new classes of men who had special aptitudes and special incentives to money-making. One of the typical features, for instance, of the seventeenth century is the importance of the exiles. In every country in Europe were men who had been driven from home by the persecution of their religious beliefs or by those political conflicts which were so nearly allied to religion. In Protestant England, Holland, Denmark, Switzerland, and Brandenburg, were French Huguenots; in Catholic France and Italy and Spain there were English and Scottish and Irish Catholics. Wherever they went these refugees formed communities of their own, half-isolated from the general business life around them, active and alive; with their own ideas striking against those they found in their foreign homes like steel on flint. Any list of the great merchants of any European country in the year 1700 will show the result. For several countries it will already include some names of the gifted race who in that and the preceding century were hunted from Spain and Portugal to be received in Holland and later in England: amongst the exiles were the Jews. So the times were bringing the capitalist, and there were causes at work which brought it about that first one branch of business and then another became capitalistic.

This was not equally so in all countries. A distinction must be made here which will recur in other connexions, between the countries which were advancing and the countries which, relatively, were standing still or dropping behind. Italy, which had been the light of Europe in economic as in so many other matters, had ceased to be so by the middle of the century. For Spain it is not, I believe, claimed that she ever was a leading nation in economic theory or practice. Though her civilization was in some respects very high, and even her political power only gradually fell away in the course of the century, from an early stage of it her economic resources were more and more ill managed, more and more were Spain and the Spanish empire passively exploited by foreign traders. The great plains of Eastern Europe, Poland, and Hungary, were but little affected by the innovations: they too were passive and ruled by tradition. In Germany, Bohemia, Sweden, and other parts the influence of change was considerable, but yet by no means so great as in the central group of sea-board countries between the estuary of the Ems and the Bay of Biscay. It was from here that the new spirit radiated through the mass. These were the active centres of economic change. It cannot be said that it had a single point of origin. There were three rays, much alike, but each with its own distinguishing qualities, the first French, the second Dutch, the third English.

The special mark of the French influence in economic life is that it is one part of an influence exerted in almost every sphere, in the arts and letters, in politics, in manners, and in thought. France has had reason in various ages to boast of her 'mission civilisatrice', but the seventeenth is of all perhaps most distinctively the French century in Europe. As the most populous country and the country which deployed the greatest diplomatic and military power, France led the way in those economic changes which were due to the action of the state. The growth of her armies, which set the pace for the armies of the rest of Europe, was a great cause of the rise of capitalism. One famous measure of Louis XIV, which was taken for religious and political reasons, did much damage to the economic prosperity of the country and handed over to other nations, which used them well, many of the best brains and strongest wills of France. This was the revocation in 1685 of the Edict of Nantes, by which the last remnant of toleration was withdrawn from the Huguenots. In spite of the efforts of Louis XIV the Huguenots escaped in thousands to Protestant countries, taking with them not only the skilled hands of industries which had been peculiar to France, but also the enterprise and ability of organizers. Their coming is a landmark in the economic history of other countries. In Holland it made factories common where they had been rare exceptions.[1] In England its results were less revolutionary, but still very marked, especially in the manufacture of silk. These facts not only show how great must have been the loss to France; they also give the measure of her previous strength, and there are sufficient indications that her example was to some extent followed abroad. That was so above all in the relations of the state with commerce and industry: the protectionist system of Colbert was imitated, more or less exactly, everywhere. Nor must we forget that it was in this century that France established her leadership in setting the fashions in dress.

The Dutch influence was more purely economic. Contemporaries in England began to be aware very early in the seventeenth century that in many branches of social organization the Dutch were far ahead of them. Pamphlets began to point out Dutch practices which the English ought to imitate or Dutch gains which the English ought to contest. Right up to the English coast the Dutch had the rich sea-fisheries almost to themselves. One of the few scraps of economic history which have become, in our time, generally known is the fact that the Dutch were then the common carriers of the world and, in particular, of the English. They had the best-managed merchant marine of the world: their ships were the cheapest to build, and the best adapted for their various purposes. Their commercial policy was well fitted to stimulate trade and to make their country 'the pack-house of the world'. In the organization of business they had no equals. It was not until well on in the eighteenth century that the insurance of English shipping came to be

[1] This point was established by Pringsheim, *Beiträge zur wirtschaftlichen Entwickelungsgeschichte der vereinigten Niederlande*, 1890.

effected at home instead of in Amsterdam. For the bread-supply of the English army which fought James II in Ireland it was impossible to find an English contractor: only the Amsterdam Jew Pereira could cope with such a task. The lowness of the rate of interest in Holland as compared with that in England was one of the most striking economic facts of the whole seventeenth century. For the practical Dutchman it pointed out England as a profitable field for investment. For English economic writers it was a puzzle: they groped uncertainly towards the truth which it is now easy to see, that this difference was a symptom and a result of the backwardness of England and the superior development of Dutch resources. Happily for us our intercourse with the Dutch people at this time was as intimate as any we ever had with foreigners before the days of railways and steam navigation. Once they had become aware of their backwardness, the English began what led the late Dr. Cunningham to call the middle and later period of the seventeenth century in our economic history, that of 'conscious imitation of the Dutch'.[1] They set themselves to overtake the Dutch, and in so doing they transformed their whole economic life.

The first thing that enabled them to do so was the immigration of Dutchmen to our shores. In greater or smaller numbers they had, of course, been coming over for centuries; but after the Reformation, the character of the movement changed. It became more local, less easily and completely absorbed and so more clearly seen and recorded. This was partly because English social and political institutions were becoming more settled, partly because amongst the immigrants there were now many religious refugees, and these refugees required special supervision by the government because they were apt both to be needy and to have contagious theological opinions. The Dutch church in Austin Friars, which traces its history at least as far back as 1550, is

[1] In the first edition (1882) of his standard work *The Growth of English Industry and Commerce* this was the title of Bk. V, cap. 2, but it was allowed to drop out from later editions. The idea had been expressed by Thorold Rogers, *History of Agriculture and Prices*, v. 65.

now the sole survivor of several churches founded in this age. After the period of persecutions the immigrants were, of course, mostly there for reasons of business. It was their interest to come away from the competition of their own countrymen to the easier opportunities of a backward country. Over they came, sometimes in defiance of decrees of their own States-General which, from 1669 to 1750, protested at intervals against the drain of skilled men from their territories. Sometimes they came in answer to encouragement from the Tudor and Stuart sovereigns, sometimes on their own initiative; sometimes to the indignation of English townsmen who feared their competition, but sometimes at the request of these townsmen themselves when they needed help. Their remains may still be seen in many places in buildings like Bourne Pond Hall at Colchester, a building of purely Dutch design put up in 1591, or in the surnames of their descendants in many parts of Great Britain and Ireland.[1]

The diversity of their occupations shows how important the movement was. First were the weavers and fullers, part of a great body of textile workers who gave an impetus to industry in London, East Anglia, and Scotland, and later, in the linen-trade as earlier in the woollen, in Ireland. There were fishermen; there were also rope-makers and other tradesmen connected with the shipping. From an early date in the seventeenth century there were glass-makers from Middelburg. There were printers and type-founders. Dutch potters established the tile-making and general earthenware industries in various parts of England. It may be doubted whether some of the 'Dutch' miners who are mentioned were not High Dutch or German: the Low Countries are not rich in mines. Yet even among the miners are some names which seem to belong to this region. However obscure the employment, if it demands ingenuity, in the seventeenth century we are not surprised if we find a Dutchman in it. When Sir William Brereton travelled in Holland in the reign of Charles I he made purchases of tiles and

[1] Cunningham, *Alien Immigrants to England*, 1897, though more than thirty years old, is still the best survey.

floor-stones, pictures and figures for supporting a chimney-piece for his home at Handford in Cheshire; but his main interest then was in water-birds, and he tells us that he imported a Dutch 'coyman' to manage his duck-decoys.[1]

In what had to do with water the Dutch had special experience, and it was in such things that they made their largest undertakings here, as indeed they did in many other places.[2] A Brabanter was at work at Dover harbour in Elizabeth's reign, and wrote a discourse on the Fens; Sir Cornelius Vermuyden, who drained Hatfield Chase and great parts of the Fens, made a considerable figure in the seventeenth century. At Canvey Island, which his contemporary Croppenburg drained, there are still two 'Dutch cottages' to be seen. Dutch workmen who made the quays there have a memorial in the name of Flushing near Falmouth. Although there is no Dutchman's name that we can associate with it, the introduction into England of the use of locks in navigable rivers came from the example of the Low Countries, and along with it, partly from the efforts of the same men, there came improvements in agriculture, of which the greatest was the cultivation of clover.[3]

Nor was the superiority of the Dutch confined to these numerous kinds of technical skill. There was much to copy in their social organization. They claim to have invented life-insurance. They certainly were before us, and were held up by various writers as deserving imitation in banking.[4] Of the Dutch influence in France much the same tale may be told, though France had in many respects less need of help from abroad. In the draining of marshes in the time

[1] His *Travels*, ed. by E. Hawkins, were published by the Chetham Society in 1844 and reprinted in J. C. Hodgson's *North Country Diaries*, vol. ii (Surtees Soc.), 1915.

[2] For the latest study of their efforts to drain the Pomptine Marshes in Italy see J. Korthals Altes in *Mededeelingen van het Ned. Hist. Inst. te Rome*, vol. vi.

[3] I do not know of any English parallel to the supervision of dairy-farms in Hanover and Schleswig-Holstein by Dutchmen.

[4] The beginning of this paragraph and the four which precede it are condensed, by the kind permission of the editor, from an article which I contributed to *De nieuwe gids* for October 1923.

of Henry IV, we find a man who, though his name was Humphrey Bradley, came from Bergen-op-Zoom, and two authentic Dutchmen of the name of Comans.[1] One of these appears also as a promoter of the new tapestry 'de marche' (with the pedal) or 'de bas lice', and for this he brought workmen from the Netherlands. There are other instances of Dutch and Flemish masters and men in the textile trades at this time, and still more two generations later under Colbert. The brothers Robais from Middelburg were *protégés* of his, and at Abbeville they employed more than a thousand people. There were dyers, rope-makers, lace-makers from Brussels,[2] Flemish makers of Morocco leather. The Delft tile-making industry was brought in. Although among the useful immigrants into France there were also Italians (for the silk manufacture), and though Colbert sent as far afield as Sweden for ironworkers, it is no exaggeration to say that the Netherlands, northern and southern, provided the principal outside influence in improving French industry.[3] In Spain, where heretics were not welcome, it was from Catholic Flanders that the textile workers and engineers to improve the courses of rivers were brought.[4]

England also, in the later part of the century, had begun to give a lead to foreign countries, but her example became strong only when she had overtaken the Dutch and French, and passed beyond them on the road of capitalist development. It was exerted chiefly in the higher regions of finance and management; but as soon as the English became a business nation, their influence abroad left its traces. One little fact is worth mentioning, because it brings us into touch with one of the manufactures which have a many-

[1] After completing his engagement in England Bradley went to Württemberg to work on making the Neckar navigable (*Resolutiën der Staten-Generaal*, ed. Japikse, x. 112).

[2] The emigration of women lace-makers from the Spanish Netherlands was prohibited in 1698.

[3] For details see Fagniez, *L'Économie sociale de France sous Henri IV*, pp. 26 ff., 85–6, 193 f., 142–3, 157, and Martin, *La grande industrie sous le règne de Louis XIV*, especially Pt. i, chs. v–vi. On the examples of Dutch trading companies see the next chapter.

[4] *Corresp. de la cour d'Esp. sur les affaires des Pays-Bas*, vol. ii, nos. 725, 462–3, 472, 776, 1018.

sided interest. The English excelled in making instruments of precision.[1] An Englishman called Hubin was one of the best-known makers of mathematical instruments in Paris in 1687, and a few years later Butterfield was the best maker there. The English had a good share in the process by which in this century clocks became common possessions, and ceased to be articles of luxury. We owe to it the first grandfather clocks. It was the great Dutch mathematician, Christian Huygens, who perfected the pendulum clock, and by inventing the balance-spring made efficient pocket-watches possible. But his elder brother, when he came to live in London as the secretary of King William III, was often in and out of the clockmakers' shops, asking questions and admiring their methods.[2] And this is significant. The clock is the modern idol. Punctuality, exactness, system, as we understand them, were becoming necessary in daily life.

The world of business, in order to move faster and more surely, liberated itself from some of the traditional ideas which had restricted its action. A great obstacle to the free progress of capitalistic ideas, and perhaps to a lower degree of capitalistic practices, had been the ecclesiastical prohibition of usury. In the Middle Ages there were signs that this could be relaxed or evaded if the exigencies of business required it, but the pressure of utilitarian demands never became so strong as to shake its foundations. The Protestant reformation[3] came about just when new financial methods were beginning to reach the stage at which the prohibition would be seriously challenged; and the profound differences of opinion among the Protestants divided them on this point. In the seventeenth century the liberal view gained ground everywhere. Bacon, in his *Essays* of 1625, treated the prohibition of usury as Utopian; he proposed instead to

[1] Buckle, *Hist. of Civilization*, ii. 193. There are some of Butterfield's instruments in the Whipple collection at Cambridge.

[2] See the *Journaal van Constantijn Huygens den Zoon*. The Englishman Robert Hooke seems to have been the first to make the latter discovery, but not the first to announce it.

[3] It seems pedantic not to stick to the established English use of these words for Lutheranism, Calvinism, and Zwinglianism. It is inconvenient to use 'Protestant' only for Lutherans and 'Reformed' only for Calvinists.

regulate it by giving general freedom to lend at 5 per cent. or less and licences for loans at higher rates. The first unequivocal assertion of the modern doctrine of interest was made by Claude de Saumaise (better known as Salmasius, the controversial antagonist of Milton) in 1638–40. Among the Catholics the difficulty of discarding the old doctrine from their theoretical books was much greater than among the Protestants, and an author of 1682 is said to have been almost the first of Catholic theologians to cavil at the old definition of usury; but before that casuistry had invented several ways round the difficulty. The time had come when the right to exact whatever interest the debtor could be made to pay was no longer to meet with any effective contradiction.[1]

We must, however, be careful not to make too much of this. It does not mean that theorists now handed over economic affairs to a ruthless rationalism, or even that the spirit of the business world had become predominantly individualistic. There were still bounds set to what was thought the proper freedom of the business man. There was a distinct and general belief that some kinds of gain were honourable and others morally not permissible. Respectability, the bourgeois virtue, was coming to take a larger place in the world. What is most remarkable and most easily forgotten is that the spirit of industry was not yet competitive. The fact of competition existed, as, of course, it exists throughout human life, but the seventeenth-century writers on trade no more avowed that competition was the basis of their system than clergymen avow that the interests of the church are best advanced by competition for preferment. Throughout the literature of the time the man of business is exhorted to shun underselling and outwitting his fellows 'and then with God's blessing and his own care, he may expect his share of trade with his neighbours'.[2]

[1] The subject is surveyed by Lecky, *Hist. of the Rise and Progress of the Spirit of Rationalism in Europe*, 2 vols., 1865; but it is set in a much clearer light by more recent studies, for which see Troeltsch, *Die Soziallehren der christlichen Kirchen und Gruppen*, 1912, a work of considerable value for the synthesis of economic, political, and religious history.

[2] Defoe, *apud* Sombart, ii. 49. Many similar expressions occur in *The Complete English Tradesman*, first ed., 2 vols., 1727.

Long before the word 'capitalism' was coined, Adam Smith had given a name to the economic policy and ideas of the age preceding his own. He summed them up as 'the commercial or mercantile system'.

'The different progress of opulence in different ages and nations', he says, 'has given occasion to two different systems of political economy, with regard to enriching the people. The one may be called the system of commerce, the other that of agriculture. I shall endeavour to explain both as fully and distinctly as I can, and shall begin with the system of commerce. It is the modern system, and is best understood in our own country and in our own times.'[1]

Its end, however, was due in no small measure to this very explanation of Adam Smith's, which is the classical example of an effective piece of economic criticism. As a specimen of economic history it is not so valuable,[2] and later writers have repeated and exaggerated the least happy of its comments, so that the mercantile system has been made to appear much more systematic and much less intelligible than it was in reality. It deserves the name of a system more truly than the capitalist system does, because it was a doctrine and a programme, rather than a mere descriptive summary of the facts of an epoch after they had come about; but even so we must be on our guard against assuming that it had anything like the consistency and uniformity which seem to be attributed to it by most of the short summary accounts of 'mercantilism' in modern books. There were plenty of controversies and contradictions within the bounds of this system. It was not the same thing for Frenchmen as for Englishmen, not the same for Englishmen as for Dutchmen. It was variously understood and applied by politicians and by merchants. It meant one thing to the apologists of the East India trade and another to the home manufacturers who tried to compete against imported eastern goods. Of these differences and divisions we shall see something as we go on; but in spite of them it is possible to say what were the common features of mercantilism.

[1] *Wealth of Nations*, Bk. IV, Introduction.

[2] See the notes in Professor Cannan's edition.

It was a system of political economy, that is to say it was a system for the regulation of economic matters by the state. It was, in Adam Smith's words, a system for 'enriching the people', and its essence is that it was to do so by means of commerce, and more particularly by the state regulation of commerce. It starts from the assumption that a people is a community with a common wealth—the wealth of a nation—and that by proper measures this wealth can be increased. It is in fact the direct continuation for the larger unit called a 'people' of the system of regulation by which in the Middle Ages the government of each separate town controlled the enrichment of that town as a whole. The aim of the multifarious ordinances of the medieval guilds and towns was, first of all, to ensure the provision of necessaries for the life and labour of its inhabitants. There must be a sufficiency of corn for consumption; equally there must be a sufficiency of raw materials for industry. A sufficiency meant not only an adequate total for all those who demanded it taken together, but also for each separate consumer or user an adequate quantity at a possible price. Thus it was not enough to control the movement of goods to and from the town. Their price, the times and conditions of their sale in the town-markets had to be regulated as well, and in order to keep an equilibrium between supply and demand it was not even enough to regulate supply in all these ways; demand—above all the demand of trade and industry—had to be kept in hand. The number of men plying each trade had to be kept within limits, and the size of each man's business, for instance, the number of men he employed. Inseparably therefore two ends were pursued together, the maintenance of the town's prosperity as a whole and fairness between its individual townsmen. To get his fair share the individual had to submit to the community, and it was from it that he derived the right to pursue his occupation on the terms which it prescribed. He was given a privilege, a privileged or protected position, and in exchange he put himself under a system of regimentation.

These two elements of protection and regimentation remained throughout the mercantile epoch the fundamental principles of economic organization, but with this great difference, that now it was the state, no longer the town or its organ, the guild, which granted the privilege and protected against the unprivileged and the foreigner. That the state should have superseded the authority of the town in this matter requires no long explanation: it was a consequence of the whole development of the power of the state which marks the essential difference between medieval and modern political history. From the time of the Renaissance, of the use of fire-arms, of the 'new monarchy', the sovereign territorial states had come to dominate the life of western Europe; if and when they chose to assert their authority few competitors were able to stand against them, and among their potential rivals it was no longer possible to reckon the towns. The rebellious burgher is a figure of the Middle Ages or the sixteenth century, and in his later appearances he was generally seen with a rope round his neck, asking a king's pardon on his knees. Now instead of the rope he wore the gold chain and furs of domestication. The kings had won; but, it may be asked, why should they have concerned themselves with commercial matters and taken the oversight of what might have been left to the same bodies which had managed it before? Why did Henry VII of England require the guilds to obtain the sanction of his judicial officers for any alteration of their by-laws? Why did Charles IX of France in 1571 take into his own hands, out of those of subordinate officers, the right of granting freedom to corporations? Why did Queen Elizabeth in her Statute of Artificers give the authority of the state to a complicated network of industrial laws? Why was it that the most thorough-going and comprehensive example of mercantilism was the work of Colbert, the minister of Louis XIV, a king who is sometimes supposed to have had a high-flying contempt for merchants and their sordid affairs? In what ways did the rulers of nations find that the mercantile system served their turn?

First and most generally it must be answered that, however much they might seem from time to time to despise economic things, they knew well enough, and were in no danger of forgetting, that all the activities of the state require a healthy economic life as their foundation. Without it they could not even keep their thrones. It was not only the warm heart but also the clear head of Henry IV that made him want every French household to have a chicken in the pot. And the idea of distributive fairness is much more than an economic idea: it forms a part of almost every far-sighted scheme for the government of a commonwealth. One of the best-known sayings in Bacon's Essays is the remark that 'money is like muck, not good except it be spread'. It is to be found not in his essay on Riches but in that of Seditions and Troubles, of which he tells us that:

> 'The first remedy or prevention is to remove by all means possible that material cause of sedition . . . which is want and poverty in the estate. To which purpose serveth the opening and well-balancing of trade; the cherishing of manufactures; the banishing of idleness; the repressing of waste and excess by sumptuary laws; the improvement and husbanding of the soil; the regulating of prices of things vendible; the moderating of taxes and tributes, and the like.'

From the primary political need for order and security he deduces the necessity for an active government supervision of every department of economic life. Not all the statesmen of those days were as clear-sighted as Bacon; but they did not need his grasp of principles to draw the same conclusions in practice. Two immediately pressing necessities reminded them from day to day of the need for national wealth. First they needed money. The whole success of the monarchies sprang from their being rich, just as their fall at the end of the old régime began with bankruptcy. In all their dealings with economic things the fiscal motive may be traced. Its part is, of course, sometimes greater and sometimes less. The intelligence with which it is applied, though sometimes very great, is more often questionable, but it never sinks so low as explicitly to repudiate the principle that the state can only be rich if the population is rich and has money to spare for it. Nor was it only money that the state wanted from its people. Its great expenditure, then as now, went for military and naval purposes; but these purposes required other things besides money, and these further needs constituted the second standing reminder to the statesmen of the value of national wealth. Men were wanted: we have touched on that question already. When they were enrolled as soldiers and sailors, they needed clothes and weapons, warships and gear, timber and sailcloth, pitch and tar, anchors and cables, for all of which there must be skilled workers to make them and a prosperous merchant-fleet to bring in the materials.

So it came about that the state became the watchful and despotic guardian of the economic interests of its inhabitants. As the seventeenth century went on it learnt to apply its whole strength to this effort. Most men believed with Bacon that 'the increase of any estate must be upon the foreigner (for whatsoever is somewhere gotten is somewhere lost)' and 'the jealousy of trade' between one nation and another was the rule before Bacon's time. Thus far, however, it had mainly been expressed in the making of protective laws or advantageous treaties. Some of the laws, like the English Acts of Navigation and the protective tariffs of Colbert, went as far in the direction of exclusiveness as it was then possible to go; but there was a further kind of commercial hostility beyond mere legislation. The great trading companies which fought and conquered the natives of the East and West Indies and the African coasts, fought also against one another. For long years there was informal war between the Dutch and the Portuguese and the English in the seas where the Dutch and English had fought the Portuguese and Spaniards in the previous century. The governments at home were slow to take up the merchants' quarrels. For many years they lent their assistance underhand, by supplying munitions and by giving diplomatic support; but they had other things to consider in fixing their alliances or enmities in Europe. About the middle of the century there came one of the great revolutions of European policy. First the quarrel of the Dutch and English, and then, a few years later, that of the Dutch and the Portuguese came to a head in a regular war in Europe. After that, throughout the later seventeenth century and ever since, economic and colonizing quarrels took a leading place, and often the first place, in the antecedents of European wars.

Thus the consequences, like the causes, of the mercantile system extended far beyond the economic sphere; but it was none the less in that sphere that it had its centre. The key to it was the enrichment of the nation. The nation, the people ruled by one state, became the economic unit. There was a tendency—not yet very far advanced except in some favoured countries like England and Sweden—to eliminate internal restrictions on movement and intercourse. France achieved a high degree of political unity, but did not yet get very far in the removal of internal customs barriers. The Dutch republic was further from political unity than any other state of that or subsequent times; it was indeed disputed whether it was correct to call it a state in the singular at all. Its economic policy, however, showed comparatively much greater coherence; but everywhere, even in England, there was a diversity of weights and measures, of local customs, and there were relics of local privileges, which excluded the possibility of anything resembling the unity and standardization which we accept as natural in the modern national scale. The state was only gradually becoming economically one within itself.

Its economic separateness from other states was more clearly affirmed. There was a tendency to erect barriers against those kinds of intercourse with other nations which seemed undesirable. No one went so far as to imagine that all foreign intercourse was detrimental. We have seen already how immigration was welcomed, and trade was welcomed too. The system was a system of regulating and even encouraging, not of abolishing, commerce. But it rested on a sharp distinction between that commerce which was, and that which was not, advantageous. This distinction was made by casting what was called the balance of trade. According to one theory those branches of foreign trade alone were profitable which resulted in the increase of the quantity of precious metals in a country. The most desirable type of foreign trade was an export in return for which the purchasing country shipped gold or silver; an import for the payment of which the precious metals had to be sent abroad was the least desirable. Between those simple cases lay a number of types of more complex and indirect transactions which were to be favoured or discouraged according to their ultimate effect on the national stock of money.

It is commonly said that the whole resulting body of theory and legislation was based on the fallacy of mistaking gold for wealth; but, as a German writer contemptuously said, the mercantilists did not labour under the delusion that gold and silver could be eaten. The explanation of their attitude seems to lie in the commercial conditions of the time. I say 'seems' because this conclusion is not universally accepted, and rests on an analysis of which the data are not easy to interpret. Its principle is that international trade in those days turned on the precious metals. Bills of exchange had long been known, and the modern trade in them, the discounting of them by third parties, had begun, but they were still used only to represent goods (including the precious metals). The capital which was increasingly required for trade had therefore to be obtained in a solid and ponderable form. It is certainly the fact that there was a contest between the trading nations for the possession of these metals, and it seems clear that the nations which were at any given time the most prosperous were those which had succeeded in getting the command of the greatest quantities of them. But questions such as these are much disputed among theoretical economists. Subsidiary reasons were undeniably present which made the English and French and Dutch—who had no mines of gold and silver worth mentioning—scheme to attract to their shores the gold and silver of America, Germany, and the East. They wanted coin to pay their armies. The Dutch also, and they alone, wanted coin and uncoined bullion in order to sell them at a profit: their policy in regard to money was exceptional. They never prohibited the export of coin, and from 1647 they virtually permitted that of uncoined bullion. In this, as in their tariff policy and in other things, some of which we have noted already, their history is a warning against generalizing too freely.[1]

[1] See Dr. J. G. van Dillen's important collection of *Documenten tot de*

The same is true of the Dutch economic literature of the time,[1] but even that shares in the main characteristics of mercantilism as I have sketched them. For more than a century past an increasing amount of attention has been paid to the economic writers of the seventeenth century, and the notion is now dead and buried that the founder of political economy was Adam Smith. It had no more truth in it than the statement of a medieval writer that Parmenides sat him ten years upon a rock and bethought him of the art of logic. There is, however, a danger of going too far the other way. These earlier writers are very attractive. Their books are readable and vigorously expressed; most of them have the great merit of being short; most of them are not dulled by academic impartiality but alive with clear-cut partisanship. They make better reading than their successors, just as an advocate's speech is generally more interesting than a judge's summing up. For that very reason they must be used with care. They are deceptive. Their statements of principle are often acute, but it is necessary to remember that they nearly all subserve a practical purpose and invoke principles simply in the interests of that purpose. To take one example, passages are sometimes quoted from these early writers in which they appear to anticipate the free-trade theorists of a later age. When taken in their contexts these passages are nearly always found to be pleas, not for any wider freedom, but simply for freedom from the restrictions imposed by some particular monopoly of which the writer or his patrons were jealous. They were all advocates. Mercantilism was a programme, a cause, an adventure. Its aim was the enrichment of the people, and its theory looked on this as a work to be done by the creative energy of men organized in a common body. It was based therefore on assumptions which were largely absent from the more sophisticated works of the later economists who tried, with the help of philosophy, to represent the economic world as regulated by mechanical laws and inevitable harmonies, in which the human being

geschiedenis der wisselbanken and the same writer's article in *Revue historique*, clii (1926), pp. 194 ff.

[1] This is surveyed by Laspeyres, *Geschichte der volkswirtschaftlichen Anschauungen der Niederländer*. 1863.

withered to the scraggy proportions of 'the economic man'. In coming back to the earlier writers with all their faults, modern economists have found that what they are still able to communicate is vitality. They lacked, however, that grasp of the organic relations of society as a whole which is necessary for any really scientific economic theory. One among the reasons for this deficiency is that lack of statistical knowledge which has already been noted. The reactions of one part of a nation's economic life upon another can scarcely be detected except by analysing figures.

IV

COMMERCE, FINANCE, AND COMMUNICATIONS

THE first impression made by the lists, of which there are many, enumerating the commodities imported and exported by the different European countries or their different provinces is that of kaleidoscopic variety. By this time there was commerce, even international commerce, in an immense number of things. At the beginning of the century, for instance, the articles exported from Naples included meat, which was shipped to Venice, the Adriatic coast, and Tuscany, almonds to Alexandria and the Barbary states, silks to Genoa and Tuscany, oils to Venice and to Genoa, wines to Rome, horses and sheep and coral to various parts. But such lists, which by themselves are merely bewildering, can without much difficulty be made intelligible if they are put into their due place in a broader picture of the world's movements of goods.

In the old days there had been two main currents of European commerce, one from the Baltic lands and one from the Levant. Each began in an inland sea and ran up the estuaries and navigable waters into the roads and streets of the western countries. The first brought the raw materials characteristic of the great plains to which the Baltic gives access: the produce of forests, timber and tar, hides and wax. The other brought raw materials of another type, those produced by a far different geographical region, spices, pepper, ivory, and precious stones; but it brought also the finished products of Eastern civilization, textiles, metalwork, articles of luxury of many kinds. Along with these goods of distant origin there followed the same trade-routes other articles which took a shorter journey, but which may be distinguished in something of the same way. The products of the Mediterranean lands were wines, oil, fruits such as oranges, lemons, olives, and figs, things which the northern countries could not grow for themselves. The importing countries paid for them as they could, the English with woollen goods, the Dutch with salted herrings, and with their services as carriers, the Swedes partly with iron and copper. Just as the Swedes had this special wealth in mines, so each other country had its more or less important peculiar position in the world's production. France and Portugal were rich in salt, and the northern countries had little success in their attempts to acquire salt at home. Spain produced much wool. England had tin and lead and alum. Thus the various countries were of use in supplying one another's wants. For the most part they were not wants in the strictest sense: except for corn and timber most of the international commerce was in articles of luxury and improvement rather than of necessity. By the seventeenth century the corn-trade had become pretty large, but it appears that only two countries depended for their subsistence on imported corn: Norway, whose barrenness had for long past had this result, and parts of the Netherlands, where the growth of population had now exceeded the capacity of the local agriculture. The great source of supply for corn was the Baltic; but France also exported corn to Spain and Portugal and sometimes to Italy. In times of war or of natural scarcity, however, even France sometimes had to become a corn-importing country, and it must be remembered that communications by land were so defective that one part of France might go short of corn while another was sending it abroad. The Baltic and northern lands were also the great source of timber and naval stores. With these provisoes, and with the general reminder that the world was then very much poorer than it is now, it may be repeated that international trade was mainly in luxuries rather than necessaries.

Its general nature had in this respect not been altered by the great discoveries of the fifteenth and sixteenth centuries. The new ocean routes carried some of the old commodities from the east in far greater quantities than had been possible for the old caravans and pack-horse trains, and also far more cheaply. They also brought from America a wealth of new commodities, tobacco, logwood for dyeing, and great masses of old known commodities which far exceeded the Asiatic and European supplies, gold and silver, sugar, indigo, tortoiseshell, and furs. They thus increased the scale of commerce very greatly and, as every one knows, they entirely changed its geography, bringing its centres to the Atlantic seaboard from the inland seas, ending the great days of the Hanse and the Italian trading republics. The new oceanic commerce all through the period of early capitalism was not a purely trading matter, but half conquest, one may say half robbery, of the comparatively defenceless natives. It was therefore immensely profitable, and as it grew in importance it contributed more and more to the change of economic organization. It built up the new accumulations of wealth which themselves became the foundation of further accumulations. In particular it brought in the flood of the precious metals on which the new system was to float: that process went through its decisive stages in the late sixteenth century. The revolution in prices which it caused was a great turning-point in the fortunes of individuals and institutions. It continued with gradually diminishing force until about the middle of the seventeenth century, as a general condition of all commerce, favouring expansion and facilitating every kind of exchanges of goods. After that, though perhaps less in Great Britain than elsewhere, the rise in prices was stayed, and the policy of governments and traders entered on a restrictive and protectionist phase in which they rather competed for what had already been gained than opened up new resources. But the level at which European economy steadied down was far higher than that from which it had started in the time of Vasco da Gama and Columbus. North America, South America, the Indies constituted, if we are thinking in terms of commodities, a great accession to the sources of supply and to the 'vent' of European industry, as the writers of the time would have said.

Here again the change in scale meant a change in organization. The seventeenth and eighteenth centuries were the age of the great trading companies, and these companies were the expression of the needs of the new age in commerce. They were created by the states, because the states could not but concern themselves in commerce and this commerce could not live without the support of the states; but they were owned and managed by private enterprise because private men were still the only source of that energy which was needed for such great undertakings. The states could make men serve them directly as soldiers or officials, but they had not yet reached the stage in which they could make economic activities a part of the public service. These were not, to be sure, the first trading companies. Association was the typical trading form of the Middle Ages: but there were fundamental points of contrast between the medieval companies and the modern. Passing over details and exceptions, we may state them thus:[1] The first function of the medieval associations in international trade was protection, the physical protection of the merchants on their journeys to fairs and the like. The associations had their chief seats abroad, where the merchants went to do their trade. They were often national in character, but companies were not formed for the home trade between one town and another. They were for the foreign trade, in which all had similar interests. Their second function was to extend to this trade abroad the same principles of just price, the limitation of sales and so forth, which we have already seen at work in municipal regulation. In this their aim was to enable the greatest possible number of their members to make a fair living. The scale of medieval commerce was so small that a trifling variation in the available quantity of a commodity made a serious change in the price, so that common control was the more necessary for this purpose. The members of the medieval companies were men, or physical persons; there were no juridical persons, no firms or corporations among them. The finances of the associations were on a basis of equality between the members; their principal item of revenue consisted in entrance fees which were the same for all. The association itself did not trade; its business was to protect and regulate the trade of its members.

When the three nations which were to be the economic leaders of the seventeenth century came to develop a considerable distant trade, new forms of organization sprang up amongst them, with many variations and from many causes, but yet with broad similarities and with broad differences

[1] See the excellent discussion in S. van Brakel, *De Hollandsche handelscompagnien der zeventiende eeuw*, 1908.

from the medieval forms. This development was to lead ultimately, long after our period, to a state of things in which a special form of joint-stock company, the limited liability company, should be the normal legal form of all kinds of business enterprises all over the world. That was still far in the future. What was achieved in the seventeenth century was that the joint-stock enterprise established itself as the form for the greater commerce, that is the company which traded for itself and distributed the profits to its shareholders in proportion to the amounts of capital which they had contributed to it.

No great institution begins at a definite moment. It must be the result of long preparation and its leading features must be to some extent anticipated before any birthday that may be selected. It is more accurate therefore to date the origin of any such institution vaguely than to date it precisely. Again a type of organization may be devised to meet certain conditions, then given up and forgotten, but revived or invented again when similar conditions return. There had been joint-stock companies in both Italy and Germany in the late Middle Ages; but those of the seventeenth century are not continuous with them. With this explanation of what is meant by the phrase, it may be said that it was in England that the joint-stock principle first definitely emerged, with the foundation of the Russian Company in 1553 and the first African Company in the same year.[1] From the legal point of view it was a fusion of the principle of the guild or association with the principle of partnership. Common measures were still taken as they had been by the medieval associations, some of them, such as the defence against armed attack, being simply the continuation of the old functions, but to these was now added the new task of common trading: the members of the association were now also partners in an enterprise. A deliberate effort was being made at that time to improve the economic position of the country and the financial position of the government by opening up new foreign trades with countries in which English trade had hitherto been little

[1] Professor W. R. Scott's *Joint-Stock Companies to 1720*, 3 vols., 1911–12, is the standard work.

developed. Russia was typical of these countries: it was more distant than the European countries with which the old 'regulated companies' had traded, and it was less civilized. The individual member of the company was so much the less likely to find his advantage in using his own capital as he thought best. Larger ships were required, but at the same time the amount ventured by the individual trader was, for this new and less certain trade, relatively if not absolutely smaller, so that instead of a number of separately owned and managed portions of the cargo, it was an economy to have the whole in one ownership.

The principle, once evolved, spread rapidly. Some of the old regulated companies survived—in Adam Smith's time there were still five, the 'Hamburgh', Russian and Eastland, which he called merely useless, the Turkey and African which he thought abusive–but the main work of the greater commerce and much other work in colonization and industry came to be done by joint-stock companies. The names of the three greatest, the East India Company, the Bank of England, the South Sea Company, sum up in themselves a great part of English history, but these were only the greatest among many. In all, good, bad, and indifferent, short-lived or long-lived, sound or fraudulent, Professor Scott reckons 49 founded between 1553 and 1680 and 56 between 1680 and 1719. The increase in the amount of capital employed by the joint-stock system was equally striking. It financed English shipping and colonization, the extension and consolidation of distant foreign trades, the organization of credit, and the carrying on of new manufactures, for instance those which were made possible by the skill of the immigrant Huguenots. Other reasons, besides the general favouring conditions already mentioned, may be ascribed for its success. It broke down the quasi-monopoly of mercantile capital as such, that is, it enabled others than merchants to put their money into trade, thus increasing the available stores of capital. It united different classes of men in the ventures, and so was able to associate the technical knowledge of the merchant with the political influence and the judgement of the man of larger affairs, who was equally needed in that adventurous and difficult stage of commercial development.

Among the Dutch the joint-stock principle developed a little later than in England and from causes which were up to a point, though not altogether, the same. Here too was the need to protect the distant trades by arming ships and erecting forts: a kindred motive which affected the Dutch and not the English was the desire to use commercial aggression as a means of injuring their enemy Spain. They often tried and often failed in the first years of the century to get the English to join them in a naval and commercial offensive in the East. Next came, as in England, the assignment of newly explored lands to the discoverers, as in the short-lived company which founded New Amsterdam. The desire of the states to raise revenue was present here as in England, though in Holland it played a less conspicuous part, the state being weaker in comparison with the merchant class. The richer merchants were able to defeat the plan for a Guinea Company in which others would have shared the profits which they were able to keep to themselves. As in England, the joint-stock form was used when capital had to be raised for an exceptionally expensive undertaking: no other method could have floated the West India Company or the projected marine insurance company which never came into being. Another motive of which the operation is seen more clearly in Holland than in England was the desire of the traders, for reasons similar to those of the firms which form modern trusts, to eliminate competition.

The Dutch East India Company was not only formed by the union of pre-existing companies but was, even after their coalescence, federal in structure. It was more like a modern trust than a simple modern company. The shareholders all got the same dividend, whatever 'chamber' they belonged to; but the separate local 'chambers' had their own directors, ships, selling-places, and so forth. This was due not solely to economic causes, but also to special local conditions. There were many towns in Holland capable of having 'chambers' in them. The political organization of the country was such that each of them could make its influence tell. The shareholders were predominantly traders, not *rentiers*, and they wanted to have the 'chambers' in their towns because of the business which they brought to the localities. The federal division into 'chambers' is thus typically Dutch. It is found even more markedly in the Dutch Northern Company than in the East India Company: the Northern Company has been called a production-cartel held together by the common enjoyment of a monopoly. The only parallels outside Holland seem to be in the plan made by the Dutchman Usselincx for a Swedish South Sea Company, and in the Prussian companies, which were much influenced by Dutch emigrants, but in which the same result was furthered by another cause, the scarcity of capital in Prussia, which made it necessary to interest all the available towns.[1]

The comparison between these seventeenth-century companies and modern trusts is misleading unless the fundamental difference is also borne in mind. Modern trusts and combines are based on voluntary agreement or on the triumph of some firms over others purely in the sphere of trading competition. In the seventeenth century something more was needed before it was possible to eliminate competition. Every one of these companies in every country owed its existence to an act of the state. Government aid, often in other forms as well, but always in one indispensable form, was necessary for them, and that indispensable form was the grant of a monopoly. It was the continuation of the medieval régime of privilege: the state granted to certain men, and to them only, the right to carry on a certain branch of business. The grants were sometimes nominally to all who would engage in a trade, but in practice the admission came to be limited to those who bought shares. The main line of criticism against the companies in both England and Holland came from those who wished to be allowed to compete against the favoured monopolists, interlopers who objected to being excluded from the same trade, or producers who wished to compete against the imported articles, as, for instance, calico-printers wished in various countries to compete against the authentic calicoes of Calicut. Never, broadly speaking, was the criticism from the point of view of

[1] The substance of this paragraph is derived mainly from Dr. van Brakel's book.

the consumer, who had to pay more for an article because the sellers were monopolists: thus the opposition to the companies differed in its turn from that against modern trusts. It was often disingenuous: the interloper often wished to derive advantage from the forts and other services of the companies without paying his share towards them.

The distinctive characteristic of the French companies[1] is their close dependence on the state. In England and Holland the state had sometimes taken the initiative, but the main impulse of foundation and expansion came from the trading classes. The French companies were formed partly in rivalry with the Dutch and partly in imitation of them. There were indeed attempts in earlier generations, but the first important efforts to introduce this type of organization were made as part of the great schemes of social and economic reconstruction in the time of Henry IV and his minister Sully. The soul of the abortive East India Company of 1604 was the Fleming, Gérard de Roy. In the last years of Henry's reign another attempt was made with ships and men from Amsterdam, but it failed when the Dutch protested against this poaching. A group of companies for trade with Africa, Asia, and America were founded by Richelieu between 1626 and 1642. One by one they fell into decay, but they were all either revived or imitated in the great mercantilist period of France, the time of Colbert, who was the minister of Louis XIV, and was at the height of his power from 1665 to 1673.

The condition of France was much less favourable for their establishment than that of Holland, and consequently their history was less successful. Most of them underwent many changes of ownership—that of (North) Africa was reconstructed or revived half a dozen times in the century—or failed and were revived only to fail again. In Asia and Africa they had not achieved much solid foothold by the end of the seventeenth century, though they, like the English companies, outdid the Dutch in the settlement of North America. They were able to do this partly because

[1] The best general survey is in the not altogether satisfactory work of P. Bonnassieux, *Les grandes compagnies de commerce*, 1892.

they had a very powerful state behind them; but this connexion with political power was not always advantageous: the wars of Louis XIV did them much harm. Colbert's Northern Company was ruined by the Dutch war of 1672; his East India Company suffered much in the wars from 1691 to 1713, which were largely wars of commerce, and was prostrate when John Law took over its management in 1720; his Africa Company was practically destroyed by the fighting against the Algerines in 1682. Thus their legacy to the eighteenth century cannot be compared with that of the English companies or the Dutch. It included the North American colonies, the Newfoundland fishery, the West Indian plantations, Madagascar, and some Indian factories. That was no small inheritance, but the North American colonies were to be lost, the Indian factories had no great future awaiting them, the sugar colonies, like those of England, were ultimately to lose their value. The more or less bankrupt remnants of the other companies might have served as a warning against the mistakes of policy which in the future were to hasten this decline. That lesson was not drawn. These remnants were for the most part absorbed in the projects of the adventurer Law, and some of them kept on a feeble existence after his catastrophe.

In structure the French companies differed from those of other countries. They were artificial creations of government. The kings took up large holdings of shares in them, and the men who surrounded the kings, no doubt not altogether of their own free will, followed suit. Colbert used strong administrative pressure to raise capital for his companies. In return the king's financial advisers had much to do with their management. The monopolies were more rigid than those of Holland, which in turn were more rigid than those of England. The companies were hampered by political interference: those of Richelieu, for instance, were not allowed to have Protestants as members. Colbert's East India Company had to govern Madagascar according to the legal *coutume de Paris*, which reminds one of the complaint made in our own time that French progress in the Sahara was retarded by the refusal of the camel to accommodate its habits to administrative regulations made in Paris. All Colbert's companies had to work according to fixed scales of prices and salaries. In France the government did more than was done elsewhere to encourage the companies by exempting them from tolls and duties; but Holland was far less a protectionist country than France or England, and Dutch duties were light to start with, so this was an advantage over the English rather than the Dutch. Some of the French companies were too ambitious and took over privileges of an unpractical magnitude, a temptation into which projectors were always liable to fall in other countries as well. It is, however, only in France that there are instances of companies handing over part of their functions to the Crown. The Levant Company founded in 1670 had the most favourable field for French enterprise, but it failed through bad trading methods and its privileges were handed over to an individual merchant in 1690. It was to private enterprise that the success of the French Levant trade in the eighteenth century was due. It does not seem unfair to say that the comparative ill-success of the French companies of the seventeenth century sprang from their failure to use private enterprise in the way in which it was used by the English and Dutch, and ultimately from the lack of a sufficiently vigorous trading community. France, after all, made demands on her citizens for the purposes of war which left little to spare for this less glorious work.

The other European countries which founded trading companies did so largely in imitation of the Dutch: how far the English example affected them is, I believe, a subject in which investigation is still needed. The Danes made an attempt at an East India Company at the instance of the Dutchman Boschouwer in 1612; this and its seventeenth-century successors did little good, but another Dutchman, Josias van Asperen, started another in 1728. Several other companies were started in the seventeenth century and the Iceland Company was important for a generation, but the flourishing period of Danish trade organized in this way did not set in until the eighteenth. The Danish East India Company was in fact only a Dutch company with an alibi; so were the

Swedish South Sea and Africa Companies, which were founded by two great Dutch organizers Usselincx and Louis de Geer. In the first half of the century the Dutch established an almost complete control over the economic life of Sweden: Dutch capital controlled in particular the mines and the commerce of the country. Reaction against this, with the general political energy of Sweden, led it in the time of Gustavus Adolphus into a marked phase of mercantilism, and amongst other steps came the foundation of an East India Company in 1626. Like Louis XIV, however, Gustavus undid his own work by his wars. The company was stifled. Gustavus's successor, Christina, revived it, but it was dissolved in 1671, and Sweden, like Denmark, had to wait for success until the eighteenth century. Prussia started late as a company-promoting country. Its African Company, founded about 1683 at Pillau and transferred to Emden, underwent a reconstruction in 1697, and sold its establishments on the West Coast to the Dutch East India Company in 1732. The Prussian East India Company, founded in 1684, with the advice of the famous French traveller Tavernier, was abortive. Companies which belong to the same general movement have been traced in yet other places, for instance Genoa. We need not stay over them. The history of joint-stock companies affords a clear illustration of the general fact to which we have already adverted, that the French, English, and Dutch were economically moving in advance of the rest of Europe.

Not less important in economic history than the changes in the organization of commerce and even more directly important for their influence on political development were the changes in finance. The two are, of course, closely interwoven, and we have already once or twice touched upon the latter of them.[1] One of the factors in the rise of capitalism was the need of large sums of money for military purposes at the end of the Middle Ages. War had become a great

[1] The work of R. Ehrenberg, *Das Zeitalter der Fugger*, deals mainly with an earlier period, but the second volume (1896) still affords the best introduction to this subject. The English translation (1927) is unfortunately incomplete.

industry which princes could not carry on with their own resources, and which they had to resign to *condottieri* and capitalists. The period from the Emperor Maximilian I (1493–1519) to King Louis XIII of France (1610–43) has been well named, after the great banking family of Augsburg, 'the age of the Fuggers'. This age ended when the need for money rose to still greater proportions, and the banker-dynasties could no longer meet it. The change which made the next step in the swelling of finances possible was the substitution of the credit of the state for the credit of private financial houses. War became an industry of the state. The only credit adequate to carry it on was the credit of the states, or more exactly of the great lending states, round which were grouped fringes of smaller, poorer, subsidized, or borrowing states, the clients of the great allies who financed their little armies for them. Money therefore came under national control, and the history of nations began to revolve, as it still revolves, round the history of national debts.

One of the causes, or at any rate one of the aspects, of the decline of Spain, that great political phenomenon of the century, was Spain's failure to adapt herself to these new requirements. Every twenty years or so the kings of Spain repudiated their public debts or settled them by compulsory conversions. They did it in 1557, in 1575, in 1596, in 1607, in 1627, and in 1647. Those years are milestones in the retreat of Spanish power. After a repudiation Spain was unable to raise more money and therefore unable to go on fighting. One great war against France ended in 1559, another in 1598; that against the Dutch was suspended in 1609, and definitely lost in 1648. The worst of the confiscatory measures were taken in 1627–32, and it was then that the financial houses which had backed up the Spanish monarchy, among them the famous Fuggers, went under. In the later seventeenth century the confusion deepened, and we shall see that Spain was then to all intents and purposes unable to bring any effective army into the field.

France began to cope with the new problem no better than Spain. By 1575 her king could raise no more loans, and in

1580 the existing liabilities were repudiated. France, however, was happier than Spain in being able still to attract Italian lenders, and they, not without anxious moments, and not without arousing unpopularity, carried her on until Sully, a really eminent financier, began to put things in better order. His master Henry IV had in 1596 assumed the burden of his predecessor's debts: but Sully's measures, though their strength lay in economy, system, and integrity, included also a partial repudiation and a compulsory reduction of interest to the low rate of four per cent. After Sully came a period of confusion in which the old system perished. The old lenders had been for the most part foreigners, and they had stood over against the finance minister in a position of independence. That state of things did not survive the state bankruptcy of 1648 and the civil war of the Fronde. After those convulsions the minister got his loans from Frenchmen who were his dependents, men on whom he conferred the valuable privilege of lending to the state.

Colbert, coming in after the ruin of an ostentatious and careless predecessor, was the man of the new system. He aimed at centralization, economy, an increased revenue from taxation, the paying off of the funded debt; but in these great tasks he made less headway than in depressing the status of the loan-mongers. In 1660–4 he carried through, against opposition to which he made some slight concessions, a debt conversion: in 1665 he fixed the rate of interest at five per cent. His finance, however, could not stand against the rising cost of the wars which, as we have seen, were so disastrous for his trading companies. The Dutch war of 1672, a turning-point in the history of European finance, drove him to raise new loans, to create and sell new offices, to anticipate revenue. His resource still enabled him to make financial reforms. In 1674 he began to collect money direct from lenders among the public, without the intermediary negotiators of loans, and so he got his money cheaper. But by 1680 he gave it as his opinion that the credit of the state ought not to be exploited further. When he died in 1683 it had been pledged far beyond that limit, and the remaining enterprises of Louis XIV were carried out against a background of deepening insolvency.

The financial history of England offers a remarkable contrast, and yet within it a remarkable analogy. While Philip II of Spain and Henry III of France were evading their creditors, Queen Elizabeth was the one solvent sovereign of her time. It was in the Stuart period that the finances, like so much else in the national institutions, went seriously wrong. James I and his successors allowed them indeed to get into the same difficulties in which the French and the Spaniards were labouring, and nothing was done to make more than a temporary improvement until the fall of the Stuarts in 1688. It would be unfair not to mention that the editor to whom we owe the monumental *Calendar of Treasury Books*, which is the basis for the history of later Stuart finance, Dr. W. A. Shaw, has set up a defence of the financial and general policy of Charles II, the pensioner of Louis XIV. He sees in the stop of the exchequer, the English compulsory conversion which resulted from the same Dutch-French-English war of 1672, not an unscrupulous act of confiscation; but a necessary operation of finance. This is no place for a discussion of his views: in all such questions there is always the difficulty of agreeing as to what is unscrupulous and what is legitimate. But the old view was that until the revolution of 1688 English finance was backward, and I am unable to give up that view. Probably no one will dispute the other old opinion that after 1688 the English finances were conspicuously well-managed and successful. Fortified by the creation of the Bank of England they stood the strain of the struggle against Louis XIV, and started England fairly on the way to empire.

The one state which throughout the century was always solvent was the Dutch republic. Although it had a large and complicated debt it never lost the confidence of the lenders. Between 1640 and 1655 the rate of interest which it found necessary to pay on its loans came down from 6¼ per cent. as low as 4 per cent. Even in the year 1672, during the war which had such ill effects on French and English credit, although the French troops had overrun their country, the

Dutch were able to raise money for the hire of auxiliary troops. After that time a short-term floating debt grew up, and early in the next century the republic, having overstrained its real resources in the great wars, was to fall into serious financial embarrassments; but, as long as the seventeenth century lasted, the signs of this coming decline were indistinct. The system of public finance was not in all respects modern: tax-farming, for instance, still continued. But it was admirably calculated to inspire confidence. The loans were subscribed direct by the original lender to the states; the states and other public borrowing bodies were corporations responsible for payment; the republic was a trade-state; the lender-class was identical with the regent-class, the ruling oligarchy. They were not passive *rentiers* but active business men whose business was dealing in loans to the states. Both as lenders and as borrowers they were on the spot and dealing with men they knew. They were the members of a thoroughly business-like community.[1]

That was really the most important point of all. Sound public finance is not likely to exist except on a basis of sound private finance; and sound private finance comes into existence when there is a healthy business community to give it employment and keep it straight. The general business world of Amsterdam was the best existing example of such a community for a period which very nearly coincided with the chronological seventeenth century. It was about 1600 that Amsterdam established itself as the great successor of Antwerp in international financial business; not till about 1700 did London begin to pull ahead. The many-sided development of all kinds of finance in Amsterdam gives an indication of the variety of the tendencies which were converging to bring capitalism forward. Various kinds of dealing were common there which must rest on a high standard of confidence. The Bank of Amsterdam, the greatest of the Dutch banks, was founded in 1609 after Italian models. It was never a bank of issue like the Bank

[1] The clearest and most recent account of Dutch public finance is that of Baasch, *Holländische Wirtschaftsgeschichte*, 1927, which has an admirable general bibliography of Dutch economic history.

of England: its more modest function was to provide a machinery for making the best possible use of metallic currency. How it did so is explained by Adam Smith in a Digression which is a model of lucidity.[1] Besides the bank Amsterdam had its Exchange. The nature of the early exchanges is sometimes misunderstood: they were essentially meeting-places, buildings for personal meetings betwen business people of all kinds for all kinds of business purposes. They do not need any technical explanation like Adam Smith's explanation of the bank: to see what they were like we need only turn to their lists of current prices. Those for the Amsterdam exchange for 1624–6 have recently been printed.[2] They begin with five different sorts of pepper, and they include more than three hundred commodities. They are the lists of a universal exchange for produce and manufactured articles.

In Amsterdam one part of the business of the exchange was the trade in stocks and shares. This began not with the state-paper, the shares in government loans, which were not regularly dealt in before the turning-point of 1672–3, but with the shares of the great trading companies. It was from speculation, not from investment and the transference of investments, that it began. By the end of the century the technique of speculation had developed many of its modern forms, time-transactions, first 'bulls' and then 'bears' appeared, and there were regular settling-days as on a modern exchange. On the London exchange options and bear sales were understood in the time of William III; though some historians are reluctant to see these as more than interesting anticipations of what was not to become important for some long time. There was little trade of any kind in stocks and shares in London before 1688. Until then East India shares seldom came into the market. During William's reign the trade developed rapidly. Macaulay has described it in a memorable passage,[3] but it has been justly said that this account is one-sided. It lays stress rightly on the untapped

[1] *Wealth of Nations*, Bk. IV, c. iii.

[2] By Dr. H. W. Aeckerle in *Economisch-historisch jaarboek*, xiii. 86 ff. (1927).

[3] *Hist. of England*, ed. Firth, v. 2276 ff.

resources of capital in the nation and the advantage of the stock-market for investors; but it reproduces from satirists and pamphleteers too much of the contemporary hostility to stock-jobbers and their devices. Fraudulent enticements to foolish investors were common; but the demand for capital had its solid basis in the needs of the government for its wars, and of the country's rapidly expanding commerce and industry.

After those of Amsterdam and London the other exchanges of the seventeenth century need only a brief notice. In Vienna, and Germany generally, their origin belongs mainly to the eighteenth century. That of Paris was becoming important. It began to gain at the expense of Lyons in the last part of the sixteenth century; but in the seventeenth France had no true stock-exchanges. There was no trade in the shares of the French companies. No doubt this was partly because they used to a great extent the capital of nobles and others who were not themselves traders, and had not the same contact with practical affairs as the English investing class.

Such in outline were the innovations of the seventeenth century in the organization of commerce. It would take us into too much detail to say more about them or to discuss the other minor changes by which they were accompanied, changes which ran down into the smallest crevices of social life. Banks and banking went through some of the crucial early stages of their growth. New classes of traders sprang up, especially various types of men who traded on 'commission', that is, not themselves owning the goods they handled, as the old merchants had done, but buying or selling them on account of some one else, very often some foreigner whom they had never seen. The many improvements in communications facilitated this development.

These improvements were due not so much to technical invention as to an extended use of the means already available.[1] Political, social, and economic conditions changed in

[1] An admirable introduction to the whole subject is the little 'popular' book of the late Vicomte Georges d'Avenel, *L'évolution des moyens de transport*, 1919.

such a way as to increase the demand for movements of men and goods and to remove many obstacles from their way. Such technical improvements as there were may be enumerated quickly. At sea the important new inventions were few. The building of merchant-ships improved, but less than that of ships of war. The chief change was that the East India trade led to the adoption of larger types. The telescope, which was perfected about 1608, made some difference to navigation. What every one wanted and many people tried to devise was a good means of ascertaining longitude; but for the present these efforts had no success. Map-making progressed steadily. At the beginning of the century the Englishman, Edward Wright, was publishing those studies by which he revolutionized the mathematics of navigation and, amongst other things, found out how to construct maps on what is called Mercator's projection. In 1665 the Jesuit father Athanasius Kircher for the first time marked the currents of the sea on a chart. Before the end of the century Edmund Halley came back from his adventurous voyage in the *Paramour Pink* without having solved the riddle of the longitude, but with the materials for his general chart for the use of seamen on which the variations of the compass were shown. On land also map-making was being perfected. In the Middle Ages road-maps and 'itineraries' or route-books had been rarities; in the late sixteenth century they had multiplied quickly all over western Europe, and in the seventeenth a considerable variety of them were in common use. By its end the best of them approached in fullness and accuracy those which we use now.[1] A number of improvements were made in the building of wagons and coaches.[2]

On the other side, in the development of existing methods, there is so much to record that only a sketch is possible. Great steps forward were made, which were carried on even more vigorously in the eighteenth century, so that by the end of the old régime the system had done almost as much in the

[1] See Sir H. George Fordham's *Studies in Carto-Bibliography* (1914) and *Road-Books and Itineraries of Great Britain* (1924).

[2] The pleasantest way of getting an idea of them is to look through Mr. Belloc's picture-book *The Highway and its Vehicles*, 1926.

progressive countries as could be done without steamships and railways. The first great division of transport is by sea. The sea as a highway is not itself capable of improvement except where it touches the land or where its bottom is shallow; but at these places governments and trading men were getting to work. Lighthouses were built: the Eddystone, to Englishmen the most famous of them all, was finished in 1699. Buoys were placed about the channels. All along the western European coasts new harbour-works were undertaken.

Inland transport by water was proportionately far more important then than it is now, and much was done to improve it by clearing obstructions from the courses of rivers and by cutting canals to connect them. In France, so the queen, Catherine de Médicis, used to say, there were more navigable waterways than in all the rest of Europe; but the civil wars of the sixteenth century, for which Catherine was partly to blame, had led to a general disorganization. Unauthorized obstructions, whether physical, like weirs and mills, or economic, like the exaction of tolls, impeded movement. Sully, the minister of Henry IV, tried to put this to rights. Navigable rivers were declared all to belong to the royal domain, and, though as a compromise obstructions dating back before 1566 were permitted in return for payments, no new encroachments were to be allowed. Much work was done on the waterways, and more was projected. Five rivers, or parts of them, were actually rendered navigable: the Vesle (a tributary of the Aisne), the Vienne, the Eure, the Ourcq, and the Vilaine. The greatest projects discussed were those for uniting the Mediterranean with the Garonne, or—the plan which was later preferred—with the Seine. A beginning was made with the Seine–Loire canal (which was opened in 1642); that between the Saône and the Rhône was planned but not made till 1783–93; that from the Saône to the Meuse was not even planned, but it was thought of; that from the Saône to the Yonne was studied but not begun till 1775. Under Colbert general and decided progress was made. Above all Colbert permitted Pierre-Paul Riquet, baron de Bonrepos, a man of equal public spirit, imagination, and common sense, to push through his plan for a canal between the Rhône and the Garonne. In 1681 this feat of engineering was completed: the Atlantic was joined to the Mediterranean. The effect of this on the cheapness of moving heavy goods may be seen by an example of nearly a century later. When Tobias Smollett travelled to Nice by way of Paris in 1767 he sent his heavy luggage by sea to Bordeaux and then, through the canal, to Cette and so to the Riviera.[1]

After France the chief scene of new canal-making was the plain of northern Germany. Here engineering was easy, but special causes hindered it. One which lasted throughout the period was the territorial division of the country between many princes, who often could not be got to agree on questions of toll and finance, and who sometimes preferred a route to go roundabout within their own dominions rather than direct through those of a possible enemy. A special hindrance was the confusion of the Thirty Years' War. We know that in that period the existing Finow canal was destroyed, and the canal between Schwerin and the Baltic seaport Wismar fell into disuse. Nevertheless the century saw much progress. The prince who deserves the greatest share of the credit for this was Frederick William of Brandenburg, called the Great Elector, the same who welcomed the exiled Huguenots from France. After him is named the Frederick William Canal, from the Spree to the Oder, which had long been in contemplation and construction, and through which the first ship sailed in 1669. Other princes also did good work: the navigation of the Rhine, for instance, was much improved by the blasting of rocks, so that large rafts of timber could now be floated down.[2] In Sweden King Charles IX cut a canal about two miles long which began the linking of Gothenburg with the Baltic.

In England the waterways were left to private enterprise. Canal-making had not begun: that had to wait till the second half of the eighteenth century. A number of acts of

[1] *Works* (1797), iii. 10–11.

[2] For German canals and roads I have used K. Kretschmer, *Historische Geographie von Mitteleuropa*, 1904, which is also very helpful for political and ecclesiastical geography.

parliament were passed granting powers for the improvement of rivers. Locks were made, for instance, in the Thames between Oxford and London: until the time of James I there were only weirs, like that which survived until a few years ago a mile or so above Oxford at Medley, a way of changing level which requires effort and involves a little danger. The Dutch waterways, together with the drainage and dikes which form a single system with them, had already a long history and formed one of the greatest works of engineering in the world. The organization by which they were controlled was an important part of the machinery of government. In their development the seventeenth century saw much progress, but it was less markedly a period of novelty than in other countries, for the simple reason that so much more had been done in Holland in earlier times.

It was cheaper to move goods for long distances by water than by land, and the waterways were the only possible routes for such very heavy burdens as siege-artillery. When Marlborough took his siege-train seventy miles by land to Lille in 1708 the feat was acclaimed as unique. Ten years earlier the states of Burgundy voted the money to buy a statue of Louis XIV in bronze. It was brought by water to Auxerre and set out on its way to Dijon by land; but it stuck in the mud, and it had to be kept in a shed for no less than twenty-one years, until the road was in a condition to bear it. That is a specimen of the stories, thousands in number, which are told about the badness of roads by land. There are whole volumes of these anecdotes about mud and floods, broken bridges, overturned coaches, highwaymen, the perils of travel, its dilatoriness, its high cost. So familiar are they that it is necessary to remind oneself of the other side. Complaints about the badness of roads in one place are sometimes evidence not only that there they were bad but also that elsewhere they were better: the man who complains has most likely formed his idea of what a road ought to be like, not by an effort of creative imagination, but by seeing a good one. And, however bad the roads were, they carried a great part of the internal traffic of Europe. The highways in and out of every thriving town were crowded with waggons, pack-animals, mounted men and women, pedestrians, flocks, and herds. Somehow or another they all managed to move, and as time went on they were gradually moving faster.

The Roman Empire had an imperial system of roads, continental main roads, trunk-roads, side-roads, cross-roads, planned as a whole for military and civil needs, laid out by good engineers, and finished with a durable surface. There were tracks and footpaths and frequented routes before the Romans, but wherever they went the Romans drilled and disciplined them into a system. Of that system, after a thousand years of use with the minimum of maintenance and patching, the Middle Ages handed over to modern Europe the worn, interrupted, dilapidated remains. The additions that had been made, as the directions of trade and pilgrimages shifted in the course of history, were not very different in quality or utility from the barbarous communications which the Romans had transformed. It was necessary to do once more such work as the Romans had done, but the seventeenth century handed the task on to the eighteenth with but little actually accomplished.

In France, as might have been expected, the first serious attempts were made, once more, by Sully. For him in 1599 the office of *grand voyer* was created, the nucleus of the administrative machinery of the *Ponts et Chaussées*, the first national highway department of modern times. Regulations were issued, inspection was carried out, some money was spent. At first the work was mainly restorative: bridges were built, main roads were drained and paved, and trees planted beside them. The countryfolk were discouraged from using the pavements as quarries and the trees as firewood. Between 1553 and 1632 there is no actual survey of the roads of France, so we do not know exactly how much Sully effected; but it is clear that it was disappointingly little. The budget of the *Ponts et Chaussées* was never large.[1] The same seems to hold good of the century as a whole: it was only in the eighteenth century, about 1735 under Cardinal Fleury, that

[1] For its history see P. Viollet, *Le roi et ses ministres pendant les trois derniers siècles de la monarchie*, 1912, pp. 476 ff. This book is a most valuable guide to all subjects connected with the French administration.

the creation of roads in the modern sense of the word began in earnest. Small success attended the attempts to get road-making done by other authorities than the state: the land-owners of adjoining property, for instance, could not be induced to undertake it.

In England there was no central department for roads, and the parliamentary legislation, which began to concern itself with them from the time of Philip and Mary, imposed the duty of upkeep on the parishes, and, for some minor purposes, on the landowners. Every man was liable to give either money or labour or materials; but, in spite of many attempts at reform, this machinery never solved the problem. The reconstruction of the English road-system was achieved by the turnpike trusts, suggested early in the seventeenth century, of which the first constituted by a private act of parliament dated from 1706.[1]

In Germany the rise of some great centres of trade like Hamburg, Leipzig, and Frankfort on the Main, and still more the consolidation of extensive territorial states appear to have increased the amount of the traffic which followed certain routes, but even in western and northern Germany there seems little trace of road-building. East of the Vistula there seem to have been no metalled roads. Even in the most advanced parts of Europe roads with made surfaces sometimes served purposes of pleasure and display rather than that of business. The old brick road through the woods between The Hague and Scheveningen, which was made in 1666, was a 'promenade', more an extension of the streets of the town than a road in the true sense. Though there are many records of journeys in land-wagons as well as in the public vehicles on the waterways of Holland, the roads there, as in most parts of Europe, do not seem as a rule to have been fit for horses to move at anything better than a walk.

For evidence of the improvement of communication we

[1] For the whole subject see S. and B. Webb, *The King's Highway*, 1913, and Dorothy Ballen, *Bibliography of Road-Making and Roads in the United Kingdom*, 1914. The first turnpike bill (for the Biggleswade–Baldock road, 1622) has been printed by F. G. Emmison in *Bulletin of the Institute of Historical Research*, 1935 (1935), 108. The first turnpike act was a public act (15 Car. II, c. 1) for the London–York road, and there were a few more in the seventeenth century.

must look rather to the way in which it was organized, and in this the seventeenth century saw one change which really deserves to be called revolutionary. This was the rise of government postal services.[1] The word 'post' is ambiguous. Its meaning is not the same when we talk about a 'post-horse' or a 'post-chaise' as when we talk about a 'postman' or a modern 'post office'. The older meaning belongs to the time when kings had established relays of horses at fixed posts on the main roads so that their messengers could 'ride post' with dispatches. At first this system was jealously kept for the service of the state; after a time it began to be understood that it was for the advantage of a king as well as every one else to let members of the public use it in exchange for a fee. That stage of development had been reached long since. In the meantime postal services of another kind had been growing up in various ways almost unobserved. Traders whose main business it was to carry some other kind of loads began also to collect, transmit, and distribute letters. In England the common carriers did it.[2] In Germany, especially in the southern parts, it fell to the lot of the guilds of butchers, whose members penetrated into the recesses of the country to buy cattle. These private posts lingered on, more or less in conflict with the later monopolists, well into the seventeenth century. For more local purposes there were also growing up municipal posts. Medieval towns had had their officially recognized couriers, but it was apparently not until the seventeenth century that the town posts, over western Europe generally, played an important part. The London penny post was founded in 1681. Of the Swiss and German towns a considerable number had their own services in the sixteenth century, and these spread out their network over widening areas. First the town would start sending letters to distant centres, then there came treaties between two or more towns for mutual postal services. One of the

[1] G. Wolf, *Einführung in das Studium der neueren Geschichte*, 1910, pp. 29 ff., gives a brief general sketch; for more detail works on the posts of separate countries must be used.

[2] See Milton's second epitaph on Hobson: 'His Letters are deliver'd all and gon.'

most astonishing examples of Dutch federalism is the fact that until the year 1752 the Dutch posts, even to foreign countries, had not risen above this municipal organization. Then at last the selfishness of Amsterdam was overcome and the states of Holland took over the services.

By that time the inter-municipal system was merely an anomalous survival. Everywhere else the state had taken the bulk of postal business into its own hands. To do so was merely an extension of the principle of permitting the private use of the official couriers. Broadly speaking the change took place from the later sixteenth century to the later seventeenth. In Germany it came early and in a peculiar form. It was done on a feudal model: the grant of the post office was assimilated to the grant of a fief. The family of the Freiherren, afterwards princes, of Thurn and Taxis, were given the hereditary privilege and duty of organizing the posts of the empire. Their connexion with postal affairs began probably in the late fifteenth century and lasted until far on in the nineteenth. Not only the empire but the Netherlands also came under their control, and in the sixteenth century they were on the way to making an international postal system of their own. But the strongest political tendency of the time was against them. The national states were determined to be masters in their own dominions in this as well as other things. First the revolt of the Netherlands took away an area from the Taxis posts. Not without a struggle the Great Elector of Brandenburg freed his dominions from them and set up a postal service of his own. The influences of the time were on that side. The English state posts may be dated from the reign of Charles I, those of France from the contemporary domination of Richelieu. It appears that those of Denmark started within a few years of the same time. The preliminary step had been taken from which all further progress became easier and more certain.

The most interesting of the further developments is the growth of international postal connexions. It is easiest to watch those that went by sea. At the middle of the century England had no direct and regular continental posts except to France, Spain, and Flanders. The normal service, as for all long-distance postal services at that time, seems to have been once a week. In 1656 a weekly service of three frigates 'to run with oars' carrying no cargo was started between London and Lisbon. How long it went on I do not know, but perhaps not more than three years; at any rate it appears that from the time of the Treaty of the Pyrenees in 1659 the Dutch, if not the English, mails for the Peninsula began to go by land. It was not till 1659 or 1661 that a direct service between England and Holland was begun: before then the Taxis post to Antwerp or Ostend took the Dutch and German mails. There then began a service between the Brill (on the opposite side of the river from the Hook of Holland) and Harwich, Dover, or Yarmouth. It started to run twice a week, but in the earlier years it was ill managed, and it seems that the services were reduced, returning definitely to twice a week only in 1677. At that time there were three packets on this line, boats specially built to carry passengers and mails, not cargo. For France there were two and for Flanders two, while Ireland had three. By 1691 there were mails twice a week for France, Italy, Spain, the Spanish Netherlands, Germany, Sweden, and Denmark; but that was in time of war, and war, though it sometimes interrupted postal services, also added to them. This is interesting because it shows that the military and diplomatic dispatches and missions of those times required a provision which was not necessary for commercial purposes. Thus in the wars of William III and Queen Anne packets ran between Falmouth and Corunna; but they were laid up after the conclusion of peace.

The progress on land seems to have been similar: modest but definite. There, of course, services were more regular, since the sailing packets were often held back by the wind for days together; but they were very slow. The statistics of the number of letters carried seem at first sight puny. In 1693 the daily number of letters between France and England (then at war) rose no higher than 110 a day or 40,000 a year, whereas in 1913 there were, counting postcards, more than 30 millions. From France to Rome the daily average was only 40. For two successive weeks in July 1661, a year of peace, the letters received in Holland from London numbered 1,545 and 1,435. These figures, however, represent an intercourse which far exceeds that of the sixteenth century, and the increase is full of promise. The significance is not merely economic; it is not merely one side of the growth of commerce. We shall find its most important results when we come to deal with the history of literature and journalism.[1]

At this point it will be convenient to consider another question which lies outside the sphere of economics, that, namely, of how the development of commerce affected the course of international relations. A partial answer has been given already. It was national commerce, furthered by the action of national states which, in assisting it, regarded one another as rivals and competitors, rather than as fellow members of a world-wide trading community. We have seen how trade-war came to be one of the characteristic activities of the time. Whatever the state of the world's commerce may be, the spirit of exclusiveness and the desire to enrich a nation at the expense of foreigners will always be apt to cause this transition from competition to political hostility, and in the seventeenth century it was inevitable. In Asia and America rivalry was primitively simple. The quick way to profits was to oust some other and weaker European nation from those rich lands. It would have been laughable to suggest that in the long run the most profitable way of dealing with a neighbour was to approach him in a friendly spirit and discover what bargains could be struck for mutual advantage. The profitable bargains in those days were bargains that paid one side only; the nearer they approximated to robbery the more profitable they were.

Two propositions were occasionally enunciated which show that this might not always be so. First was the idea that there was room in the undeveloped parts of the world for all the European peoples, room and to spare for each of them to use its expansive energies without getting in the way of the others. The Dutch and the English began to reckon up the cost of their trade-wars and to doubt whether the rewards of

[1] Below, p. 331.

victory made up for the burden of debt and taxation and the losses of merchant shipping at sea. The merchants and the governments negotiated for an 'accord' between the Dutch and the English East India Companies. At one time the plan was for what would now be called a division of spheres of influence, at another it went as far as planning an actual union of the two companies. Although much effort was spent over them, these negotiations led to nothing. The proposals generally originated from the party which was consciously weaker, while the other party, which still had good hopes of gaining by a vigorous prosecution of its own ambitions, was unwilling to surrender any chance of expansion. Of the other commercial treaties of the century it must be said in the same way that they did little to mitigate international rivalry, and what little they did was due rather to consciousness of inability to go on struggling than to an enlightened appreciation of the benefits of good understanding.

The most important of these treaties relate to tariffs. When the French made peace with the Dutch and had to make concessions in order to get peace, they would promise (as in 1678) to withdraw an unfavourable tariff and restore one that permitted the Dutch greater openings for trade. When it suited them they went back on their concessions. There were indeed occasions when something like the later spirit of free trade actuated a government. Of these the most interesting is that of the Anglo-French commercial treaty of Utrecht in 1713, which was overthrown on party grounds which were also the reasonings of the commercial interest: then, and in general, the English trading community was obstinately anti-foreign. In England there is a striking paucity of utterances of the second of the two propositions to which I have referred. It was not unknown; instances of it can be exhumed from the pamphlets of the time, but it was a maxim not generally or widely believed. It is the maxim that the interest of a trading nation is peace. This is the wider principle underlying the attempts to eliminate rivalry between the nations, and it is frequently invoked in Dutch writings. Partly this was because the Dutch, in the second half of the century, though not yet in a state of decline, were commercially on the defensive. They were suffering from the wars, and, although they were probably not losing ground, they were not progressing like the English or even like their smaller rivals the Swedes or the Hamburghers. Moreover they were on the whole less of a fighting nation than the English. I do not mean that they fought less bravely or less well. Comparisons of that sort are hard to make, but if one had to give a decision on the point, it would be, on their records of the seventeenth century, a very close thing between the two nations. But in Holland the constitution, the social order, though they were capable of magnificent exertions of defence, were ill adapted to armed aggression.

Armed aggression, when all is said, was the heart of commerce. Nowhere was there less of humanitarian or tolerant feeling. To investigate the details of seafaring and colonial life is to find oneself in a world of tough men, exposing themselves to great risks, and putting up with great hardships, never slow to take the shortest way with other men whose presence might mean danger. It was not a life for delicate susceptibilities. Even in navies there were only the roughest beginnings of the chivalry of the sea, and it must be remembered that, in the literal sense of the word, at sea there had never been any chivalry, there had never been knights or a knightly code. It was an age of pirates and wreckers, press-gangs and mutineers. The tougher the seafaring man, the longer he lasted, and so with the seafaring nation.

The roughness of maritime and commercial life may be illustrated from the slave-trade. There had been slave-traders in Europe in the Middle Ages, but when African negroes began to be imported into the American colonies a new era of boom began for the man-hunters of the Guinea coast. The maritime nations eagerly contended for the trade. Genoa lost it to the English, Dutch, and Portuguese; the French tried but failed to gain it when the grandson of Louis XIV became the ruler of the Spanish colonies. We know what its horrors were in the succeeding century: in this they were so far from stirring pity or indignation that they were not even recorded. The days of protest were, however, at hand. From the time when George Fox visited Barbados in 1671 some of the Quakers began to feel compunction about both the slave-trade and slave-owning, and they addressed some exhortations against them both to their own society and to the world in general.[1] The English Puritan leader, Richard Baxter, in a book published in 1673, which may have been influenced by continental Catholic authors, although he permits slavery itself under strict conditions of justice, condemns the slave-hunters as the common enemies of mankind. Those who buy slaves from them 'and use them as beasts, for their meer commodity, and betray or destroy or neglect their souls, are,' he writes, 'fitter to be called incarnate Devils than Christians.'[2]

In the Catholic countries and their colonies, the tradition which mitigated the hardships of the weaker races was never lost from the earliest days of conquest, and there were seventeenth-century writers who applied it to negro slavery. It was indeed from Christianity that the great humanitarian movements of the next century took their first energy, not, as is often supposed, from the newer rationalistic social criticism which came to be associated with them and often to be hostile to the churches. It does seem, however, that sympathy with suffering became wider in the seventeenth century.[3]

[1] See G. L. Beer, *Old Colonial System*, i. 322–3, and various pamphlets such as the *Exhortation and Caution . . . against Buying or Keeping Negroes* published in 1693 by the party of George Keith, afterwards famous as 'the Christian Quaker'.

[2] *Chapters from a Christian Directory*, selected by Jeanette Tawney, 1925, p. 33.

[3] One curious instance may be mentioned. The custom of tying a plough to the horse's tail prevailed in Ireland until it was forbidden by a statute of Charles I. This alleges as its reasons not only the damage to the breed of horses, but also 'cruelty used to the beasts', the first mention of such a consideration, we are told, in any English law. (10 & 11 Car. I. c. 15; Lecky, *Ireland in the Eighteenth Century*, i. 336.)

V

INDUSTRIES

If we wish to find a link between the development of industry and the wider intellectual life of a community, it is natural to seek it in the history of mechanical and chemical invention.[1] That history has, indeed, peculiar difficulties. Just as genealogy has been falsified by the pretensions of family pride, so the history of many a great invention has been obscured by the rivalry of various countries or towns, each of which was ambitious to have the credit for it. Another difficulty arises from the slowness of communication in remote times. The claim to priority was often made quite honestly because the earlier appearance of an invention in some distant country was unknown. The first introduction of a device from abroad was often mistaken for the inventing itself.

In the seventeenth century the face of European life was being changed by the gradual dissemination of processes and devices which had been hit upon in the sixteenth or earlier. The paving and lighting of streets, the practical use of the diving-bell for work on wrecks, the use of forks at table (which the Englishman Coryat *furcifer*, who introduced them here, first saw in Italy in 1608),[2] the artificial cooling of drinks, the stopping of bottles with corks are all examples of customs which were not altogether new but which made their way over most of Europe in this century, having before that been confined to narrow parts of it. The same is true of the more strictly industrial processes of glass-making and tinning, and the important method of refining gold and silver ore by quicksilver. Saw-mills also were not new, but they were not introduced in the shipyards of Zaandam until 1596, into Sweden until 1653, nor into England until 1663, when they had to be abandoned because of popular opposition, an incident which was repeated at Limehouse as late as 1767 or

[1] For this subject J. Beckmann, *Hist. of Inventions and Discoveries* (numerous editions), is still useful.

[2] *Coryate's Crudities*, ed. of 1776, i. 106–7.

1768. The stocking-frame appears to have been invented in England about the end of the sixteenth century. At first the attempts to acclimatize it abroad were not successful, but by 1696 parliament prohibited the export of these, by then much improved, machines, from which it may be inferred that their use was becoming common abroad. Some of the inventions which came into widespread use were revivals or adaptations of what had been known to the ancients. Such was the hodometer or waywiser, for measuring roads by a wheel, which the Romans used, but which was first applied to a systematic measurement of English roads in the famous survey of Ogilby in the reign of Charles II.[1] Writers of the seventeenth century tended to suppose that almost everything that was useful or ingenious had been known to the ancients.

It would be absurd to attempt an enumeration of all the really new inventions of the century, but enough of them may be mentioned to illustrate some general principles. Altogether there were a great many, and this is not surprising, because when active and intelligent men are engaged on practical tasks, they will hit upon new contrivances. This century did not differ much in this respect from the sixteenth: both were times which added a number of little conveniences and elegances to daily life. The seventeenth has to its credit the making of ruby glass, cut glass, etched glass, the speaking-trumpet or megaphone, 'Turkish paper,' velvet paper with a pile, fire-hoses, fountain-pens, one of the best kinds of sympathetic ink, sugar of milk. It began a new era in expensive amusement with ices and champagne. Of improvements in the processes of the more necessary industries, however, there is much less to say, and in this the seventeenth century seems to be very different from the eighteenth. There were certainly improvements. The art of calico-printing was brought in from the East. Dyeing made considerable advances. In Holland and France some changes were introduced, or at least invented, in the methods of

[1] Ogilby's *Britannia*, a folio volume of maps, was published in 1675. John Evelyn mentions the waywiser in his diary of 13 July 1654 and, as attached to a carriage, 6 August 1657.

corn-milling. The Dutch worked out a number of new devices for dealing with ships, such as the 'camel' for raising them in the water. The Dutchman Blaeuw gave his name to a new and better type of printing-press. The sum total of these improvements seems, however, to be small in comparison with the general energy of the age, and this requires to be explained.

Few of the inventions we have named owed anything to the scientific inquiries for which the century is famous. The one outstanding example of inventions by a great scientist is the improvement of watches and clocks by Huygens. In the metallurgical industries science gave some help, for instance, in making it possible to give a milled edge to coins; but even in metal-working, and still more in other industries, inventions were for the most part made by 'artists', craftsmen, not by men of science. William Lee, the reputed inventor of the stocking-frame, was a man of education, but his figure is almost legendary, and there is nothing to connect him with scientific studies such as mechanics. One of the two men who, shortly after the end of the century, perfected the steam-pump, Newcomen, was an artificer; but the other, Savery, was an engineer-officer, deserving to be classed as a scientist, and these two only put the final touch to a long process of research which had occupied some of the best minds of Italy, Germany, France, and England. This, however, was unique; few of the other inventions of the seventeenth century sprang from the effective application of science. Some of them were vaguely foreshadowed by more or less fantastic theoretical inventors, whose paper-projects must not be taken too seriously. Most of them were not in touch with the makers of things. The most famous of these men, the Dutchman Cornelius Drebbel, seems to be an exception, but he too is a mysterious figure, and it is hard to believe that he made a submarine boat and travelled under water without artificial light from Westminster to Greenwich.[1] He does, on the other hand, seem to deserve the credit

[1] See Boyle, *Works*, ed. Birch, iii. 174, and Birch, *History of the Royal Society*. For French projects and experiments with submarines in 1634–41 see la Roncière, *Histoire de la marine française*, iv. 612–13.

for some improvements in the telescope, and his discovery of cochineal red is one of the landmarks in the history of the dyeing industry. He was one of the few men who applied science to industrial purposes. The worlds of business and of science were still far apart. What is more, the world of business itself was full of self-contained units, which jealously shut off their knowledge from one another, and consequently from the scientists as well. Trade secrets were vastly more important than they are now. Trades were still mysteries. Even an ambassador of the most distinguished scientific dilettante of the time, King Charles II, failed to elicit, on behalf of the great Mr. Boyle of the Royal Society, the German glass-blowers' secret of making convex mirrors without foil. Most of these secrets were embodied in the workmen who had learned them by practice and tradition, and so they were easily kept.

There were also forces from outside which were opposed to technical developments. It is often said that in the Middle Ages the guilds resisted their introduction, and it is less commonly remembered that in the age when corporations were declining and the supervision of industry was passing into the hands of the state, the new authority regarded them with little more favour than the old. There are a number of instances of legislation against them. Where machines threatened to reduce employment, the state sometimes intervened against them, as in the English proclamation against machines for making needles and brass buckles.[1] Perhaps a fear of riotous opposition was the chief motive of the widespread attempts to prohibit the use of the 'develishe invention' of the ribbon-loom, a machine on which sixteen or more ribbons could be woven at the same time. Its origin is somewhat obscure: some say that it was invented or perfected in Leyden about 1620, but it, or something like it, seems to have been common in England by 1621. At all events its use was circumscribed by resolutions of the Dutch states-general in 1623 and again in 1639 and 1661. It was prohibited in Nuremberg in 1664 and in the Spanish Netherlands in the

[1] Steele and Crawford, *Tudor and Stuart Proclamations*, nos. 1368 (needles, 1623/4), 1653 (brass buckles, 1632/3).

same year, in Cologne in 1676, in which year there were still disturbances against it in England.[1] Later in the century and early in the next, successive emperors prohibited it in the empire and the Austrian dominions. These prohibitions cannot all have been faithfully observed, but it seems they had much effect in retarding the spread of the machine.[2] A different motive for such prohibitions was protectionism. In the interests of the established textile industries and of the importers of Indian goods, calico-printing was for a time forbidden in both France and England. In Paris, Lyons, and Languedoc, as in several German states at different times, the use of indigo in dyeing was prohibited because it was imported from abroad.

These various causes probably suffice to explain the comparatively minor importance of industrial invention in the seventeenth century. The most effective contact between industry and the intellectual development of the time was not in technique but in organization, and even there, as generally happens, finance and commerce were ahead of industry, and the changes in industry for the most part filtered down through them. Old methods, like book-keeping by double entry, which had been gradually making its way since it was discovered in the later Middle Ages in Italy, helped in the increase of the scale of all business operations. New methods like insurance and the publication of lists of current prices came to supplement them. Above all the expansion of markets and of supplies called for an increase of production and for such changes in organization as could bring that increase about.

The increase was achieved in many industries and in many places, not only in the three countries which were generally farthest advanced. A good deal of progress was made in some industries in the creation of factories. In the industrial revolution of the late eighteenth and early nineteenth centuries, one of the most prominent changes was the triumph

[1] Hale, *Pleas of the Crown*, i (1736), pp. 143* ff. The attorney-general stated that the 'engine-looms . . . have been used above these sixty years'.

[2] For an account of the ribbon-loom see the late George Unwin's chapter in Wadsworth and Mann, *The Cotton Trade in Industrial Lancashire* (1931), pp. 98 ff.

of the factory system over the older dispersed cottage or workshop unit in industry, and it was closely bound up with the triumph of large power-driven machinery over the simpler tools and machines. The classical example of the transition from the earlier to the fully developed form of capitalism in industry, that which occupied the largest place in the books which blocked out the main lines of its interpretation, was the fall of the hand-loom weaver and the rise of the weaving-shed. So much were the two processes intermingled that it came to be widely believed that the new machinery was the cause of the new unit in organizing work; it is still generally believed that the machine made the factory. It is, however, important to remember that the factory has also independent origins of its own. There have been large factories for the carrying on by many people under one roof of simple handicrafts which required nothing but tools, or of others which used one-man machines. The earliest buildings of the kind are to be found in the distant past. What is characteristic of the factory as a form of organization, the concentration of a comparatively large number of workers in one place and under one employer, seems to be something specially modern only in certain textile processes, especially spinning and weaving.

At times and places where spinning and weaving were still carried on in the households of the workers, the later finishing processes of textile-manufacture, dyeing, fulling, like machine stocking-making, were already carried on in considerable establishments. Outside the textile trades there are still more striking cases, especially in some of the industries which started late, when the spirit of capitalism was already in the air. Printing-works, saw-mills, sugar-refineries, breweries, distilleries, soap-boiling and candle-making works, tanneries, various chemical works for preparing substances such as dyes, calico-printing works, lace-workshops, rope-walks, were all in our period well on the way to large-scale organization.[1]

[1] In many of the larger establishments, however, labour was not simply controlled from above, factory-wise, but through subordinate employing masters, sub-contractors for hands.

Shipyards naturally lent themselves to this arrangement. It seems to have prevailed for the works where coaches and the more costly kinds of furniture were made. Mines and quarries, especially those which belonged to sovereigns or landowners who owned the whole of them, also tended very early to be exploited by single employers with many hands. Much of the work done on metals after the ore was extracted, was also done under conditions far removed from those of the old-fashioned handicraft organization.

Modern research is doing much to establish precisely what point each of them had reached at definite times and places, and for many branches of industry a continuous general history, if not already written, is in sight. Until we have a good many such histories it will be premature to say much about the causes of this tendency; but some things may be said with confidence. The tendency towards capitalism in industry not only lagged behind the same tendency in commerce, there was even a sort of opposition between the two. Industrial capital had to contend against a special obstruction: the desire of commercial capital to control industry as well as commerce. It has indeed been maintained, as it seems convincingly, that the joint-stock system was originated in England not only by the great commercial companies, but also quite independently by the new corporations of small trading and producing masters in industry which were characteristic growths of the late sixteenth and early seventeenth centuries.[1] Co-operative joint-stock enterprise was, along with monopoly, the means by which the small masters tried to make up for their lack of capital. The London felt-makers in the early years of the century had several ventures for which they appealed to outside lenders of capital. But the small masters were not the men of the future. They were 'the protagonists of industrial democracy' under Elizabeth and the early Stuarts, but they were champions of a losing cause.

Their attempts to set up independent organizations were a symptom of the break-up of the great amalgamated companies. In each of these by the end of the sixteenth century

[1] G. Unwin, *Industrial Organization in the Sixteenth and Seventeenth Centuries*, 1904.

the many crafts had been united under the rule of an oligarchy which was, in every case, an oligarchy of traders, buyers, and sellers, rather than of makers. There were some circumstances which favoured the new secessions, especially the migration of certain crafts to the suburbs of London where the old companies' privileges could not be made effective. Other and weightier causes, however, worked against them. Like all other organizations they sought protection in the form of monopoly from the Crown; and the Stuarts did give them their countenance, for instance in the charters of the felt-makers and glovers, partly from a disinterested desire to encourage them, and partly from interested desires to conciliate them and to raise revenue, as in the instance of the superfluous beaver-makers' company started under Charles I. But royal intervention always tended towards monopoly, and monopoly was in the long run unfavourable to the small master. Thus, although in the seventeenth century industrial capital won for itself an equal place as an organized interest alongside of commercial capital, at the same time in doing so it passed out of the hands of the small master to assume new forms in the hands of a new class of manufacturers, who might be traders to some extent, but whose principal function it was to be employers and organizers of labour.

A partial parallel may be drawn between this development and the course of events in France. There too the Crown helped industrial capital to free itself from the control of commercial capital. That control was exercised at the beginning of the century by the powerful corporation of the *merciers*. These *mercatores* had got into their hands the control of all the *six corps de marchands*, the six corporations (not always the same six) which had in their hands all wholesale and retail trade in cloth of gold, of silver, silk, serges, cloths, *menues merceries*, goldsmiths' and silversmiths' wares, jewellery, ironmongery, *épicerie*, and druggists' goods. The *rois des merciers* had long had the right of selling to all merchants and artisans the *lettres de maîtrise*, which constituted them masters, besides which they raised other dues from them and appointed the *gardes-jurés* or wardens whom the corporations had formerly appointed for themselves. The *merciers* and the *fripiers* (a less influential but more curious and anomalous body of traders, whose name is akin to our word 'frippery') were much hated, but they had acquired their power because there was a real social need for a trading class, not themselves producers, who should adapt supply to the growing complexity and capriciousness of demand. King Henry IV made some attempts to restrict them to this function; but French industry did not take its stride forward into modernity until the time of Colbert.

The industrial policy of Colbert sums up so much of the economic history of France and embodies so much of the spirit of the seventeenth century that it will be best here to sketch it as a whole and not merely in its bearing on the new forms of organization.[1] We have already had occasion more than once to mention Colbert's name. After a varied business experience he became the minister of the most ambitious monarch of his time. He served the ambition of Louis XIV with all the driving force of a masterful character. He had few prejudices, and a real sympathy and enthusiasm for energetic men. His ideas were sufficiently concrete and simple to lift him out of the ruck of those wild-cat projectors with whom the courts of Europe teemed. His policy was to increase the amount of circulating medium in France by encouraging agriculture, so as to create a demand for manufactures, while he also wished to create and foster these for their own sake. He believed that at the beginning of the seventeenth century, two generations before he began his work, manufactures in France gave profit to an infinite number of people, that money did not then flow out of the kingdom, that in 1600 and even in 1620 and later there was no cloth manufacture in England and Holland, and that all the wool of Spain and England was brought to France to be spun and woven.

[1] The old work of P. Clément, the editor of Colbert's papers, *Vie de Colbert*, is largely superseded by C. W. Cole, *Colbert and a Century of French Mercantilism*, 2 vols. (1939). G. Martin, *La grande industrie sous le règne de Louis XIV*, 1889, is episodic rather than comprehensive. In some respects valuable is a work of mainly legal character, dealing more with the eighteenth century than the seventeenth, A. des Cilleuls, *Histoire et régime de la grande industrie en France*, 1898.

These convictions made him believe that his task was to bring back by sound laws and administration a state of things which had actually existed. Every one of them was historically incorrect, but there is no reason to suppose that he would have acted differently if he had known the truth. His policy was the policy of his age, the policy of protection and regimentation.

Of his tariffs, the most famous part of his protective system, something has been said already from the point of view of commerce. They did not, indeed, apply to the whole of France, which was not yet a fiscal unity; but that scarcely diminishes their importance. The tendency of Colbert's earlier measures was towards a lightening of burdens. The tariff of 1664 freed from duty all raw materials except fuel. After that his system changed. The tariff of 1667 amounted almost to a general prohibition of imports. It led to a tariff-war with Holland, in which the treaties of 1678 and 1697 represent truces, and there was no real settlement till 1713. With England it was the same: in 1678 the English prohibited all imports from France. This prohibition seemed to the English, in the light of the theory of the balance of trade, to be advantageous on purely economic grounds. It was continued in full force until 1693, and, after that, broke down only piecemeal. As we have already noted, the tariff settlement with England could not be completed in 1713.[1] Portugal equally was driven into tariff-war with France, and this was one of the antecedents of the Methuen treaty of 1703 by which Portugal, as has been said with some exaggeration, saved her colonies by an economic merger with the British empire. So much did Colbert's tariffs contribute to the general intensification of protectionism throughout Europe that it would be difficult to say whether their effects on French manufactures were beneficial or not.

It would be difficult, or rather it would be impossible, for there could not, in any case, be any means of disentangling the effects of the tariffs from the effects of all the other measures and influences of the time. Amongst these came first the other kinds of protection given by the state; but these were given sparingly. The chief advantages given to particular manufactures were honorific rather than sub-

[1] See p. 58 above.

stantial. Colbert dispensed official titles and diplomas; money and monopolies he reserved for infant industries, especially those imported from abroad, and he well knew the disadvantage of spoon-feeding. Such public money as was spent on loans or grants to manufacturers came, in fact, not from the king but from local provincial estates whom the minister urged on to the work. There were grants of sites and buildings for factories. The small masters in the towns and country-side shared in none of these favours, but on the other hand they were more free from supervision than the subsidized capitalists, and their share in the national output was considerable. For the instruction of employers, as well as for the profit they might make, Colbert established a few state factories which were models of method and arrangement. The tapestry factories were the most famous.

The supervision, the regimentation, of Colbert is, on paper at least, the supreme historical example of state interference with industry for economic ends. The social motive of nineteenth-century industrial legislation has led to still more thorough-going and minute codes of regulations; but that motive was not yet at work. The French Crown was not the workman's friend; what it wished to protect was production. Some of the regulations arose partly from the same protective principles as the tariffs and subsidies, for instance, the ferocious but ineffective prohibition of the emigration of skilled workmen to foreign parts. But the general ground of the regimentation seems to have been the belief that the sale of goods could be ensured by enforcing a high standard of quality. That idea was part of the legacy of the Middle Ages. It was still a part of the generally accepted current opinion about industry. It survives, if feebly, in our own age, and it will never die out altogether, because it is the offspring of the instinct of creation, of which the converse is the hatred of bad work. But it may be stated in such a way as to contain a fallacy. A well-made article will not find a buyer unless there is a demand for it, and an economic demand means a demand at the time and place and price where it will pay the maker to sell it. Modern critics have accused Colbert of falling into this fallacy. It is not a fallacy into which the money-maker is likely to fall, and they have seen in Colbert's battles with the manufacturers the collision of the money-makers who saw through it with the idealist whom it deluded.

Colbert believed that success had justified his way of using authority to vanquish the obstinacy of the manufacturers. Under the minister himself and the provincial *intendants* was a hierarchy of inspectors and magistrates, combined not quite harmoniously with a system of assemblies and officers elected by the master-manufacturers themselves, all with their allotted shares in the paternal work of surveying and disciplining industry. Everything that was made and every process of making it had to conform to a standard, and every artifice of administrative activity was used to make sure that it did so. It was a hard fight. Officials in those days had their special imperfections. They were lax. They feathered their own nests, and often the best way of doing that was to make a corrupt bargain with the manufacturer who wished to fall short of what the regulations exacted. Some of them, however, took the manufacturer's side for reasons of principle. Within two years of Colbert's death an *intendant* held that 'le plus grand secret est de laisser *toute liberté* dans le commerce. Jamais [les manufactures] n'ont si fort dépéri, dans le royaume, et le commerce aussi, que depuis qu'on s'est mis en tête de les augmenter par des voies d'autorité'.[1]

The evidence shows clearly enough that in some instances demand and sales increased in proportion to the decline from exactness in following the regulations. After Colbert's death, under a succession of inferior ministers, the life went out of the system. There was an unquestionable industrial decadence, and, as the eighteenth century opened, manufacturers and theorists alike sought the remedy for it more and more in the relaxation of control, even of control by tariffs. The days of free-trade theory were not far off, and free-trade theory, when it came, was to condemn the ideas of Colbert unsparingly on economic grounds. That was perhaps not fair, and certainly not historical. The fate of Colbertism and its practical results were not determined

[1] des Cilleuls, p. 208.

solely by economic factors. Three points alone need be mentioned now, but there are others like them, and these three would perhaps suffice to prove that in the overthrow of Colbert's economic schemes the greatest part was that of disturbances from outside the economic world. First there was the religious reaction to which we have more than once referred already, the revocation of the tolerant Edict of Nantes. Second, in consequence of the government's chronic need for money, there were derangements of the machine such as the creation of numerous official positions for inspectors and the like, not where and because they were needed, but for the mere sake of the fees they paid on buying their appointments. Third, and greatest of all, there were the wars. Much harm is often wrongly ascribed to mistaken policy or to administrative incompetence in the seventeenth century which ought to be laid to the charge of war. The cessation of sea-borne commerce when the Dutch and English frigates and privateers were on the trade-routes, the drain of taxation, the fall in the purchasing-power of the home market which Louis's wars inevitably caused, made it impossible for Colbert's work to be completed or continued. The ambition which he served was his undoing.

So much for his place in French history. In the history of all Europe too, as we have seen, he led the way in innovation; but outside France the fate of Colbertism was different. Where there was a strong political machine in a country relatively backward in economic development it set the note for a long period of time: the obvious example is Brandenburg. Here industrial progress could not be other than artificial, but the kings were strong enough to foster it. More vaguely the same may be said of Russia, the huge bulk of which was beginning to respond to the economic teachings of the west. But in the countries of established wealth the influence of Colbert's example was much fainter. His tariffs, it is true, provoked and almost commanded retaliation; but his encouragement of industry by other means found little imitation, and indeed it is scarcely too much to say that it was in essence a survival from the last phase of economic policy rather than the prelude to a new phase.

The late Dr. Cunningham, whose authority stands high, gave the title 'Parliamentary Colbertism' to that part of his book [1] which deals with the history after the Revolution of 1688. It is a striking phrase, because it calls at once to mind the sharp contrast between the despotic administrative machine which enforced the will of Colbert and the antiquated, if well managed, British constitution, where there was little centralization and little unity of action. It suggests that in their two completely different ways the governments of the two countries were trying to do the same thing; and Dr. Cunningham held that the fostering of industry was the prime object of economic policy during the period of Whig ascendancy. It is true that this came in the eighteenth century, especially under Sir Robert Walpole, to be the aim of the adjustments of the tariff; but in the late seventeenth century the tariff was still dominated by the idea of trade balance, beside which the motive of encouraging manufacture had a secondary place. And beyond the tariff Colbertism did not affect parliamentary policy. It is in fact from the Revolution of 1688 that it is most convenient to date that great revolution in economic policy by which the state, though it continued to handle commerce according to the maxims of protectionism, began to allow industry to take its own course. The old fabric of guilds and corporations was allowed to fall into decay; their regulations were neglected or evaded; the regimentation of industry by the State was abandoned. Without any fuss or theoretical discussion, the principle of *laisser-faire* became the basis of the industrial régime.

In Holland Colbertism had even less influence, though for different reasons. Its pale reflection may indeed be seen in the tariff; but that is all. The federalism of the constitution of the republic had its economic counterpart: the guilds were still on a municipal basis. The only national bodies were one for the trade in *lakens* or cloth, in vigour from 1616 to 1643, and the Amsterdam college of commerce, founded in 1663, which lasted only two years. The makers of *lakens* for the province of Holland had regular provincial

[1] *Growth of English Industry and Commerce*, 6th ed., vol. ii, p. 3.

organization from 1645; but this represented mainly the large producers of the towns and it was opposed not only to the competition of the country-side but also to guild restrictions in general. The guilds and the numerous other standardizing authorities, which affixed the town-mark which all textiles had to carry, were advantageous to the small producer, because they guaranteed him against unfair competition; but they were a nuisance to the big man, and it was maintained on his behalf that he was in any case averse from malpractices because the reputation of his products was so important to him that in his own interest he would keep up a high quality. At the beginning of the century Dutch industry was restricted by the regulation of the number of workmen, machines, and so on to the household scale, in the medieval spirit; at the end much of this restriction had gone, but the prohibitions of industry in the country-side were upheld, no doubt in the long run to the general disadvantage.

Elsewhere the movement of industry from the towns was one of the notable features of the century, and although there are special causes for it in special places, it happened over such a wide area that it may be cited as a proof that, in spite of and beneath all political and other diversities, Europe really had a common economic history. New industries were started in the country, and old ones transplanted there. In the Spanish or Southern Netherlands, it took place before and about the beginning of the century. Their separation from the Northern Netherlands, when the latter successfully rebelled against Spain, had brought about the cessation of the maritime commerce of the Scheldt and consequently the loss of some important markets and economic decline. Yet the seventeenth century, though the Scheldt remained closed, saw a revival of prosperity, and this was due to the rise of large industries outside the towns. Not only were the country villages free from the hampering and obsolescent restrictions of guilds, they were also nearer to wood and water, the two growingly important sources of power. In France, Germany, and England also the country gained at the expense of the towns.

This was part of a greater complex of changes in the local seats of industry. Industry was not only being dispersed over the country-side: at the same time it was tending to be more concentrated in favourable localities. In the Middle Ages there was in a sense very little local specialization of industry: specialization seems at first sight to be characteristic of a world like ours, where communication is so rapid and easy that the one place where production can be carried on in the most favourable conditions can undersell all its competitors everywhere in the world, while every place can have access to the desirable products of every other. In the Middle Ages, when things could not be moved so freely, this was not so, and small areas had to be economically more self-contained. At first each village was almost an economic unit: there came in from outside only a few luxuries and a few things of which the production is limited by nature to special places. Gradually the area widened, and there came specialization, though not of the kind we know now. It was part of the manifoldness of medieval life that every place of any importance had its speciality. We have only to think of the scores of household words—Lincoln green, Kendal green, Worsteds, Cambrics, Toledo blades, Ripon rowels—to see that their very isolation enabled particular places to become famous for special products. Improved communications meant larger markets, and so the superiority in competition passed to the places which could best provide large quantities of their wares. After the Middle Ages there was thus some concentration of particular industries in particularly favoured places. In the German iron-producing centres there was a tendency for the manufacturing processes to be collected round the mines. From one side this is an example of the removal of industry from the towns: the metal industries, with their progressing technique, needed more fuel and water-power than could be conveniently had in the towns. Medieval industry and the industry of the age of steam were predominantly urban. It is to the intermediate period that the scattered factories and manufacturing households by Yorkshire streams or Silesian pine-woods specially belong. But concentration had not gone very far by the end of the century. It was checked, amongst other things, by the break-up of old international markets, for instance, in weapons and in those goods of which the movement was restricted by tariffs. It ran counter to the strongest tendency of industrial geography in the seventeenth century, that towards a national industry.

The processes of industry were changing, and its scale, and its local distribution. There was also going on, conditioned at every point by these changes, sometimes favoured by them and sometimes hindered, but in the long run destined to prevail, another change of far greater moment, a change in its human relationships. When we talk now about industrial problems we think first of the relations between masters and men, of the condition of the working-class; and this aspect of industry assumed greater importance during the seventeenth century. The rise of capitalism meant a change in the industrial function of the individual man. The old guilds had not been purely philanthropic or exceptionally enlightened: like most other human institutions they had been meant to serve their own members rather than the outside world. They stood for the town against the country, for one town against another, sometimes for one craft against another; and, as we have abundantly seen, their time was passing. But when the nation became the economic unit, something of the old system was continued and extended in the new. In particular, the new paternalism of the state tried at first to keep to the principle of fairness between the individual men in the trade, fairness between master and master, but also, what could not be abandoned without favouring some masters at the expense of others, fairness between master and man. Industry and trade were still largely organized in corporations. The corporation was an organic whole of which the welfare was inseparable from that of the members. Membership in it meant a guarantee of subsistence and reasonable promotion, a guarantee which implied also the renunciation of unlimited gain and especially of gain at the expense of the other members. The master might not employ more than a certain number of journeymen. Therefore, on the one hand, he could not take away all the business of the other masters, nor, on the other hand, could he keep all his journeymen for ever in their dependent and subordinate status. Not that the master was the only party whose freedom was hemmed in. The man had to submit to a long apprenticeship, to a fixed rate of remuneration, to a personal tutelage. He could not transfer his services to another master merely to better himself or to find a more congenial employer. In France, England, and Holland alike we still find the regulation that a workman is to have a sort of *bene decessit* before he leaves his master. It was a guarantee on one side against poaching by the master and on the other against the advancement of the man.

In the Middle Ages there had been exceptions to all these rules. In the seventeenth century they were ceasing to be rules altogether. Their decay led to social unrest and to some obscure agitations and experiments which form part of the prehistory of the labour movement. The unrest had indeed little in common with the labour movements of a later age. It was surprisingly destitute of theory. Broadly speaking there was no socialism in it and no theoretical humanitarianism, no demand for a better social system, and no appeal to a doctrine of what social systems owe to the individual man. It is not difficult to find passages in pamphlets of the seventeenth century which seem to belie this; but the history of ideas, as much as any other branch of history, must keep anticipations and survivals in their proper subordinate place. Its business is with breathing realities, not with embryos and ghosts. The anticipations of socialism in the seventeenth century are embryonic, and even so they are to be found chiefly in periods of political and intellectual upheaval like the English interregnum when, in the ferment of questionings and projects, everything was doubted and everything, from women's suffrage to communism, irresponsibly suggested. The social discontent of the seventeenth century was in the main inarticulate. So much is this so that we seldom know whether or where and to what degree the rise of capitalism raised or depressed the material standard of working-class life. Modern historians have disputed these questions. Such questions about the pre-statistical era are likely long to remain disputable. Here there is not even, as there is with some earlier examples of social unrest, such as the English agrarian discontent of the sixteenth century, a literature of protest which supplies, if not figures, at least definite assertions that the life of the poor was becoming worse.[1]

What we do know for certain is that in the rough and tumble of the seventeenth century, when law and order were far from having reached their modern perfection, the discontent of the journeyman was one clear cause of disturbance. In France the Crown had to mediate in disputes between masters and workmen. There are a number of records of workmen's 'conspiracies' and riots, though not so many, we are told, as in the eighteenth century. They arose from immediate, practical grievances: in 1688 at Thiers between three and four hundred paper-makers demanded the fixing of their hours of labour, their holidays, and the amount of food to which they were entitled. In Holland the social murmuring was inextricably mixed up with politics and religion. It found expression in the communistic ideas of certain sects, and in political agitations in times of war, especially the agitations worked up in favour of the house of Orange against the republican oligarchy. Direct and simply economic agitation was less common, but it existed. What called into being the provincial organization of the *laken*-makers was most probably a strike of the year 1638. In England the story is much the same: political parties and religious sects gained strength from a feeling which also led to sporadic strikes and riotings.

Sporadic protests do not constitute a social movement, and there was no social movement. What we know of the workmen of the seventeenth century makes it clear that they were not such men as could well have bound themselves together in the pursuit of a positive aim. Most of them we may suppose to have been ignorant and light-minded men, content with a bare subsistence, and thinking themselves

[1] For the seventeenth century, however, agrarian discontent in England has not yet been studied so widely and thoroughly as for the sixteenth: among historians as among contemporaries it has been overshadowed by political quarrels.

lucky when chance brought them something more that they might spend in crude enjoyments. Workmen of more serious inclinations turned to religion the energies which would later have been spent in social movements. The vitality of religious feeling, the absence of political democracy, and the low level of education all contributed to make a working-class movement impossible. The world was still loosely knit, and there were outlets enough for the ambition of the exceptional working-man. Much had to alter in industry and also in religion, and in education, before working-men were to band themselves together as members of a class with common interests and common aspirations. They had not yet reached even the stage of effective combination in single trades and districts. The old corporations in which masters and men shared together were fallen or falling; the new unions of workmen alone were yet to be born.

In England, especially during the Puritan revolution, the journeyman element within the companies made itself heard; but after the Restoration of Charles II the slight results of this were swept away. Nothing remained possible now for the journeymen except to form organizations of their own. In London they had the court of aldermen against them and in the later years of the century the movement came to nothing. It was so throughout the country. The continuing industrial combinations which are known to have existed were on the side of keeping wages down, not bringing them up. In Holland workmen's combinations were forbidden. The prohibition seems to have had a result which followed from similar measures in later times: it drove the combinations underground and led them to take on a secret if not conspiratorial character. Stricter prohibitions followed: in 1692 in one instance such assemblies were even threatened with the capital penalty. As in the milder case of England, the repression was successful. In the other countries of Europe there is little evidence that it was attempted, for the very good reason that there was nothing to repress. Nor was there, except in England, as yet any sign of the great change in social policy which was to be one of the causes of the estrangement of working-men from their rulers. English industry, as we have seen, was handed over towards the end of the century to the principle of *laisser-faire*, and this was a change which affected not only the attitude of the state to industry, but its attitude to the 'condition of England question' in its other aspects. The paternalism of the Tudors and Stuarts, which Bacon had so cogently expressed, had many failures in its record, and it came quietly to an end. A sufficient measure of law and order, and a hitherto unexampled national prosperity were obtained without it, and there was reason enough for contemporaries to think that to continue it would be wasted effort. On the Continent regimentation was still the aim of governments. Under the one system as under the other there were as yet neither the indignation nor the means of protest which made the life of the industrial worker the leading ethical problem of nineteenth-century politics.

VI

COMPARATIVE CONSTITUTIONAL HISTORY

COUNTING each of the federal states as one we may say that in the seventeenth century there were in Europe more than a score of sovereign states. The number varied slightly with events like the recovery of its independence by Portugal. A number of states which formed single units for purposes of international politics were not units from the point of view of the student of constitutions. England and Scotland, from their personal union under James I till the union of their parliaments under Anne, had two constitutions, and Ireland a third, not to mention the Channel Islands and Man, or the county palatine of Durham. Constitutional unity was scarcely to be found except in minor states, and in some of the federal states it was doubtful whether the federation or the component part was the unit even for international purposes. It was a controversial question whether the United Provinces of the Netherlands should be spoken of as one state or seven. The Holy Roman Empire was gradually ceasing to deserve the name of a state, and in 1648 by the treaties of Westphalia all the essential attributes of sovereignty were recognized as belonging to its members. These members numbered altogether, from great princes down to free towns and petty knights, more than three hundred. The government of each, however small, had its virtually separate organization; so that if we set out to make a comparative study of the specimens of constitutions which can be found at this time, we start with a bewildering wealth of materials, and the hope of detecting any development common to all seems distant. That there really was such a development, not merely a number of points of resemblance but a genuinely common tendency, is a striking illustration of the unity which underlay the evident diversities of the map of Europe.

Wherever a number of similar political communities exist side by side, there will normally be copying and borrowing of one institution or another, and in the Middle Ages, as in any other time, there were pattern-states and imitative states. The varieties of detail arising from local conditions were so great that to a modern eye it seems at first sight that the grammar of medieval institutions, like that of the Basque language, consists entirely of exceptions; but, in spite of this, it is true that there was a normal European method of organizing the work of government. In the larger states this consisted of a grafting of the unifying principle of monarchy upon the broader groundwork of feudalism. The tenure of land, hereditary, but in a sense contractual, was the benefit in return for which the ruling classes rendered military service, and carried out the administration of justice and the general work of government. Ecclesiastics formed another feudal body, with their own courts and taxes and hierarchy, a body of which the relations with the lay body were never in a perfectly stable equilibrium or altogether free from doubts and controversies. As towns grew up, they also attained a status of their own, with their own courts, and to some extent with their own control over taxation. Every authority was limited and liable to come into collision with the others, and, according to the local circumstances, the result might vary in any direction. There were strong hereditary monarchies which left very little play to the church or the towns or the nobles. At the other extreme were city-states which owned only a nominal imperial overlordship and themselves ruled over a subject nobility. The proportions of the different ingredients varied indefinitely, but their nature was everywhere the same, and in the later Middle Ages there had everywhere grown up a new type of institution through which they worked together.

This was the system of estates. Every country of western Christendom, from Portugal to Finland, and from Ireland to Hungary, had its assemblies of estates. There was every variety of internal arrangement in the number and composition of the houses, their procedure, their competence, as well as in their relations to the royal power; but it is pretty generally, though not universally, true that in these assemblies there were either present or represented the nobility, the ecclesiastics, and the burghers. In a more or less flourishing condition these estates everywhere survived until the beginning of the seventeenth century, or the last years of the sixteenth. Nowhere, however, had they reached the position, which is normal to the parliaments of European countries in the age after the English and the French revolutions, of being the authority to which the executive government is responsible. In one country or another they might from time to time, with or without success, claim some control over taxation, or over the appointment of ministers, or even over high matters of policy like wars and alliances. In some countries, though not possessing in theory an exclusive right to do the work of legislation, they had become the usual channel for it in practice. But the machinery of government was still, in monarchies, the king's, and where the estates got a hold over it they generally sowed the seeds of present or future dissensions with monarchy.

The king's control over government was indeed still precarious. He lacked the means of complete authority and the administration was only gradually approaching the stage in which it would be properly amenable to control. The concentration of armed force in the royal hands was imperfect. Not a single western country had a standing army: the only one in Europe was that of the Turks. Feudal levies and mercenary troops were apt to follow the will of their own immediate leaders, and the feudal forces had in some places a legal right to do so even against the king. Side by side with the civil government of feudalism there had grown up a royal machine, a body of civil servants, law-courts, chanceries, secretaries; but nearly everywhere it was still rudimentary. The division of functions between departments and their subordination to one head had not been made logical and firm. Offices tended to slip from the royal authority by becoming hereditary, privileged, feudal. In Protestant kingdoms where the Lutheran system prevailed the church had been subjected to the state, but the Roman Catholic church was an independent international power, and, at the beginning of the century, it was still possible that Calvinism might become another.

In reviewing economic changes we have already seen that

the social foundations were shifting in such a way as was bound to make this old superstructure untenable. The divisions of classes were changing. The agricultural wealth, which had been the material strength of feudalism, was now faced with the rivalry of the more mobile wealth of the capitalists. In England, France, the Netherlands, Germany, even in Naples, men of finance and commerce were able to acquire titles of nobility. They made it their practice, as they still do, to buy the lands and marry the daughters of the older aristocracy, but, however much they perpetuated the trappings and even the traditions of feudalism, their political influence was inevitably new in kind. Since it rested on money, it could scarcely grow without a similar growth in the money-power elsewhere. Its first clear tendency was to depress the political power of all those classes which were not comparatively rich by the new and rising standards. Democratic ideas in the modern sense play a very small part in the seventeenth century. Few men seriously proposed to extend any sort of franchise to labourers, and no such proposal had any more influence on events than to create a temporary disturbance. The ease with which Oliver Cromwell put down the levellers and the failure of the peasants' rising in Switzerland about the same time are typical of the period. Much as they were changing, aristocracies were tending to consolidate their power. The English landed gentry, the patriciates of the Swiss cantons, the regent class in the Dutch republic, the *noblesse de la robe* in France, were new nobilities which owed their power to the general tendencies of the time, and, though the nobilities of other countries as they underwent transformation met with great obstacles to their power, it remains true that there was a general tendency towards a growth of aristocratic influence.

The tendency manifested itself most plainly in an opposition to monarchy. This too was general. Ranke pointed to one of its most striking examples in the deposition in 1661 by its members of the head of the most strictly autocratic body in the world, the Society of Jesus.[1] In the political world it found expression in conflicts between kings and estates. Practically

[1] *History of the Popes*, Bk. VIII, c. ii.

everywhere in these collisions it was the aristocratic element, even in a rather narrow sense, which gave its force to opposition: for the towns it was, as we have seen, a period of political decline. What is, at first sight, more surprising is the further fact that the outcome of these collisions was normally favourable to monarchy: the instances in which aristocracy or the partisans of the estates succeeded were exceptional.

A summary of the facts will clear the way for the explanation. First the cases may be taken in which the estates had to give way before the rising royal power, and that power became virtually absolute. In Spain the decisive steps had been taken shortly before the beginning of the century. When Philip II came to the throne he found the *cortes* of Castile largely shorn of their liberties; those of Aragon he first restricted and then suppressed. In the Spanish kingdom of Naples, parliamentary proceedings had long been almost empty forms, their sole purpose being to vote supplies and to arrange the incidence of taxation in the way least inconvenient to the barons. Even the forms of parliamentary assembly were abandoned after 1642. The revolt which was, a few years later, begun by Giulio Genoino and led by the ridiculous Masaniello, originated in a kind of liberalism, but merely proved the impotence of any such spirit. In France, the absolute system was gradually built up after the confusion of the civil wars, first by Henry IV, then by Richelieu. The states-general met in 1614 for the last time before the revolution of 1789. The provincial estates were thoroughly tamed. In 1648–53 another body, the *parlement* of Paris, a law-court, but with a certain legislative function and staffed by a hereditary caste, formed the nucleus of the light-headed revolutionary movement of the Fronde. After its ignominious failure Louis XIV reduced the *noblesse de la robe* to complete subordination, and the old *noblesse de l'épée* to a state of highly expensive futility. In Portugal the victory of monarchy was slower but not less complete. The country broke away from Spain in 1640 after a subjection which had lasted for two generations. During that period the Castilian rulers had broken their sworn promise not to impose taxes without the consent of the *cortes*, so that, as opposition always tends to enlist on its side any repressed and disfranchised force, there was an element of 'liberalism' in the rebellion. In 1668 the *cortes* compelled the regent to make peace with Spain. Their triumph was, however, short. The same regent dissolved them because they attempted to control expenditure, and declined the crown because they claimed the right to dispose of it. In 1697 they met for the last time.

Among the Teutonic peoples liberty fared little better. The Great Elector, Frederick William, made himself the real founder of the power of the Hohenzollerns by repressing the estates of his two chief possessions, Brandenburg and Prussia, and by making his revenue independent of their consent. The Habsburgs had many provinces, in some of which, as Carniola, Styria, and Carinthia, the work was already done. By crushing their Protestant subjects in the Thirty Years' War they were enabled to draw the teeth of the estates in those which remained. In Bohemia, Moravia, Silesia, the estates lost many privileges, and above all, that of electing their king. The Hungarian crown became hereditary in 1687. In Denmark in the sixteenth century a king had failed to make his rule hereditary; but in 1660–5 his successor succeeded not merely in accomplishing that, but in imposing a *kongelov* or *lex regia*, which is famous as one of the most consistent legal expressions of the principle of absolute monarchy. It is interesting to notice that the author of this law, Peter Schumacher Griffenfeld, was influenced by English political thought, though he was not apparently, as has been supposed, a follower of Thomas Hobbes, but rather of the high church divine right theorists.[1] Across the straits in Sweden a similar consummation was reached by a different road. There the king's authority was to some extent limited by that of the senate, a privy council of which the members were appointed by him, but held office for life and took their oaths not to him but to the estates. In the last quarter of the century Charles XI, with the support of the estates, repudiated this limitation, obtained unlimited legislative authority, and made himself absolute.

[1] See Professor Brinkmann's review of K. Fabricius, *Kongeloven*, in *English Historical Review*, xxxvi. 622.

There were several countries in which the course of events was very different. In England, after a civil war, and a subsequent revolution, constitutional monarchy was established, and the ground was prepared for the full development of responsible government. In the Dutch republic a complicated and archaic system emerged from the war of independence, in which the estates kept most of the power in their own hands, and allowed only a restricted, though not permanently and effectively restricted, authority to the stadtholders, the successors to lieutenants of the king they had thrown off. Even in the Southern Netherlands, which remained obedient to the Spanish crown, obedience was purchased by leaving to the estates a simulacrum of their authority in finance and policy. In Hungary, although, as we have seen, the monarchy became hereditary, the estates survived, and when the Habsburgs recovered the greater part of the kingdom from the Turks, they were to find themselves faced by a constitutional and national opposition.

The constitution of the Holy Roman Empire fell into hopeless dilapidation. In the elective system the princes had a lever for diminishing the imperial power: each emperor at his election had to give away something of his sovereignty. The division of the empire between Catholicism and Protestantism was organized in such a way as to permit either confession to paralyse any attempt at action by the diet. At the end of the Thirty Years' War the princes got recognition of their sovereignty and the right to make alliances with foreign powers. The only links of the empire were ineffectual: it meant little that in 1663 the diet instead of being intermittent began to be in permanent session all the year round and from one year to another. When a group of German princes accepted the guarantee of Louis XIV for their rights and territories against any encroachment of the emperor, the dissolution of the empire was heralded. At the end of the century it may be called a limited liability con-

[1] The chief exception to the rule that the princes prevailed over the estates was Württemberg.

federation, a federation of which each of the leading members had greater interests and possessions outside it than inside. The emperors themselves, the Habsburgs, were partly to blame for the decline of the empire precisely because Hungary meant more to them than Germany. The Spanish branch of their house renewed its voice in the empire in the sixteen-seventies by sending a permanent representative of the Burgundian circle to the diet at Ratisbon. The electors of Brandenburg were kings in Prussia. The elector of Saxony was king of Poland—another state in which 'republicanism' prevailed against the advance of monarchy. The elector of Hanover was heir-presumptive to England. One group of German provinces belonged to the king of Sweden, another to the king of Denmark. Not only the emperor's monarchical authority but the whole machinery of the federal government was in decay.

This, however, formed no exception to the rule that the general progress of the time was towards absolutism. On the contrary, it was an instance of that rule. It was just because the members of the empire, from the emperors downwards, were bent on establishing their own sovereignty that they dismembered the authority of the empire. How must the rule be qualified when we consider the real exceptions, Poland, England, Holland, and so forth? In the first place we may notice that, even when the outcome was the curbing of monarchy, the same contest between monarchy and the estates took place. In England it was but narrowly won by the cause of liberty, and, on the whole, the issue is not simplified too much if we say that it was won because the anomalous, insular monarchy of England had gone through a more varied experience and fostered a more widespread political capacity among its subjects than any other. In Holland monarchy had to wait another century for its turn, but that state too was exceptional partly because of the strange vicissitudes of its political history, and partly because of its unique economic conditions. One factor which helped 'liberty' in both Holland and England was religious division. Protestantism had the upper hand in both, but in each there was an important Roman Catholic minority and a vigorous variety of sectaries and schismatics who had to be granted a grudging and not quite consistent toleration. Religious uniformity has at least a consanguinity with political submissiveness. Holland had other points in common with the other republic of Switzerland. Both were small. The conditions favourable to freedom could hardly have been found extending over wider areas. Moreover, both Holland and Switzerland were doubly small: they were broken up into still smaller units. They were federal. The amount of unity which they imposed was very slight.

In Poland and Hungary the social power of the landed class was too little influenced by the new economic forces for monarchy to find the necessary tools. Poland is always cited as an awful example of constitutional inefficiency, especially because of its *liberum veto*, a rule then recently introduced, by which any single noble in the diet could negative any proposal. This was only the last addition to a system in which central control was at a minimum, and the independence of the individual members of the feudal class, however impoverished, was allowed to go to extreme lengths. The political decay of Poland proved that it was utterly out of date. The same may be said of the small old-fashioned republics like Genoa and Ragusa. Although they survived, it was merely because a series of chances provided them, for the time being, with sufficient allies or protectors whenever their independence was threatened. They had a respite from absorption, but that was all, and this was true even of Venice, although Venice was still regarded in the seventeenth century as a model state. James Harrington in England was one of a body of writers who in various languages recommended its institutions for imitation:[1] they failed to see that in the future they would be inadequate to protect the venerable republic.

The general tendency consisted not merely in the triumph of monarchy, but in the rise of a particular type of monarchy. It may be called the French type of monarchy, not only because it reached its strongest and most logical expression in France, but also because it was consciously and de-

[1] Especially in his *Commonwealth of Oceana* of 1656, often reprinted.

liberately copied elsewhere from the Bourbon model. The later Stuarts in England envied and tried to emulate the powers of their cousin Louis XIV. The Elector Frederick III of Brandenburg, a prince of distinguished conjugal fidelity, wishing to do his business exactly as Louis did, is said to have added to his establishment a lady who had the title and the court functions, though not the pleasures, of being his mistress.[1] The departmental organization of administrative work and the supervision of local government by the central power were widely imitated from the French example, and it was monarchy as Louis XIV left it which made the enlightened despots of the next century.

It is misleading to summarize in a single phrase any long historical process, but the work of monarchy in the seventeenth century may be described as the substitution of a simpler and more unified government for the complexities of feudalism. On one side it was centralization, the bringing of local business under the supervision or control of the government of the capital. This necessarily had as its converse a tendency towards uniformity. A central government to be able to compare a number of subordinate organs with one another and to make them all serve the same ends, needed to make them work alike. We shall see in detail how this double tendency transformed military institutions and made the standing army both the type and the instrument of the new order. In intellectual life we shall see the same movement expressed in the academies. First France under Richelieu and then in succession the other monarchies adapted for the encouragement and disciplining of letters a form of association which had been devised spontaneously, without the notion of control from above, by literary men themselves. This compulsory purchase of prosperity and recognition at the expense of the loss of freedom had its counterpart in the arts, in ecclesiastical history, and in the mercantilist regulation of economic life. It was, in fact, everywhere in the life of the time; but its central achievement was the diminution of the feudal element in the state.

The feudal nobility lost its functions, and first among them

[1] M. Philippson, *Das Zeitalter Ludwigs des XIV* (1875), p. 210.

its military functions. In France it was concentrated at Versailles, where Louis XIV practised the art of government by spectacle and taught his nobles that all their ambitions must depend for their fulfilment on his favour. Elsewhere the change was less striking, but fundamentally much the same. A nobleman, instead of leading his vassals to the wars, took service in an army and went through a regular course of promotion from one rank to another on the recommendation of his superior officers. The nobility threw off a branch which is continuous with it but unlike it, the officer-class. In the same way in civil government, although ancient hereditary offices retained some of their dignity and emoluments, they lost most of their real significance: if a nobleman wanted political power he had to win it in the service of the state, or, which is much the same, of the Crown. Step by step the Crown ousted the feudal lords from their rights and privileges. If they were impoverished, if they were refractory and liable to punishment, if they were ambitious, the king's servants knew how to take advantage of the opportunity. The extent of their victory may be gauged from the change in their character: it has been observed that in the seventeenth century the French *intendants*, the officials who controlled the provinces for the central government, were *des gens de lutte*: in the eighteenth that type of man was no longer needed, and they were *des gens de bon ton*.

In dealing with economic matters we have already had to notice some of the administrative departments which grew up in France. This growth was somewhat different in other countries, but it too was a general movement. It was general but not quite universal: the Dutch republic, that curiously antiquated organism, was exempt from it as it was from the centralizing tendency generally. In England also it had anomalous forms, especially a looseness of central control over local administration, a closeness of contact of the estates, the parliament, with government, a system of putting at the head of a government office not a man but a board, the board of trade, the lords of the treasury, the admiralty board, and others. But the growth of bureaucracy —not its origin but its progress—was one of the characteristic seventeenth-century movements in most of the more thriving countries. The state made more and more concerns its own: its growing needs and its wider outlook impelled it to be no longer content with limited functions of police and defence, but, especially on the economic side, though not on that alone, to take under its care one department after another in the life of the nation. Administrative departments proved determined enemies to immunities and anomalies: their progress was not to be reconciled with the feudal spirit.

How toughly rooted that spirit was all over Europe is, however, shown by its persistence. Despotism in the seventeenth century, in spite of the energy and continuity of its efforts, fulfilled only a small part of its programme. Even the eighteenth century, in which the impetus of the new enlightenment was added to these efforts, left the greater part of the task to the more drastic methods of the revolutionary period. There were directions in which the feudal spirit, as fast as it was lopped and felled, seemed to push up new suckers from its buried roots. In France, for instance, the new bureaucratic class themselves held many of their offices by hereditary succession. The seventeenth century saw not only the decay of the old nobility, but the establishment of the judicial and administrative caste, one of the strangest of institutions, which was a sort of prosaic, civilian feudalism. The ministers who allowed this to come about did so neither gladly nor inadvertently: financial necessity brought them to it. On the frequent occasions when new methods had to be devised for raising money, it was easiest to resort to the vicious practice of creating a new office and selling it, making it a good capital investment by allowing it to pass to the buyer's heirs. This was a peculiarly French abuse, but it is only one example among many of the fact that the old régime could not afford more than limited instalments of reform. And in addition it must be remembered that the new monarchy was only partly new. It was up to a certain point opposed to feudalism, but it was also itself a product of feudalism, and, as the world was to discover in the time of the revolutions, it was in a sense the great stronghold of the feudal spirit.

It was hereditary: we have seen that in the seventeenth century the survivals of the elective system were wiped out in every country except the two doomed organisms of Poland and the Holy Roman Empire. The hereditary principle may be defended or adopted on public grounds as the most satisfactory way of selecting a ruler: that is one ground on which we retain it in the British Commonwealth to-day. In the seventeenth century, however, monarchy was more than hereditary. It was dynastic: the kings and their families formed a caste apart, higher than nobilities and difficult of entry even for the greatest *parvenu*. The legitimation of his bastards by Louis XIV was a notable disparagement of noble blood in comparison with the blood royal. Whatever theorists might say in explanation of the nature of royal power, kings did normally regard their kingdoms first and foremost as the possessions, the estates, of their families, and of themselves as heads of their families. Critics of the old order in international affairs have often shown how disastrous and absurd it was that the issues of war and peace, of independence and national subjection, often revolved on the chances of births, deaths, and marriages among this inbred and not very healthy stock of royalties.

Contemporaries also knew that the dynastic system meant that the interests of rulers and their subjects must be more or less widely divergent. Sir William Temple, who knew his Europe as well as any one, assumed as a matter of course that the two interests were distinct. There was not even any one class whose interests permanently coincided with those of monarchy. From time to time kings relied on the support of one class or another, and, as aristocracy, whether expressing itself through the assemblies of estates or otherwise, was their most usual opponent, it sometimes appears as if they had a natural affinity with other elements which tended to resist aristocratic privileges and pretensions. Charles XI of Sweden and Frederick III of Denmark relied on the peasants against the nobles: the house of Orange could raise the mob against the Dutch regents; the Stuarts have been almost plausibly represented as tory democrats. More than once the regents of Naples resisted the nobility: the second duke of Ossuna even armed the mob against them. From these and similar instances it is sometimes inferred that, before the real emergence of democracy, the kings were the leaders of the poor and unenfranchised against their oligarchic oppressors. A broader view must, however, lead to the rejection of this theory. There were other occasions on which kings showed themselves favourable to aristocracy and indifferent to the lower populace. Only when its claims were exorbitant did they turn against the nobility, and never once did they attempt anything so radical as the extinction of all aristocratic privileges and power. Aristocracy was part of the established order, and when kings were not openly and avowedly against it, they were for it. Even when they were driven to work against it, the mob was not their only or their most congenial ally. Ecclesiastics of various kinds had their share even in those revolutions which have been mentioned: the clergy were actors in the Danish *coup d'état*, the Calvinist ministers were the most valuable supporters of the Dutch stadtholders, and the Stuarts prospered most when they retained the loyalty of the Church of England. Monarchy needed allies and it found them where it could, but not always in the same place. Its own interest was distinct from all others. It might reconcile or it might divide; it might take a position of national leadership or foster one part of the community in order to hold down another. It was consistent only in fidelity to itself.

The contradiction between its modern and its archaic aspects is reflected in the various kinds of support which it received. It is doubtless true that its development is closely related to the economic movements of the early capitalistic age; but its rise was not solely or even mainly due to economic causes. When kings were popular leaders there is no lack of evidence to prove that, along with hopes of material betterment, they aroused a far stronger sentiment of personal loyalty and devotion. The simple faithfulness of the peasant, the soldier, the labourer cannot be analysed and needs no explanation. It is born of one of the primary instincts of mankind. Akin to it is the chivalrous service of military commanders like Tilly and Montrose. The latter sentiment, however, is not one for which the seventeenth century is conspicuous. It is hard to think of generals of the first rank who gave examples of it. Most of them, like Turenne and Condé, Wallenstein and Marlborough, had, in the matter of loyalty, questionable records: they were still near to the type of the feudal magnate or the *condottiere*. For strong expressions of monarchical faith one must look to words rather than deeds. The clergy of every creed and country, when they happened to be on the monarchical side, strained the language of submission to the utmost. The doctrine of the divine right of kings, after a long and eventful history, had reached a condition in which its theoretical groundwork had become unworthy of the intellectual atmosphere of the age, but its emotional force had reached its apex. It is sometimes said that the divine right of kings was the form taken in the seventeenth century by the theory of sovereignty. This is inexact, because, as we shall see, there were many writers of different schools throughout the century who expressed that theory in well-considered and, we may say, modern terms. Nor is it historical to emphasize the more reasonable side of a doctrine which had its still more prominent side of adulation and spurious mysticism.

In spite of this, the last word about the supporters of monarchy must be that, upon the whole and except for those countries and occasions which have already been characterized as anomalous, they included the best and most enlightened elements of society. In France, almost throughout the century, the opposition to monarchy, whether practical or theoretical, was interested, factious, destitute of breadth and statesmanship. In the disastrous end of the reign of Louis XIV there is a liberal spirit in the writings of Fénelon and some of his contemporaries; but Fénelon remained a monarchist, and when the chance came after Louis's death for the experiment of a new system, it was only to show how small an element this spirit was in the oligarchic sham-liberalism of St. Simon and the clerical *esprit de corps* of Gallicanism.[1] Even in Poland it appears that the wisest men were, though in vain, on the side of an increase of royal

[1] See below, p. 308.

authority.[1] At a later stage we shall return to the development of political thought. At present, looking at thought and action together, we may say that the experience of the seventeenth century caused republican ideas to be generally discarded, and led both men of action and men of thought to throw their influence on the side of the kings.

[1] See Dyboski, *Landmarks of Polish Literary History*, p. 36 (on Lucas Opalinski and Andrew Maximillian Fredro). I have no first-hand knowledge of Polish literature.

VII
ARMIES

DURING the whole course of the seventeenth century there were only seven complete calendar years in which there was no war between European states, the years 1610, 1669–71, 1680–2. In the first of these years great armies were on the move and shots were actually exchanged, a great war being averted by the narrowest margin. In the third period of peace there was war between Russia and Turkey, which perhaps may be reckoned as European war, so that on a strict calculation the years of general peace were no more than four. Several of the great powers were at war for more than half the whole period. The wars in which two powers fought a simple duel were few and comparatively short: the commoner type of warfare was that between two groups of allies. War, therefore, may be said to have been as much a normal state of European life as peace, and the history of armies was one of the hinges on which the fate of Europe turned.[1]

The first striking fact in this history is the great increase in the size of armies, in the scale of warfare. In a well-known passage of his *Siècle de Louis XIV*[2] Voltaire says that from the siege of Metz by Charles V, which was in 1552, until Louis's time more than a hundred years later, no general found himself at the head of an army of 50,000 men. Fifty thousand is a small army by the standards of the twentieth century, two modern divisions, but it was far above the reach of the commanders in the Dutch war of independence or in most of the operations of the Thirty Years' War. Alva

[1] The best general book is Delbrück, *Geschichte der Kriegskunst*, vol. iv, *Neuzeit*, 1920. Among works on separate armies the following are specially useful: for France, André, *Michel le Tellier*, 1902, which in some respects supersedes Rousset, *Histoire de Louvois*, 4 vols. 1862–3; for England, Sir Charles Firth's masterly *Cromwell's Army*, 3rd ed., 1921, and Walton, *Hist. of the British Standing Army, 1660–1700*, 1894; for Holland, Ten Raa and De Bas, *Het staatsche leger* (unfinished), 5 vols., 1911–21; for Spain, S. M. Soto, conde de Clonard, *Historia organica*, 10 vols., *s.a.*

[2] Cap. 2.

marched ten thousand men from Lombardy to the Netherlands. The rebels under William the Silent never had more than about 45,000 men and the Spaniards about 60,000 on their muster-rolls, though not as one moving force. Thirty thousand marched with Gustavus Adolphus in 1631. In 1627 and 1630 Wallenstein is thought to have had about 100,000 in pay;[1] but when Richelieu complimented his master on having surpassed this figure he seems to have exaggerated. During the reign of Louis XIV the French army increased until at last he was able to command a force which surpassed anything which had been seen since the greatest days of the Roman Empire.[2]

Louis set the pace for his opponents. It was only the wars against him which made it necessary for the English to become a military nation. The measure of what they could do was given by the civil wars, in which it was thought that something like 120–140,000 men were under arms on the two sides together. From a small beginning under Charles II the standing army grew steadily. William III during his war went as high as about 90,000 soldiers of all kinds, and, after the drastic reduction to about 20,000 consequent on the peace of Rijswijk, the British army in the war of the Spanish Succession reached something like the limit of the national capacity. As it was with the British, so it was with the other armies of these wars. The Great Elector of Brandenburg, who, when he made peace in 1640 kept about 2,000 men enrolled, left his successor a well-found force of 29,000.

Not every state in Europe could add to its forces thus. The Spaniards, who at the beginning of the century were the leading military nation, had great difficulty in 1640 in raising an army of 15,000 to cope with the Portuguese revolt. The empire was gradually ceasing to be a military state at all. In 1681 it had a paper army of 40,000, but in April 1689, although the empire was at war, there was no imperial army. The members of the empire were divided into armed and unarmed states. The Magdeburg Concert of October 1688 gave

[1] For this and other particulars of his armies see Loewe, *Die Organisation und Verwaltung der Wallensteinischen Heere*, 1895.

[2] See Gibbon, *Decline and Fall*, ed. Bury, i. 18.

the unarmed states the duty of providing winter quarters and contributions while the armed states fought in their own right as separate belligerents. In 1697 the unarmed circles of the west and south-west formed the Frankfort Association and were admitted to the grand alliance, but the military history of the empire after the Treaty of Westphalia is to all intents and purposes that of its greater component states. Northern and eastern Europe also felt the increased strain of war, but they did not put very numerous armies into the field. The armies with which the Great Northern war was fought do not appear to have been large: its name comes from its long duration and perhaps from the vast area of the operations. Charles XII is said in 1718 to have reached 60,000. There is no reason for taking seriously the statements that Mazeppa had 100,000 Cossack horse and that the Turks marched 190,000 men to the Pruth in 1711. In any case these were not troops organized in the European way.

These exceptions do not vitiate the general statement that armies were increasing. The numbers engaged in single battles were greater; the total numbers under arms in Europe were greater; the proportion of the available men of military age who became soldiers was probably greater. In the eighteenth century it was not infrequently said that a people could support an army of one per cent. of its population.[1] This figure represents, roughly speaking, the achievement of the more strongly organized states in the time of Louis XIV. This was the beginning of that swelling of armies which went on until our own time. In the time of Louis XIV there seems to have been one great bound forward. During the eighteenth century the process continued, above all in Prussia; then, in the time of the French Revolution and Napoleon there was another bound, followed by a continuation all through the nineteenth century. But there is a difference between the two epochs of rapid development. The second is easy to explain. Fundamental changes in the

[1] Montesquieu, *Grandeur et décadence des Romains*, cap. iii (1734), see also Adam Smith (*Wealth of Nations*, Bk. V, ch. 1, pt. 1). According to Gilbert Elliot, it was commonly reckoned that one-fifth of a population were fit to bear arms (Fitzmaurice, *Life of Shelburne*, 2nd ed., i. 383).

political and economic organization of Europe made it possible. Universal service, conscription, was one of the results of the French Revolution and of the answering nationalisms and revolutions by which the other nations of the Continent fitted themselves to fight beside or against the French. The new means of transport and food-supply which accompanied the industrial revolution gave the material provision for this new political possibility. Armies grew and changed as the world changed and grew. It is at first sight not so easy to see in the history of the seventeenth century any political or economic alteration adequate to explain the earlier change in armies. The 'old régime' seems to be a comparatively uniform period, an age without revolutions. The truth seems to be that the greatness of the later changes has thrown the earlier out of perspective, that precisely in this growth of armies we have a proof of how much Europe was altered by the two sets of changes, economic and constitutional, which we have already considered. The growth of absolutism and the progress made by the state in controlling all its subjects are nowhere more strikingly illustrated, as we shall see, than in the affairs of armies.

The crucial point was finance. Not only the change in size, but all the other great changes in armies during this period were made possible because the states became richer. They developed an efficient taxing system, and this was made possible both by economic changes, by deliberate political effort and invention, and by the pressure of military necessities. Just as the modern state was needed to create the standing army, so the army created the modern state, for the influence of the two causes was reciprocal. It is seen most strikingly in Prussia, where the 'Intendantur der Armee', created in the seventeenth century, became the nucleus of the central government, the trunk from which not only the ministry of war, but the ministry of finance, the ministry of the interior, and most of the ministries of the present day are derived. In France the process was less simple, but not less real. The growth of the administrative machine and of the arts of government was directed and conditioned by the desire to turn the natural and human resources of the country into military power. The general development of European institutions was governed by the fact that the continent was becoming more military, or, we may say, more militaristic. The exceptions prove the rule. Of the two great powers which escaped the rise of absolutism, one, the Dutch Republic, failed to keep pace with the growth of armaments and, as a consequence, ceased to be a great power altogether. The other, Great Britain, continued to be a great power even on the mainland of Europe, and was able to do so because economic prosperity came to her rescue when it was deserting the Dutch. For in the intensity of international competition even absolutism could not do without the new wealth: the suppression of internal liberties availed nothing in poverty-stricken Spain.

It was not only the size of armies which responded to the new conditions and helped to modify them. Their relation to the state changed just as much, and also their organization and the art of war. It was the period of the rise of standing armies. When it began no purely European state had a standing army, that is to say an army maintained in peace-time as well as in war, consisting of professional mercenary soldiers. The only army of that kind in Europe was that of the Turks. It does not necessarily follow from this that the Turks still had a military superiority over the Christians: during the long period when the Christians were building up a similar organization there were no serious encounters by which the fact could be tested. But it was perhaps from the example and the menace of the Turkish troops that the Christian powers first derived the idea of organizing their armies in this way. Before tracing the steps by which they did so, we must see clearly what their systems were beforehand.

In most countries there were considerable relics of two obsolete kinds of armies, the old national militias and the feudal levies of the Middle Ages. In England, for instance, theoretically all able-bodied men were liable to serve in the militia, and attempts were made to keep the machinery of the militia in working order. If the Armada had landed its troops, the militia would have been the only defence against them. Militiamen actually were under fire at Landguard Fort in one of the Dutch wars. But in the real military history of the century the militia is negligible. Even more was this so with knight-service: it meant nothing in 1600 and it was formally abolished in 1660. In France the feudal levies survived, but in an inglorious decay. In 1674 the *ban* and *arrière-ban* were called out, but found to be useless. When the experiment was repeated in the next year it was merely as a financial measure, not to raise the troops, but to raise money by letting them buy themselves off. In the later stages of his reign Louis XIV had recourse to a revival of the militia system, but that too was soon modified so that its essential nature altered and it became merely a device for recruiting the regular army.[1] In Germany it was the same. To the end of the Thirty Years' War theory and practice were at variance. Theoretically there were feudal service and militia, but in practice the wars were carried on by mercenaries. The real armies everywhere throughout the period were made up of mercenaries. At the beginning they were normally engaged for the campaigning season and paid off at the end of it. Their commanders were contractors who undertook to supply a certain number of troops in exchange for a certain sum of money, and the obedience of the men was rendered primarily to their employer, the commander. In military organization the period before Louis XIV may be characterized generally by saying that wars were carried on with the men and money provided by private *entrepreneurs*.

In the sixteenth century several different causes had been at work in the dominions of the Habsburgs which tended towards a different military system. The *Defensionsordnung* made at the diet held at Bruck in 1578 by Charles of Styria founded the system of a frontier-militia: it made all Inner Austria (Styria, Carinthia, Carniola, Gorizia) into one defensive unit on paper, and instituted a compulsory levy, of which the expense was to be divided between the archduke and the states.[2] This was the foundation of the defensive

[1] See Girard, *Racolage et milice*, 1921.

[2] A. Steinwerter in *Zeitschr. des Hist. Vereines für Steiermark*, xvi. 51 f. (1918).

system of the next two centuries; but it was not enough to give security against the Turks. From quite early in the sixteenth century there had been writers and statesmen who had seen that it would be more efficient and more economical to keep troops on foot through the winter instead of paying them off. Instead of starting every campaign with fresh troops, it would be possible to have some sort of continuity of training. Regular pay would be cheaper than intermittent but heavy expenditure on levying and disbanding. Both in the Reichstag and in the diets of the hereditary dominions the Habsburgs pressed for the regular financial provision which would have enabled them to make these reforms, and, although the jealousy of the states and their well-founded fear that the change would undermine their own power prevented any great advance, some corps were actually kept on a permanent footing through the winter in the later years of the Turkish war which ended in 1606.[1]

Professor Delbrück is of opinion that the first true standing army was that of the Spaniards, who had to keep an army continually active in the Netherlands even in the intervals of their French wars. The same changes took place in the German states during the course of the Thirty Years' War. One after another the princes began to keep standing forces, and by the time of the wars of Louis XIV it was normal for a sovereign to have an army in the winter and in time of peace. From his reign France had also the device, when an army had to be reduced to a peace footing, of paying off the private soldiers from part of it but retaining the *cadres* of officers and other commanders, so that it could easily be restored to its former strength.

The internal structure of the standing armies was necessarily very different from that of the earlier forces. The office of the colonel sank from the independent position of a contractor to that of a regimental commander, one of a hierarchy, with general officers between him and the commander-in-chief. The old *Landsknechten* had elective and temporary commanders. Now that service was for longer periods and the armies were recruited from worse materials, these tended to

[1] Eischmann, *Die Anfänge des stehenden Heeres in Österreich*, 1925.

give way to something like the modern professional hierarchy of officers. In Wallenstein's army there was still no fixed corps of officers; the difference between an officer and a private was one of degree. There was no set proportion of officers to men and the functions of different ranks were not precisely defined. The idea of seniority of rank throughout the army and the whole plan of systematic promotion have been traced back to changes made in the French army in 1675 after the death of Turenne. All these things developed in the course of the century, and in some countries, especially in France and Prussia, there also grew up the tendency, which had become almost the rule by the end of the century, to restrict the holding of commissions to persons of noble descent, or of such exceptional wealth and influence as to be able to get the officials concerned to give them fictitious certificates of noble origin. The modern idea of an officer class is thus derived not directly but indirectly from the medieval ideas of knighthood and nobility. The officer derives his authority from his commission. He is essentially a servant of the state, and the state, in order to establish itself, had to destroy the power of the feudal knight. The transition from the feudal force to the modern cavalry units is one side of the process of which the rise of the officer is another. Both may be regarded as phases of the rise of military discipline. Regulations, punishments, and the rest of the apparatus of discipline were developing from a very rudimentary stage. Uniforms for the common soldier were introduced in England in the New Model Army of the Civil War; in France by degrees in the reign of Louis XIV. There were examples of them in the sixteenth century, and some troops dressed according to their fancy even in the eighteenth; but the general European adoption of uniform was a seventeenth-century process. No one who has ever worn a uniform can doubt that it was a decisive step in the history of discipline.

The rise of uniform was not only part of the rise of discipline; it was also part of a great change in the relations of armies to states in which the rise of discipline was a factor and a result. The states were gaining control over the armies. In the management of armies three classes of commodities have to be supplied in large quantities, arms and ammunition, provisions, clothing. During the earlier Middle Ages the individual soldier, whatever his rank and the nature of his obligation to serve, knight or militiaman, came with his own armour and weapons, his own clothes and his own supply of food. Nowadays the soldier is dressed, fed, equipped, and armed as good as entirely by the state. It is easy to see how this accords with the needs of modern warfare, warfare which requires the largest possible number of men to act as much alike as possible. The tendency was inevitable as soon as mass-armies took the place of the armies of chivalry. It began with the pikes of the Switzers and with the introduction of firearms. Weapons had to be standardized, and after them the men behind them. Supply became a problem too big for private enterprise; the state had to take over this as it took over the rest of the control of armies. Professor Werner Sombart holds that the victualling of troops by the state seems first to have been done in Spain in the seventeenth century; [1] the evidence on this point is not yet, however, complete. Direct provisioning by the state, though it was tried in this and other instances, did not anywhere become the regular system. What came to prevail was a mixed system by which the state provided for the soldier on the march and in the field, and gave him money to provide for himself in quarters. To do their part, and to keep up the great arsenals and magazines of food which the large scale of warfare made necessary, the states became great buyers, and this was one of the controlling causes of change in the organization of industry and commerce.

The achievement of state control was a hard task, and it meant great changes in both armies and states. At the beginning of the century the states were impotent against the *condottieri*. The Emperor Ferdinand II with all his dominions could not raise an army equal to that of the landless adventurer Count Ernst von Mansfeld. Wallenstein by successful business transactions built up wealth enough to become the greatest of the military *entrepreneurs*, and the time soon came when princes followed his example by in-

[1] *Krieg und Kapitalismus* (1913), p. 121.

creasing their wealth and using it in this way. After his death Wallenstein's regiments became the nucleus of the Austrian army. Maximilian of Bavaria, Michel le Tellier and his son Louvois in France, the Great Elector in Brandenburg, all succeeded in making this step to the modern army with its corresponding political machinery. When le Tellier became secretary of state, an office which he held from 1643, to be followed by his son till 1691, the French army was without order. It did not belong to the king. Commissions were sold by the outgoing officer, as doctors' practices are still sold in England: this system lasted till the French revolution, and in England it lasted till 1871. In the seventeenth century it could only be limited and regulated. The higher officers were so powerful that the king could not control them: they were now suppressed. Regiments were too many and too small. The cost of the upkeep of troops was divided between the king and the officers. The pay, which was insufficient, was handed over to the captains, who made as much out of it as they could. By false musters they drew pay, as Falstaff did, for more men than they had. This abuse is said to have been corrected in France by 1678. No country was free from it in the earlier part of the century, and it is heard of in England at least as late as 1708.[1] Le Tellier founded the *intendants de l'armée*, who, inferior only to the commander-in-chief, brought an efficient administrative despotism into the army. Inspection spread obedience, uniformity, and efficiency: the name of Martinet, the first inspector-general, has become a household word. From a congeries of isolated regiments and independent companies the French army gradually became a true army, knit together by a system of higher formations and commands. The process was not completed. The division and the army corps, formations of all arms under a single, subordinate command, were not yet possible, but in the century European armies generally advanced a good way on this road.

By all these and many other changes armies became at once more efficient and more manageable. Some of the greatest political events of the sixteenth century were caused

[1] Luttrell, *Brief Historical Relation*, vi. 385.

by mutinies or the desertion of large bodies of troops. After the middle of the seventeenth and until the French revolution these things were seldom of any importance. Once more the crucial point was finance. In the reign of Charles II, Sir James Turner, the original of Sir Walter Scott's Dugald Dalgetty, could still write that although the Dutch states-general paid best of all the governments, armies were still universally ill paid.[1] That evil, the mother of mutiny, of looting, and of desertion, was being overcome. The state was not yet the soldier's friend. It was not in his interests but in its own that it tried to eliminate the innumerable frauds which were practised on him by his officers. It wanted to become his only master, and it was succeeding. Armies were for the most part becoming instruments which the states could trust to carry out their policy. In England the change was dramatically effected when General Monck put an end to the intervention of the army in politics and made it submit to the restoration of Charles II. He told the officers that 'nothing was more injurious to discipline than their meeting in military councils to interfere in civil things': and it is significant that he had had his training in the Dutch service, in which, as he said, 'soldiers received and observed commands, but gave none'.[2] One by one the armies of Europe were coming up to this standard.

The armies became state armies, but they did not yet become national armies. They were controlled by the organism which came into existence specifically for the purpose of controlling them, but this state-machine, if it was something broader than the personal following of the monarch, was just as remote from the people as a whole. This separation reacted also upon the idea of war, when, for instance, Hugo Grotius tried to restrict its evils by asserting the principle that it is a matter for soldiers alone and does not concern the citizen. How little of paradox there was then in this view may be seen from a consideration of the system of recruiting. Throughout the period armies were not national in the sense of being made up of subjects of the states for which they fought. Every power employed foreign mer-

[1] *Pallas Armata* (1683), p. 198.

[2] Firth, pp. 383–5.

cenaries. There were, indeed, in this respect some differences of degree between different powers, though the general statement is true of all. Purely economic causes made one kind of distinction. The poorer countries for the most part supplied troops to the richer. Most famous of recruiting-grounds was Switzerland, whose infantrymen had transformed European warfare at the end of the Middle Ages. At the beginning of the war of the Spanish Succession, Swiss infantry had still the attraction of demanding only 20 rix-dollars as a bounty on enlisting when the standard rate was 25.[1] All through the century Scotland and England, also comparatively poor countries to begin with, supplied the states-general of the Netherlands with soldiers; but the Dutch themselves, presumably because they were comfortable at home, were less easy to enlist for foreign service. The Venetians raised 3,000 troops in those parts in 1616, but in 1625 and 1645 their attempts had very little success.[2] Not much more than half of Gustavus's troops were Swedes or Finns by birth: he had men from all over the Baltic region and many Scots. In the cosmopolitan army of Wallenstein there were fierce rivalries between the German officers and the 'Romanen'. Louis XIV had English, Irish, Scottish, German, Spanish, and Swiss units. Professional soldiers of whatever rank moved freely from any one army to any other.

A tendency may be traced which prepared the way, though it did not yet do more than prepare the way, for the modern system by which men serve for the most part only in the armies of their own countries. It was beginning to be a concern of the state's where its subjects took service. Long before this time the Swiss cantons had begun to exercise a sort of control, which has been called a 'monopoly', in this matter, and a good many states in the seventeenth century made laws restricting the right of their subjects to serve where they pleased, or treaties permitting foreign powers to enlist them. In Germany the vicious system grew up by which the minor princes used their authority to establish

[1] Petition of the Raad van State, 31 January 1701, in Vreede's edition of Dijkveld's letters, *Tijdschr. voor gesch. van Utrecht*, 1849, p. 150.

[2] For 1645 Geyl in *Bijdragen*, 5th ser., v. 173 ff.

themselves as traders in troops. Too poor to keep armies as the great powers did out of taxation, but at the same time desiring to have armies for political reasons, they financed them by hiring them out as organized bodies to the great powers for use in their wars. The trade was sometimes so profitable as to make a contribution to their general and not merely their military finances.[1] Even the kings of Denmark hired out in this way troops which fought as auxiliaries in the quarrels of strangers, in which their masters were not belligerents. It was mainly by this quicker and easier method, not by the direct recruiting of foreign individuals, that the large foreign contingents in the armies which fought against Louis XIV were made up; but, if this system is another example of the progress of state control, it is the crowning proof that the quarrels in which they fought were not the individual concern of the men who carried arms.

It was not held that an army of foreigners was inferior to a national army. On the contrary, even in those countries in which there was compulsory (though, of course, not universal) military service, the natives were compelled to serve merely because no other way was available for making up the required strength. There were compulsory levies in Spain from 1637, and Gustavus Adolphus introduced a limited conscription for the Swedish peasants. The use of compulsion by Louis XIV in his later years has already been mentioned. About the same time the voluntary system ceased to be equal to the demands for men made by the rulers of Brandenburg-Prussia, but the development of compulsory service there, though it begins in the war of the Spanish Succession, belongs really to the eighteenth century. William III had to impress soldiers in Scotland. There may be other exceptions, but in the main the armies were recruited voluntarily.

Their separation from the general public was increased by the fact that they were always enlisted for long service. Soldiering was a trade in which men spent their lives. Once persuaded or tricked or even kidnapped into it, a man was likely to stay in it for a long time. In France in 1666 a

[1] See Braubach, *Die Bedeutung der Subsidien für die Politik im spanischen Erbfolgekriege*, 1923. This system was practised by Spain in the Thirty Years' War and the Dutch loans to German princes had a similar effect.

minimum of four years was indeed allowed; but the young man who does his military service and then returns to civil life is not a figure who is often met in the seventeenth century. Little is heard of either minimum or maximum age-limits. Commanders preferred old soldiers because they were better at their work. Not very much progress had, on the other hand, been made in the building up of that separate world of institutions in which the soldier of our own time lives, and which does so much to make his mind unlike that of the civilian. There were as yet few barracks anywhere in Europe: the soldier was billeted on the civilian. In France and England at the end of the century a beginning had been made in the provision of military hospitals and of institutions for the disabled and aged veterans; but only a beginning. The army was indeed still extending its control over what had been regarded as semi-civilian services. The artillery and engineering services were assimilated into the armies of the more advanced countries in the course of the century. The commissariat services, which increased vastly in importance with the establishment of magazines, vast stores of provisions for the armies, were still civilian. In the course of the century progress was made towards the provision of food and supplies by the state, and apparently Spain went first and farthest in this. But the soldiers still to a great extent fended for themselves. An army moved with an enormous crowd of sutlers, women, and other camp-followers and masses of their impedimenta. It had not yet lost all resemblance to a confused tribal migration.

To describe tactical methods or armament, or other technical military matters in detail would take too long and would lead us too far from our general plan; but it is to our purpose to show how the art of war was connected with other kinds of activity, how, in fact, it was an integral part of the work and thought of the time. The connexion is not to be sought where it might seem most natural to look for it. Of the considerable number of books which were written on military subjects, not many have much value either as evidence of what was the military practice, or as examples of thought and writing. Few had much practical influence. The points of contact between the art of war and the other arts and sciences were mainly in the minds of men of action.[1]

The most striking thing we have to notice is that it was in the seventeenth century and not until the seventeenth century that the spirit of the Renaissance added the last province to its dominions, namely warfare. It is true that in the high days of the Italian revival of learning Machiavelli had written out an art of war which was intended to revive for modern use what the ancients had understood of it; but neither on the side of organization nor on that of operations did he succeed in his aim. The study of Roman military methods had been a source of inspiration for military reformers since the early sixteenth century; but neither its practical application nor the study itself had reached any notable success until the Dutch war of independence. It sprang into life in the hands of Justus Lipsius, who taught in Leyden and Louvain.[2] Its application was the work of his contemporaries, the two cousins, Maurice of Nassau, stadtholder of Holland, and William Louis, stadtholder of Friesland.[3] Some of their reforms sprang directly from the renewed study of Roman military methods, amongst others the least successful of all, which was the provision of shields for the footguards, and one of the most successful, the training of the soldiers in digging, which they did for themselves instead of having it done for them, and with excellent results not only in the field but in discipline. William Louis used lead soldiers, the first recorded 'war-game'. But the real Renaissance influence made itself most clear in the attention which Maurice paid to inventions, especially scientific inventions. The telescope was brought to the stage of practical usefulness during his later campaigns and in his own country. He was probably the first general who climbed a church tower to look at the enemy through a glass, and after the truce of

[1] An interesting though somewhat superficial treatment of the subject is in Blanch, *Della scienza militare*, ed. by A. Giannini, 1910.

[2] His *De Militia Romana* is dedicated to Philip III of Spain, and his *Poliorceticon* (1596) to the elector of Cologne.

[3] There has been some controversy as to whether some of their innovations were not copied from France: for the present purpose this difficulty may be overlooked.

1609 he presented one of these new instruments to his opponent, the Archduke Albert.[1] He had the first practical time-fuse and so was able in 1592 to use hand-grenades. He brought in the curb-bit for cavalry chargers. He was a friend of the versatile mathematician Stevin, who made great advances in the art of fortification. He induced the university of Leyden to add fortification to its studies. But besides being good at the intellectual side of his business, Maurice was a fighter, an organizer, and a man of common sense. In planning fortifications he used the most advanced devices of surveying, but his characteristic method of attacking them, quite unlike the methodical investment of his old opponent Parma, was a powerful concentration of artillery and a sudden assault. Simultaneously with Henry IV of France he gave firearms to his horsemen, who thus sacrificed the characteristic cavalry advantages but needed a shorter training, and could do with less perfect horses than the old lancers. He standardized armament, reducing the weapons of the infantry to two, the pike and matchlock.[2] He stiffened discipline and made epoch-making improvements in drill. He made much use of sham fights and even in winter quarters his troops were trained. Companies of infantry which had previously been independent he grouped in regiments, though this reform and still more so a similar change in the cavalry could not be quite completed. As a result of all this, the army, though smaller than it had been before his time, was constantly victorious.

Under his brother and successor, Frederick Henry, the victories went on, but there was great confusion in discipline

[1] See H. A. L. Hensen in *Mededeelingen van het Nederlandsch Historisch Instituut te Rome*, iii (1923), pp. 199 ff.

[2] The longbow had ceased to be the national weapon of the English in the last years of the sixteenth century. Bowmen vanished earlier from the western and central parts of the Continent; but bows and arrows were supplied for Buckingham's expedition to the Isle of Rhé in 1627. In the same year the London long-bow makers' company in a petition to the City Corporation said that there were only four of them left, with no apprentices; but bows and arrows were ordered for the defence of Oxford in 1642 and they were actually used by some of Montrose's men in 1644 and by Lochiel's Camerons in 1652.

and administration. Later still, in the period when the Dutch had no captain-general, things were still worse and all the typical evils of seventeenth-century armies flourished. Everything was neglected, corrupt, inefficient. Absenteeism among officers, false musters, promotion for incompetence, diversity of armament and even of drill were symptoms of the decline which ended in the disaster of 1672 and the revival under William III. The Dutch lost their primacy, and other nations took the lead in scientific warfare; but scientific warfare had come to stay. From this time the contrast between the forward and the backward countries was shown as sharply in armies as in any other sphere. The Swedes under Gustavus Adolphus made great improvements in tactics, in armament, especially of the artillery, and in organized mobility. After them the French became the leaders. In 1686 a French diplomatist describing to Louis XIV a review of the Dutch army by William III and the Great Elector wrote: 'effectivement, Sire, on croit être dans l'armée de Votre Majesté.'[1] It was possible for soldiers to remain far behind the times. Though the bayonet came into general use in the time of Louis XIV, and its improved form, the socket-bayonet, was spreading in his later years, as late as 1706 the Saxon army met Charles XII of Sweden with the pike. But such neglect entailed a heavy penalty. It was not a mere absurdity that in the time of Louis XIV, when Vauban had shown what could be done in adapting fortifications to sites and in methodically attacking those of an enemy, fortification became one of the regular parts of the education of a gentleman. Military education itself was becoming a serious matter. The great generals were not mere leaders of troops: they had to know geography, diplomacy, the sciences of statesmanship. As these advanced in complexity, the armies, down to the lowest ranks of command, showed a corresponding movement away from their barbarous simplicity and isolation.

[1] Rébenac in *Urkunden und Aktenstücke*, xx. 1132 ff.: the report has other expressions amplifying this. Brunot in his great *Histoire de la langue française*, v. 232, mistakenly gives the date as 1656 and the writer's name as Rebersac.

VIII

NAVIES[1]

ONE of the great changes of the seventeenth century was the rise of the navies. In the preceding century the great sea-power had been Spain, which had been victorious in the Mediterranean and for a long time immune from attack in the Atlantic. The maritime power of Spain and her Italian allies had, however, suffered blows from which it was never to recover. After the defeat of the Armada Spain was still able to offer some resistance to her enemies, but she never learnt the lessons which might have enabled her to hold her own. In the Middle Ages the Mediterranean had been a separate world of sea-warfare, the world of the many-oared galley; but early in the seventeenth century the sailing warship with its broadside of guns made its appearance there and the galley lost its supremacy. This technical revolution made it possible for Britain ultimately to become a Mediterranean power. The navy of Spain, during the seventeenth century, was in a state of decadence. In the earlier part of it she had some good ships, but on the few occasions when her fleets went into action they were invariably worsted. In the second half of the century their decline went farther. In the war of the Spanish Succession the Spaniards themselves hardly fought at sea, and by the end of it they had practically no navy left: the Bourbon kings of Spain had to create a new one from the beginning. But, more than that, Habsburg Spain in the strict sense of the term had never really possessed a navy. She never had an organized maritime force provided and governed by the state for the purposes

[1] There is no satisfactory general history of the British navy: the best bibliography of works relating to it is Section III of the admirable *Bibliography of British History, Stuart Period*, ed. by G. Davies, 1928. For the Dutch navy the standard work, J. C. de Jonge, *Geschiedenis van het Nederlandsche zeewezen*, 2nd ed., 5 vols., 1856–62; for the French the still unfinished *Histoire de la marine française* of C. de la Roncière, 5 vols., 1899–1920. Although in some respects superseded by later works, the late Admiral A. T. Mahan's *Influence of Sea-Power on History, 1660–1783* (first ed. 1896), is still very important.

of war alone. Neither, at the time of the Armada, had her opponents. The small nuclei of specialized men-of-war which belonged to the states-general and to Queen Elizabeth were surrounded by a miscellaneous crowd of pressed and hired merchantmen, more or less well adapted for the different tasks of warfare. Beyond money and commanders and dockyards the state directly supplied few of their requisites. The minor operations of commerce-destroying were carried out by privateers, privately owned ships, authorized by sovereigns to do this work and subject to a supervision so elementary that they were often indistinguishable from pirates.

The three wars between the English and the Dutch began a new era. The first, from 1652 to 1654, was fought entirely at sea. It was the first war outside the straits of Gibraltar in which there was a succession of big battles between the fleets. Its experience showed that in future the naval battle must be an affair of purely fighting ships: the pressed and hired merchantmen disappeared from the line of battle. That line was becoming in other ways more an organized body. Discipline was codified. After the war, in the English fleet fighting instructions were so drawn up that the combat now came under regular tactical principles, instead of being managed merely at the discretion of the commander helped out by a few traditional rules. From this new beginning progress was rapid, especially under the stimulation of Anglo-Dutch rivalry. One change which was also taking place in armies came to the navies as well, the formation of a regular corps of officers. In the British navy the way was prepared for this under Charles II by the creation of the half-pay list and the ending of the custom of appointing distinguished landsmen to high commands: it was completed by the reign of Queen Anne. By that time the big ship had also established its place in naval warfare. The larger vessels could not safely be navigated in the stormier months from September to May, but in the summer they dominated the scene. Smaller ships of war were eliminated from the line as the merchantmen had been before them. When Louis XIV became a dangerous factor at sea he increased the size of ships and made a number of improvements in naval architecture

The English and the Dutch were driven to bring themselves up to the standards he set, and thus the closing years of the period completed the transition from the world of Drake to a world not very remote from that of Nelson.

Differences of *matérial* were not an important factor in deciding the results of naval war. It has been remarked that the methods of construction used by the different powers in the latter part of the seventeenth century differed less widely than at any preceding period. In the battle-pieces painted by the two van der Veldes, father and son, about 1672–4, the ships of the various nations are scarcely distinguishable except by their ornaments. In organization, however, there were remarkable contrasts. The demands made by a navy upon the state and the community were up to a certain point similar to those made by an army. Men, money, guns, ammunition, and provisions had to be found. There must be strategical direction and discipline. To that degree the extension of state control over navies in the seventeenth century is closely parallel to its extension over armies. It has been said that the Stuarts made the English navy a truly national force, and, if the work of the Protectorate is included in this estimate of the Stuart period, it represents much the same process as the work of le Tellier and Louvois in the French army. Richelieu centralized the admiralty and subordinated the navy to the civil power. The growth of navies in size also runs parallel to the growth of armies, though here the correspondence is less close. At sea the increase of forces was less general and less steady. Continental states, when they wanted to restrict their expenditure, almost always economized on their navies rather than on their armies. Every state had an army, and every land frontier was vulnerable; the number of dangerous naval powers was small, and the Dutch were the only continental nation who believed that their interests in trade and colonies were as vital as those which could be protected by an army on land. Only the island-state of England could do without an army altogether.

The growth of navies in size, though important, was thus irregular. Its course was also affected by some other facts which made it quite different in its political and economic aspects from the growth of armies. The navies had certain special requirements. First, they must draw their personnel not from the general population but from the seafaring classes, the fishermen and mariners of the coasts. Either they must make their service more attractive than that of the fishing fleets or the merchant marine, or they must use some sort of compulsion. The latter was the universal method. The English had the press-gang, a crude system, very erratic in its operation and lending itself to serious abuses. They supplemented it with the system of embargoes, practised also by the Dutch, under which merchant-ships were held in port until they had made up the naval crews by surrendering a certain proportion of their men. This plan, too, always caused friction and discontent; and when it was carried out successfully it often had the effect of creating a shortage of seamen in the merchant service, and so irritating the traders, for whose special benefit navies were popularly supposed to exist. Neither the Dutch nor the English adopted the French plan, though in England it was much canvassed in the time of William III, of an *inscription maritime*. A register of all seamen was kept, and they were divided into classes to be allotted for service in the navy and in merchant-ships. Theoretically this should have been a much more effective and less irregular system; but it appears that the discontent created by harsh administration did much to neutralize its good effects.

Shipbuilding and the maintenance of ships required a far larger organization than any of the subsidiary services of an army, and a more developed technical efficiency. In periods of administrative slackness or corruption they might easily become paralysed, and to keep them in motion the government had to be not only rich but vigilant. For the large fleets of the time England, France, and Holland all had to use large quantities of imported materials. The great source of supply of naval stores was the Baltic: the forests of Sweden and her subject provinces supplied masts and planks, pitch and tar, while hemp for cables and flax for sailcloth were imported from Russia. It was sometimes an anxious matter for policy to keep this trade open: the friendly or hostile attitude of the Baltic states themselves might react on the shipyards. The encouragement of the rope-making and canvas-making industries at home, the protection of English oak-woods, or the granting of bounties to exporters of timber and tar from the American plantations did something to mitigate the dependence of England and Holland on the Baltic; but throughout the period foreign policy as well as finance had to take a hand in the task of keeping up the fleets. On finance the strain was considerable. Even in the reign of William III when Great Britain maintained a far larger army than ever before, the cost of the navy was greater than that of the army. It is well within the mark to say that every sailor at sea cost twice as much as a soldier in the field.[1] The effort required to equip and man a navy was therefore proportionately far greater than that needed for forces on land.

This explains the fluctuations in the size of the fleets. At the beginning of the century the Dutch were at war with Spain and therefore had a considerable number of ships in commission. During their twelve years' truce from 1609 to 1621 they kept up a respectable force, and in the period of the English wars they made a huge effort. Those wars, of which the second and third were land wars also, not only strained their resources, they also inflicted heavy damage on their commerce; and the latter part of the century saw a decline in the relative importance of Holland as a naval power. Her administration, divided between five local admiralty colleges, was unsatisfactory, and in the wars against Louis XIV she had not only to conduct land operations, but she was able to shift an increasing share in the naval burden to her ally England. In the war of the Spanish Succession her navy was in decline. She always fell heavily short of the contingents which she owed to the allied fleet, and in the last three years of active operations she could with difficulty put out a dozen or so of ships when the English contributed some sixty.

In this stage the decline of the Dutch navy was not due to

[1] *Report on Public Income and Expenditure*, 1869. The point is brought out even more clearly in the tables of expenditure in Brit. Mus. MS. Harley 3274.

pressure from the French, for the naval greatness of the French in this century had been fitful and uncertain. At the beginning France was not a naval power at all. Richelieu began to create a new French navy where there was none, and, though he laid down the lines of administration and made effective use of his ships against the Mediterranean pirates, everything fell to pieces in the period of confusion and inefficiency after his death. Colbert had to start afresh. He instituted dockyards, had his ships and their component parts built in France instead of in Holland, and concentrated on the naval services all the means of stimulation which he applied to commerce in general. In his time and the next few years after it, France caught up with the older maritime powers in the regulation of discipline and tactics. She organized a regular corps of officers, and, as we have seen, naval recruiting. Louis XIV knew better than his successors how to use the fighting qualities of seafaring men, and the most famous sailor of his kingdom was Jean Bart, the son of a fisherman and with a fisherman's manners, who spoke only Flemish, not French, but whose genius raised him to high command and to the rank of a nobleman. On the whole, however, the French navy was more an artificial creation, more purely military, less a product of a sea-going people than those of England and Holland. The rule that naval officers must normally be of noble blood was seldom relaxed: in England there was little of such prejudice and in Holland naturally none. Naval operations were always subsidiary to the military ambitions of the French kings, and therefore the great effort begun by Colbert was not long maintained. The new French fleet was ready to play a part in history soon after William III invaded England, soon after, but not before. Having missed by a handsome margin its chance of preventing that decisive stroke, it had the chance of cutting William off from Ireland and from the continental war. At first for some years it did pretty well, and at Beachy Head it scored a creditable success, but the defeat of La Hogue in 1692 closed this chapter in its story. During the remainder of that war France attempted nothing but minor operations at sea, and in the naval fighting of the war of the Spanish Succession she was worsted.

By that time the English navy had gone through vicissitudes in some ways resembling those of the French, though its general history was more like that of the Dutch, except in the important particular that it was more variable and interrupted. Under King James I there was practically no British navy: the good ships of Queen Elizabeth rotted at their moorings. The king and his ministers did indeed institute inquiries and form plans, but it was left for Charles I to carry them to a practical outcome. Charles unfortunately for the navy, if fortunately for his country, was short of funds. By the famous levies of ship-money he raised enough to equip a squadron and send it to sea, but that source of revenue soon dried up, and his domestic troubles put an end to the naval revival. Where he had failed, the Commonwealth succeeded, and Robert Blake, an Oxford graduate who had been a merchant, a member of parliament, and a soldier, commanded the British fleets of the new era. After the Stuart restoration the continuous efficiency of the navy, the navy of Samuel Pepys, was the most respectable feature of British policy. It had its lapses, as when the Dutch sailed up to Chatham, for which the government was to blame rather than the sailors; but if the four big naval wars from 1665 to 1713 are looked at as a whole, they show a steady advance in strength and skill. When France slackened in her efforts at sea and Holland overstrained her resources, England brought her new economic strength and political efficiency into play, with the result that at the end of our period France and Holland together had about one-third and England alone about an equal proportion of the world's force of ships specially equipped for purposes of war.[1]

The remaining third was in the hands of Spain, Portugal, Russia, Denmark, and Sweden. The Portuguese navy took little part in European wars: its main work was in connexion with colonial trade. The navies of the three Baltic powers were on a smaller scale than those of the North Sea and Mediterranean, and the naval history of the northern inland sea was from time to time dominated by the intervention of the stronger powers from outside. Thus in 1659 the English

[1] Charnock, *History of Marine Architecture*, iii. 27.

and the Dutch, in an interval of peace between themselves, sent a fleet to enforce a settlement upon Sweden and Denmark, whose war was interrupting their northern trade. In the eighteenth and nineteenth centuries this process was to be repeated with variations. When they were left to themselves the three northern powers formed a separate naval world and their fleets controlled the communications of the armies which fought for the dominion of the Baltic Sea. Denmark at the beginning of the century had a not inconsiderable naval force. It never went into action until 1630, and then again not until 1643, when a fleet of fifty sail, some of them of fifty guns, put out against the Swedes. The Swedes had at first been of no account at sea, and in 1617 had very few warships to accompany their transports to the attack on Riga; but Gustavus Adolphus raised their strength well above that of the Danes, whom the Swedes beat in 1644. After the death of Christian IV in 1648 the Danes dropped out of serious competition and the naval domination of Sweden was well maintained until the time of the great northern war which began in 1699. By then it had a more serious rival. One of the supreme instances of the political genius of Peter the Great was his perceiving that Russia's ambitions needed the support of a navy. All the world knows how he learnt the crafts of shipbuilding in Holland and Deptford, and how he collected from the west the experts he needed to build his fleet and sail it and fight it. More even than that of France his navy was an artificial creation; but he made it the leading force of the Baltic, with the prospect of becoming not merely a local power but one which the western states would take seriously into their calculations.

The growth of the navies was made possible by the union of the two intimately allied tendencies which caused the growth of armies, progress in wealth and progress in the power of the state. As commerce grew, the trade of preying upon commerce, the trade of the privateers, also grew, but here too the states were able to tighten their hold. Commerce-destroying is the natural weapon of the weaker party in a naval war. That side which had the stronger fleet would be able to close the seas to the commerce of its enemies, but its own merchant shipping would invite attack from the swift sailing corsairs who could escape the vigilance of fleets. The greater the volume of a nation's commerce, the more it rewarded this form of attack. For these reasons privateering reached a great height in France. Dunkirk, on the flank of the channel trade-route, was the greatest centre of the enterprise, and it was there that Jean Bart was born. In the war of the Spanish Succession there were more than a hundred Dunkirkers at sea together, and French privateering reached its zenith, a height which it was never to equal again. At the same period the English and Dutch privateers were also more numerous than they had ever been before. Many of them, in all nations, were violent and lawless men; but privateering was better regulated and less like piracy than in the days of Drake. Commissions were granted under stricter rules. Larger bonds were given by the captains to be forfeited if these were infringed. The admiralty courts enforced the arrangements agreed upon in a number of maritime treaties, and the system of privateering was gradually becoming what it remained until the days of steamships, a decent auxiliary to the work of the navies. It serves, however, like the great trading companies, as a reminder that there were limits to the capacity of the state in the seventeenth century to absorb all the energies of its subjects under its direct authority.

IX

INTERNATIONAL LAW AND DIPLOMACY

It has been shown that warfare, both by land and sea, was coming more under the control of the state, was becoming both more regular in its methods and more subject to single political purposes. This development of warfare was only a part of a wider movement in the relations of states, affecting equally their peaceful dealings with one another and the conduct of those negotiations in which they settled whether there should be war or peace. The sovereignty of the state was becoming more and more the key to the general organization of Europe. Energies which had previously been controlled from a variety of centres—feudal, ecclesiastical, communal, or what not—were becoming polarized about the state, and the states therefore necessarily elaborated the technique of their dealings with one another.

The clearest sign of this is the change in the content and reputation of international law. In the Middle Ages there had been a number of national or municipal courts which dealt with questions of what we should call international law, and a number of codes or collections of rules, especially for maritime questions, which were accepted as authoritative by these courts, though their authority had narrow and almost fortuitous geographical limits, and for the most part each nation judged such matters according to rules of its own. There was little in the way of rules generally received by all nations, and little, although in the writings of theologians and jurists there was something, of an established body of theory. In the later sixteenth century the theoretical literature grew and improved.[1] The neo-scholastic authors of Spain contributed much to it, and there began to be, besides the works of theory, handbooks for practical use. In this stage of the development the writer who is perhaps the most important and certainly the most interesting to English readers is Alberico Gentili, an

[1] For this the best general guide is E. Nys, *Les origines du droit international* (1894). For the subject of this chapter in general, Holdsworth, *Hist. of English Law*, vol. v, pp. 25–60, is valuable.

Italian exile for religion, who settled in Oxford to teach law and died in London in 1608. His books are typical of the way in which international law has been built up by the union of academic study with the experience of practice in the courts. His *De Jure Belli* of 1598 is a solid and scholarly treatise, but he was no mere theorist. For many years he had been consulted by the English government and had pleaded in the court of admiralty: amongst his works is a posthumously published volume of notes on his cases as standing advocate in London for the king of Spain.[1]

Even Gentili writes not like a pioneer but like an accomplished master in a well-cultivated field: there is no need to argue against the mistaken statement still current in some works of reference that the science of international law was founded by a still later writer, Hugo Grotius. The work of Grotius, *De Jure Belli et Pacis*, was published in 1625.[2] It was one of the great books of the seventeenth century, but there has been some pardonable controversy about exactly wherein its greatness consists. It does not lie in its originality; indeed it would be truer to say that it lies in its laborious avoidance of too much originality. Instead of turning his back on his predecessors, Grotius worked from the point they had reached: he used the traditional method, which was not long to outlast his time, of piling up from every possible source all the arguments and quotations that could be brought to bear on his subject. He owes much to his precursors, and he adequately acknowledges the fact. The modern reader, who cannot but be wearied by Grotius's endless recitation of passages from the Bible, the classical poets and historians, the Christian theologians and former jurists, is apt to overlook the fact that he also used, so far as he could, the kind of materials which a modern writer would prefer. He drew on his own

[1] *Hispanicae Advocationis libri duo*, 1613.

[2] The best text is that edited by P. C. Molhuysen. For English readers the most convenient edition is still that, with abbreviated translation, by Whewell, 3 vols., 1853; an excellent account of Grotius in English is that in *The Collected Papers of John Westlake*. A stimulating essay, though not well translated, is C. van Vollenhoven, *The Three Stages of the Law of Nations*. The useful *Life and Works of Hugo Grotius* by W. S. M. Knight is less satisfactory on the critical than on the biographical side.

experience as a practising lawyer gained before he had to leave his own country and go into exile. He used in his work the remarkable treatise which he had written for a professional purpose at the age of twenty-one, *De Jure Praedae*, on the right of taking prizes, of which the greater part was not published until 1872. He referred to a collection of maritime laws. It is an exaggeration to say that he has no concern whatever for contemporary or recent precedent.[1] He may have deliberately avoided controversial allusions, and he may have done so not for any unworthy reason, but to raise his book to a plane of permanence and impartiality. But if his allusions to contemporary matters are collected together they are not inconsiderable, and their number should be judged in comparison with other authors of his time, whose practise in this matter was not that of our own. In general he seems to have used everything which, by the standards then prevailing, was necessary for a wide, philosophical view of his subject; and the use he made of these materials was to combine them into what had not existed before, a regular department of jurisprudence, with clear limits marking it off from the others and with a logical division of its component parts. He rightly claimed to be the first to treat it 'universim ac certo ordine'. As a systematizer he had faults; but it is primarily because his book was a contribution, in the accepted manner of the time, to the systematic arrangement of the subject that it attained its unequalled reputation.

There were limits even to this reputation. To Spain and Italy it scarcely extended. In the Austrian Netherlands the book was censured on religious grounds.[3] But in the Protestant countries and France, in the countries which in the seventeenth century were those of action and progress, it stood very high. With some intervals of neglect it has lasted well. The editions and translations have been many. It was the first book on international law to win a place in the general literature of the world, the first to have more than

[1] Knight, pp. 218–19.

[2] See the opinions quoted by Vicomte Ch. Terlinden in *L'Université de Louvain à travers 5 siècles*, pp. 217–20.

a merely professional importance. It found its way into all large libraries. On the one hand this was due to the fame of Grotius himself. By birth a Dutchman, living as an exile in France, and employed as a diplomatist by the Swedish crown, he was an international man: he stood between nations as he stood also between the warring creeds. He was famous everywhere as a classical scholar, as a poet, as a theologian, as a historian. Whatever subject he had chosen, he could have made his book famous; but this book was helped by its subject as well. International law was appealed to more often, observed more carefully in practical life: a book like this was needed. And it was helped by the impetus of the ideas which are the driving force of its intricate and sometimes perplexing machinery. First, it is remarkable among the great political books of the century in expressing a strong humanitarian spirit. In the next age the protest against oppression and the crusade against cruelty, deliberate or inadvertent, were to become constant preoccupations of the great leaders of thought: it was not yet so. Grotius saw, when he compared the events of the Thirty Years' War with those of the Dutch war of independence during which he was born and spent his boyhood, a growing *immanitas*. He was not, however, a fanatic or a prophet. He wrote for ordinary men, or at least for ordinary kings and ministers, and he was able to do so because his desire for peace went no farther than was possible to a man whose supreme demand was for justice. His book is a plea for the spirit of law in international relations both in peace and more especially in war, a plea and also a programme.

Succeeding writers did much to improve the symmetry and aptness of the various elements to which Grotius had given what may be called a scientific unity. As he left it, it still wanted even a satisfactory name. He called it 'ius illud quod inter populos plures aut populorum rectores intercedit'. It was not until long afterwards that Jeremy Bentham invented the name of 'international law'; but another Englishman, who was only a few years younger than Grotius, Richard Zouche, Gentili's next successor but one in his Oxford chair, used the Latin equivalent, 'ius inter gentes'. That was not the only improvement made by Zouche. His book *Juris et Judicii Fecialis Expositio* has been, probably too hastily, called the first treatise on positive international law. Where Grotius was mainly pre-occupied with natural law, the divinely ordained rules which are proper to the social existence of man, Zouche, who was a judge as well as a professor, came down closer to the facts and concerned himself chiefly with treaties and customary rules which could be enforced by the courts. Other writers of the seventeenth century similarly worked at what Grotius gave them; but it was not until the eighteenth that there was any real departure from the leading principle of his method. This method was to apply to the relations between states the fundamental principles of the law which exists within states.

Its starting-point was the assumption that states were sovereign, that international law was the law between sovereign states. What the political theorists of one school were elaborating as a theory of the nature of the state, the international lawyers of all schools took as their initial assumption: 'Qui rex est regem, Maxime, non habeat'. Gentili wrote: 'Non est Principi in terris iudex aut ille Princeps non est, supra quem capit alius locum primum. . . . Necessarium itaque iudicium armorum inter hos fuerit.' These words are not very different from those of Grotius: 'Summa autem illa dicitur [potestas] cuius actus alterius iuri non subsunt, ita ut alterius voluntatis humanae arbitrio irriti possint reddi.'

Grotius then held that a sovereign state was subject to no human authority whatsoever outside itself. He held this because it was in his time a hard fact: kings and republics would not recognize any such authority, would not tolerate any interference from outside. They were busily ridding themselves of all the survivals of feudal suzerainties and immunities which might still provide pretexts for interference on the part of their neighbours. By the end of the century there was almost everywhere something resembling a direct, simple, and complete supremacy of the prince over all persons and matters in his dominions. So far as they concerned the relations of states, the far-reaching claims of the papacy were now merely archaic. The reformation had freed the Catholic powers from them as well as the Protestant. Even in diplomacy the declining influence of the popes rested on persuasion rather than authority. In the negotiations for the treaty of Vervins of 1598 a pope had exercised the decisive influence. At the great congress of Westphalia his successor was represented but could do no more than protest against the treaties which were made. At the treaty of the Pyrenees the next pope was not represented, and was hardly consulted. The papal fiefs of Sicily and Sardinia were disposed of by the powers at Utrecht as if the papacy had not existed. After 1660 few popes were European statesmen.

Little or nothing was left of the political structure in which the medieval dream of the unity of Christendom had found a transient and precarious embodiment. The ideal of unity found few advocates, and those without influence on the life of their age. Not a single man of the first rank as a writer or thinker gave it anything more than incidental and perfunctory encouragement. Among those who did treat it seriously two, however, were authors of respectable eminence and statesmen of great importance. The duc de Sully, the old right-hand man of Henry IV of France, great in finance, in diplomacy, and in war, devoted his time in retirement to writing voluminous and untruthful memoirs.[1] In passages scattered through the later-written portions of these he attributed to his old master a 'Grand Design' for remodelling Europe by the balancing of the powers of the various sovereign states and their union in a federation with a common army for operations against the enemies of Christendom. The details of the scheme are interesting for their combination of various elements. There is a genuine aspiration to peace and order, but along with it a survival of the old idea of crusades against the infidel, and there is a regard for the interests of France which can only be called ambitious. The scheme had never been Henry's, and, great as has been the attention paid to it, it is really only one of the most notable of the curiosities of politics. A shorter and far less celebrated work written at the end of the century is free from the

[1] For their value and for particulars of the editions see H. Hauser, *Les sources de l'histoire de France, XVIe siècle*, vol. iv, no. 2574.

ambiguities of aim and presentation which cloud the work of Sully, and was written by a man who combined as few men have done the experience of great affairs with personal humility and simplicity. This was William Penn. His *Essay towards the Present and Future Peace of Europe* [1] is easily shown to have been useless as a practical plan for a confederation of the world. The government he projected for the world was to have no executive. The pamphlet had no influence on contemporaries. It does not appear even to have influenced the subsequent projectors of world-commonwealths, and its relation to the facts of its own time is one of contradiction and protest. The works of Sully and Penn belong strictly to the pre-history of the movement towards international organization: they prove, not that it had begun or was about to begin, but that some exceptionally gifted men were beginning to see that it was needed. Its remoteness is illustrated by the way in which Grimmelshausen introduces a plan for universal peace into his novel *Simplicissimus*, the book which describes more powerfully than any other the miseries of the Thirty Years' War.[2] The plan itself is a caricature, but not an extravagant caricature. It might pass well enough for an ironical rendering of some hope that had actually passed through the mind of some German theorist during the war. What is bitter is the way in which the author introduces it into his tale: he puts it in the mouth of a wandering lunatic.

For the time being, and indeed for a long time still ahead, international relations could be organized only in such ways as the existence of jealous separate sovereignties permitted. Under that limitation some progress was made. The body of the rules of international law grew in bulk and was much improved in such qualities as adaptability to the varied circumstances which resulted from the rich experience of that century of expanding intercourse. A large number of treaties were concluded by which two or more powers agreed to

[1] 1693–4, and several times reprinted.

[2] The anonymous English translation of 1912 is good and omits little except quite worthless matter. It was the work of the late Rev. A. T. S. Goodrick.

observe certain rules between themselves. Often, indeed, there were differences between the rules accepted in this way by one set of powers and those accepted by others. The disagreements were so great that they gave rise to wars. The question of the rights of neutral shipping in time of war, for instance, was one amongst the causes which drove the English into wars with both the French and the Dutch. And, although in the settlements of these questions one treaty often followed the lines laid down by another between other powers, it is impossible to trace any decided progress towards the general acceptance of any one system of regulating them. At the end of the century, as at the beginning, the Dutch stood, on the whole, for the principle of restricting the interference of war with commerce and allowing as much commerce to go on as was not directly to the advantage of their enemies alone; while the English stood for the principle of suppressing and diverting and controlling commerce in every way that could be made harmful to their enemies and tolerable to the rest of the world. The great controversy between belligerents and neutrals went through some novel and remarkable phases, but it cannot be alleged that it was any nearer solution at the treaty of Utrecht than at the time of the Spanish Armada. What the seventeenth century did for international law as a factor in the life of states was not so much to make their relations more legal and regular in their main lines as to give them a great body of experience in the regular and legal handling of minor questions. In big things, even in the larger matters of international law, each state was a law to itself, but in small things each tended more and more to follow a generally accepted system of forms.

One department in which this tendency was strong was in the perfecting of the machinery of diplomatic intercourse. Like so many other institutions, the system of standing diplomacy had its beginnings in the Middle Ages; but its rise to being a characteristic feature of the states of Europe belonged to the sixteenth century, and was a necessary consequence of the growth in that period of the sovereign state for which foreign policy is a constant function, a matter of necessity, whether for ambition or for defence or merely for handling the growing mass of economic and other everyday business. That stage had already been reached, and in the seventeenth century the network of embassies and minor missions was continually spreading and thickening. The circle of states which had to be taken regularly into account in political calculations was widening for every statesman, and the amount of current business was in every way increasing. There were, therefore, more diplomatists, and they were getting more of the specialized training and attitude of a profession. France set the example. The French administration was in all its departments a model for the rest of Europe, and in none was its eminence more marked than in this. It reached its best level in the time of Louis XIV, when French diplomacy had to undertake tasks of the most exacting difficulty, and was able to solve them in a series of negotiations which were the envy of its opponents. The extraordinary intellectual ascendancy of France seemed to be embodied in her best ambassadors: men like the comte d'Avaux, whose dispatches became a text-book for the next century,[1] were not merely talented individuals, but also they had the prestige of a tradition, the style of a great school. They and the secretaries of state whom they served had devised a thoroughly efficient routine of instructions, reports, dispatches, and memoranda. No other country at that time approached them in the technique of their calling.

This calling, even in France, had not yet completed its progress towards becoming a profession or a 'service', completely differentiated from all others. On important occasions at the end of Louis's reign a mission to him or from him to a foreign prince might still be entrusted to a general, or to an ecclesiastic; other powers lagged behind France in this as in other ways. Earlier in the century negotiators had been in all countries much less a specialized class of persons: to take only well-known names, the president Jeannin was a judge; Rubens and Gerbier were painters. They, however, were employed for extraordinary missions. The resident

[1] For the editions see E. Bourgeois and L. André, *Les sources de l'histoire de France, XVIIe siècle*, vol. ii, no. 1173.

envoys and ambassadors, who did the daily work of diplomacy, were for the most part men who spent their lives in this work. It was not thought so desirable as employment nearer the person of the prince: it was a kind of honourable exile, not very remunerative, and very willingly exchanged for any moderately dignified ministerial position at home. Most of the men who discharged it belonged, however, to the ruling classes. The more spectacular missions were reserved for noblemen of high rank, and there were noblemen's sons and other persons of quality amongst the regular diplomatists. Philip IV and the archduchess Isabella did not care to employ Rubens because he was a painter, just as Queen Anne, because his birth was low, would not give Mat Prior the highest employments although he was a professional diplomatist as well as a distinguished author. Promotion, as everywhere in those days, went by merit or favour and not by rule: the hierarchy was even more rudimentary than in armies. There was, however, a considerable number of men who were regularly employed in foreign affairs and only in these, either constantly abroad or with spells in the directing department at home.

A number of books were written to lay down the principles of their craft, some of them historical or legal text-books, others attractive collections of advice and reminiscence.[1] They give an idea of the mental equipment which was thought necessary for the career. It was such as could be picked up from observation and reading by a young man who could get himself attached to the person of an ambassador abroad: secretaryships paid by the state were not unknown, but no sovereigns maintained more than a few of them. A knowledge of the Roman civil law was desirable but not essential, and the number of trained civilians who take part in the diplomacy of the different states was not great. Legal questions were commonly referred to the sedentary civilians of the courts. There are scattered instances in the seventeenth century of attempts by governments to institute a regular training for diplomatists. Torcy in

[1] For a readable survey of the latter class see the essay which gives its title to M. Jusserand's *School for Ambassadors.*

1712 started a course of instruction under M. de St. Parest; but it was not until later in the eighteenth century that this tendency got far. The regius professorships of modern history founded by George I at Oxford and Cambridge are part of it, like the school kept at Strassburg by Schöpflin and Koch. The need for such innovations illustrates the way in which, as we shall notice later, the universities were losing touch with public life. It is significant that, in the time of William III, Lord Halifax, anxious to get a recruit for diplomacy, wrote to the president of Magdalen to ask him not to insist on Joseph Addison's going into orders. 'His arguments were founded upon the general pravity and corruption of men of business, who wanted liberal education.' [1]

A curious symptom of the development of diplomacy towards maturity is the attention paid to questions of etiquette. Formalities still play a greater part in this sphere than perhaps in any other except those of court and ecclesiastical ritual; but in the seventeenth century they reached a fantastic elaboration.[2] They fill a great part of the considerable literature on the rights and duties of ambassadors. The footman's quarrel at Utrecht was immortalized in *The Spectator*,[3] and the street-fight in London in the time of Charles II between the followers of the French and the Spanish ambassadors showed to all the world that precedence was worth bloodshed. The number of such disputes, more or less serious, was infinite. Ministers were constantly occupied with titles, with the forms of address and correspondence, with the right to take the hand of a foreign representative in his own house or elsewhere, with the arrangement of places at table, with all the pedantries of ceremonial. Disputes were more often deliber-

[1] Aikin, *Life of Addison*, i. 57–8. A generation earlier Sir Joseph Williamson, after whom Addison was named, had a plan for sending young men abroad at the expense of the Crown to fit them for the public service. Two whom he sent were Dr. William Lancaster and (Bishop) Nicholson, both members of Queen's College, Oxford, of which Williamson had been a fellow.

[2] There is probably a connexion between this and the spread of court formality in general in the sixteenth and early seventeenth centuries from Spain through Italy to the rest of Europe.

[3] No. 481.

ately ordered than spontaneous: they were useful as methods of delaying business or of picking a quarrel if a quarrel was wanted. It was easy enough to avoid them if dispatch or harmony was preferable; but it is characteristic of the age that they should have been so prevalent even as means to other ends.

One environment was specially favourable and famous for them, that of the congresses. To put it in another way, the use of congresses was a new method of diplomacy, for the working of which, etiquette, amongst other things, had to be altered and adapted. Only one kind of earlier gatherings, the ecclesiastical councils of the later Middle Ages, bore a resemblance, and that by no means a near resemblance, to these congresses. Their origination is one of the great landmarks of the century.[1] In former times the representatives of three or four powers had sometimes met in one place; but it was not until the time came for winding up the Thirty Years' War, which had involved almost all Protestant and Roman Catholic countries, that there was any general European congress. That settlement was effected by the congress of Westphalia, an assembly not merely impressive in comparison with any that had been seen before, but more impressive than any other before the fall of Napoleon. It met while Grotius was still alive. In the two towns of Münster and Osnabrück—in two towns because the difficulties of precedence which would have arisen if they had met in one—there were gathered together representatives of most of the sovereigns in Europe except the outlying kings of England, Poland, and Denmark, and the tsar of Russia who was in Europe geographically but scarcely in any other sense. They made the great body of treaties in which the problems of one generation were solved and those of two more set. From that time to our own the diplomatic history of Europe has stridden along from one congress to another. That of Utrecht which closed the era of Louis XIV was reckoned the ninth from this beginning.[2]

[1] For congresses in general and some other points mentioned in this chapter see Satow, *Guide to Diplomatic Practice*, vol. ii, cap. xxv and *passim*.

[2] The Pyrenees 1659; Oliva 1660; Aix-la-Chapelle 1668; Nijmegen 1676–9; Frankfort 1681; Rijswijk 1697; Carlowitz 1699; Utrecht 1712–13.

In the treaties of Utrecht solemn recognition was given to a principle which was to supply for a long time to come both pretexts for making war and the theoretical basis of treaties of peace, a principle which was, in fact, to be accepted as the ostensible aim of the foreign policy of every important state. This was the principle of the balance of power. We shall have occasion in a later chapter to see how it suited the prevalent habits of thought, and how closely it is related to other doctrines current at the time.[1] For the present it must be treated solely in its direct bearing on international relations. So long as it meant that no one power must be allowed to tyrannize over the rest, it was a healthy and admirable idea; but unhappily it lent itself to a different interpretation. It has been defined by a great French historian thus: 'Il se forme ainsi entre les grands États une sorte de société en participation: ils entendent conserver ce qu'ils possèdent, gagner en proportion de leurs mises, et interdire à chacun des associés de faire la loi aux autres.'[2] It had a variety of different forms. On one side it was an analysis of the actual constitution of Europe. An early example of it may be quoted from an English writer, which is interesting because it describes not one general equilibrium of Europe, but a number of separate systems. In the *Observations on his Travels* in 1609 ascribed to Sir Thomas Overbury occurs this passage:

'For the relation of this state [France] to others, it is first to be considered that this part of Christendom is balanced between the three Kings of Spain, France and England, as the other part betwixt the Russians, the Kings of Poland, Sweden, and Denmark. For as Germany, which if it were intirely subject to one monarchy, would be terrible to all the rest, so being divided betwixt so many princes, and those of so equal power, it serves only

[1] See p. 213 below.

[2] Sorel, *L'Europe et la révolution française*, i. 33–4. This masterly volume is the best introduction to the diplomatic history of the period. For our immediate subject Dupuy, *Le Principe de l'équilibre et le concert européen* (1909) and Meinberg, *Das Gleichgewichtssystem Wilhelms III und die englische Handelspolitik*, are worth consulting, and among contemporary works D'Avenant's *Essay on the Balance of Power* and *Essay on Universal Monarchy* (1701).

to balance itself, and entertain easy war with the Turk, while the Persian witholds him in a greater. . . . England is not able to subsist against any of the other, hand to hand, but joined with the Low Countries, it can give law to both by sea, and joined with either of them two, it is able to oppress the third as Henry VIII did.'

The idea of a balance of power at sea, distinct from that on land, half expressed in this passage, is to be found in other works of this and the next century.[1] Usually, however, a single general European equilibrium was meant; and this was represented not merely as in fact existing, but as something to be consciously striven after and artificially manipulated by diplomacy. It was not indeed a new invention of statesmanship to attempt this. There are well-known examples of such an endeavour in the sixteenth century—that of Wolsey is the most famous—and David Hume was quite right in pointing out that 'the utmost refinements' of the theory could be traced as early as Demosthenes.[2] What was new in the seventeenth century was the general and official adoption of the formula. Before it found its way into treaties it appeared in the preambles of English acts of parliament. We have seen that it was foreshadowed by Sully.[3] Fénelon, the typical liberal of the latter part of the century, praised it as the only means of preserving the general peace and welfare. Though he was protesting against the ideas of Louis XIV, it was not long before the unrepentant French monarchy resorted to it as a justification.

In contrast with other schemes for preserving peace and order, it seemed to have the advantage of facing the facts. It admitted that every state wanted to prevail over its neighbours, and was prone to use its power for ambitious ends. It offered to provide the means by which these ambitions could be made to neutralize each other. Thus it was advocated as a conservative principle. Just as the alliances against Louis XIV were ostensibly meant to restore the settlements of older treaties, so each adjustment of the

[1] Molesworth, *Account of Denmark* (1694), 3rd ed., p. 175; *Bedford Correspondence*, iii. 126.

[2] *Essays*, Part II, no. vii.

[3] p. 129 above.

balance of power was professedly meant to protect the *status quo* against aggression. In practice, however, it was not a static principle, but a method of regulating and facilitating change. The balance of strength, of which the ordinary basis was territorial possession, was restored, when an aggressor was brought to terms, not by restoring the *status quo*, but by a new construction, in which the several great powers had strength in the required proportions, but not in the old quantities or in the old places. The balance was redressed at need by annexations. The states of Europe fell into two classes, on the one hand the great and growing, on the other those which were declining and at the expense of which the greater were able to add to their possessions. As each strong state gained, its rivals sought for what were later called 'compensations'. Once partition had started, it was bound to go farther. The public claims of the balance coincided with the separate interests of the states which upheld it; the upholding became profitable to these public-spirited powers themselves, so that one rapacious power could lead the world to a rapacity like its own.

If the states had disinterestedly tried to preserve the equilibrium they would thus, in spite of themselves, have perpetuated the universal scramble for territory. The method of the attempt was the formation of alliances, and it has been observed[1] that all 'systems' or groups of states organized in this way tend to become aggressive. By acquiring power they expose themselves to the temptation to use it without the provocation of an attack from outside. Thus, even the formula by which the diplomacy of the seventeenth century tried to put the best light on its intentions was deceptive. It had in it very little of a rational attempt to manage the world's affairs for the general advantage. The smoothness of its professions and the expert plausibility of its apologists easily lead a modern reader to overrate the real quality of its statesmanship. In reality it was penetrated by the spirit of what the French call 'une politique d'aventure'. Only in the countries which were governed by assemblies was it in any serious sense responsible to public opinion, and, even in those, foreign affairs, except when they touched

[1] Bernard, *Four Lectures on Diplomacy* (1868), p. 70.

economic interests, were often and easily kept in the hands of ministers and courtiers. Callières, who had been one of the French plenipotentiaries at Rijswijk, wrote a sentence which was to remain true long after his time: 'La plupart des grandes affaires ont été conclus par des Ministres envoyez secrètement.'[1] It had been so in the treaties of Westphalia, of the Pyrenees, of Rijswijk: it was to be so at Utrecht. The great congresses were something more than a mere façade, but they were not all they seemed to be.

This defect in the conduct of international relations was not accidental. It was intimately related to the whole state of civilization at the time. A sounder and more enlightened diplomacy could not have been produced while the state of politics and especially of political knowledge remained as it was. Alliances and wars were necessarily speculative. The absence of statistical information which we have already noticed as one of the governing conditions of economic life extended, needless to say, also over the political sphere. In the middle of the eighteenth century Lord Chesterfield, as good an authority on this point as could be wanted, wrote to his son: 'There is one part of political knowledge which is only to be had by inquiry and conversation: that is, the present state of every power in Europe with regard to the three important points of strength, revenue and commerce.'[2] In the rest of their correspondence there are abundant proofs of it; but by Chesterfield's time the stock of information available for the public and the machinery by which more could be procured for ministers had far outdistanced what it had been even at the end of the previous century. Huge misconceptions of the strength of an ally, the weakness of an enemy, the obstacles to a campaign or the value of a conquest were almost inevitable in the days of Charles XII and Peter the Great, as in those of Philip II and Queen Elizabeth. Such uncertainty encouraged the spirit of speculation, which on its good side meant adventure and enterprise, on its bad the abandonment of honesty and responsibility. There were far-sighted statesmen here and there; but they had to work with a clumsy, erratic, and dangerous machinery.

[1] *De la manière de négocier* (1716), p. 239.

[2] 1/2 March 1748, no. lviii in Bradshaw's edition.

X

FRONTIERS

In the political relations between European states the central questions appeared to be the questions of territory. From the dynastic marriages and from the wars the chief gains that were desired were territorial, and in the treaties the most disputed clauses were nearly always those about cessions and annexations. Many a schoolboy has learned by heart the names of the provinces and bishoprics which changed hands at this treaty or that, and even this skeleton knowledge has its value. It gives the stages by which some powers grew and others dwindled. It explains the political map of Europe, and it gives the basis of the wealth and military strength of the several states. But there is more to be learnt from these territorial changes. They too have their relations with many apparently remote departments of human life.

Those which took place in the seventeenth century form a part of the transition from feudal Europe to the modern Europe of sovereign states. By the beginning of the century the conception of sovereignty had been completed by jurists and political theorists and it had almost established its dominion in international and 'municipal' law. The authority of the state within its borders was to be exclusive of all other authority, so that conversely any given plot of ground must be under one sovereignty and not more than one. If any one other than the sovereign had any rights over it, whether of ownership or whatever kind of feudal superiority, they were to be regarded as conferred by the sovereign and revocable at his will. As a legal theory this could, no doubt, be so stretched or relaxed as to serve for any existing condition of things. A feudal lord might continue to exercise over his inferiors the same rights as before, provided only that he now recognized them as derived from the sovereign rights of his overlord and not resting on any validity which that overlord could not challenge. But the legal theory had come into existence as the counterpart of a change in the facts. It was the expression of the determination of sovereigns to get something more than a merely theoretical recognition of their rights, something for which the theoretical recognition was merely a lever, namely, a real obedience. Feudal Europe had not been organized in such a way that obedience to one superior and one only had been the primary defining feature of each man's position. To make it so had been one of the tasks of jurists, of constitutional reformers and of many others; but it could not be made so without a great clearing up and rearrangement of boundaries.

The dominions of medieval kings, like those of their vassals and like the estates of great modern landowners, were scattered and interrupted. Everywhere there were immunities where the king's writ did not run, overlapping and divided jurisdictions, disputed boundaries, enclaves. The need for consolidation, like the need for centralization, had not yet been felt. When it came to be felt it caused a two-sided process, of which the shiftings of the frontiers of states make one aspect. Among the irregularities in the boundaries of a kingdom those were the most difficult to deal with which affected the interests of some powerful overlord, especially if he were a sovereign elsewhere. If a neighbouring sovereign owned an inlying enclave, or an inconveniently intrusive salient, or even had some ill-defined feudal rights over a village, the assertion of sovereign rights against him would probably become a matter of high politics; but it was merely a part of the general task of asserting them against every one, at home or abroad, sovereign or subject, in order to establish real unity in the realm.

How closely the two sides of the process are intermingled may be illustrated from the way in which historians treat the change which in 1642 altered the status of the principality of Sedan. This is sometimes stated to have been a separate sovereignty; but another way of explaining its standing is to say that it was rather a 'frontière',[1] that is a frontier province of which the ruler had specially great though not quite sovereign powers. Whether it was or was not a sub-fief of

[1] P. Viollet, *Le Roi et ses ministres*, pp. 48, 51; *L'Art de verifier les dates*, xii (1818), 300 ff.

the French crown came to be disputed. It was certainly under the immediate lordship of the dukes of Bouillon, and the dukes of Bouillon held some of their possessions of the bishops of Liége, who were princes of the empire. In 1651 the ducal family ceded Sedan in exchange for certain counties and duchies of France. How exactly this cession is to be interpreted is a point on which the modern writers do not agree: the ambiguity of its previous status is reflected here, so that sometimes it is counted as an annexation of foreign sovereign territory and sometimes as the addition of a piece of French land to the royal domain. This legal doubt does not affect its political importance. The celebrity which the name of Sedan acquired two centuries later, when the ruler of France was captured there by the Germans, is a sufficient reminder that it was a district of great military importance. The town of Sedan itself is at the point where there is a great meeting of roads. Three roads into Germany diverge from here, one of the roads to Aachen, the road to Strassburg, that to Luxemburg; westwards runs the road to Paris, and southward that to Dijon. Not only is it a nodal point for roads; it is also at a crossing of the Meuse. It was therefore the aim of Richelieu to get control of it, and even if the theoretical sovereignty was French already, the practical change was none the less decisive. There are a number of other cases more or less similar both on the French frontier and on those of other states, or even well within them, away from the frontiers. The little principality of Orange, which was absorbed by Louis XIV, lay about eighty miles within the French boundary, and its sovereign was Louis's bitterest enemy. That was a simple annexation. But besides such real enclaves there were the quasi-enclaves, and other immunities descending in a graduated scale of independence down to commonplace feudal exemptions from this or that branch of royal authority. The task of clearing up all this feudal debris was one whole.

One consequence of this was that the frontiers not only changed their geographical position but also tended to change their character. Some of them remained much as they had been, ill defined, indented, economically and politically inconvenient. The eastern and southern frontiers of the Dutch republic, down to the end of its existence, had all sorts of irregularities and anomalies. There were detached pieces of Dutch territory away from the rest; there was a joint dominion with the bishop of Liége in Maastricht; there were Spanish fiefs embedded in the Dutch lands. That was because there was never any thorough-going settlement of the line. Where the frontiers were settled by decisive wars of the seventeenth century, they were tidied up, much as the boundaries of English counties were tidied by the reforming legislation of the nineteenth century. They were simplified. It is significant that the modern principle of 'opting' for nationality made its first appearances in the time of Louis XIII and XIV: in the terms of surrender of various towns in the Spanish Netherlands, from 1640, and in the treaties of Utrecht and Baden (1713 and 1714) the inhabitants of the places annexed to France were given the right to choose whether they would stay where they were and become Frenchmen or pack up their possessions, move over the new line and remain Spanish subjects or Germans as they had been before.[1] The growing size, cost, permanence, and military value of fortifications in the age of Vauban is another symptom of the change in the character of frontiers. We may say that a frontier was ceasing to be an area and tending to become a line. The word or its equivalent in other languages had at first both meanings. The Austrian 'frontier' against the Turks in the sixteenth century was not a boundary, for the territorial limits fluctuated constantly: it was the special military organization prevailing in those districts which were responsible for defence. As the modern states became more consolidated such arrangements grew obsolete. All parts of a realm must now take their share in defence and send up their contingents when the enemy encroached. The regular administration became more established and more active; it dealt with all the inhabitants and not merely with the great feudatories who ruled them; it

[1] Fauchille, *Traité de droit international* (8th ed., 1922), vol. i, pt. i, p. 859, enumerates seven such agreements, of which six belong to the period 1659–1715.

needed to know exactly how far its authority extended. The tendency therefore was towards a linear frontier. As yet, however, it was a tendency imperfectly fulfilled. For completion it had to await, amongst other things, the progress of map-making. I have not been able to discover a case of a frontier fixed literally on the map until the year 1718. To the treaty made between the emperor and the states-general in that year there was annexed a map of the boundary of Flanders, to which the plenipotentiaries set their signatures and seals. An engraving of this map, with the signatures and seals, was published.[1]

Although the changes of frontier brought with them these various kinds of improvement and modernization, we must be on our guard against laying too much stress on this element. Even in some examples where it is conspicuously present, it does not go very far towards explaining the changes. Its application is always governed by a greater fact in the relations of states. The 'Chambers of Reunion' of Louis XIV afford a case in point. In the Treaty of Münster, one of the treaties which constituted the peace of Westphalia of 1648, France acquired from the empire a miscellaneous mass of sovereignties and overlordships in Alsace. They were typical of the confused transitional stage of decadent feudalism and imperfectly developed state-supremacy. So great was their intricacy that it was not finally straightened out until after the French Revolution: it will be remembered that difficulties arose from the application to those feudal lords in Alsace who were vassals of the empire of the law of 4 August 1789 abolishing feudal burdens. At the time of the original cession the crucial clause was drafted ambiguously, some of the towns, nobles, and ecclesiastical feudatories being expressly left in possession of the privileges which they had previously obtained from the house of Austria. Here was material for an infinity of collisions between these guaranteed rights (which were not enumerated) and the sovereignty given to France, an aggravated case of the need for definition

[1] Kluit, *Primae lineae historiae federum Belgii Federati*, i (1790), p. 90. I do not know when it became customary in different countries to affix plans to conveyances of land.

and settlement which existed more or less acutely in so many other places.[1]

Louis XIV decided, thirty years later, to clear it up. He commissioned three Chambers of Reunion, with the function of reuniting to his crown all those rights and superiorities in the frontier regions which had been allowed to pass out of its hands. Those in the region of Alsace were to be dealt with by the conseil de Breisach; another existing court of law, the parlement of Besançon, dealt with similar matters in the newly annexed Franche-Comté, the old imperial free county of Burgundy, and a new body was set up at Metz to adjudicate over those in Lorraine, the county of Bar, and the bishoprics of Metz, Toul, and Verdun. In form their task was reunion, the sorting out of the feudal inconsistencies and contradictions; but this form, as the whole of contemporary Europe knew, was a hypocritical pretence. In fact their work was to incorporate as much as they could, and especially the places of strategic value. Not only was Louis judge in his own cause. There was further the patent fact that this procedure, begun promptly after the ending of one of his great aggressive wars by the Treaty of Nijmegen, was a way of carrying on in nominal peace the expansion which he was for the time being unable to prosecute by fighting. It inevitably led to a renewal of the alliances against him.

That is the most striking illustration of the general truth that the governing factor in the reconstruction of frontiers was the desire of the strong powers to expand. Europe was going through one of those recurring stages in its history in which the *leit-motif* is the contest between the strong and the weak. Economic, political, intellectual forces had combined to set up a sharp division between those states which were capable of attack and those which had to stand on the defensive. On the one hand were the modern countries, like France, where a strong central government had at its disposal a large population and stores of taxable wealth. Among her immediate neighbours France had none to reckon with which approached her in these respects. The empire was

[1] For a clear explanation of the questions see J. E. Hamilton in *History*, new ser., xiii. 107.

a loosely united confederation in which the central authority amounted to almost nothing. For military and diplomatic calculations it was not the empire itself which had to be considered, but the several units of which it was composed, and, as it happened, of the states from which France wanted to acquire territory the only one which was strong and powerful was the Habsburg agglomeration. Among the small, weak, old-fashioned states, which were destined sooner or later to be absorbed, and even before their absorption to be satellites of their bigger neighbours, one class deserves special mention, the ecclesiastical principalities. Even in the sixteenth century three of these had come under French influence, Metz, Toul, and Verdun. In the territorial settlement of Westphalia it was partly from the bishoprics that the ambitions of Brandenburg-Prussia, Hanover, and Sweden were gratified. Those which survived through the eighteenth century went down in the next great era of territorial redistribution, that of Napoleon. Their long respite was in part due to the fact that the great German powers which emerged from the Westphalian settlement in a condition to continue their expansion turned most of their energies eastwards against another kind of weakness. The Turks failed to keep pace with the western progress and the Habsburgs made rich gains at their expense. Poland began in the later seventeenth century to be one of the victim-states. Not only the rising power of Brandenburg-Prussia menaced her, but, on the other side, the vast population of Russia, into which Peter the Great infused enough of the western discipline to set it in motion against the weak.

These eastern changes present a very different appearance from those of the west. In exhausting and fiercely contested campaigns in Flanders or in the Alps or at the foot of the Pyrenees the French might push forward their line by a day's march, while Peter and Charles XII swept forward or backward over extensive provinces. To account for this there was a difference in the political conditions and also a difference of geography. In the west there was a more closely knit system of alliances, a greater possibility of rallying numerous and well-found forces in opposition to any threat of change, and this had its counterpart in tougher natural and artificial obstacles, ranges of mountains, and where there were no mountains, a network of fortresses. In the east alliances were less stable and calculable, less like the systematic agreements of solid investors than the improvised and speculative combinations of adventurers who have nothing to lose. The country too seemed to favour this state of things. Vast featureless plains lay open to conquest and offered little impediment to military movements which still resembled the raids of nomadic barbarians. Of a later age it has been said that the frontiers of Prussia were her armies, but it was true already that all across the great northern and eastern lowlands it was by armies and not by frontier-lines that the extent of each state was determined. Here the changes of boundaries were accompanied to a far lower degree by the clearing of the feudal undergrowth. It is impossible to overlook the fact that they record the fluctuations in the rivalries of conquering states.

These rivalries have been cloaked at different times under different pretexts suited to the changing atmosphere of political discussion. Side by side with the liquidation of feudalism there was another type of theoretical justification which, like that, was plausible because it contained a germ of truth. This was the doctrine of natural frontiers. Its great days were not yet come. It was to reach a far higher influence in the eighteenth century, when the idea of nature came to play a great part in all branches of thought; but it does appear before that, though only casually and by way of anticipation. I do not know of anything in the seventeenth century which can be called a reasoned exposition of it. Expressed in general terms, it is the doctrine that the boundaries of a state ought to conform to natural features, that they ought not to be 'illogically' unrelated to the lie of the land. It is much easier to formulate it definitely for one country than for all countries, and so the classical example of it is the doctrine that the frontiers of France ought to be the Rhine, the Alps, and the Pyrenees. This is to be found in seventeenth-century writers;[1] but with them it is mainly

[1] See Sorel, *L'Europe et la révolution française*, i. 319 ff.

an historical theory: these were the limits of ancient Gaul. There was no studied attempt to prove that these natural limits were necessary for the satisfactory organization of political and economic life in the country.

We know that these arguments in our time are often insincere. Lord Balfour once drew attention to the interesting fact that in every recorded case the natural frontiers of a country embrace a greater extent of territory than its actual frontiers.[1] This is so even in our own time when the idea of natural frontiers is supplemented and controlled by another which emanated from it, that of frontiers based on racial or national identity. Of this we find in the seventeenth century scarcely even the beginnings: only one or two phrases foreshadow it and the notion of natural frontiers merely furnishes pretexts, well-sounding reasons alleged in justification of courses adopted on other and more questionable grounds. It does not help us to understand why the statesmen acted as they did, and it was not yet sufficiently current to throw much light on that public opinion before which they tried to justify their conduct. It has just enough importance to deserve to be mentioned, and an industrious collector could possibly assemble a fair number of texts in which it was employed. At any rate, the earliest example I have seen in which the term 'natural frontier' occurs in the English language uses it in a metaphorical, almost a paradoxical way which implies that it was already familiar to the reader. The passage is well worth quoting, though it hardly bears on our immediate subject. In 1677 Andrew Marvell wrote of the 'Spanish-Nether-Land, which had always been considered as the natural frontier of England'.[2]

The actual achievement of the century in altering frontiers is best shown either in maps, which are provided amply in

[1] At the Philosophical Congress in Oxford, 28 September 1920.

[2] *Of the Growth of Popery and Arbitrary Government*, in *Works*, ed. Thompson, i. 461. The Dutch ambassadors in England in 1674 pointed out that the Spanish Netherlands were without 'natuerlycke ofte artificiale frontieren' (*Correspondentie van Willem III en Bentinck*, pt. 2, i. 401); but this is a different sense of 'natural', meaning defended by natural features, not fortifications.

the historical atlases, or in a tabular form.[1] Either of these methods gives both a quicker and a clearer conspectus of the growth or diminution of states than is possible in continuous prose. A few words may, however, be said here which will serve as a commentary on such maps or tables. The two states which made the most notable advances were France and Brandenburg-Prussia. France gained rich provinces which made her frontier more defensible in some parts, and in others provided starting-points for further forward movements. The provinces gained by Henry IV from Savoy in 1601 brought the frontier north of Dauphiné forward from the line of the Saône, in comparatively easily traversed country, to the rocky gorges of the Rhône. The peace of Westphalia and the reunions, although they did not quite complete the absorption of Alsace, made France mistress of the left bank of the Rhine from Switzerland two-thirds of the way to Mainz. Switzerland and Alsace were separated from France by a wedge of territory, more than two hundred miles from north to south, of which the northern portion formed the imperial duchy of Lorraine and the southern the Franche-Comté or free county of Burgundy which belonged to Spain. Both these provinces were now, in the military sense, at the mercy of France. Lorraine was occupied more than once, and small portions of it were annexed; but in 1697 its dukes were restored to most of their possessions, and its annexation was held over by France as one of her tasks in the eighteenth century. Franche-Comté was easily and definitively taken by Louis XIV. In the Spanish possessions to the north, in Flanders, the old prize-fighting stage of Europe, where every yard was stubbornly contested, he had to recede, as we shall see, from the high-water mark of his conquests; but there he kept a strongly fortified and easily defensible artificial frontier. At his death the eastern and northern frontiers of France were far stronger than they had been at his accession. The line now showed few weaknesses and irregularities. Geneva and the little principality

[1] A table of the provinces annexed by Brandenburg-Prussia with their area is given in Meyer's *Historischer Handatlas*, 1911, and a similar table for the Habsburg possessions in Léger, *Histoire d'Autriche-Hongrie*.

of Montbéliard or Mömpelgard interrupted it. Lorraine and some districts of Alsace remained to be incorporated when circumstances permitted. These were, however, only small shortcomings in the great work of consolidation which France had accomplished on this side, as also against Spain in the direction of the Pyrenees.

The progress of Brandenburg-Prussia presents a contrast. Instead of rounding off a block of territory, the electors of Brandenburg, one of whom gained the title of king of Prussia as a reward for his service against Louis, were collecting detached pieces scattered about northern Germany from the Dutch frontier to the Polish. They took, of course, what could be had, whether it was by getting partial recognition of a dynastic claim, as in the Cleve duchies about the lower Rhine, or by taking bishoprics as their share in a general bargaining, as at Magdeburg, Halberstadt, Minden, or Kammin in Pomerania. Their dispersed possessions which to the first glance look even more confused than the scattered strips of a medieval agricultural holding, had their own geographical plan. There were three main blocks of land, the electoral mark of Brandenburg in which was Berlin, the duchy of Prussia, to the east, and the smaller, richer, and less consolidated possessions towards the Rhine. Each of these blocks was growing. The political testaments written by the heads of the house of Hohenzollern for their descendants show how opportunities were foreseen and watched.[1] Other acquisitions outside these three nuclei had their place in the programme. Minden was a bridge over the Weser, one of the main points on the great road from east to west which connected Berlin with the lower Rhine. Magdeburg was one of the most important crossings of the Elbe. These scattered dominions were ceasing to be a mere feudal agglomeration and beginning to look like the framework of a great kingdom.

In this, as in many other things, the history of Savoy is analogous to that of Prussia. It is true, as we have seen, that she began the century by losing outlying territory to France; but even in that settlement she made good her possession of

[1] See the very convenient edition by G. Küntzel and M. Hass, *Die politischen Testamente der Hohenzollern*, 2 vols., 1919–20.

Saluzzo, which was on the Italian side and closer to the heart of her dominions. In 1713–15 she gave up the Barcelonette valley on the west side of the Alps; but she could afford to lose it. Her dukes had freed her in the course of the seventeenth century from the danger of tutelage to France which was symbolized by the French occupation of the fortresses of Pinerolo and Casale. They began to make modest advances eastwards, their first bites at the Italian artichoke.

Like the dukes of Savoy, but on a far greater scale, the Austrian Habsburgs had both gains and losses. They too might count the gains as balancing or outweighing the losses, indeed it was in 1718, with the Treaty of Passarowitz, that their possessions reached their greatest territorial extent. Like Savoy, Austria was turning from west to east, but here the analogy ends, for, while Savoy was becoming more Italian and preparing for a future in which she was to become more homogeneous, Austria, in diminishing her German possessions, was taking on responsibilities on the Danube so various that they were ultimately to prove impossible. The reconquest of Hungary, the allegiance of Transylvania, the large share of Austria in the dismembered Spanish empire, with other minor gains, materially did more than compensate for losses in Alsace and other parts of Germany. For the generation following the Treaty of Utrecht they kept Austria in the front rank of the great powers. With the changes of territory in the north we shall be occupied later,[1] and we need not here notice minor transferences between greater or lesser powers. For European, as distinguished from national, history the gains of France, Prussia, Savoy, and Austria were the significant changes of political geography.

It must, however, be remembered that territorial extent is not the whole of the strength of a state. A larger and even a more populous territory may be more loosely controlled. Even when only frontiers are thought of, their position is not the only point to notice. Often it is more important to ask what lies beyond them. France not only moved her boundaries forward, she also conducted a policy which

[1] Below, pp. 167–70.

surrounded her with a ring of harmless neighbours, either well disposed towards her, or held in check by herself or her allies. The Dutch, once their boundaries were laid down in the Treaty of Münster and some consequent agreements, neither corrected them nor extended them as much as their political influence might have allowed. This was partly because they had reasons of internal policy which made them averse from expansion, and partly because they trusted to arrangements beyond the frontier to secure the same advantages of defence which a larger territory might have given. They not only had their allies; they also got their 'barrier', or rather barriers, for the same system which protected their southern frontier existed also on a smaller scale to the east. It was the system of obtaining from their neighbours the right to maintain garrisons in their fortresses. A weaker neighbour, with little interest in defending itself and little power to do so, would be a danger if a stronger power lay behind. The southern Netherlands were a danger-zone for the Dutch. The Dutch were allowed to buttress their resistance against France, while at the same time keeping them in a state of economic weakness which prevented them from becoming dangerous competitors.

The barrier system was thus a system of making a weak neighbour strong against one's enemies. It was a variant of the system of buffer-states. In the end it proved a failure, and it must be regarded now as one of the blind alleys of political history. The future may relegate to the same class the other variants of the same idea. Specimens of these also may be found in the seventeenth century. Such are neutralization as applied to single towns, as Sabern (though not yet to states), the limitation of armed forces by treaty (imposed by France upon Lorraine and upon Savoy). The part which these devices play in the history of that time is, however, trifling. They serve merely as forecasts of the future, and reminders that a change of frontiers is only one among a number of ways in which the relations of states may be altered. The history of frontiers is part of a larger whole which cannot be recorded in maps or tables.

XI

THE INTERESTS OF THE STATES [1]

THE history of diplomacy, although it is sometimes said to be the easiest branch of historical writing, ought to be classed amongst the most difficult. It is true that in the modern centuries for which the materials are abundant, it is generally possible to make a connected narrative of the negotiations on a particular question without having to solve any problems more abstruse than those as to which events preceded others and which followed. A narrative of negotiations is, however, only a beginning, and even that will probably suggest the need for a critical treatment of the authorities. The bulkiest of these are the dispatches of diplomatists. Such writers are naturally anxious to present their own conduct in the most favourable light, and often, whether innocently or purposely, they exaggerate their own influence if things have gone favourably, or misrepresent that of others if things have gone ill. They habitually treat diplomacy as a highly skilled game in which the decisive turns are given by their own adroitness. Writing at short intervals and reporting on the events of a week or a day, they can scarcely escape taking short views and losing the proportion of great and small events. A history of diplomacy based on such materials may be consecutive, but it is almost bound to be superficial and ill balanced. On the other hand, there are

pitfalls for the historian who reduces the personal factors to their due place. He may without much difficulty discover some great forces which were embodied in the international relations of a period. In the seventeenth century, for instance, as we have seen or shall see in later chapters, dynastic and religious and, later, commercial considerations had much to

[1] For the subjects of this and the following chapter the best text-books are the two volumes *Geschichte des Europäischen Staatensystems* by W. Platzhoff (*1559–1660*) and M. Immich (*1660–1789*); but they should be used in conjunction with the admirable volume by E. Fueter in the same series which covers the period 1492–1559. The brilliant sketch from the French point of view, E. Bourgeois, *Manuel historique de la politique étrangère*, vol. i, 9th ed., 1925, begins with 1610.

do with the wars and the alliances. The historians who have recognized the influence of these great forces have, however, often stated their view in such a way that the actual course of events seems to lose its significance. It has been said of Sir John Seeley, who was one of them, that there was 'too much predestination' in his account of Europe.

In the search for links between the general forces and the particular events, it is well to pay some attention to the books, mostly short, which were written at the time to survey the relations of the European states. One of them, which is known as *The Observations of Sir Thomas Overbury in his Travels*, but which has every appearance of being the work of a member of a British diplomatic mission, we have already noticed.[1] Others were written by British and foreign diplomatists at different times. The earliest which treated of Europe as a whole seem to belong to the period of Richelieu. One of the most famous was the work of the duc de Rohan, *De l'Interest des Princes et Estats de la Chrestienté*, first published in 1638.[2] This was succeeded by a considerable number of similar works of greater or less value and interest which, by their titles, excite the hope that they contain a contemporary *rationale* of international politics. To that, however, they contribute in reality little. The spirit of the time was matter-of-fact: very few generalizations about the nature of the interests of states were current. What these authors for the most part gave was a statement of the pretensions of each state against its neighbours, whether they were legal claims or mere ambitions, with some historical information about the previous attempts to prosecute these claims. Instead of offering a theoretical or systematic account of these matters, they give a rough-and-ready historical account.

In one way that is interesting as pointing forward to the greater use of the historical method in all kinds of political studies in a later period: it is exceptional in the seventeenth century to find anything explained by its previous history.

[1] Above, p. 136. One of the manuscripts (Bodleian MS. Tanner 93, fo. 70) has the appearance of being an office document.

[2] This work and others of its class are discussed in Meinecke, *Die Idee der Staatsräson*, 2nd ed., 1925.

But that must not be emphasized too much. These writers for the most part lacked the power of generalizing or theorizing. Like the other men who were concerned with the practice of diplomacy, they were concerned first and foremost with the ups and downs of the struggles for power. The state of those struggles at any given moment was one of the conditions which determined many things far distant from the sphere of international politics. Thus the narrative history of political relations will always have its value, and this must not be forgotten if, for another purpose, we put ourselves at a point of view from which the details can be merged in a generalized outline.

Thus seen, the seventeenth century presents six great movements. The first was well on its way when the century began, the decline of Spanish power. The second also had its roots in the past, and was closely connected with the decline of Spain: it was the disintegration of Germany. The third, a consequence and a cause of the first two, was the rise of French domination, which had its sequel in the European combinations against France. A fourth followed from the second and third, the decline of the old Baltic powers, Sweden, Denmark, and Poland, before the rise of Prussia and Russia. This prepared the way for a fifth which was still only partially fulfilled, the fusion of the Baltic and Eastern questions in the general European struggles. A sixth, also protracted into the future, was the fusion of these European struggles themselves with the maritime and colonial struggles in Asia, Africa, America.

From the time when nation-states were first concentrated from the feudal nebula of the Middle Ages, there has been a succession of efforts to produce some supra-national organization. It is in this light that we must regard not merely the nascent efforts of internationalism, but some of the selfish efforts of states. The first and in some ways the greatest of these efforts was the rise of the Spanish power. That power was not, as appears when we read of the part taken by 'Spain' in European affairs, the power of a national state, but the power of an international organization. The Spanish kingdoms, the Netherlands, the kingdom of Naples and Sicily, the duchy of Milan, the Habsburg lands in and adjoining Germany, the Castilian conquests in America were all ruled by Charles V, who also became head of the Holy Roman Empire. They were held together only in a personal union; but there have been many instances in which such personal union was a stepping-stone to constitutional and organic union: to contemporaries in the sixteenth century it looked as if this league of nations [1] under Charles V might well be the beginning of a new kind of world-empire.

That prospect by 1601 seemed remote or impossible. The Reformation had divided the world so effectively that the first question which the politician now had to ask about a country was, what was its religion, and the Spanish power lay within the Catholic half of Europe. The house of Habsburg had been driven to separate into two branches, a Spanish and a German. Half the Netherlands had become independent. But the Spanish was still the greatest power in the world, and it was still essentially an international power. It dominated Italy more firmly than ever. It still held the southern Netherlands as a *place d'armes* from which it could invade either Germany or northern France. In its main stronghold, the Iberian peninsula, it had been strengthened by the conquest of Portugal, and that conquest had brought with it the Portuguese colonial empire, that is, the whole of the European establishments in the Atlantic and the east which had not previously belonged to Spain. The relations of the Spanish with the Austrian Habsburgs were still intimate. The two branches followed a careful policy of intermarriage by which if either line should become extinct, its inheritance would fall to the other. It was not until this policy broke down by a series of unforeseen accidents that the political co-operation of Spain and Austria came to an end: they never fought on opposite sides in a war until the outbreak of the war of the Spanish Succession in 1702. Lastly, there was no religious division within the Spanish dominions.

[1] This phrase, so familiar now in another sense, is used deliberately here, as it was by General Smuts in his pamphlet of 1918, *The League of Nations, a Practical Suggestion*, because it emphasizes the similarity between two apparently opposite principles.

They were free from that weakness by which all their probable enemies were hampered, and there was no knowing that the time might not again come when, as in the days of Philip II, only a few years before, they would have the support of the rest of Catholic Europe in a bid for still greater power.

In 1601 two wars, already of long standing, were in progress, but both nearing their end, in which Spain was the loser. That which had begun more recently of the two was the war with Elizabethan England. It was almost entirely a maritime war, a war of sea-fights or of brief raids on shore with no sustained fighting on land. The English had proved themselves great fighters, and had inflicted much loss and irritation; but they had made no conquests, and their hopes of establishing colonies had come to nothing. Latterly, on their side, the war had been unprofitable and badly planned. In the beginning, sixteen years before, it had been a war of defence against Spain as the leader of the international Catholic reaction. The danger had been averted, and when James I succeeded to the English throne, it was merely at the dictation of common sense that he made peace. By doing so he left in isolation the persistent enemy of Spain which had been at war even longer than England. The Dutch, however, though they had needed English and French help in the earlier days of their war of independence, were now strong enough to stand alone. They had for a good many years established themselves as a state, and turned what had been a civil war into a regular international contest. Recently they had begun a new phase in their warfare by carrying on trade and hostilities in the eastern seas. The Spaniards, seeing their colonial possessions threatened, and checked in attempts to succour them, were brought to make a Twelve Years' Truce in 1609.

At the time of this truce Spain had lost little in military efficiency, and, although her financial and economic difficulties were plainly visible, her political prestige remained very great. She was still, at least in appearance, the first power of the world. She had made her concessions to the Dutch only in the provisional form of a truce. Only a year after the truce was made there came the murder of Henry IV of France, and the only power from which the Spaniards had anything serious to fear entered on a period of domestic divisions which made her internationally impotent for the next fourteen years. By marriage alliances she came within the circle of Spanish influence. Spain had a chance of economic and administrative reconstruction.

Her failure to take it had far-reaching consequences. When the Thirty Years' War broke out in Germany in 1618 she was no better off than she had been at the time of the truce of 1609; but her international tradition drew her into that distant war for three separate reasons. She intervened to support the Habsburg power and also to support the Catholic cause. When the Dutch truce expired, the Dutch would not renew it, so that their war of independence was resumed, but this time with a series of diversions in Germany. Very few years passed before France, under the strong hand of Richelieu, began to come back into the arena. First she obstructed the communications between the Milanese and the lands of the Austrian ally. Next, through the succession of a Frenchman as duke of Mantua and the occupation of Piedmontese fortresses she began to acquire influence over strategical points commanding the roads into the Milanese from the east and the west. Then at last she threw all her regenerated energies into a great war. At the battle of Rocroi she broke the spell of Spanish military superiority. When the Dutch and German wars were ended by the peace of Westphalia in 1648 the French fought on, and not alone. Portugal had rebelled in 1640. Oliver Cromwell sent his fleet to the West Indies and his Ironsides to Flanders. The French war which lasted till 1659 completed the ruin of Spain, and, when she yielded Portugal her independence in 1668, Spain, though still holding her Indies, her Netherlands, and her Italian possessions, had become in war and politics a second-class power, a victim. In the three wars which she had to fight against Louis XIV for the defence of the Netherlands, she had to depend on the treasuries and even on the armies of her allies. Her international bundle of possessions could be held together only on sufferance, because the strong powers grudged one another the gains they could have wrested from her.

The Thirty Years' War, in the course of which Spain suffered some of her most damaging expenses and reverses, though it involved at one time or other almost every state in western and central Europe outside Italy, was primarily German. It was not one war but a series of contests in which the issues changed and the parties to the quarrels changed with them. What provides a thread of continuity through the whole period from 1618 to 1648 is the fact that the house of Austria was fighting practically the whole time; but the aims of its campaigns were radically different at different stages of the war. The trouble arose from the constitutional and religious condition of Germany. The Holy Roman Empire was by this time almost wholly German. It retained over its non-German provinces in Italy, Franche-Comté, and elsewhere a suzerainty which had no practical importance except in rare events like the failure of a line of heirs, as in Mantua, which we have just noticed in connexion with the rivalry of France and Spain. Although German, the empire was not, however, and never had been, in the least like a national state. It retained the trappings of the old universal empire of Rome, but apart from trappings and theories, it was a federation in which the federal organs had a minimum of authority. There was a diet which resembled a congress of ambassadors more than a parliament. There were courts which heard cases and never came to a decision. There was a system of raising federal armies which could only with the utmost difficulty be made capable of coercing a refractory prince of the second rank.

The emperor himself was, by a habit now of long standing, elected from the Habsburg house, because that family was the only one rich enough and powerful enough in its own dominions to make any use of the poor remains of power left to the imperial office after centuries of feudal encroachment. He was like the incumbent of a living which was too poorly paid to be held by any one without private means. These difficulties had been increased by the religious schism, which had led first to civil war, and then to an uneasy peace, in which the two sides were held back from further aggressions by being organized in the diet in two *corpora*, each of which could prevent any innovation by the other. For a generation past the progress of the Counter-Reformation had threatened this equilibrium. A number of ecclesiastical states and properties had been acquired by the Protestants in ways which were either contrary to the terms of the religious peace of 1555 or at least open to legal cavil. To recover these losses and to prevent similar losses in the future naturally became the aims of the Catholic party. Political circumstances, however, prevented these quarrels from coming to a head as early as might have been expected. A civil war implies two sides of which each must be firmly enough organized to stand the strain of fighting. Catholic Germany did not reach this point until certain changes in the Habsburg power were completed.

The hereditary dominions of the house, regarded by its members as the endowment of their family, had been divided on the death of the Emperor Ferdinand I in 1564 into three parts, each of which maintained a separate line of rulers. As it happened, two of these branches were of short duration, so that first one inheritance and then the other fell to the third line; but as long as the division lasted the power of the family did not act as a single unit, and the ultimate reunion of the dominions in 1606–8 was an event of such moment that it began the rise of Austria as a great power. Its effect was increased by the fact that Ferdinand of Styria, afterwards emperor as Ferdinand II, put an end to a period of uncertainty in Habsburg policy which had at times bordered upon ambiguity.

He threw his weight altogether on the Catholic side. Nor had he to rely solely on Catholic support in the first great problem that confronted him. Bohemia, one of the outlying Slav members of the empire of which the chartered privileges had been violated by the Counter-Reformation, broke into revolt, and the revolt was supported in Lower Austria itself, as well as by the half-barbarous Calvinist prince of Transylvania, Gabriel Bethlen. Frederick, elector palatine, the leading Calvinist prince of Germany, was irregularly elected to the Bohemian throne where the Habsburgs had sat for nearly a century. Three causes were in danger: Catholicism, the Habsburg *Hausmacht*, the imperial authority. Ferdinand was able to save them all, though he could do so only by buying Lutheran support at the expense of the prospects of Catholicism, and by buying the support of Catholic princes at the expense of his authority as emperor. Unhappily for Germany foreign rulers had a double interest in these contests. The system of international dynastic alliances provided the parties with friends on whose alliance they might reckon. We have seen that the Spanish Habsburgs responded to this call, and by so doing brought their enemies the Dutch into the German war. Frederick less successfully appealed to his father-in-law James I, to his wife's uncle Christian IV of Denmark, and to his brother-in-law Charles I of England. These marriages which led to foreign intervention were closely connected with the division between Protestants and Catholics: there were few royal mixed marriages in the first half of the century. Thus the two old supra-national tendencies, the dynastic and the religious, brought foreign armies to German soil, the English, the Dutch, the Danes, the Swedes. By 1629 Ferdinand was in a position to oppress the Protestants. He set about taking from them all their gains of ecclesiastical territory, and they were only saved by the invasion of the 'Protestant hero' Gustavus Adolphus of Sweden in 1630. Ferdinand abandoned his extreme policy, offering to the Protestants other than the elector palatine, tolerable terms which most of them accepted. But in the Swedish intervention, if not before, the more modern motive of national ambition was as much concerned as the old supra-national motives; and when, soon after, Sweden's Catholic ally, France, intervened as a principal in the war, national ambition was predominant. It had the easy task of dismembering an organism in which national feeling had never yet been embodied in political institutions.

The absence of nationalism from Germany may be measured by the rise of a power still more alien than that of the foreigner, the power of armies which were virtually free from all political ties, which were controlled by no constitutional machinery and bargained with the territorial state as independent equals. In the early days of the war the mercenary Ernst von Mansfeld had set the example. Wallenstein had carried the system to its highest point. From 1625 to 1630 he was the emperor's strongest support: the jealousy of the princes, fomented by France, led to his dismissal. Two years later the Swedish victories compelled Ferdinand again to entrust his cause to this uncontrollable force; but this time it was the emperor himself whose jealousy was aroused, and it was only the murder of Wallenstein which saved him from military tyranny. But although that was averted, the fearful devastation of the German cities and countryside had its counterpart in political collapse. The peace of Westphalia was guaranteed by two foreign states, France and Sweden. In Germany, however, it did make an internal settlement. It established once more the equilibrium of the three confessions. Exhaustion, growing indifference, the rise of ideas of tolerance combined to make it last thenceforward with few interruptions of any moment. The political settlement left Austria a stronger power than it had been at the beginning of the war, but left it with its back turned on the wreck of the imperial constitution and with less interest for its remaining possessions in western Germany, where France was a menacing neighbour, than for those in eastern Germany and beyond, where the weakness of the Turk was soon to invite attack. Several of the princes, Protestant and Catholic alike, had gained strength as Austria had gained it, and now figured in the calculations of the great powers. They were, however, not great powers themselves. They pursued no aims far from home; their horizon was limited to Germany, and even when they took part in the European combinations, it was in order to get as their share in the spoils of victory German territories or titles. For them, as for the great neighbouring states, Germany had become little more than a reservoir of recruits and a field for annexations.

The power which profited most from it in the latter respect was France, the rise of which, as we have already seen, was the complement of the decline of Spain and the disruption of the empire. France is the first clear example in European history of a national state which over-shadowed the whole politics of Europe without passing from the national form to an international form like that of the Spanish or even the Austrian power. Whereas Philip II held in personal union half a dozen separate inheritances, and Ferdinand was a duke in his homeland, king in Hungary and in Bohemia, here a count and there a margrave, Louis XIV wore a single crown. His relations with his German neighbours, it is true, seemed at one time to foreshadow a system of subordinate client-states beyond his frontiers, but in the end it was not until a century later, not until the time of Napoleon, that France transcended the national form and became herself the head of a league of nations. In the circumstances of the time this was a strength and not a weakness: France was less embarrassed by the claims of dependants and less vulnerable through the weakness of outlying possessions than Spain or Austria or eighteenth-century England. Her rank among the European states was based on the solid facts of population, wealth, and geographical compactness.

In 1610, when Henry IV was stabbed, she was about to assert it. That event threw her back into internal confusion; but when Richelieu, the great minister of Louis XIII, came to power in 1624, there was soon an end of the weaknesses of the Crown and of the divisions caused by the nobles and the Huguenots. Consequently there was a beginning of success abroad. Not that Richelieu himself reaped the crop. His blocking of strategic points about the Spanish possessions in northern Italy led to nothing for the time being, and little in the future. His intervention in Germany changed the whole character of the war there, but at the time of his death there had been neither a striking victory nor any conquest of German land. In his famous *Testament Politique*[1] he had to congratulate his master not on any extension of his realm but on the greatness of his armies and the gains he would make when his enemies came to terms. After Richelieu's

[1] This was published in Holland in numerous editions in duodecimo, of which the first appeared in 1688. Curiously enough, they are more trustworthy than the modern attempts at critical editions (see P. Bertrand in *Revue historique*, cxli. 40, 198) except that of L. André (1947).

death in 1642 this consummation was delayed. The war entered upon a glorious stage, and in 1648 the peace of Westphalia gave France a rich accession of German lands, which, besides their own value, made her able to occupy Franche-Comté and Lorraine whenever she pleased. But the Spanish war dragged on. From 1648 to 1653 the civil disturbances of the Fronde shook the power of Richelieu's successor, Mazarin, and made his country impotent abroad. The recovery, however, was quick and complete. In alliance with the English protectorate and aided by the Portuguese, the French broke down Spanish resistance, and the Peace of the Pyrenees in 1659 marked plainly the fact that France had become the first power in the world.

Even before that date, shrewd observers had foreseen that the progress of France might excite jealousies like those which had withstood the ambition of Spain. Rohan wrote thus: 'Si les Rois de France et d'Espagne sont en guerre ouverte l'un contre l'autre, le Roy de la grand[e] Bretagne doit se souvenir que c'est de ces puissances-là seulement qu'il doit prendre ombrage, et que si l'une avoit réduit l'autre en estat de ne luy plus nuire, il seroit incontinent la proye de la victorieuse.' In 1647 during the English civil disputes the editor of an edition of Rohan's book, not foreseeing the curious reversion of Oliver Cromwell to the Elizabethan war with Spain, speculated on the possibility of an attempt by the English and Spaniards together to check French progress in Flanders.[1] As it turned out, that combination did not come about in diplomacy until the Triple Alliance of 1668, and then it lasted only for a moment. It did not become the basis of a military alliance until 1689; but by that time a similar process had occurred at so many other European courts that Louis XIV found himself at war against a vast coalition which he had to meet without a single ally.

During the thirty years since the Treaty of the Pyrenees France had never lost sight of her designs against the Spanish Netherlands. On the thinnest of dynastic pretexts they had been invaded in 1667, and portions of them annexed which

[1] The two passages may be found in the 1670 edition of *Maximes des princes*, beginning at p. 111 and p. 114.

any eye could see were meant to be taking-off places for another advance. The Dutch, the ancient allies of France, having shown disfavour at these proceedings, were themselves invaded in 1672, and the English, who had twice made war on them for commercial reasons in the previous twenty years, were induced by Louis to join in his attack. That gave him his first experience of serious opposition. The Dutch, under William of Orange, having withstood the first shock, were able to call Brandenburg, the emperor, and Spain to the rescue. England deserted Louis, and at the Treaty of Nijmegen in 1678, though he gained still more of the Spanish lands, he reached the limit of his expansion. It was not yet, indeed, clear that this was so. Spain had to withstand him alone when he made another attack a few years later; but he did not push it home. He had roused Germany against him to an extent that would have seemed impossible twenty years before. In the earlier years of his reign he had created an interest there, and had set himself up as the protector of the states of southern and western Germany against the emperor. The first attempt to shake off Louis's power in Germany was, however, unsuccessful. From 1679 to 1686 he exercised a domination over Germany, annexing even the free imperial city of Strassburg without let or hindrance. But he went too far. William III took up the policy enunciated some time before by the pamphleteer and diplomatist François de l'Isola,[1] and worked for a union of the Dutch and Germans against France. In the dramatic year 1688 Louis once more invaded Germany, with another trifling dynastic pretext and a plan for setting up his nominee in the frontier electorate of Cologne; but by doing so he left the way open for William to sail to England and to bring British ships and men and money to cement the European coalition.

The Nine Years' War which that coalition sustained cost France some of her gains, but it was indecisive. Its sequel was the war of the Spanish Succession, which raged from 1701 until 1713. In this, with some minor changes in the composition

[1] His most famous pamphlet was *Le Bouclier de l'état et de justice* of 1667, an anonymous reply to Louis's pretext for the invasion of the Spanish Netherlands.

of the two opposing parties, all the old questions continued to be disputed; but they were overshadowed by another great problem, the greatest that was ever raised by the old dynastic internationalism. The line of the Spanish Habsburgs came to an end, and their inheritance was disputed between rival claimants. Throughout his reign the policy of Louis had turned on the fact that this question was bound to arise. Whether in pressing forward, as he did against the Dutch, or in holding back, as he sometimes did, the prospects of the coming crisis of Spain were what decided his course. The crisis had now come. All the great powers were concerned, France and Austria on dynastic grounds, Great Britain and Holland because the future of the Spanish Mediterranean and colonial possessions affected their colonial and commercial interests. For many years before the death of Charles II of Spain there had been attempts to settle the matter by a partition, and, the Spanish possessions being held together by nothing more than a personal union and a now outworn tradition, there seemed to be no insuperable objection to the principle of partition. At the critical moment, however, Louis was led by the Spaniards to try to obtain the whole inheritance for one of his grandsons, a younger brother of the ultimate heir to the throne of France. The long war frustrated this attempt, and the principle of partition was applied. The French claimant received Spain itself and the Indies, but had to make considerable commercial concessions to the English. The Austrians took the Spanish Netherlands and most of the Italian possessions, thus aggravating the miscellaneous and international character of their dominions. The Dutch, whose energies had been severely taxed in the war, gained nothing worth mentioning; but considerable pickings went to France's mountain neighbour, Savoy.

Compared with his greatness twenty years or so before, these terms were humiliating for Louis, but they did not stand for a change in the position of France in any way comparable with the change which the century had brought about in the position of Spain. The decline of Spain was the undoing of an international combination; the check to

France was the setting of limits to the advance of a national state. France did not sink to the position of a second-class power, but remained along with Austria and Great Britain in the first rank. During the next two centuries other great powers were to arise, and these belonged rather to the new national type like France, than to the old complex type like Spain or Austria. Besides the territorial redistribution which set the stage for the international contests of the next age, the struggle against Louis XIV had another permanent result of great importance. It gave Europe, in the successive alliances and coalitions, much experience of organized co-operation. It prepared the way for the still more arduous co-operation in the great wars of a century later, and though the lessons thus learnt were applied only for military ends, they have their place as preliminaries to international co-operation for the ends of peace. Just as the League of Nations had amongst its ancestors the conferences of the allied and associated powers, so the congresses of allied princes summoned by William III at the Hague, for what he conceived to be the enforcement of international right, are among the true lineal forbears of modern international organization.

In the sketch of international relations which has been given in this chapter, scarcely any allusion has so far been made to the Baltic powers. One or other of them did, indeed, take part from time to time in the affairs of western and central Europe. Denmark and Sweden fought in the Thirty Years' War. Sweden, the third member of the Triple Alliance of 1668, was the ally of Louis XIV in his next war, and Brandenburg, though also concerned in the Baltic question, was a party, as it suited her, to the alliances for and against Louis XIV throughout the period of his German wars. Yet, although the two political systems came into contact in these ways, none the less they remained separate. In the last two wars of Louis XIV, his greatest wars, Sweden and Denmark were neutral. Sweden was the mediator for the peace of Rijswijk, and ten years later Charles XII at the height of his military reputation had the sense to resist the advances of the two sides in the war of the Spanish Succession, when they were bidding against one another for his alliance. The north did not form a system to itself. Holland and Great Britain needed to keep open the Baltic trade, and so their mutual rivalries and their wars against France involved them in northern affairs. The French also regarded Scandinavia as the flank of their far-flung encirclement of the Habsburgs: whenever they could they brought together a chain of alliances from Turkey through central Europe to Sweden. Northern affairs were closely connected with those of eastern Europe, since Russia and Poland faced the Turks on one side and the Swedes on another; but the northern problem had its own history, almost separate from the west and not merged in the east.

At the beginning of the century the leading powers of the Baltic region were Catholic Poland and the two Lutheran states, Denmark and Sweden. Denmark then included not only Jutland and the islands, but Norway, Jemteland, and the Herjedal in the centre of the Scandinavian peninsula, and the maritime provinces round its southern extremity. She thus controlled both sides of the entrance to the Baltic and exacted toll from all shipping that passed through. Sweden, her old enemy, had Finland on the eastern side of the inland sea, and was thus ready, when her internal state made expansion possible, to advance both in Scandinavia and along the Baltic shores. A dynastic connexion with Poland provided her with the excuse for attacking that third Baltic power. It so happened that though they depended on the Dutch in the first half of the century for the development of their economic resources at home, the Swedes became under the leadership of a line of warrior-kings the pre-eminently military state of the time. War became their chief national industry. By it their kings were able to control and reward their restless nobility. From 1611 to 1721 they fought five wars against the Danes, and three against the Poles. Until 1660 they had a dazzling series of successes. Gustavus Adolphus not only took Ingria and Livonia, with its great port of Riga, and the less important province of Carelia. His victories prepared the way for the conquest of Jemteland and the Herjedal, and for the annexation by the Westphalian treaties of the economic keys of Germany. With the exception of Danzig and Hamburg the Swedes overshadowed all the great ports from the mouth of the Weser to the Gulf of Finland. They were masters of the Baltic. Charles Gustavus took Bleking and Halland, thus controlling one side of the outlet, and freed Swedish shipping from the toll. He even pushed down for a time from the mountains to the North Sea coast of Norway. But the line he reached in 1660 was a maximum from which his successors had to recede. Sweden had outrun her real strength. She had reduced Denmark and Poland to the level of minor powers; but her hold on the bridgeheads in North Germany was precarious. She could neither expand them so as to make them safe nor build up armies and sea-power sufficient to reinforce them against attack from strong states in their hinterland. By exhausting herself and her two old rivals she had provided the opportunity for another military state which was to become even more Spartan than herself, and a Slavonic power which was to grow more powerful than Poland had ever been.

Brandenburg-Prussia during the Thirty Years' War had narrowly escaped the closing of all her possible avenues of ambition. The Swedes threatened to cut her off from Pomerania and the Baltic; Poland stood in the way of the linking-up of her central and eastern dominions. By withdrawing from an unequal contest against Sweden she was able to make acquisitions at the peace of Westphalia which were the beginning of great advances. She supported Charles Gustavus against his enemies, and even had to acknowledge his suzerainty in place of Poland's over East Prussia; but by adroitly changing sides the Great Elector soon became sovereign there and independent of both. In 1675 his chance came to make war on Sweden in alliance with Denmark, and the battle of Fehrbellin, though no great matter in itself, was a defeat for the Swedish arms, an event of significance similar to that of Rocroi or St. Gothard.

The diplomatic support of France delayed the dismembering of the Swedish dominions; but the Great Northern War which began in 1699 and lasted until 1721 could have had only one outcome. It was not a single war, but a succession of attacks on Sweden by shifting combinations of allies.

The first was the flotation of the Livonian Patkul, half patriot and half adventurer, a combination of greedy powers who hoped to have easy work against Charles XII, a wilful boy of seventeen. The boy revealed himself a hero, and a scientific soldier of a very high order. He dispersed the first coalition, and, until he was shot in the trenches before the Norwegian fortress of Frederiksten in 1718, he never ceased to be terrible to his enemies and unmanageable for the peace-makers; but he could not save his inheritance. Not only had Brandenburg-Prussia grown in strength. Russia, from which Gustavus Adolphus had easily conquered the Baltic provinces, had been no more formidable to Charles XII at the outset of his wars; but his victory at Narva had taught its lesson to the tsar, a man even more remarkable than Charles himself. As Russia reformed her strength, it was seen that Sweden could not prevail in the end, either alone or with the Turks or other allies. The peace of 1720–1 saw Prussia in possession of part of Pomerania west of the Oder. Sweden lost another German province in the bishoprics of Bremen and Verden at the mouth of the Elbe. Ingria, Carelia, Esthonia, and Livonia went to Russia: the Baltic was now dominated from the east.

XII

RELATIONS WITH ASIA BY LAND

THE fortunes of the northern powers were thus involved in the contest between western and Asiatic civilization, which was being waged by land from the Adriatic to the Baltic. A glance at the map will show that it was not a simple contest. Its first element was the Turkish question. In the southern part of the arena, but only in the southern part, the west was in direct contact with the Ottoman empire, a state which was typical of Asia if anything can be typical of so various a continent, or which, at least, was as completely outside Europe, as foreign from it, as any state with which it has ever been in contact. It is true that in conquering the lands and capital of the old Byzantine empire, the Turks had become in a sense its political heirs. As the masters of the eastern shores of the Mediterranean, they stood in a relation to the European powers which sometimes obviously resembled that of their geographical predecessors, and it had now for a long time been normal to find them taking their part in international politics as allies of Christian states. Internally also they had inherited something from the Byzantine system: the personnel of their administration was mainly made up of Greeks, Slavs, and Albanians, with a few Italians. The Greek church, under the patriarch whose seat was still at Constantinople, remained in docile submission to the sultans as successors of the emperors. But there was no more real continuity in this than there was in the use of the great church of the Holy Wisdom as a mosque. What the Turks took over from the former régime was only what they esteemed so little that they did not trouble to rebuild it. They had not become Europeans and they were not destined to assimilate western ideas for at least another two centuries; nor, on the other hand, had they now anything of moment to teach to the west. In this they were far different from the Saracens of the central period of the Middle Ages, who had handed over some of the richest of the materials of the Renaissance. The Turks had been to Moslem civilization what the barbarian invaders had been to that of the Romans.

It has often been said that their empire was an army of occupation and not a political power. That is perhaps to put the matter too simply, but it expresses well the contrast as it must have appeared at this time. The Turks had a standing army before there was any in Europe. In quality it was not equal to the armies of Europe. Especially in its artillery and in all kinds of technical skill it was inferior; but it had great advantages. Its pay was regular, its musters full, its commanders spoke to their men in their own languages, and its discipline worked better than that of the west. The social basis of the military institutions was entirely different. The Ottoman Empire was the only state in Europe which had no legal distinctions of status between different classes. It is probable that about one-third of its inhabitants were Turks; but it was religion, not race, which distinguished the ruler from the ruled. Islam was not intolerant: at the price of a tribute it conceded a contemptuous toleration to Jews or Christians as separate communities; but it excluded them from power. No obstacles, however, were set in the way of conversion. Renegades were numerous, and even for those Protestants who continued to bear it the Turkish yoke was more tolerable than that of the Catholic Christian powers. Taxation was light. The extent of the empire was enough to provide men and money in abundance, and that although its economic condition was backward. There was little industry. External commerce was in the hands of foreigners. For more than a generation the Turks had been virtually powerless at sea, and in this century the North African corsair princes, who nominally owned the sultan's suzerainty, though they gave some trouble to the western seafaring powers, did so in the pursuit of their own purposes. As allies of their overlord, for instance against the Venetians, they were untrustworthy, and often ineffective.

The western nations had their factories in the Turkish ports, and the system of capitulations had been established, by which these trading communities were extra-territorial, subject to a jurisdiction of their own and exempt from that of the Turks. Their relations with the Turkish authorities were often unsatisfactory. They often had to complain of arbitrary exactions and breaches of their privileges; but their presence was profitable to their hosts as well as themselves, and the Levant trade, though at times difficult, went on by sea without long or serious interruptions. Trade was not the only kind of peaceful intercourse. Christian missions were established, especially by the French, and the political relations of France with the Porte led to some slight importation of French ideas; but these influences effected very little. Islam and Christianity are the two amongst the world's religions which are least likely to lose their adherents by persuasion, and the Turkish social structure, based upon polygamy and slavery, was almost impervious to western influence.

The European possessions of the sultans were less important in their eyes than those in Asia, but they covered an area roughly comparable with that of France or Spain. They included the whole of the Balkan peninsula, and to the northward of it they ran as far as the lower Danube. Where the Danube falls into the Black Sea, the Turks held the whole of its delta and beyond they had Bessarabia and Jedisan, that is the coastal plain as far as the estuary of the Dnieper. Here began the lands of their feudatories, the Crim Tartars, but the Turks had also the south coast of the Crimea and the eastern side of the Straits of Kerch, which give access to the Sea of Azof. It was not only towards its mouth that they had territory north of the Danube. For many years they had held the district ruled by the 'ban' of Temesvar and the rich plains of the Theiss, the Drave, and the Save, which together made up the greater part of the old kingdom of Hungary. Bosnia and Herzegovina were theirs, though the Venetians had strips of the Adriatic coast as parts of their little empire, which also included most of the Greek islands and Crete. In the rough quadrilateral of which three sides were enclosed by the Danube and the two blocks of Turkish territory to the north of it were three tributary Christian principalities. Wallachia and Moldavia had princes who were elected by their estates, though their election was confirmed by the sultan, and they owed a tribute to the Porte. Poland claimed a suzerainty over them. Transylvania, the more mountainous region which fills up the angle between them, had also an elected and tributary prince; but he owed a nominal allegiance to the Habsburgs as kings of Hungary. Between the Habsburgs on the west and the Crim Tartars on the east a single power marched with both the Turks and the principalities, the 'republic' of Poland, which stretched from the Baltic to within a hundred miles of the Black Sea and the Sea of Azof.

Poland was the most easterly of the western lands. Its wide plains, with their sparse population, their few towns, and their loose political cohesion, were, indeed, very different from the populous, busy, and wealthy countries to the west. Its outlying parts, especially the Ukraine of the Cossacks, were untouched by European customs. Lithuania, the eastern part of the kingdom, was, with its Uniat Church [1] a borderland between east and west; but fundamentally the institutions of Poland belonged to the same genus as those of Spain or England. There was a monarchy, with a diet, a feudal nobility, privileged towns, universities, Jesuit schools, Renaissance architecture, a learned literature in Latin, all the essentials of the western mind. The Protestant Reformation had spread into Poland, as the Latin Christianity had done before it. All the historic influences which had made the country what it was were known and intelligible to the Latin and Teutonic peoples, and neither the Poles nor any one else doubted that they belonged to the true western tradition.

At their eastern frontier, however, that tradition ended. There began a dominion, already of prodigious extent, which was neither European nor Asiatic, but something of both, and something that was all its own. Russia was Christian, but its Christianity had come to it from Byzantium and not from Rome. The patriarchate of Moscow had only recently obtained a national independence from that of Constantinople, and in beliefs and ritual, as well as in church government and discipline, it was separate from Roman Catholic and Protestants alike. The Latin language, and even the

[1] See below, p. 312.

Greek language, had no part in Russian culture. The emperor used the title of tsar, the most distant of all the echoes of the name of Caesar, but his monarchy was of the Oriental type. He was nearer to the Moguls than to the Bourbons. Western artificers, builders, and gun-founders had been introduced into the country in the later sixteenth century. Englishmen and Dutchmen had found their way along the river-routes inland from the Baltic and from the White Sea to the Caspian; but this intercourse was not different in kind from the intercourse of the west with the remoter parts of Asia. Until this period Russia was external to western civilization. It had been important to the maritime powers as a field for commercial exploitation, and to its continental neighbours as a military power and a possible field for conquest. Its internal history in the earlier part of the century scarcely forms a part of our subject. Towards the end of our period western civilization set out on a course of eastward expansion overland as well as by sea. Russia became one of its abodes and one of its points of departure.

At the beginning of the century the wars and the clashes of civilization in eastern Europe had not reached the stage of being so involved together that there was one 'Eastern Question'. That phase, which has lasted down to our own time, was brought about during the course of the century by changes which were not yet foreseen. The Turks were familiar enough with wars against the Venetians, the Habsburgs, and the Poles, but, although they had already had difficulties with the Russians, there was no war with them until 1678. The Poles had a long history of wars against the Russians and much experience of trouble from the sultan's *protégés*, the princes of Transylvania; but until 1682 their Turkish wars were quite separate from those of the emperors. Hitherto in all the wars the initiative had been with the Turks. Their European empire was at the greatest territorial extent that it ever reached, and there was little to indicate that in the future it would yield before Christian attacks and leave the Christian powers with the task of sharing its spoils. The spell of Turkish victory had indeed been broken by the naval battle of Lepanto, which confined them to the eastern Mediterranean beyond the Sicilian narrows, but the position of the Turks on the European mainland had not yet been seriously impaired.

Already, however, internal decay had set in. The line of the great sultans was ended; discipline in the armies was relaxed; the power of the outlying pashas was growing; the once dreaded janissaries were losing their military importance. But the west had scarcely begun to take advantage of all this. The Venetian republic, retaining only the shadow of its former power, was living on friendly terms with the Porte, and so continued until 1644–5. The emperor was fighting on the Danube, and in 1601 his task was made easier: far away in the enemy's rear Shah Abbas, the greatest of all the rulers of Persia, threw all his forces into the attempt to win back the lost Persian provinces from the Turks. His great conquests, and the revival of the morale of Persia which followed, made one of the milestones in the decline of Turkey. When the Habsburg emperor made peace in 1606, he was able to do so on another footing than that which had been possible to his predecessors. Instead of being imposed by the Turks, the treaty was examined by both parties and mutually agreed. It relieved the emperor from the humiliation of paying an annual tribute, to which he had been subjected in 1547; but that was all. He did not simply free himself from the tribute; he could only buy it off with an indemnity. No Turkish territory was ceded. And, although the Persian war continued fitfully, the Habsburgs did not again take the field against the infidel before the outbreak of the Thirty Years' War, which put it out of their power to do so with any effect. A short war with Poland in 1620–1 did the Turks no serious damage. After that they enjoyed more than twenty years of peace on their European frontiers, and were able in a series of campaigns in the sixteen-thirties to win back great provinces from Persia, and terminate the brief revival of that power.

Their western troubles began again with the outbreak of war against Venice. This war, the war of Candia as it was called, from the name then used for the island of Crete, was forced on the Venetians by the Turks. They found their pretext in the use of this Venetian island by Maltese corsairs in their depredations on Turkish shipping. The war lasted until 1669, no less than twenty-four years. It ended with the loss of Crete by Venice and with a considerable spread of Mohammedanism among its population. This successful result was due to a sudden recovery of vigour in the administration of the empire, especially in military affairs. The appointment as grand vizier in 1656 of Mahomet Kuprili, a man of Albanian descent, inaugurated a period of energy which may be reckoned as lasting, under himself and his two sons who succeeded him in the office, until the death of the younger son in battle in 1691. The revival, however, though genuine was insufficient. Even when it began, the western enemies had made such progress in technical skill of all kinds, as well as in administrative efficiency, that the Turks were now for the first time, what they were long to remain, a backward power. Now, therefore, when the final result of the Thirty Years' War had strengthened the Habsburgs and at the same time diverted them from the pursuit of ambitions in Germany, they were able to renew the war with far more favourable prospects.

Disturbances in Transylvania, which had been put down a few years before, revived in 1663, and led to the intervention of the emperor. In the next year, with the aid of a small French contingent, he inflicted on them at the abbey of St. Gothard on the Raab their first defeat on European soil. This led to a twenty years' truce. Transylvania, however, remained tributary to Turkey and the Turks gained the districts of Waradin and Neuhäusel. Nor was the emperor yet able to follow up his encouraging success. He remained at peace with the Turks for eighteen years, during which the policy of Louis XIV, whose co-operation with him had been only momentary, gave him constant anxiety and for a time actual war. This postponement of the Habsburg advance was not, however, a period of peace for the Turks. They were engaged first, in 1672–6, in a war against Poland, which they undertook on behalf of the rebellious Cossacks of the Ukraine. In this they conquered Podolia, the fertile district north of the Dniester and extending beyond the Bug, of which Kaminiec is the capital. It was their last considerable gain of land in Europe. Within two years of this settlement the Cossacks, whom the Turks had liberated from

Polish suzerainty, abandoned their alliance and sought that of Russia. The Turks made war on both, but fared badly, and in 1681 had to make a peace in which they recognized the Russian supremacy over a wide expanse of the Ukraine on the left bank of the Dnieper from the Desna to the Turkish territory on the coast. This was the last in a series of moves by which the Russians got control over the Cossacks from the Desna to the Don. They were building up a dangerous power in close proximity to the Turks. Hardly had this important step in their advance been concluded, when the grand vizier Kara Mustafa, whose tenure of office interrupted the Kuprili line, plunged into a war which was to turn the gradual decline of Ottoman power into a disastrous collapse.

It began as a simple war of aggression, the affairs of Transylvania once more providing the pretext. The Turks marched forward against the Habsburgs, and the march took them to the walls of Vienna. Only once before, in the great days of their victories, as long ago as 1529, had they penetrated to that bulwark of Christendom, the capital of the emperors. It seemed as though the whole future of the west was once more threatened. The Holy Roman Empire, weakened by the long wars against Louis XIV, was in no condition to save itself and Europe, and Louis himself, who had gravitated back to the traditional French alliance with the Turks, did not repeat the gesture of sending his troops to defend the faith. The quarter from which help did come was one which had been improbable and even suspect. At that time the elective throne of Poland was occupied by John III, John Sobieski, a brilliant soldier, who combined the parts of hero and villain in the national history. He had been the tool of France in the affairs of Poland, when Poland was a link in the chain of alliances with which Louis encircled the Habsburgs. He had been a traitor to his country in the war with Sweden, and it was his factious, even rebellious, conduct which had primarily brought about the disasters of the Ukrainian war against Turkey, though he himself had partially retrieved them by a series of striking victories. Of late years, since he had been king, the French support had been slipping away from him. France would not second his attempt to set up absolute monarchy in Poland. By a momentous coincidence his estrangement from France ripened at the time of the Turkish threat to Vienna. He signed a treaty with the emperor and brought an army to raise the siege. Two months after the investment of the city the relieving army appeared and fell upon the besiegers. The battle was decided by a charge of the Polish horsemen, led by their king in person. Vienna was saved. The last great offensive of the Turks was broken.

The war now assumed a new character. In the first place, it was waged by a combination of the Christian powers. Austria, Poland, and Venice made an alliance against the Turks, and in their treaty they made arrangements for the partition of a great part of the Turkish dominions. Nor was this as presumptuous as such arrangements often are. The Turks were driven back in two theatres of war. The Venetians reconquered the Morea, and though they failed to maintain themselves in Athens and Chios, they held the Morea firmly, and the Venetian revival in Greece lasted for more than a generation. While this flank attack was being pressed home, the Germans were hammering at the centre of the enemy's front on the Danube. By 1687 they had recovered the whole of Hungary. In the next year Transylvania returned to Hungarian suzerainty, and a boundless prospect of conquest seemed to lie open. Once more, however, the affairs of the west reacted on those of the east. With the outbreak of the Nine Years' War the emperor found himself fighting on two fronts. His ally, William III, besought him to suspend his advance against the Turks and concentrate his resources on the struggle against Louis XIV. The emperor hesitated and let slip the most propitious moment for making peace; but even so he was able to secure huge territorial gains. Two years after their Treaty of Rijswijk with Louis XIV, the sea-powers as mediators brought about in 1699 the Treaty of Carlowitz, which marked the first stage in the withdrawal of Turkey, and the first great surrender of Ottoman prestige. It was the first peace which the Turks had received from the hands of mediators. It ceded the Morea to Venice. To Poland it restored Podolia. To the Habsburgs it gave Transylvania and all Hungary except the Banat of Temesvar.

It was not only on the Turkish side that this treaty marked a new era in the eastern question. It registered also the last territorial gain of Poland, and the last effective participation of the Poles in the Turkish wars. The delivery of Vienna was, in fact, the last service of the old Poland to Europe. By the time when it was done, the chronic internal anarchy and corruption of the country were already incurable, and the subsequent years of the reign of John III were darkened by treasons and rebellions for which his own earlier career had set the example. At intervals, for some time before, the idea of a partition of Poland among its neighbours had been held up by patriotic Poles as a warning to their countrymen, or jotted down amongst the secret memoranda of foreign diplomatists as a possible bait for attracting allies. It was now approaching the region of practical politics. A few months after the Treaty of Carlowitz was signed, the Great Northern War began, and we have seen how this completed the reduction of Poland to the rank of a second-class power.[1] Three powers were ultimately to divide the Polish dominions among them, Austria, strengthened by her acquisitions from the Turks, and the two new Baltic powers, Brandenburg-Prussia and Russia, which were also to share the inheritance of Sweden. Of these two it was Russia which came to dominate the politics of Poland.

Both Russia and Poland were concerned in the problem of Turkey and the Ukraine as in that of the Baltic. Their common frontier was more than a thousand miles in length and it ran through a country of steppes and forests and marshes which nevertheless permitted the march of armies. Both were inhabited by Slavonic peoples, and there was little to distinguish the speech of the White Russians and Little Russians, as they are called, the peasantry in the old Lithuania which formed the eastern and greater part of Poland, from that of their kinsmen across this scarcely visible boundary. The victory at Pultava began a period of Russian domination over Poland, and the Saxon kings who feebly

[1] Above, p. 169.

reigned there, with one short interruption, from before the Great Northern War until the eve of the dissolution of the kingdom, were Russian puppets.

The eastern question of the eighteenth century may be formulated in simple terms. It was the question who was to occupy the room of the Turks as they were gradually extruded from Europe. We have seen already how it came to assume this form, but we have only seen in part how it was that the two competing claimants were Austria and Russia. Austria had resumed the first place and Poland had resigned the second, but the rise of Russia to a position co-ordinate with that of Austria had been gradually prepared by an almost unnoticed growth, and was now completed by one of the supreme surprises of modern history. The growth of Russia in the seventeenth century had been virtually unseen by western eyes because it was in great part Asiatic. A steady stream of settlers and traders had been moving since the late sixteenth century, as it has moved ever since, out over the Urals into the waste lands of Siberia, where it encountered no opposition other than that of scattered nomadic tribesmen. It had not ceased in the darkest periods of Russian political history, in the 'Troubled Times' at the beginning of the century, which followed the death of the tsar Boris Godunov. It had gone steadily forward, and the Romanov dynasty, which began its long rule in 1613, had not allowed these swarms to form new hives of their own, but had kept its authority over their remotest vanguard. As early as about 1639 Russian pioneers arrived on the shores of the Sea of Okhotsk, north of Japan, and a few years later a party sailed round from the river Kolyma on the north coast of Siberia through the Bering Straits. By the end of the century Russia had the greatest extent of territory that had ever been united under a single crown. It included the whole of northern Asia from the Urals to Kamchatka, and the way lay open from it to the regions of desert and mountain farther south. It is true that the resources of this empire could not be mobilized and brought to bear on a single point as could those of the western powers; but they did provide inexhaustible and constantly increasing reserves of strength, and their pressure made itself felt, however indirectly, wherever Russia had to cope with opposition. In the west, however, where military opposition was most serious, it could do little to counteract the deficiency in technical skill and in discipline, for in both of these, in the first half of the century, the Russians were inferior to a far greater degree than the Turks. The Swedes made short work of them in all their wars before Charles XII. Their Ukrainian wars against the Turks were affairs of cavalry, resembling the Turkish wars with Persia rather than European fighting.

Until the last few years of the century the indications that Russia was to take a greater part in the Turkish question are to be sought not in improved military methods, but in changes of political aims. The first Russo-Turkish war, in 1676–81, was a local, isolated collision, almost altogether apart from European politics. The second came in 1686, when Russia took advantage of the war on the Danube to renew her own attack. It brought her into relations with Austria: in 1689 she lent her support to the emperor. At Carlowitz Russia was not included in the treaty, but her representatives took part in the negotiations and she obtained an armistice which led to peace in the following year. She had thus, by participating in an international congress, won recognition as a member of the European system. The great change in her own being which was to justify that recognition had, however, barely begun. In a few years it was to make her not merely a member of the system but indisputably one of the great powers. This was the revolution of Peter the Great.

A great English statesman of a later age, speaking to justify the British advance in Asia, used the memorable words: 'When civilization and barbarism meet, it is inevitable that the latter must give way.' It has not always been inevitable, and there is no need to fortify with instances the statement that barbarism has sometimes triumphed; but the advance of civilization has truly enough been irresistible while western ideas and institutions have been permeating the whole world, a movement of which it may be said that its force could first be seen when the Turks began to be driven back across the plains of Hungary. By sea and by land the movement had begun, and it had used one method only, that of conquest. If a miracle had not happened, it might have been expected that in the long run the same method would subjugate the immense plains of Russia and Siberia. Their barbarism had inevitably to give way, and it did give way; but the miracle happened, and it gave way not to the old method of conquest, but to the new method invented by Peter the Great, the spontaneous adoption of the western institutions and ideas by an eastern ruler. At the moment when the course of history had brought his country face to face with the strong forces of the west, he westernized his country, and made it able to hold its own with any power in the world. The conditions were in a sense favourable to the experiment. His most dangerous western rivals were past their prime. Poland had relinquished her attempts to conquer Russian territory as long before as 1667. There was no lack of allies to assist in dismembering the artificially extended possessions of Sweden. The two growing powers of central Europe, Austria and Prussia, were neither of them immediate neighbours of Russia, nor were they as yet jealous of her advance. Yet this does not detract from the greatness of Peter's work. With almost superhuman energies he accomplished an almost incredible revolution. No one man since Charlemagne had made so deep an impression on the political history of the world, and possibly none except Napoleon has done so since. Only one other eastern nation has yet certainly repeated the achievement, and the smaller, easier revolution of nineteenth-century Japan was itself one of the wonders of history.

Peter's personal character was not attractive. It is usual to say that the scale of his crimes and vices was colossal, and though the picture is overdrawn for effect it is not altogether untrue. At all events he got what he wanted for his country, and rose to the level of genius not only in his power of getting it, but in his insight into what was wanted. He seems to have been born with a passion for the technical and mechanical arts, and he saw that they were the key to the efficiency of the west. As a young man he learnt the use of the astrolabe, and geometry and fortification. After his first victorious campaign he made the famous journey in which he learnt gunnery at Königsberg, shipbuilding at Zaandam and Deptford, not to mention anatomy and engraving. Ships he had already built and commanded; for he had discovered the second secret of the west, one that made his technical acquirements all the more significant, the secret of sea-power. He built and launched a ship on the White Sea when he was twenty-two. His first warlike expedition was for the capture of Azov, at the mouth of the Don. This and his new naval station of Taganrog beside it were the starting-points from which he intended to impose his will on the Turkish sultan, the overlord of the Crim Tartars and all the hordes which impeded trade and progress in the direction of the Caspian. In the Baltic also, as we have seen,[1] he made a fleet. He conquered the whole Baltic coast-line from Riga to the Gulf of Finland; and the situation of his new capital, Petersburg, was a proof that the new Russia was to look westwards over the water.

It was to be transformed in all its political and many of its social institutions. The national dress was compulsorily abandoned. The old administrative hierarchy was gradually superseded by a new machine on the western model: in 1711 the system was completed by the introduction of the 'administrative senate'. Ten years later the holy synod, a government department, superseded the old patriarchate, and a complete Erastianism was established. Much remained to be done by Peter's successors: he was only fifty-three when he died. But the criticism which is most commonly made on his work is false or superficial. It is said that he went too fast, and that his plans were fundamentally unsound, because they meant the introduction of alien civilization which could never be really fused with the Russian character and traditions. As Rousseau put it: 'Il a d'abord voulu faire des Allemands, des Anglais, quand il fallait commencer par faire des Russes.'[2] Had he gone to work more

[1] p. 122. [2] *Contrat social*, Bk. II, c. 8.

gradually, it is urged, he could have made something more Slavonic and therefore more solid. It is not that he was lacking in national feeling. On the contrary, it was one of his leading aims to keep Russia for the Russians; and though he imported thousands of skilled men, whether scientists or soldiers or artificers, he never took the easy way of handing over the country to the foreigner, but kept the immigrants as teachers and subordinates, and governed his subjects by means of their own countrymen even more than the western sovereigns were wont to do. The criticism is against his ideas, not against his choice of men; and it must be said of it that it is a condemnation of the known by comparison with the unknown. Peter could not wait. If something had not been done quickly to give his empire cohesion and efficiency, it would have become one of the victim states, like the Asiatic monarchies which did not awake, or it would have fallen to pieces among feudal nobles and Tartar hordes. And if he had no choice of time, neither had he a choice of instruments. The superiority of the west was in knowledge and skill, and it was these which he imported. Navigation, metallurgy, and even some parts of political economy do not require to be adapted to the idiosyncrasies of national character, and when Peter took the leap to civilization from barbarism he had to make for the only civilization that was accessible. He was resisted by men who could not appreciate his aims, not by men who had better ideals of their own. Only a morbid taste for imputing blame to great men can lead historians to bring up in judgement against him the subsequent sufferings of his country.

The additions which he made to the effective force of Russia had impressive results, as we have already seen, in the direction of the Baltic; but they left as yet little mark on the Turkish question. On that side Russian progress was delayed. One reason for this delay was the Great Northern War. When the Porte declared war against Russia in 1710 at the instigation of Charles XII of Sweden, Peter's military operations were badly conducted, and though his army got off more lightly than he deserved, he had to restore Azov in

1711. The treaty of 1711 was followed by a 'definitive' treaty in 1713, and Russia took no further part in war against the Turks until 1736. In the later years of Peter the Great she was even in alliance with the Turks against Persia, at whose expense she made valuable conquests. She left the other Christian powers to their own devices. The Turks took the opportunity to recover the Venetian conquests, and though the emperor Charles VI made an alliance with Venice in 1716, the Morea was already lost, the Venetian revival in Greece was ended, and the successes of the Austrians on land brought no advantage to the republic. For the Habsburgs they provided, in the Treaty of Passarowitz of 1718, a still more triumphant sequel to the Treaty of Carlowitz. The Banat of Temesvar was acquired, and, with it, a strip of Bosnia along the Save, western Wallachia, and best of all Belgrade, the crossing of the Danube, and the gate to Serbia. Northern Serbia itself was taken. This was the greatest territorial extension of the Austrian power. It closed the great seventeenth-century process of Austrian advance, in which the emperors owed little to allies and feared nothing from rivals. When the next series of wars began, the conditions prevailed which lasted through the eighteenth and nineteenth centuries. Austria was a declining power, and the chief enemy of the Turks was Russia.

A word must be said about another difference between the eastern question of the later seventeenth century and that of the eighteenth and nineteenth. Ultimately the Turkish inheritance in the Balkan peninsula was to go to neither of these great powers, but to the once subject nationalities, the Greeks, the Roumanians, the Bulgars, and the Southern Slavs. None of these formed a fully independent political entity until the nineteenth century, and in the seventeenth there was scarcely anything to indicate that they ever would. South of the Danube there was no trace of national sentiment or of political action by the Christian population. The difference between it and its Turkish masters was conceived of as a difference of religion, and for a long time to come the community of religion was to be the only lever by which the Christian great powers were to stir up a party for themselves in the Turkish possessions. To this period belong their first small attempts to do so. The Venetian successes in Greece were partly due to the support of the inhabitants and were partly counteracted by a relaxation of the Turkish oppression of the Christians. The French had been recognized, since their first Turkish alliance in 1535, as having some rights over the Holy Places in Palestine. Louis XIV at one time lost these rights in consequence of a commercial dispute with the Porte, and in general they have little importance during the period. The French capitulations, however, served as an example to other powers. In 1689 the Austrians claimed to extend their protection to the Albanian Catholics. Before the death of Peter the Great, the 'Greek' priests in Turkey, that is the priests of the orthodox church, had begun to ask for Russian alms and protection. Russian envoys had visited Montenegro, and the prince-bishop of Cetinje, the ruler of the little state, had gone to Russia for his consecration.

Religion did not offer any foothold for Russian or Austrian influence in the three tributary principalities, in all of which there was religious diversity and toleration. The princes of Transylvania had to swear to protect no less than five religions, the Catholic, Lutheran, Calvinist, Orthodox, and Anabaptist. Religion instead of being a help was therefore an impediment to their absorption by the Catholic and intolerant Habsburg power. The attachment of the Transylvanians to their liberties meant that there was a standing incompatibility between their wishes and those of their would-be deliverers, and the struggles between the two, which may be best regarded as a chapter in the history of Magyar liberties, approximated to a contest between alien absolutism and constitutional nationalism. At the beginning of the century the dependence of the Transylvanian princes on their nominal overlords the sultans was slight: the country was mountainous and difficult, and the sultan got no more from it than his tribute, his right to confirm the elections of the princes, and its independent help against the emperors. Stephen Bocksay, at the beginning of the period, obtained from Austria his own recognition as a sovereign prince, and religious and constitutional liberty for royal Hungary. As the permanent result of his three wars against the emperor, Gabriel Bethlen won seven additional Hungarian counties for his principality. Like his successor, George I Rákoczy, he was enabled to maintain the liberties of his country mainly by the fact that the Thirty Years' War was going on. They won no battles, and their demands were conceded rather because they were troublesome than because they were strong. George II Rákoczy was foolish enough at the time of the Kuprili revival in Turkey to try to get for himself the Polish throne. This led to a Turkish occupation and the effective reduction of Transylvania to the position of a feudatory province. It refused, however, to aid the Turks in the war of 1663–4, and after that, though its territory was reduced, it enjoyed an immunity of more than twenty years from any Turkish invasion other than border raids. The absorption of Transylvania into Habsburg Hungary after its recovery from the Turks was accompanied and followed by such ruthless reaction that in the time of the war of the Spanish Succession, when the emperor was hard pressed by the French, there was a national Hungarian rising under Francis II Rákoczy which lasted for eight years and ended in a confirmation of the old privileges. After this there was a period of harmony between the Magyars and their masters.

Moldavia and Wallachia, which together with Transylvania, once more detached from Hungary, formed the great Rumania of a later day, had a very different story. They lay far more open to Turkish pressure, and it was not until 1699 that the Habsburg frontier came into touch with theirs. Their princes were freely chosen by the clergy and nobles until 1618 in Moldavia and about a century later in Wallachia, when the sultans began to appoint Phanariotes, or Greeks of Constantinople, with the natural result that the thrones came to be practically sold by auction. Some progress in civilization was made, but the principalities suffered much in the wars from Turkish exactions and Tartar depredations, and the declining Polish power was unable to help them. They were incapable of effectively helping themselves, but the rise of Russia opened a new hope for them too, though it was still a distant hope, and the alliance of the Moldavian prince with Peter the Great in 1711 ended disastrously. None of these stirrings deserves to be called a national movement, and the same must be said of the efforts of the Cossacks in the Ukraine. The Cossack war against Poland which began in 1648 is nowadays sometimes called a Ukrainian national movement, and its leader, Bogdan Chmielnicki, is given the title of a national hero. Such an interpretation is in reality an attempt to read into the past a modern idea, which it is desired to find there in order to confirm its validity in the present. The seventeen regiments of half-nomad horsemen who followed Chmielnicki over the steppes no doubt hated the Poles and Russians and Turks impartially though in turns. Chmielnicki, however, belongs not to the line of national liberators, but to that of the chieftains like the bandit Styenka Razin, whose name still lives in Russian folk-song and folk-tale, or the hetman Mazeppa, the treacherous ally of Charles XII. Their spirit was not the complex and mature national sentiment which, for good and ill, made history in the great and settled countries of the eighteenth and nineteenth centuries. In the seventeenth, south-eastern Europe could show only the undeveloped elements of that sentiment: it was full grown only in the countries where the state has assumed something of its modern form.[1]

[1] See the very illuminating first four chapters of C. A. Macartney, *National States and National Minorities* (1934), which contrast the 'political nationality' of western with the 'personal nationality' of eastern Europe. The latter, which in effect was group-nationality within the state, was connected with the widespread medieval custom by which a man 'took his law with him wherever he went'. The states of the west crystallized around solid national nuclei; the unassimilated national minorities at their peripheries (such as the Welsh, Bretons, or Frisians) were ruled by assimilated upper or middle classes. The lower classes of both the peripheries and the centres were unenfranchised and did not aspire to power. The coming of democracy changed all this.

XIII
COLONIES

WESTERN civilization had its home in a restricted region, far less than the whole, of that little Europe which takes up so small a portion of the globe in comparison with the great land masses of Asia, Africa, and America. To the east and south it covered a far narrower space than the old Roman empire, and if it extended to Ireland, Scandinavia, and north-easterly regions of the mainland which the Romans had never subdued, it was not equal in its total area to the dominions of the Antonines. Divided and subdivided into a mosaic of kingdoms and principalities and republics, it seemed also to lack that unity which had been the great historic achievement of Rome, when the poet apostrophized her with the words 'Urbem fecisti quod prius orbis erat'. Yet this appearance was deceptive, and although the outward unity of a single law and a single allegiance was lost, the long reconstruction of the Middle Ages had established a more profound unity of civilization. Never before had so large an area been so much at one in institutions, in beliefs, above all in knowledge. Even the religious schism of the Reformation and the divergent growth of national sentiments and vernacular literatures had not checked this common life. The wealth of local diversities still had its roots in subterranean springs which communicated their nourishment to all parts alike, and the western spirit of that age, the spirit of science in action, was entering on those achievements which set it beside the Roman spirit as one of the great forces in history.

The little area to which it belonged was bounded on the west by the Atlantic and on two other sides by the inland seas, the Mediterranean and the Baltic. All round its coasts the gulfs and bays and the estuaries of navigable rivers gave easy access to the sea, and communication by water, besides being one of the causes of the similarity of one part with another, gave the opportunity for the vast adventure of expansion overseas which had already begun, and which was to be the means of filling all the habitable world with new stations, whether homes or mere camping-places, for this civilization. The westerners were masters of all the seas of the world. With inexhaustible heroism they had been exploring, step by step, for generations, and charting as they explored, so that by the beginning of the century the navigable globe, with the exception of some secluded places like the Arctic and Antarctic regions, and the greater part of the Australian coasts, had been visited and mapped. The first great modern period of discovery was, indeed, drawing to a close.[1] The Portuguese and Spaniards had almost done their work. In the earlier years of the century the Spaniards did indeed explore the upper Amazon and make new discoveries among the Pacific Islands. The Portuguese, in the time of the subjection to Spain, found their way to the highlands of Abyssinia and discovered the sources of the Blue Nile. But the chief task of the two nations overseas was soon to be the maintenance of their possessions against the advances of the English and the Dutch. These had begun their heroic age of sea-travel in the days of the Tudors and Philip II, before they became colonizing powers, and it fell to their lot to make the principal additions to geographical knowledge in the seventeenth century. The French also, like them, brought fresh energies to the work, and helped to carry it on from the points which the sixteenth-century sailors and travellers had reached.

Exploration for merely scientific purposes was, of course, almost unknown: trade and settlement were the two leading objects, to which missionary enterprise may be added as a third for the Catholic countries throughout the period and for the Protestant from its later years. Now that the great lines of geography were understood, for the most part the pioneer had succeeded the explorer, and expeditions on the grand scale were taken only in the regions where great geographical mysteries remained to be cleared up. The first of these was the Arctic. In the earlier part of the century the Dutch and the English,

[1] E. Heawood, *History of Geographical Discovery in the Seventeenth and Eighteenth Centuries* (1912), is a good text-book but without bibliography.

who still had to fight their way into the eastern seas against Spanish guns, were much taken up with attempts to find a way round them through the Polar Seas. The Russian trade through Archangel and the whale fisheries of Spitzbergen gave them their introduction to these regions, and taught them the art of navigating among the ice. They made valiant efforts to find a north-east passage along the coast of Siberia, and then a north-west passage between Greenland and America. The stories of these endeavours are worthy of their place in the epic cycle of sea travel; but the desired discoveries were not made, and the fields thus opened up for trade were of secondary importance. Exactly what was new in these discoveries is a matter of some uncertainty. The best opinion seems to be that Henry Hudson, one of the heroes of the search for the north-west passage, an Englishman who sailed under both English and Dutch auspices in different voyages, has been given too high a place among the actual finders of new lands. Nor were the voyages in the Arctic followed up until long afterwards.

It was in the Pacific that the greatest progress was made. The northern coasts of Australia were known, though incompletely. The Dutch explored the western and part of the southern coast. It was assumed or conjectured that they were a projection from a great southern continent, 'terra australis nondum cognita.' Here was a second major problem, and this problem was solved. The most important among a series of voyages was that of Abel Tasman, who sailed from Batavia, the Dutch capital of Java, in 1642. He discovered Tasmania and the south island of New Zealand, and by circumnavigating Australia, though he did not sight its eastern coast, he proved that it is an island. This journey added more to the knowledge of the earth's geography than any since the first journey round the world. The Dutch had other great enterprises to their credit. They were the first to sail round the southern extremity of America, which they named after the little town of Hoorn on the Zuider Zee. Others of them, driven south by storm, sighted portions of Antarctica.

They did not, however, work out their great discoveries in

detail. It was left for the late eighteenth century to push forward the exploration of the Pacific and even to discover that Tasmania is separated from Australia by the sea. For the Dutch explorations had outrun the demand. Australia was too distant and too large for the little Europe of those days to settle it, too poor to attract the great trading companies. The impulse which had led the northern nations into these searches proved to be short-lived, and about the middle of the seventeenth century there came a pause in geographical discovery which lasted for more than a hundred years. No doubt this relaxation of effort was due to the concurrence of several causes. The period after the peace of Westphalia was one in which the seafaring nations had to use much energy nearer home. It was the time in which the maritime rivalry of the English and Dutch was fought out by battle-fleets in the narrow seas. The great wars which began with Louis XIV may partly account for the lack of explorers. But what chiefly distinguishes this period from those before and after it is that commercial policy was restrictive, not expansive, and that colonization had for the time being more empty lands at its disposal than it could use. It was when Europe, as a result of economic changes, once more sought outlets for a superfluity of men and goods that the work was resumed.

The trade and colonization of which geographical discovery was a by-product were made possible not only by courage and enterprise, but by another factor which accompanied them so inseparably that it is easy to overlook its presence. This was the superiority of the westerners as fighters. Many of them perished at the hands of savages or of the civilized peoples of the east, and they had constantly to face dangers from men as well as from the elements; but when they were prepared and on their guard the white men could defeat any other men in the world. Their superiority lay in two things, neither of which could be closely copied as yet by any of the other races, technical skill and discipline or organization. When they met primitive tribes like the North American Indians, they could be sure in the long run, apart from casual reverses, of taking the land they wanted and holding their own. When they reached populous empires like those of Asia, their course could not be so simple; but their military superiority served them equally well. Not indeed that they were yet for a long time to rout great Asiatic armies as Clive was to do at Plassy. Their operations were on a smaller scale; but they were always governed by the factor of force, even when it was latent. When Sir Antony and Sir Robert Sherley presented themselves in Persia in 1598 they took a gun-founder with them, and they undertook a reorganization of the army of Shah Abbas.[1] In India, when the Mogul's governor reoccupied Surat after one of the raids of the Maratha chieftain, Shivaji, he found that the English factory had held out when the town had fallen. He offered its commander a sword of honour, but the Englishman laid down his pistol, saying that he was only a merchant, and asked for a merchant's reward in privileges for trade.[2] As allies or auxiliaries, even as military advisers, the Dutch and English could insinuate themselves where they could not come as conquerors; but it was their command of force that enabled them to do so. The limits of their colonizing efforts were therefore set by a combination of economic and military factors.

It is usual to divide the European colonies of that time, as of modern times generally, into the two classes called 'colonies of settlement' and 'colonies of exploitation'.[3] The distinction is not so clear as is sometimes supposed, nor are the names altogether happy. Any colony implies some degree of settlement, and no one would give the name of colony to such temporary resorts as the whaling-stations in Spitzbergen. 'Exploitation' is also an ambiguous word: we talk about exploiting natural resources, which may be done in either type of colony, and when we talk about the exploitation of native peoples the word has a flavour of disapproval

[1] Sir P. Sykes, *History of Persia*, 2nd ed., 1921, ii. 176 does not give the authority for these statements, but there is no reason to doubt them.

[2] J. Sarkar, *Shivaji and his Times* (1919), p. 117.

[3] The most comprehensive work (but without bibliography) is P. Leroy Beaulieu, *De la colonisation chez les peuples modernes*, 6th ed., 1908. The *Koloniale Geschiedenis* of H. T. Colenbrander (3 vols., 1925–6) has excellent short bibliographies.

which is not wanted in a classification of this kind. In spite of these defects we shall, however, find the distinction useful. The first type, the true colonies, are settlements of white men with their wives and children who form regular civilized communities. They are to be found where there is a suitable country and climate, and where the resistance of the natives can be overcome so as to permit of sufficient immigration. Canada was such a colony.

The second type is that in which a small number, often wholly or predominantly male, set themselves down amongst a native population. It prevails in tropical countries unsuitable for European family life and in countries with a stable political organization capable of controlling the influx of Europeans. Under it are included the small and simple establishments like the factories or trading centres, sometimes coupled with forts, which were set up in India in the seventeenth century; but the class also includes the tropical plantations in the West Indies where the settlers controlled the labour of a whole coloured population. For some of the instances, such as the tobacco and sugar colonies, one is tempted to use the name of mixed colonies of settlement and exploitation, but the fact is that none of these names can be used very precisely. Just as any colony implies settlement, so there were in the seventeenth century practically none which had no 'exploited' population whatever. Settlement and exploitation are not the exclusive characteristics of one colony or another, but elements one or the other of which predominated in each of them. It is in this sense that we shall use the terms.

At the beginning of the seventeenth century there existed only one colonial empire, that of the Spaniards, which, since the conquest of Portugal, included the colonies of the Portuguese. It comprised colonies of both types. In America the Spaniards ruled over large native populations, but they had formed communities which had all the apparatus of western civilization. Throughout the sixteenth century the emigrants from Spain to America had averaged between one and two thousand souls every year. Their great cities had almost the appearance of European towns. There were cathedrals, monasteries, printing-presses, schools, and universities. To Spanish literature, it is true, the colonists had made scarcely any independent contribution; but that was the only respect in which New Spain fell conspicuously short of Spain itself. Amongst its exports to Europe were not only gold and silver and natural products, but works of art and ornamental objects of household use. Mexico and, in a less degree, Peru and Chile, were outlying parts of Europe. In the West Indies and the Philippines the climate was tropical and the products, such as sugar, were got by organizing native labour which, since the supply was inadequate, was supplemented by the importation of negroes. The colonies there were consequently of the exploiting type. To that genus belonged also the settlements of Guiana and most of the Portuguese establishments. The principal Portuguese exception was Brazil, the first colony to be founded in America for agricultural purposes, its mineral wealth being at first unknown. Round the coast of Africa, from Elmina on the Guinea Coast to Mombasa and Melinda north of Zanzibar, the Portuguese had forts and harbours for their trade. In Indonesia they had a somewhat firmer hold, though of the same essential kind, and they monopolized the profitable trade in spices, commodities of considerable importance to Europe in the days when most of the Continent lived through the winter on salted meat. In India proper the Portuguese also had their stations, of which Goa was the most important. Here they had attempted a form of colonization which failed so completely that it was seldom imitated by other nations and never by the English. Albuquerque, the founder of the Portuguese empire in India, tried to make up for the shortage of Portuguese immigrants by mixed marriages with the natives, hoping by an infusion of European blood to extend the Portuguese rule. The only result was the creation of a large half-caste population which was neither European nor Asiatic.

The varied and vast assemblage of lands under the Spanish crown was the only existing European colonial empire: no other European state as yet ruled over an inch of land in any other continent. It is also in a sense true to say that the

Portuguese and Spanish colonies had already attained their utmost extent. In those which were settlements, the population was destined to increase, and the frontiers to be pushed forward from the coasts into the inhospitable or unexplored interiors; but that process was akin to the steady development which was going on in the European countries themselves. No new colonies were founded by either of these nations. The first stage of their expansion, the stage of acquisition, was over. The Portuguese indeed had overshot their strength, and there were already signs of decline in their possessions. Goa sank in importance after the destruction of the neighbouring capital of Vijayanagar in 1565. The cruelties of the inquisition and the arrogance of their civil and military authorities undermined the position of the Portuguese there and elsewhere. It needed no acuteness of perception to see that the Portuguese colonies might easily become the prey of more active peoples, and some of the Spanish colonies offered the same prospect to aggressive Englishmen like Sir Walter Raleigh. The first great chapter in the colonial history of the century was in fact to be the seizing of parts of the one old empire by Dutch newcomers, in whose wake the Englishmen soon followed. It must, however, be remembered that what the Dutch and the English acquired in this way were only colonies of exploitation. The great settlements were unshaken. Neither Dutchmen nor Englishmen took an inch of Mexico or Peru or Chile. The Dutch failed in their long struggle for Brazil. The entire losses of the Spaniards in the century came to only a trifling fraction of their empire. Those of the Portuguese were more substantial; they lost all their richest dependencies.

It was the Dutch who first succeeded in the attack, though the Elizabethan Englishmen had pointed the way. The great companies of Holland had, as we have seen, the double object of trade and of damaging the national enemy in distant seas. Their methods were those of the Portuguese, first the trading voyage, next the factory, and then the fort. They took what they could from the Portuguese, or from native princes. The latter had to let them in either as allies against other natives or against the Portuguese, or else as plain enemies. By about 1660 their empire was made. That is to say that, although they have developed and extended their colonies from that time until the present day, they have not taken on any considerable new possessions. In the same way, although it is equally true that they developed and extended what the Portuguese had begun, their empire was based on what they took from their forerunners. They established a factory in Java in 1597. In the early days of their eastern trade they were in constant rivalry with the English, who were also trying to force their way into the Portuguese preserves. The English got a footing in Bantam, Jacatra, and Japara, in Macassar, and in the Moluccas. In all these places the Dutch encountered difficulties in their trade with the natives, and they ascribed these difficulties mainly to the English. It was thus the rivalry with England rather than that with Portugal which turned their commercial enterprise into an imperial channel.

The real founder of their empire was Jan Pieterszoon Coen, a man equally strong in war and in administration, who was the most determined opponent of the English in the East. The result of his work was not only that the Dutch became an imperial power, but also that they won the first round of the contest against England in the eastern seas. Coen became governor-general in 1617. His first success was the defeat of a powerful combination of natives and English in Bantam. On the ruins of the town of Jacatra he founded the new capital, Batavia. His rule was marked by ruthless massacres of the natives, and by the practice, typical of the realism of the new capitalistic spirit, of 'limiting output' by devastating the spice-bearing trees. The most famous stroke against the English was done in the time of his successor. In 1619 they had acquired the right to have representatives at Batavia and at Dutch places in the Moluccas. Four years later some of them were accused along with some Japanese of conspiring to seize the Dutch fort at Amboina, the greatest entrepôt of the spice-trade. On the strength of confessions which, if genuine, were at least extracted by torture, nine of them were executed. Retribution came a generation later; but for the time being the massacre and the policy of which it was the expression were successful. The English dropped out of the race for empire in the Malay Archipelago and concentrated the main effort of their eastern trade in Hither India.

Further progress was made by the Dutch in the following years, especially after 1627, when Coen again became governor-general. The Mahommedan sultan of Mataram, who ruled over eastern and central Java, was ambitious of acquiring the whole island, and sent a large force to besiege Batavia. Coen died during the siege, but the Javanese were completely defeated, and the Dutch were thenceforth firmly fixed as the predominant power in the island, though the empire of Mataram lasted far on into the eighteenth century. The aim of Coen to make real Dutch settlements was, however, not fulfilled. The conditions were such that only colonies of exploitation were possible.

One after another, small military and diplomatic successes over the natives built up Dutch power, and there was at least one spectacular success in the conquest of Ceylon from the Portuguese which was begun in 1636, mainly done in 1656 and completed in 1658. Of their Asiatic and Pacific empire the Portuguese retained nothing except Goa and Macao at the mouth of the Canton river, which the Dutch had twice failed to capture. The Dutch, besides Ceylon and Cochin had (until 1662) the island of Formosa as an outlying possession convenient for their trade with China and Japan. Mauritius and the Cape of Good Hope were valuable places of call for their East Indiamen. The central nucleus of their empire was in Indonesia, where they were supreme and had no European neighbours worth mentioning except the Spaniards of the Philippines. On the mainland of the Malay Peninsula they held Malacca, the predecessor of Singapore. South and east of it they had Sumatra, Java, Borneo, the Celebes, the Moluccas, the western end of New Guinea. Not that these great territories were completely subdued. The mountains and forests of the interiors and the impassable places generally in both the greater and the smaller islands remained in the hands of native rulers. The

Dutch were only there for utilitarian reasons, and they assumed only so much of political authority as they needed for their trade. It was necessary, indeed, to govern the coastal regions directly, and to maintain control over the princes of the hinterland by diplomatic agents; but there was no long-sighted policy of development, still less of government in the interests of the natives. Quick returns were wanted, and they were got by restricting, not by encouraging, production. The trade and shipping of the natives were allowed to languish: Dutch monopoly overbore them. The native princes were allowed to misgovern as they pleased so long as they remained peaceable and fell in with the Dutch commercial measures. Empire was not yet the white man's burden.

It is significant that, although the Dutch East India Company regularly sent out ministers of religion to its eastern establishments, they did not undertake missionary work among the natives.[1] Conversions to Christianity were not unknown, and in Ceylon, where Roman Catholicism had been introduced by the Portuguese, thousands of natives were given the form of baptism; but, apart from such apparent exceptions, the new colonial powers were conspicuously devoid of the missionary tendency of the old. Some of the cruelties and errors of the Spaniards and Portuguese had been committed in the name of Christianity; but that name was also linked with courageous protests and generous services. From the earliest times of the Spanish empire the ideal of the conversion of the newly discovered heathens had been present in men's minds, sometimes in a pure and disinterested shape, if sometimes perverted to be the instrument of mundane designs. The missionaries, especially the Jesuits, had penetrated into every corner of the known world, and had been amongst the pathfinders into the unknown. They had done much to make the expansion of Europe into an ex-

[1] See Knappert, *Geschiedenis der Nederlandsche hervormde kerk*, i. 213 ff., and H. L. Osgood, *American Colonies in the Seventeenth Century*, ii. 413. Professor Knappert informed me that he afterwards came to think his judgement in the passage cited too severe: references to a number of sincere, though not very effective, Dutch missionary efforts are given by Latourette, *History of the Expansion of Christianity*, vol. ii.

tension of western civilization as well as western rule, and the reflections to which their experience gave rise had done much to revise the current prejudices about the nature and degree of the superiority of the Christian over the pagan world. One of the tributary streams of European humanitarianism and rationalism was flowing in from the Jesuit colleges of America.

It was a stream which as yet drew little from the Dutch or the English colonies. In a sense this was partly because their colonists were Protestants. After its first rapid spread in the sixteenth century Protestantism had made no converts, and in Europe it has, broadly speaking, never again made any. The Roman church, on the other hand, had reconquered much of what it had lost, and the missionary spirit was equally alive at home and abroad. In the congregation *De Propaganda Fide* it had a strong central organization, completed in the seventeenth century, and all the necessary departments of missionary work, including printing and linguistic training were amply provided. There were, however, what may be called accidental reasons which kept the Protestants out of the field besides the essential differences in their religious outlook. It was their traders, not as with the Catholics, their governments, who made the conquests. The traders were utilitarians: it was even believed that the Dutch, as Swift tells in *Gulliver's Travels*,[1] would insult the emblems of Christianity in order to obtain their entry to the trade of Japan. The comparatively small efforts of the Protestants in the century were only preliminaries to their real missionary labours. Grotius exhorted his contemporaries to the work. Dutch scholarship and Dutch printing came to the aid of the Catholics in the great enterprise of translating the Bible into Arabic. An Englishman put Grotius's *De Veritate Christianae Religionis* into the same tongue. Dutchmen and Englishmen produced Bibles in the Malay languages. One of the early colonists who went out to join the Pilgrim Fathers did the same and much more for the language of the 'Massachusetts Indians'. This great and good man, John Eliot, though his work ultimately failed, was well supported from England, where a society raised money for the purpose. The reign of William III saw the

[1] Part III, cap. xi.

foundation of three English missionary societies, the Christian Faith Society for the West Indies and the two more famous bodies which still continue, the Society for Promoting Christian Knowledge and the Society for the Propagation of the Gospel in Foreign Parts.

Their foundation was an index of the reaction of her new position as an imperial power on the religious and intellectual outlook of England. We have seen how the English were worsted in their first rivalry against the Dutch for the seats of the spice-trade. That failure had the effect of making the English East India Company concentrate its attention on the sub-continent to which we give the simple name of India. Here their relations with the Dutch were but little disturbed, and although until 1650 the Dutch even here were the pioneers, the English were able to set up forts and factories more or less after the Dutch model. At Surat the two nations traded side by side. In 1639 the English, on the unpromising site of Madras, founded what is now the third city of India. The first two were in English hands before the end of the century. Calcutta was obtained from the Moguls in 1690 at the conclusion of an unofficial war. Bombay had been peacefully handed over a generation before by the Portuguese. Their power in the east had been declining throughout their long war of independence against Spain. Even before the war began, the Mogul Shāhjahān had driven them out of Hugli. In 1652 Muscat on the Gulf of Oman was taken by the Arabs. The Dutch and the English now controlled the external trade of Arabia, whose inhabitants rose to comparative prosperity and were more friendly with them than with their Turkish overlords.

The Portuguese decline in Africa and Asia could not be stemmed, and in the hope of saving something from the wreck and keeping the independence of the mother country, King John IV handed over, as the price of an English alliance, the two expensive possessions of Tangier and Bombay. The English government did not retain the first long, and did not appreciate the value of the second for some time; but the English traders were alive to their interests, and the period of English commercial imperialism had begun. The

Commonwealth, when it fought the Dutch republic, had exacted an indemnity for the massacre of Amboina. Oliver Cromwell, in the course of a foreign policy which, from the European point of view, seemed ill informed and ill advised, had blundered into the capture of Jamaica from the Spaniards, and the restored monarchy of Charles II had found it necessary to retain this prize. In the two Dutch wars of his reign further colonial gains were made, but these were of another character, and they symbolize the great contrast between the Dutch empire and the British.

With a single exception the Dutch colonies which have hitherto been mentioned belong to the class of colonies of exploitation. That exception is the Cape of Good Hope, but it was by an afterthought that the Cape became the settlement of a population of Boers. It was first occupied simply for the purposes of a calling-place for ocean-going ships. The genius of the Dutch turned to the tropical lands, and they lacked the resources, especially the supply of men, for peopling new countries. Not that they made no attempts in that way: New Netherland, running inland from New Amsterdam at the mouth of the Hudson River, was a prosperous offshoot of the republic. But it was small beside the French and English settlements by which it was surrounded on three sides. The French in Canada, from the time of Henry VI, had done a wonderful work. Samuel de Champlain, a naval officer, after a remarkable journey through Mexico and the West Indies, began in 1603 a series of travels in Canada which made great areas of it known to Europeans. He and his successors opened up and settled the country on the banks of the St. Lawrence. The *habitants* clung to their Catholic religion and French laws and customs so firmly that they have retained to this day, through strange political vicissitudes, a character and a unity of their own. In comparison with the French, the English were later comers. Their early attempts to settle in the temperate zone were unsuccessful. But the eastern shores of America were awaiting the settler, and circumstances brought it about that there were to be developed in England new impulses to settlement previously unknown in Europe.

Englishmen attempted in the reign of Elizabeth to make homes for themselves in Virginia, the same region in which they successfully did so in the reign of James I. The adventurers who carried out these expeditions, and to a lesser degree those who financed them, resembled up to a point their contemporaries of the English and Dutch East India Companies. The maritime element and the commercial element were much the same, whatever the geographical field to which they applied themselves, and the natural conditions of those parts of America which the Spaniards had not effectively occupied necessarily led in Virginia as in Canada to the method of settlement. There was no productive native population with which to trade. There was no strongly organized native resistance to immigration. In what afterwards became the tobacco colonies the climate led the English to take the position of masters of coloured labour, and during the first half of the century they acquired a number of places of this kind, which became the permanent residences of English families, but were economically similar to the older tropical colonies. In the period of the first two Stuarts, the Bermudas, the lesser Antilles, Barbados, British Honduras, and the Bahamas were quietly occupied, and they entered on their days of great prosperity on the basis of sugar-growing by slave labour. The social condition of these colonies, when compared with those of the Dutch, mirrors to some extent the distinguishing features of the England of that time. The Dutch planter was primarily a man of business; the English planter had much of the territorial squire about him. It must be remembered that the English out-distanced the Dutch as colonizers before they overtook them in economic organization at home; and the reason of this is that the qualifications for effective colonization were not merely economic. In the factor of organized force the English had perhaps an advantage: they were less ready than the Dutch to make their terms with native princes. But the chief way in which their political condition influenced colonizing activity was in providing a supply of men who were better satisfied with a moderate subsistence in America than with mere material comfort at home, if that material comfort entailed political and religious subjection. The more northerly English colonies of America, the colonies of pure settlement, were made by a new kind of colonist, the man for whom economic gain was a minor consideration.

That this was the historical significance of the Pilgrim Fathers is well known. They were neither the first nor the last of their kind. Huguenots had made the first French attempts to settle in America, and the stream of religious refugees still moved westwards in the eighteenth century. Although it was incomplete, religious liberty was more nearly approached in New England and in Maryland, so long as it was a Roman Catholic colony, than anywhere in the British Isles. The line of English settlements, interrupted at only two points, stretched by 1664, from the French border in the north to South Carolina. It provided room not only for almost every possible religious belief, but also for many varieties of social and political types. From England it was but loosely controlled. The governments of Charles II and his successors set up a machinery of boards for collecting information and co-ordinating policy. Its work was by no means contemptible; but the distance of the colonies, the spontaneity of their growth, and the English habit of doing without symmetrical or centralized organization gave them the great blessing of constitutional variety. Some, the proprietary colonies like Maryland and Pennsylvania, were little monarchies ruled by British subjects. Some, like the New England colonies, were little republics with almost powerless British governors. The spirit of liberty throve in this group of states much as it did in the group of provinces which made up the Dutch republic.

The two breaks in the chain of British colonies were closed in consequence of the Dutch war of 1665–7. Each was made by a patch of Dutch territory. The less important of the two was New Sweden on the Delaware, which had been wrested by the Dutch from the Swedes who, as we have already seen,[1] took part, like the Brandenburgers and the Danes, in the colonial enterprise of the century, but without lasting results. The more important was New Netherland. Modern

[1] Above, p. 240.

writers are sometimes surprised to see how light-heartedly the Dutch allowed New Amsterdam to become New York. They were not, however, in fact throwing away their chances. These two settlements had no great future under the Dutch flag. The small territory of the republic had not the men to provide for further emigration, and there were signs that the Dutch empire had reached its limits. The attempts on Brazil had definitely failed. European wars were closing in on the States. It was none too bad a bargain to get final possession of Surinam and Polaroon, with a satisfactory clarification of the Navigation Acts.

England and France thus remained the two North American powers, and before the end of the century they had begun to come into collision. In the reign of William III the European war extended to the line of forts which the English had built, when they came up behind the French from Hudson Bay. The French in the time of Colbert had begun to grasp the importance of New France, and under the intendant Talon and the governor Frontenac it made headway against the Indians and grew in population and prosperity. The French flag was carried past the Great Lakes to the Mississippi. In 1682 the city of St. Louis was founded, and it was possible to travel in French territory from the river St. Lawrence to the Gulf of Mexico. It was the English, however, not the French, who saw most clearly that European war should be made the means of acquiring colonial possessions. At the Treaty of Utrecht they made the first great forced additions to their empire: Nova Scotia, Newfoundland, the territory round Hudson Bay, and in the West Indies St. Kitts. In addition they took naval bases in the Mediterranean and lucrative commercial concessions from Spain. They had provided themselves with strong positions for that struggle against the French in east and west which was to be their main business in the eighteenth century.

The outline of general colonial history in the seventeenth century may thus be stated very briefly. At the beginning there existed one colonial empire, that of the Spaniards and Portuguese. The rebellion of Portugal dissolved it into its two component parts, and these two parts had for the present very different fates. Spain retained hers with only the loss of some minor points. That of Portugal fell into something resembling dissolution: the best and richest places were lost. Three new colonial powers arose. The French had a single temperate colony of settlement, but that great and full of promise; in the West Indies and in Madagascar, as at Réunion and Cayenne and Pondicherry, they had made a beginning with settlements of the tropical type. The English were in a position not very different from that of the French. They also had made a start in India, in the West Indies, on the west coast of Africa, and at St. Helena. In North America they had a line of colonies where rivalry with the French had already begun. The marvellous destiny of the English colonies in America was only very imperfectly visible, if visible at all. Their population numbered not much more than two hundred thousand white men. Harvard College was founded at Cambridge, Massachusetts, in 1636 and three years later, in the same town, came the first printing-press in British America. There was no newspaper until 1690. To European observers these settlements were still interesting as adjuncts of the European economic system rather than as separate centres of western civilization, with a life of their own.

XIV
POLITICAL THOUGHT

WE have seen that one of the propelling forces in the revival of military science was the historical study of the methods and writings of the ancient Greeks and Romans. Justus Lipsius, the leader in this study, also turned his attention to the problems of political obligation and the organization of the state.[1] He collected and arranged passages on these subjects from the best classical authors, and the books in which he did so were received by the educated world with the attention due to his learning. They were several times reprinted and they found their way into all considerable libraries. Yet their influence was negligible. They did little if anything to further the solution of the political problems which were engaging men's minds. For this purpose the method which had proved so useful in the art of war was inadequate. A lack of boldness in Lipsius himself, a compliance with the absolutist and intolerant principles of the government under which he was living when he wrote one of these books, were no doubt partly to blame for this, and a further explanation lies in the large borrowings of previous writers from the stock of political wisdom left behind by the ancients. The principal reason is, however, another. In the military sphere, by adapting them to certain specific new conditions such as the use of firearms, the principles of antiquity could be made to supply a key to the needed reform. In politics the new environment was too deeply different for any such adaptation to serve the purpose. The political experience of the world had become so rich, and its greatest problems were so completely without precedent in the ancient world, that a volume of quotations from writers like Tacitus was trite and superficial in comparison with the results of direct and original observation and thought. There were others who followed the method

[1] *Politicorum sive Civilis Doctrinae, libri sex*, 1589, and *Monita et Exempla Politica*, 1605. An English translation of the former by William Jones of Newington Butts was published in 1594.

of Lipsius, and the great Hobbes translated Thucydides for his political lessons; but more than this was needed. Classical examples proved to be of only a limited value, and in this they shared the fate of Biblical examples. Through a great part of the century many writers took the Hebrew monarchy as the type of what monarchy should be. Visionaries looked forward to the rule of the saints, the fifth monarchy foretold in the book of Daniel. Milton wrote of the prophets

> As men divinely taught, and better teaching
> The solid rules of Civil Government
> In their majestic unaffected stile
> Then all the Oratory of *Greece* and *Rome*.[1]

But the two sets of teachers were alike reduced to comparative neglect. One after another the writers of the century discovered that the traditional principles did not cover the new facts. They could, for instance, no longer be satisfied with the classification of constitutions, as monarchies, aristocracies, and democracies, which was already old when Aristotle used it. 'Nor', wrote Sir William Temple, 'will any man who understands the state of Poland and the United Provinces, be well able to range them under any particular Names of Government that have yet been invented.' [2]

The wealth of political experience brought a multiplicity of political literature. In the best works on the history of thought, the arguments of the greater writers are one by one analysed and discussed, and it is shown how each answers his predecessors and is himself answered by those who follow, so that the whole seems to move forward with the orderly sequence of a debate. Such an exposition, in the hands at least of reporters like T. H. Green,[3] does not falsify the history, but gives its essence. At the same time it must be remembered that this debate, like others, had an

[1] *Paradise Regained*, iv. 353 ff.

[2] *Essay upon the Original and Nature of Government* (1673), in *Works* (1760), i. 31.

[3] In his *Lectures on the Principles of Political Obligation*, first published in *Works*, vol. ii (1886), and afterwards separately.

audience, that there were interruptions, asides, pieces of by-play, whispered hints which find no mention in the formal record. The great political theorists were few in number. In the highest rank it would perhaps be wrong to include more than three in the whole century and the whole continent: Hobbes, Spinoza, and Locke. Each of these had a realistic grasp of the facts of political life, and also a critical knowledge of the import of his interpretation of them, an understanding of what his argument implied and how it was related to the other parts of his view of the universe and of human nature. Grotius falls short of them in system and consistency; the systematic and consistent Althusius is deficient in the criticism of his fundamental principles; Campanella has no hold on the world of practical life. These latter writers, however, and others who like them fail in one way or another to reach the first eminence, have their place in the evolution of thought, as have many others who handle only subsidiary questions or treat the leading problems incidentally or with small success. Mere pamphleteers, of whom, as we shall see, there were hundreds, often struck out, to meet the exigencies of short-range controversy, the rough shapes of ideas which were afterwards to be embodied in the considered discussions of the masters. Somewhat above the pamphleteers were several classes of writers whose books were often acute and fruitful of new insight. There were academic compilers, who arranged the conclusions of more original minds for the use of teachers: in this class we may include even such a heavy folio as the work of the Spanish Jesuit Suarez,[1] the principal writer of the neo-scholastics, who held to the conclusions and the elaborately systematic plan of St. Thomas Aquinas. There were also writers on statecraft. Their aim was to show princes and politicians how to get what they wanted, not to discuss theoretical questions about the nature of their offices or their title to obedience. The best things in this kind that have been written since Machiavelli are in Bacon's *Essays* of 1598–1625. Nor could a full history of political thought leave out of account antiquarian jurists like Selden, economists like

[1] *Tractatus de Lege ac Deo Legislatore*, 1619.

Pieter de la Court,[1] divines like Bossuet, mere satirical story-tellers like Grimmelshausen[2] or Swift.

This multiplicity of political literature is, of course, increased by the differences between the histories of the different states. Spain, under the influence of the counter-reformation, could carry on the Thomist ideas of the Middle Ages. France, no less monarchical, stood in a different relation to the church, while the Protestant countries were divided between absolute monarchies, republics, and anomalous constitutions which were neither. The more philosophical writers were, indeed, naturally less affected by these national peculiarities than those whose business was with more immediate and practical affairs, and, furthermore, in these higher regions thought was still international, and its circulation was only partially obstructed by religious divisions. Most of the more serious political works of the first half of the century were written in Latin. Hobbes, like Bodin in the previous century, put out his ideas both in Latin and his native tongue; even Locke did not write only in English; the great French authors of the second half of the century could dispense with Latin translations because their own language was by then itself an international vehicle of thought. Political thought did not go forward in separate national compartments, but each writer was aware of what was being done in other countries.

Partly because thought was international and partly for another reason, it is unnecessary to say much about the writers of some of the chief countries, amongst whom even those of France may be included.[3] The prevailing phase of monarchy was unfavourable to political speculation. It confined the ingenuity of writers to an orthodox point of view. Until the latter part of the reign of Louis XIV they did no more than to perfect the theory of absolutism. After that,

[1] His principal work, the *Interest van Holland* of 1662, was published in an English translation in 1702 and 1746 with the title *The True Interest and Political Maxims of the Republic of Holland* but with the name of John de Witt as the author.

[2] See above, p. 130.

[3] For these writers see H. Sée, *Les idées politiques en France au XVII*[e] *siècle* (1923).

it is true, there set in a reaction, but it did little more than to proceed some way in directions where writers of other times and nations had previously explored much farther. Frenchmen did something for the advocacy of religious toleration, and much for the theory which underlies it. They exposed some of the fallacies and disadvantages of absolute monarchy, but the alternatives they had to offer, whether in theory or in practice, were ineffective. St. Simon,[1] the most acrimonious writer against Louis XIV as a man, stood for an archaic and unworkable principle of aristocratic government. Archbishop Fénelon, whose *Télémaque* has high literary merits, was a humane and philanthropic thinker. He exposed the essential contradiction between the interests of the people and the interests of a bad king; but he had, roughly speaking, no remedy for it except that kings should become virtuous and enlightened, and that aristocratic assemblies of estates should exercise an intermittent control. For the most part, the best French thought of the time foreshadows the benevolent despotism of the eighteenth century, which has been called the death-bed repentance of monarchy: a movement of great importance, but historically, and still more from the point of view of theory, a movement that came to an end and led to no distant consequences. For their ultimate influence those writers were more important who, unlike most of the French, saw that constitutional organization is the firmest link between good intentions and wise administration. They are the forerunners of the liberalism of the eighteenth and nineteenth centuries, a tendency in which France at times took the lead but which does not trace its ancestry to the France of the *grand siècle*, and was to come thither later as a foreign importation.

The political thought of any age consists of the interpretation of political facts by the mind of that age, and political literature therefore shares the general intellectual characteristics of the time. In the seventeenth century the dominance of the mathematical and scientific tendency manifested itself in more ways than one. We shall see later how it transformed the language and arrangement of political, as

[1] See below, p. 280.

of other, books. In their substance also it brought great changes. In the first place, it added new departments to political thought. A name which serves as a link between scientific and political studies is that of a wonderfully gifted man who was one of the early fellows of the Royal Society, Sir William Petty. We have seen that he worked at the figures of population and trade and such-like matters, and he deserves to be called the inventor of the application of statistics to public affairs. In his time the invention was still rudimentary, but the steady process had begun by which the quantitative method has become one of the foundations of the sciences and arts of government. What is more, Petty's work, like that of most of the great inventors, came at the time when the world was ready for it. Other workers in various countries were engaged on similar researches: Dutchmen were busy at the actuarial calculations on which life-insurance was based; Frenchmen began to investigate the relation between their system of taxes and the taxable resources of their country. Outside the economic sphere, to which the statistical method is readily applied, there was the same attempt to arrive at certainty by means of theorems at least superficially resembling those of mathematics. The idea of equilibrium was taken over from mechanics. Harrington enunciated the doctrine of the balance of property. Not only theorists but even men of action held that constitutions should be made to work by a system of balance: Oliver Cromwell harped on the word in one of his speeches.[1] We have seen that the lawless confusion of international relations was reduced to a deceptive appearance of order by the doctrine of the balance of power, the European equilibrium. Although these theories had little in them that was truly scientific, they stood for more than a mere borrowing of the scientists' vocabulary. Beneath them lay a serious, if misguided, attempt to explain by weighing and measuring, by adding and subtracting.

There is a kinship between them and another tendency of

[1] Speech IV in Carlyle's *Letters and Speeches of Oliver Cromwell* (ed. Lomas, iii. 420). This was in 1655. He used the expression in the previous year (*ibid.*, iii. 384). See also the letter of 1693, ascribed to Godolphin, in Dalrymple, *Memoirs* (1790), II. i. 38: 'a new election . . . will throw the ballance too much on the one side or the other.'

the period, that towards the comparative study of political phenomena. Studies of the actual constitutions of different countries, of which there are few earlier examples, now became common. Particular attention was paid to states like Venice, which were supposed to be models of good government, but no state was neglected. There was a definite desire to collect and compare all the available information of this sort. A French nobleman, Pierre d'Avity, in 1614 put together a mass of material, of very unequal value, in his work *Les empires, royaumes, estats . . . et principautez du monde.*[1] A far more useful collection was in the series of little duodecimo volumes published by the Elzevirs and other Dutch firms, which are catalogued in old libraries under the general heading 'Respublica'. Some of these were well-known existing works like Sir Thomas Smith's *De Republica Anglorum*, but others seem to have been written specially for the series. Altogether more than fifty of them were published; and a learned German, Werdenhagen, supplied in 1632 a general *Introductio Universalis in omnes Respublicas*. What is now called 'comparative politics' had come into being, and its point of view was expressed by Sir William Temple in the preface to his *Observations on the United Provinces*, one of the most famous of the books of this type.

'I believe', he says, 'it will be found, at one time or other by all who shall try, That whilst Human Nature continues what it is, The same Orders in State, the same Discipline in Armies, The same Reverence for things Sacred, And Respect of Civil Institutions, The same Virtues and Dispositions of Princes and Magistrates, deriv'd by Interest, or Imitation, into the Customs and Humours of the Peoples, will ever have the same Effects upon the Strength and Greatness of all Governments, and upon the Honour and Authority of those that Rule, as well as the Happiness and Safety of those that obey.'

The study of politics is to proceed from the assumption that the same cause will always produce the same effect, the fundamental postulate of science.

[1] An English translation by Edward Grimeston was published in 1614; for a favourable estimate of its place in the development of the anthropological point of view see the article of Dr. Myres cited in p. xiii n., above.

Hobbes and Spinoza and Locke, thinkers who considered what human nature in its various aspects is, worked out their political theories as parts of general philosophy, and made this same assumption. Hobbes explains it in the beginning of his *Elementa Philosophica de Cive* (1647), and indeed it is implied in the title. It appears to have been about this time that the idea of a science of politics, and the application of the word 'science' to it, became current in various countries.

Some of the writers who put forward this idea had in mind rather the art of statecraft than a theoretical body of doctrine; but it is interesting to note the expressions that they used, and, incidentally, to note that they connected this idea of scientific politics with the teachings of the Greeks and Romans and with historical study. Henry Nevile, a pamphleteer whose later work consisted in adapting the principles of the republican Harrington to the altered conditions of a restored monarchy, wrote in 1681 of 'that great Science of the Governing and Increasing great States and Cities' as it had been taught by Aristotle, Plato, and Cicero.[1] In the same book he says: 'The Politicks or Art of Governing is a Science to be learned and studied by Counsellors and Statesmen, be they never so great; or else Mankind will have a very sad condition under them, and they themselves a very perplexed and turbulent life, and probably a very destructive and precipitous end of it.'[2] And 'whosoever sets himself to study Politicks, must do it by reading History'.[3]

In three ways the conditions favoured the development of this science as they had favoured it in the times of ancient Greece. There was a considerable variety among the known constitutions of different states; there were revolutions which led to the questioning of accepted political maxims; there was the need for drafting new constitutions for the colonies which went out from the older states. The leading problems which demanded solution were, however, those which had been set by the sixteenth century. The period of religious and political strife which was ushered in by the Protestant Reformation was one of the great revolutionary periods of

[1] *Plato Redivivus*, p. 25. [2] p. 89. [3] Preface.

political thought. By the time of the Counter-Reformation, the French wars of religion, and the Dutch revolt, a number of arguments had been circulated which were to form the greater part of the stock in trade of the controversies of the seventeenth century. The main lines in particular for the discussion of the social contract and sovereignty had been plotted out. It was left to the succeeding age to carry on the work thus begun.

The social contract theory, nowadays needlessly despised, is the most telling way in which the relation of the individual to the state can be expressed. It is one of the theories in which political science has been influenced by jurisprudence. A contract, in everyday law, is an agreement freely made by two parties in which each of them undertakes to do something on condition that the other also does what he in turn promises. To put the argument for political obedience in the form of saying that the relation between the subject and the state is contractual or similar to a contract has the attraction of seeming to solve the riddle of reconciling the need for obedience with the desirable condition that government should rest on the consent of the governed. If it is by his own promise, explicit or implied, that the subject is bound, then he may be reconciled to the possibly unpleasant consequences of fulfilling his obligation. Unfortunately, as writers of different views built their several structures on this same scaffolding, it proved that the social contract could be twisted to bear quite opposite meanings. The contract was not an historical event, and little attention need be paid to the half-hearted efforts of some old writers to give it an historical foundation. It was an explanatory and symbolic fiction; the essence of the theory was not that there had been, but that the relation of the parties was as though there had been, a contract. There was, however, nothing which necessarily indicated exactly who had been the parties, or exactly what had been the terms on which they had agreed. When the theory was first revived in the sixteenth century, the emphasis was laid on the mutual character of the obligation. The parties were supposed to be kings on the one part and their subjects on the other. Whatever the king's promise was, there was some duty which he owed to the subject in exchange for allegiance. Thus there were Huguenot writers under Catholic kings, and equally there were Jesuit writers against heretical monarchs, who demonstrated that the states which persecuted their friends had broken their agreements and so forfeited the right to obedience.[1] The social contract was thus a ground for resistance and rebellion. The more extreme of these *monarchomachi*, or opponents of monarchy, even advocated the right to kill a tyrant. That phase, however, ended. On the Catholic side it was extinguished, perhaps in consequence of the general indignation at the murder of King Henry IV of France by a religious fanatic. It had a brief rebirth a generation later when the English opposition sentenced Henry's son-in-law, Charles I, to death. It is said that during his trial Oliver Cromwell 'entered into a long discourse' with the Scots commissioners 'of the nature of royal power according to Mariana and Buchanan.'[2] The sentence on Charles, drafted by the Dutch jurist, Isaac Dorislaus, is reminiscent of the Catholic scholastics, and the apologists of the execution repeated the arguments and reprinted the pamphlets of the sixteenth century.

Even before that century had ended the social contract idea had been adapted to the requirements of a theory of obedience. Richard Hooker, the apologist of the Elizabethan settlement of the Church of England, in his *Laws of Ecclesiastical Polity*, of which the greater part had been published in the last decade of the sixteenth century,[3] had pointed the way in this direction. Hooker knew his Aristotle, and so he regarded human society as being, to use the most dangerously ambiguous of all political terms, 'natural'; but with this explanation he combined its opposite, the contract theory, by which it is the product of a made, artificial agreement. 'Forasmuch', he says, 'as we are not by ourselves sufficient to

[1] The short study of Treumann, *Die Monarchomachen*, 1895, is a useful guide.

[2] Burnet, *History of his own Time*, ed. Airy, i. 42, on the authority of an eyewitness, Lieut.-Gen. Drummond.

[3] For its somewhat mysterious literary history see the article on Hooker in the *Dictionary of National Biography*.

furnish ourselves with competent store of things needful for such a life as our nature doth desire, a life fit for the dignity of man; therefore to supply those defects and imperfections which are in us living single and solely by ourselves, we are naturally induced to seek communion and fellowship with others. This was the cause of men's uniting themselves at first in politic Societies, which Societies could not be without Government, nor Government without a distinct kind of law from that which hath been already declared.' [This refers to what we should call moral law.] 'Two foundations there are which bear up public societies; the one a natural inclination, whereby all men desire sociable life and fellowship, the other an order expressly or secretly agreed upon touching the manner of their union in living together.'

Although there are yet other views which Hooker seems momentarily to entertain, his leading idea is that this second foundation is the basis of law. He takes a pessimistic view of human nature: 'We all make complaint of the iniquity of our times: not unjustly for the days are evil. But compare them with those times wherein there were no civil societies . . . and we have surely good cause to think that God hath blessed us exceedingly, and hath made us behold most happy days.' The object of the social contract was 'to take away . . . mutual grievances, injuries and wrongs'. Man's nature since the Fall is so corrupt that 'utterly to take away all kind of public government in the world, were apparently'—that is, evidently—'to overturn the whole world'. The contract, like other legal arrangements, is binding in perpetuity, and it does not impose any limit on the authority of the sovereign.

For Hooker these matters are only preliminary to his main theme, the vindication of episcopacy and of the ecclesiastical legislation of Queen Elizabeth against the Calvinistic Puritans who wished to free the church from all secular interference. The state control of religion is usually called the 'Erastian' position, though it does not seem to have been held by the Swiss divine, Thomas Erastus (1524–83), after whom it is named.[1] Both Erastianism and the political doctrine which sees the social contract as the foundation of

[1] The various forms of Erastianism are distinguished in a chapter of the *Studies in English Religion in the Seventeenth Century* (1903) by the Rev. H. Hensley Henson, afterwards bishop of Durham.

law and the means of escape from the evils of the state of nature were expressed in their most uncompromising form by Thomas Hobbes of Malmesbury. Between Hooker's time and his the Tudor monarchy had broken down under the bad management of the Stuarts, and civil strife burst out on the question of where the sovereignty lay in the English constitution. Hobbes wrote many books, illuminating many branches of thought: the greatest of them is *Leviathan*, which was published nine years after the outbreak of the civil war.

The curious title of this treatise is metaphorical. Leviathan is the state, the supreme power which men have set up over themselves, and the name is chosen because we are told of Leviathan in the book of Job that there is no power on earth that may be compared with him.[1] Hobbes, in that time of confusion turned, as Jean Bodin[2] had turned in the confusion of the French civil wars, to the idea that the peace of a country must be established by uniting in one strong hand all power, civil and ecclesiastical, legislative and administrative. In dealing with international law we have seen how the conception of sovereignty as complete independence from external power, whether of the papacy or of a suzerain state, had become the prevailing doctrine. Similarly, sovereignty on its other side was now regarded by Bodin and Hobbes as supremacy over everything within the state, over all persons and all laws. Before Bodin's time the word 'sovereign' had been used loosely of any authority that was the highest of its kind. Thus in France there were three sovereign courts of law; in England in the fifteenth and sixteenth centuries so unimportant a person as a mitred abbot had been officially referred to as a sovereign.[3] For Bodin, although he allows some exceptions, there can be only one sovereign, the absolute and perpetual power in a state, bound not by human laws but only by God and the law of nature. Hobbes, unlike Bodin,

[1] So the Vulgate: the Authorized Version says in the same place merely that his heart is as firm as a stone. The whole chapter (Job xli) is full of phrases which may be applied in Hobbes's sense.

[2] *Six livres de la république*, 1577. The Latin version is Bodin's own, but the English by Richard Knolles (1606) is not good.

[3] For instances see Sir Roger Twysden, *The Government of England*, pp. 16–17.

is a philosopher, and he carries this principle with the utmost consistency into every department of political organization. There can be no anarchy if there is a single power to make regulations and compel submission. To fulfil his purpose of keeping the peace the sovereign must therefore control the armed forces, control opinion by governing the church and education, permit no rallying-points for competing loyalties in autonomous corporations, above all, permit no division of authority between the different organs of government. In England the king, lords, and commons are no more than three separate factions. The nature of a sovereign is that it is irresponsible. No man or body of men can have rights against it. In power it is irresistible, ruling the subject body and soul; that is as it should be, for 'the good of the sovereign and the people cannot be separated'.[1]

In thus sweeping away the belief in the accountability of rulers and the other belief, equally common in the seventeenth century, in the independence of the spiritual power, Hobbes was building on foundations quarried from the new scientific spirit of his age. He had been an amanuensis of Bacon, a correspondent of Descartes, a friend of the materialist Gassendi. With such associations it is not surprising that he took a rigidly determinist view of human nature. Just as Newton explained all the movements of physical bodies by the single principle of gravitation, so Hobbes and the other determinists of the seventeenth century explained all human action by the one principle of self-interest. 'Will', says Hobbes, 'is the last appetite in deliberating.' Society rests on purely egoistic passions. When these have free play in the state of nature, the life of man is 'solitary, poor, nasty, brutish and short'. The social contract is a single act by which men agree together, once and for all, to resign their liberty to the sovereign which they create by that act. This is, as Hobbes describes it, a covenant

[1] This does not mean that Hobbes's doctrine is 'totalitarian'. In accordance with his individualist premisses he holds that laws which are 'not needful' are 'not good', and thus his Leviathan is indifferent to everything that does not affect peace and security. In this sense he anticipates the point of view of *laisser-faire.*

of all with all, but it is not a revocable contract, void if the sovereign breaks it. It is an unconditional delegation of powers to him. The sovereign is no party to it. To talk of his breaking it has no meaning, for all obligation is subsequent, not previous to it. 'No law is unjust.'

Except for certain insoluble difficulties in his position, Hobbes works out his argument with rigid consistency, and he even appears to be more consistent than he is. As his theory of the passions is purely egoistic, he has no right to use the notion of obligation; but he constantly tries to get on his side the prejudices and associations of words like 'ought', by using these words without reminding the reader of the peculiar sense they have in his system. The word 'unjust' has for him no meaning except 'what is contrary to the will of Leviathan': to use it obscures the essential contradiction in the attempt to base absolute non-resistance on self-interest. If Hobbes's psychology is accepted, then government has no foundation except a *de facto* foundation: successful resistance has just the same *de facto* foundation. Leviathan is by definition a power sufficient to coerce men and keep them in awe. Hence 'the obligation of subjects to sovereign is understood to last as long as and no longer than the power lasteth by which he is able to protect them'. It is no wonder that Hobbes's doctrine failed to become the orthodox defence of monarchy. He admits that its greatest difficulty is 'that of the practice', for such a Leviathan as he conceived had seldom, if ever, existed. Doubtless he was right in retorting that few states had ever been free from civil wars and seditions; but if these dissolved Leviathan, then the successful rebel was always in the right. Hobbes's argument was valid only against unsuccessful rebellion: it came to no more than the argument of a contemporary who, advising his fellow countrymen to submit to the victorious Puritans, used the words: 'He that spits against the wind spits in his own face.'[1]

Another passage in which Hobbes reveals his weakest

[1] Antony Ascham, *Discourse of what is Lawful during Confusions and Revolutions of Government* (1648), pt. II, c. ix, sec. 6. This expression was already current: the *Oxford Dictionary of English Proverbs* gives an example of 1612.

point is that in which he grants to a man condemned to death the right to resist the hangman. He may do that because, on the principle of self-interest, no one can make a covenant to sign away his own life. But if this is so, why should any one make a delegation of any other rights? Why should it be impossible to renounce life and yet possible to renounce any chance of the good life? This weakness is detected by Spinoza. In his *Tractatus Politicus*, published after his death, which came in 1677, that great man gave what may be called, in spite of the fundamental differences between their respective metaphysical systems, a stricter version of Hobbes's determinist politics. At one crucial point he does indeed break away. The end of the state is for him as for Hobbes 'pax, vitaeque securitas'; but there is a difference between the mere absence of war and real concord, so that when Spinoza speaks of peace he has in mind 'vitam humanam . . . quae non sola sanguinis circulatione et aliis quae omnibus animalibus sint communia, sed quae maxime ratione, vera mentis virtute et vita definitur'. This is consistent with Spinoza's following Hobbes in ignoring the element of consent in government and devoting all his attention to the other side of it, command and obedience. There was no popular control in the Dutch republic, of which he was himself a denizen, the state in which sovereignty pressed less hardly on the individual than anywhere else.[1] So much did he profit from this circumstance that his own writings could probably not have been published in any other country. Yet he follows Hobbes in denying any rights to the individual against the state, in the assertion, to use modern words, that all rights are social. That he did so is on the one hand due to the cast of his own mind, on the other to the predominance of the problem of security in the political life of the century. Men were to pursue high ends, but under the state and not in defiance of it.[2]

[1] We must no longer say that he was acquainted with John de Witt or enjoyed his protection; see Dr. Japikse's article in *Bijdragen voor vaderlandsche geschiedenis en oudheidkunde*, 6th ser., vi (1928), 1 ff.

[2] This is very different from the liberal point of view of the *Tractatus Theologico-Politicus* of 1670: see A. Menzel, *Wandlungen in der Staatslehre*

Such were the principles of the two classical writers on the side of authority. Around them swarmed the inferior exponents of divine-right theories, but of them little need be said. In this age the doctrine of the divine right of kings was rather a popular, uncritical, belief than the work of great thinkers. It is, indeed, an error to suppose that there is anything absurd or eccentric in it. If the name of God is taken broadly as meaning a moral order of the universe, an idea which, in the seventeenth century, was seldom expressed by any other word, then all positive and optimistic theories of the state are theories of divine right. 'Vox populi, vox dei', for instance, is a divine-right slogan. The more elaborate theory that kings ruled by right divine had been invented as a counterblast to the papalist doctrine of the later Middle Ages: it was to the kings that the divine right was attributed because they were leading the opposition to the papal claims. Since those days the fortunes of monarchies had given rise to an absurd perversion of the doctrine by which it was made to support monarchy against the interests of the subject. In this stage it is stated thus in an Address of the University of Cambridge to King Charles II in the year 1681:[1]

'We will still believe and maintain that our kings derive not their title from the people but from God; that to him only they are accountable; that it belongs not to subjects, either to create or censure but to honour and obey their sovereign, who comes to be so by a fundamental hereditary right of succession, which no religion, no law, no fault or forfeiture can alter or diminish.'

Sunk to the level of mere adulation, this theory has no place in the history of serious thought except as a stimulus to contradiction. That contradiction was, of course, not mere denial but counter-argument. The opposite doctrines, those which made the consent of the governed a necessary element

Spinozas (1898), reprint from *Festschrift zum siebsigsten Geburtstage S.E. Dr. Joseph Unger* (1898).

[1] I take this quotation from the late Dr. Figgis's book, *The Divine Right of Kings* (2nd ed., 1914), p. 6, which with his other book, *From Gerson to Grotius*, 1907, forms the best English introduction to the political thought of the period.

in government, had consequently their own development parallel to that of the theories of authority. It would be misleading to call these theories democratic,[1] since only a few extremists thought of all men whatsoever as the members of the state. Some such extremists there were, and, as in revolutionary periods everything is questioned and everything suggested, there were even some who put forward the idea of women's suffrage; but for the overwhelming majority of the liberal thinkers of the seventeenth century citizenship was to be limited to a narrow class, usually a propertied class, but sometimes the class of the godly. In making the consent of this citizen body the foundation of government, they were preparing the way, but not doing more than to prepare the way, for the later and truly democratic view, according to which every individual man as such ought to be given political rights and functions. Three streams may be distinguished in their thought. First there was mere opposition. It is always the tendency of a party which is not in power to appeal to some great unenfranchised force. Thus in democratic countries a beaten party will often try to revive the monarchical tradition, while in monarchical countries, such as were those of the seventeenth century, the party with its way to make will tend to aristocracy or democracy. Contemporaries were well aware that anti-monarchical doctrines were apt to be advocated for such opportunist reasons: Filmer shrewdly pointed it out when he said of tyrannicide that 'Calvin and Bellarmine both look asquint this way'.[2] Beneath their opportunism, however, these two great antagonists had a second thing in common: they both carried forward something of the medieval doctrine that law implies assent as well as authority. It was no longer possible for natural law or the law of God to be enforced by the courts as overriding positive law: to that extent the modern state had won its battle. But it had not rooted out from theory the Aristotelian principle that in

[1] I do not mean to disparage the valuable book of Mr. G. P. Gooch, *English Democratic Ideas in the Seventeenth Century*, 2nd ed., ed. by H. J. Laski, 1927.

[2] In one of the opening paragraphs of his *Patriarcha*, posthumously published in 1680.

the best state laws, not men, will rule. That idea survived the polemics of Hobbes. As Catholics ranged themselves more and more on the side of monarchy or obedience, it became more exclusively the ally of a third anti-authoritarian force, the Protestant individualism. It was an inevitable, if unforeseen and undesired, consequence of the Protestant revolution, that where the individual had loosened the power of ecclesiastical authority, he should also shake that of secular political authority. The main line of development of the theories of consent thus lies for this time in the Protestant countries. It is there that great writers were able to vindicate the belief that there is nothing abhorrent to the nature of society in the withdrawal of popular support or even in active opposition to a government.

A writer who must be named as one of the leaders in this argument is Johannes Althusius (Althus or Althusen) who lived from 1557 to 1638.[1] The influence of his book *Politica Methodice Digesta* was limited. It is true that there were five editions in his lifetime and three posthumous issues, and that it was published in five different towns; but from its rarity it appears that these editions must have been small, and in character it is essentially a professorial text-book. It gives a systematic, indeed an over-formal, rendering of the anti-monarchical social contract theory as the sixteenth century had known it; but for Althusius this is no longer only a theory which can be used to justify revolutionary opposition, it is a positive doctrine of the foundations of the state. Taking for granted the existence of society as a going concern, Althusius sees it as made up of individuals who agree to the prescribed terms on which its benefits are available.

His book is famous for some distinguishing ideas to which its author gives comparatively little prominence. The first of these is its 'federalism': Althusius thinks of the state not as a single unit but as a multicellular body, an interesting antici-

[1] The work of O. von Gierke, *Johannes Althusius*, 3rd ed., 1913, although it has faults, is very valuable both for its immediate subject and for the general history of modern political thought. There is an important discussion of Althusius in Dr. P. S. Gerbrandy's lecture *Political Stability, National and International* (1944).

pation of an idea which has become important in our own age. Some of those who have prized his book most highly have misunderstood this, and several English writers have taken him as the theorist of Dutch federalism. His theory of political obligation is the best statement of the view of the Calvinistic elements in the Dutch republic, who never entirely succeeded in making their view prevail; but he probably had a wider area of political fact before his mind. He was a German, and although he knew the Dutch republic well, he knew it from outside. The federalism he had primarily in mind was that of the Holy Roman Empire. What is really original is his clear distinction between the state and the other associations. He makes the state a sub-division of the political community. Sovereignty he attributes to the people, and he maintains that its exercise may be delegated and even divided among a plurality of persons: these theses he maintains against Bodin. But he smothers much of his thought in formalism, that is in the attempt to classify all forms of association in mutually exclusive divisions and, with a great lack of historic sense, to explain all irregular types as divergences from very empty and generalized normal forms. His view of the relations of church and state is Erastian. In this he represents the modified form of the Calvinist system which prevailed in Germany; but he is behind the best liberalism of his day in that he upholds the state's right and duty of religious persecution.

The cause of toleration had indeed made considerable advances before Althusius wrote. Before the end of the sixteenth century there had been practical politicians in more than one of the western countries who deprecated the infliction of death for heresy and advocated the toleration of all forms of Christian belief. In Germany it was so easy to move from a Catholic to a Protestant state or vice versa that executions for heresy ceased. In the Roman Catholic countries tolerance advanced, though unequally. France, indeed, ceased to allow the Calvinists the liberty they had enjoyed. Heretics and blasphemers were still put to death, on the rare occasions when they appeared, in Spain and Portugal; the last such execution in Scotland did not occur until 1696, in England there was none after 1612, in France none after 1748. There were small principalities in eastern Europe[1] where there was full religious equality for all Christians and even for Socinians; but no western country granted full political rights, full citizenship, without regard to creed. In the Protestant countries, however, diversity of belief became much commoner. The machinery of repression fell into disuse. The Reformation had changed the problem of church and state. At first, in most countries, the settlement had been on the lines of the formula 'cuius regio eiusdem et religio'; there was to be freedom for each sovereign to choose his own religion, but each state should enforce uniformity among its own subjects. Even in the countries of the Calvinist confession this had resulted, as we shall see, in a more or less complete supremacy of the state over ecclesiastical concerns. Within the territorial states, however, there grew up independent sects, and in the more tolerant countries the practical problem came to be not how could the church maintain its freedom against the state, but how could there be free churches side by side with the state church. As early as 1631 Roger Williams, the Welsh founder of Rhode Island, was advocating unlimited toleration even of Jews, Catholics, and infidels. He was, however, an isolated forerunner. The statesmen of Europe could not be converted to that view until thought had progressed in many of its branches. The most notable single book on that side was not published until 1681, the long *Commentaire Philosophique* in which Pierre Bayle discussed the Biblical text 'Compel them to come in'. Bayle's first concern was to write against the forcible conversions, such as the 'conversions by dragoon' of Louis XIV; but he had the courage to go even farther than most men openly went even in tolerant Holland, where he had himself taken refuge, and to advocate the toleration of atheists. Among earlier writers that one who had the greatest passion for liberty, John Milton, did not propose to extend tolerance so widely, and even John Locke, whose plea for toleration appeared later than Bayle's, fell short of him in this respect.

[1] See p. 187 above.

Milton in his *Areopagitica* of 1644 addressed the Long Parliament in favour of uncensored printing; and in doing so, as in many other passages of his works, he drove the argument for freedom down to its fundamental principles. It is true that he wished to limit toleration to 'neighbouring differences or rather indifferences', but with him the argument for toleration had broadened out into a general argument for liberty. In *Comus* he had written of virtue that 'she alone is free', and the strict correlation of virtue, reason, and freedom runs through all his work, verse and prose alike. He shows that the system of licensing the press implies 'the grace of infallibility and incorruptibleness' in the licensers, that the prohibition of bold books can but lead to the 'laziness of a licensing church'. Above all, it 'hinders and retards the importation of our richest merchandise, truth'. The commission of the licenser enjoins him to let nothing pass if it is not received already, and 'if it come to prohibiting, there is not aught more likely to be prohibited than truth itself, whose first appearance to our eyes bleared and dimmed with prejudice and custom is more unsightly and unplausible than many errors'. In true virtue freedom is itself an ingredient, for 'reason is but choosing', and 'they are not skilful considerers of human things who think to remove sin by removing the matter of sin; that virtue, therefore, which is but a youngling in the contemplation of evil, and knows not the utmost that vice promises to her followers and rejects it, is but a blank virtue, not a pure'. Milton had his inconsistencies. He was no theorist, but a prophet, and with prophetic insight he coined the noblest phrases of seventeenth-century political thought. The appeal against the authority of the state was thenceforth not to a competing authority, whether of an ecclesiastical hierarchy or of a natural law embedded in juristic treatises; it became an appeal to freedom. Freedom of opinion was the first stage. Freedom to live and to pursue happiness was soon to claim the worship that Hobbes demanded for peace and security.

From Milton's golden words it is a long descent to the prosaic reasonableness of John Locke, yet Locke too was a great man, and he owes his position in the history of political ideas to the fact that, in a disappointed and sobered world, he gave a workable version of Milton's ideal. Besides being a doctor, a theologian, a philosopher, a civil servant, and a drafter of colonial constitutions, he was the thinker of the English Whigs. The restored monarchy of Charles II raised up against itself an opposition which had to restate and again maintain the principles of resistance to arbitrary government. Locke did this in a thoroughly English way, matter-of-fact and fair, and in a way suited to the times, moderately, and without pedantry. It was also without romance. Locke wrote that 'the commonwealth is a society of men constituted only for the procuring, preserving and advancing their own civil interests'. In his *Letters on Toleration*, of which the first and most important was published in 1689, he maintained that there should be both freedom to express opinions and freedom to associate for religious purposes. He wished to exclude the magistrate from all religious matters. 'This chiefly because the power of the civil magistrate consists only in outward force, while true and saving religion consists in the inward persuasion of the mind, without which nothing can be acceptable to God, and such is the nature of the understanding that it cannot be compelled to the belief of anything by outward force.' There is nothing really new in this: the distinction between *actus transeuntes* and *actus immanentes* had been drawn in the Middle Ages; and Locke excludes from toleration those who deny the existence of God as well as those whose opinions are contrary to civil society and those who claim, in virtue of their religious belief, any sort of civil power and authority. But his argument served as a justification for an attitude which in practice was soon to go beyond this temporary compromise.

Where Locke shows a more genuine confidence in freedom is in his second *Treatise on Civil Government* of 1690. Here he is the apologist of the English Revolution of 1688: he writes 'to justify to the world the people of England', and for this purpose he lays down 'the true original, extent'—that is a significant word—'and end of civil government'. The form which his doctrine takes is the social contract, the destructive type of that theory, in which it justifies the accountability of the ruler to the people. In contrast with Hobbes, he begins from a comparatively optimistic view of the state of nature. He calls it a state of liberty but not of licence. He does not make it a golden age of noble savages, but a state in which there are natural law and natural rights, of which property is one. It is not a state of war. War may occur in it, but it is compatible with peace. It is the same as the lawless but not necessarily warlike relation of sovereign states. The law of nature prescribes truth and the keeping of faith as duties of men as such, so that the social contract is not quite the beginning of all morality, but is itself made binding by this prior law. Society is founded not to escape from war but to end inconveniences and the risk of war. Men give up their equality and 'executive power' for the object of preserving liberty and property. Locke lays himself open to objections by laying down the exact terms of the contract and by a feeble attempt to treat it as an historical reality. He repeatedly says that 'government has no other end than the preservation of property'. That is to limit its scope doubly, both by excluding religion and other matters, and by protecting property itself against communistic or confiscatory interference. His definition of property is famous: he regards it as the product which a man gets by mixing his labour with a part of the common stock and thus appropriating it to himself. It has a respectable ancestry in Roman Law but a most disreputable descendant in the Marxian theory that a man has the right to the whole product of his labour: Locke himself avoids any such conclusion by naïvely including in a man's property not only the product of his own labour but also that of his horse and his servant, that is to say his employee.[1] In fact his individualism has here led him into hopeless errors. In trying to protect property he has represented it as a mere natural right, failing altogether

[1] Locke's work on the allocation of land in Carolina may have influenced his formulation of the theory of property. There is no evidence that he was acquainted with an interesting work by the American colonist John Winthrop, where, as in some other works, the natural right over the earth is distinguished from a civil right 'by enclosing, and peculiar manurance'.

to see what Hobbes saw to the exclusion of everything else, that it is a social, in fact a legal, creation.

The intentions with which men resigned their natural liberty can, according to Locke, only be fulfilled if the state has a certain constitution. An absolute monarchy will not do, because in it the monarch will be in a state of nature in respect of his subjects. There will be no judge between sovereign and subject in the event of their falling out. Therefore 'the first and fundamental positive law' must be the establishment of a legislature chosen by the public, which must be supreme, because that is implied in the nature of a general law and in the foundation of society on consent. The legislature may, like the British parliament, be summoned by the executive and be in session only intermittently, from time to time; but it must be supreme. The executive must be distinct: this is the germ of the famous eighteenth-century dogma of the separation of powers. The legislators must not administer their own laws because they might do so with partiality to themselves, and, on the other hand, an executive must be more a permanent and standing authority than a legislature need be. The executive, in turn, must not be allowed, by extending any power lawfully belonging to it of summoning or dismissing the legislature, to make itself supreme over that legislature. Society is an enterprise for specific purposes, and government 'a fiduciary power to act for certain ends', a trusteeship. The contract is tacitly renewed by every one who, being born into the society, does not renounce his allegiance, a renewal well likened by a later writer to the refusal of a person who is carried aboard ship in his sleep to escape by jumping overboard. But if government exceeds its powers, especially if the executive encroaches on the legislature, then the contract is terminated. When the government gives up or forfeits its powers, but only then, every one may fall back on his supreme right of self-preservation. Locke has also the usual arguments of common sense against unconditional obedience. His doctrine of revolutions has weaknesses similar to those of the rest of the work. It is grounded in natural rights, and it does not succeed in its attempt to provide a definite test of when a government has justified revolution against it, a decision which must always rest on a judgement of the concrete circumstances at a particular time. It did, however, end the dominance of the crude and simple doctrine of the sovereignty of kings. It reaffirmed the belief that the original sovereign is society as a whole, and that the powers of government are derived from this.

Locke's doctrines, with all their hesitations and inconsistencies, became an accepted orthodoxy in England in the eighteenth century, one of the periods in which English thought exercised its greatest influence abroad. He was the main ancestor of all the individualistic liberalism typical of the eighteenth century in England, France, and America, and one of the forerunners of the various schools of liberal thought in still more modern times. His influence was partly due to his habit of writing with little reference to preceding speculation, and with an easy assumption that no previous knowledge was needed to understand his arguments. None the less he did hold together, if somewhat loosely, the principal threads of the liberal thought of the century of which he saw the end. He convinced the world that the purpose of government was the public good. He established the respectability of tolerance and of revolution in moderate measure.

XV
MATHEMATICS AND SCIENCE

THE subject of mathematics is to many people distasteful, if not alarming; but something must be said about it here, though with the least possible use of technical language, because it held the central position in the history of seventeenth-century thought. This was not only one of the greatest periods of progress in mathematics, but it was the period in which mathematical knowledge had the greatest influence on knowledge in other spheres, and consequently, we may say, on life in general. It is unnecessary to say much about the reason why this great period of mathematics came when it did. In the remote past these studies had owed their origination to practical needs. They had sprung from the desire to measure land or to calculate debts. It was still possible for some practical need to set a mathematician's mind to work: Kepler found out how to estimate the contents of a tun of wine; and Pascal and Fermat dealt with the problem of the just division of stakes in an unfinished game, each of them, in the process, making remarkable discoveries. But these outside stimuli were of hardly any importance. For a long time mathematical knowledge had been pursued for its own sake, and it was already the supreme example of the disinterested search for truth. Even without the casual hints to which some of the great discoveries were attributed, they would doubtless have been made, and to search for external causes for them would be as foolish as believing the fables about Newton seeing the apple fall[1] or Descartes watching a fly as it crawled across the ceiling. The main truth is that the several branches of mathematical inquiry were pursued by one man of genius after another, each starting where the last left off, and that they had already reached a point whence the next steps led to great revelations

[1] Since these words were published, a new authority for the story has appeared in Stukeley's *Memoirs of Sir Isaac Newton's Life*, ed. A. H. White (1936); but though I cannot guess what, if anything, Newton really told Stukeley I see no reason to alter the text.

and to the uniting under general rules of many truths which had before been apprehended only separately and not in their connexion. The proof of it lies in the fact that some of the most important discoveries were approached by different thinkers along separate lines, and were at last enunciated by two or more men working independently of one another.

Mathematical knowledge, as it is taught and learnt, consists largely of devices for calculation; but these devices, from a very early stage, have been worked out as belonging to certain bodies of theory which are called the branches of mathematics. The progress of each of these has, however, been accompanied by the increasingly clear knowledge that they are mutually connected, and that truths which had seemed to belong only to one may be expressed in terms of the others. In both these respects in the late sixteenth century and in the seventeenth so many advances were made that it is impossible even to give a list of them here.[1] There were a considerable number of mathematicians who are universally regarded as belonging to the first rank, and amongst these only a few can now be named. It will be convenient to mention by preference those who are also important in other respects than as pure mathematicians, since that method will give clues to the relations between mathematical and other studies.

The progress of pure mathematics was general: it is difficult to think of any respect in which some improvement was not made. Notation, the language of mathematics, was much simplified and amplified: the familiar signs $> < \times$: :, for instance, were introduced, besides the use of brackets, and the decimal system, a form of which was devised by Stevin, whose contributions to military science we have already noticed.[2] The converging efforts of several great men in the first half of the century brought logarithms into use. Logarithms are the best example of a calculating device

[1] I find it impossible briefly to describe the state of mathematical knowledge at the beginning of this period without assuming some slight acquaintance with mathematical terminology. I therefore omit that attempt. The reader who has the small amount of technical knowledge needed will find an admirable summary in the *Cambridge Modern History*, vol. v, ch. xxiii, by W. W. Rouse Ball and Sir Michael Foster. At the end of the volume there is a good bibliography for the whole of the subjects of my present chapter.

[2] Above, p. 113.

which can be employed by a person who does not understand the principles on which it depends. The slide-rule was invented, a well-known instrument by which the results of logarithmic calculations can be read off without actual calculation.[1] In innumerable kinds of scientific, technical, and even purely business calculations, slide-rules and tables of logarithms are in constant use, and any one who has used them knows how much they simplify operations.

They could not, of course, be invented except by men with a deep knowledge of the principles on which they rest, principles which they studied not only in their bearing on the relations of numbers, but also in their bearing on trigonometry. These studies were amongst those which led to the greatest discovery of the century, the turning-point at which mathematical knowledge in general fixed its course for about two centuries to come. This was preluded also by new methods in geometry, amongst which we may name that of René Descartes, whose greater fame as a philosopher we shall have to consider in another chapter. Descartes imported the idea of motion into geometry. He drew attention not merely to the properties of figures but to those of curves, lines of which the relation to two fixed lines at right angles to one another may be expressed by equations, so that every point on the curve has the geometrical property expressed in the equation of that curve. This idea, coupled with the previous application of algebra to geometry, gave rise to co-ordinate geometry, to which belong the curves or graphs so familiar in scientific and statistical writings. By the time this and other contemporary improvements had been reached, the ground was ready for the great achievement, the calculus. The calculus is, as its name tells, a system for calculating, and it may be called the supreme example of a system which can be employed to advantage only by those who understand it. Nor can it be understood without some effort: it is a body of knowledge which can all be applied to obtain precise results, but which is as far as possible from being a collection of rules of thumb. It deals with the

[1] Early slide-rules may be seen in the Lewis Evans collection of early scientific instruments in Oxford and other similar collections.

relations between variable quantities. It provides the means of solving an endless variety of problems of which the general character is that they involve ascertaining the relations between changing quantities. When it is remembered that geometrical relations could, since Descartes, be represented as expressions of movements, and so could be dealt with by the calculus, it will be seen that it provided an almost universal, though still imperfect, method for all difficult calculations, and a better theoretical framework for all the previously acquired stock of knowledge about mathematical relations of all kinds. The modest pride which most people feel when they begin to grasp its principles from simplified text-books is an index of the greatness of its discoverers, to whom they are as the passenger in a Cunarder is to Columbus.[1] Yet it was not exactly a discovery, but rather a completion and a synthesis. There was a controversy, which cannot be remembered without regret, as to the relative shares of credit due for it to Leibniz, whom also we shall encounter as a philosopher, and Sir Isaac Newton. They both deserve, as do several forerunners, of whom one was Pascal, the highest gratitude and admiration.

Nothing is easier for us, who live in a scientific age, than to see that the results of these mathematical discoveries have ramified all through human society. At one time it was necessary for those who preached the utility of the mathematics to point to their direct application to daily life. Newton showed how to make optical lenses of other than spherical forms, and he served his country well as master of the Mint. His great Dutch contemporary, Christian Huygens, improved the telescope and pendulum clocks, and invented the balance spring for watches.[2] Pascal made the first calculating machine. But these are toys in comparison with the sum of the influence of these men. That must be traced through the different branches of applied mathematics and science. Several of the greatest pure mathematicians of the century

[1] The best way of taking the first step to the historical study of the calculus is to use G. W. Brewster, *Commonsense of the Calculus* (reissued 1925).

[2] See p. 19, above.

were also great in such allied subjects as mechanics, optics, and astronomy. In mechanics Stevin did good work. His younger and far more famous contemporary Galileo Galilei did much to clear up the fundamental principles of the science: all the world knows that he studied the pendulum and the velocity of falling stones. He was the first to discover that a pendulum of fixed length, whether it swings through a long or a short distance, takes the same time for its swing. He experimentally disproved the elementary error of Aristotle that heavy bodies would fall in a vacuum more rapidly than light bodies. He did much to clear up the theory underlying facts like these. It is, however, common to indicate the importance of his work by saying that he anticipated Newton's first two laws of motion, and possibly also the third: the earlier achievement is estimated by its approach to the later. Newton's complete and coherent system of dynamics, expounded in his *Philosophiae Naturalis Principia Mathematica* of 1687, was his greatest single achievement. The *Principia* took its place at once as one of the world's great books, and its publication marked an epoch in the study of the action of force on bodies. One particular set of bodies had, from the earliest times, been a favourable subject for this study, those which are picturesquely called the heavenly bodies. Astronomy, the oldest of our exact sciences, had entered on its new era in the early sixteenth century, when Copernicus worked out his system according to which the earth and the planets revolved round the sun. Since then progress had continued, both in the accumulation of observed facts, in which the telescope gave its aid, and in their mathematical interpretation. Copernicus, indeed, had not fully proved his discovery, and his system did not win general acceptance among scientific men until it was improved by the astronomers of the late sixteenth and early seventeenth century. Johann Kepler, the son of one of Alva's German mercenaries, perfected the geometrical scheme of the solar system and added much to the power of astronomical prediction. Newton, with the new methods of calculation, was able not only to recognize that the law of gravitation was the key to the theory of all this, which Sir Christopher Wren and others also independently recognized; but he was also able to do what none of them could do, and give the proofs of the discovery.

Going through the other branches of scientific knowledge, we find in almost all of them great names and notable advances. It is true that the farther we recede from pure mathematics the less striking these are; but they are very remarkable even when mathematical methods are scarcely used at all. In chemistry there was vigorous work all over Europe. Alchemy was left behind, and chemistry, though it was directly useful for medicine and metallurgy and other purposes, was disinterestedly pursued as a science. By the middle of the century, by improved manipulation and observation, there had been collected a great mass of information about the character of different substances. In particular, gases had been recognized as being distinct from air and vapour. The importance of the balance had been grasped, the importance, that is, of quantitative method. Balances, however, had not reached anything like a modern standard of accuracy, and another defect of apparatus held chemistry back, the ignorance of how to make glass vessels which would stand pressure without bursting. The greatest reputation in chemistry was that of the Hon. Robert Boyle, one of whose works, *The Sceptical Chymist*, published in 1662, is still often read. Boyle swept away a tangle of alchemical theories and groundless traditional conceptions, insisting on the importance of experiment and sound deduction. He treated chemistry simply, and, for the time being, adequately, as the study of the composition of substances, and he made some effective applications of his own methods. When he is said to be the father of modern chemistry, it is not, however, meant that the science had yet altogether entered on its modern period. His successors were still hampered by misconceptions similar to those he had dispelled, and chemistry had much spade-work still to do in the eighteenth and nineteenth centuries.

Among the biological sciences, those concerned with living bodies, the most forward were naturally those which dealt with the human body and supplied knowledge to the physician and surgeon. These too had leapt ahead in the age of the renaissance. They had made a fresh start when, as their chief method, they substituted actual dissection for the study of classical texts. They now profited from the improvements in apparatus and method in other sciences. When Galileo was a professor at Padua, an English student was there who afterwards rose to great fame as an anatomist and physiologist, William Harvey. The discovery which Harvey announced in his book *De Motu Cordis et Sanguinis* (1628) is usually, though not with complete accuracy, described as that of the circulation of the blood. There can be no question that it is of capital importance. From the point of view of method and of the history of science in general it is remarkable, though there is nothing mathematical in it, as turning on the employment, the first employment in this sphere, of a quantitative argument. Harvey traced the course which the blood follows through the body by watching how much of it passed through the different stages. He made many other contributions to knowledge, including some of considerable interest in the department of embryology, and his was a period of activity in all the studies on which he touched. The impulse given to biological studies by him and his predecessors and successors soon made its influence felt outside the circle of those immediately useful to medicine, though for some time to come it was in that narrower region that it chiefly told. Not only the underlying theory of medicine profited from it, but there were great advances in medical practice.

In our own day it is a well-understood axiom that human biology is a part of general biology; but the full realization of that fact was impossible until the two had been brought together under an evolutionary conception, and in the seventeenth century, such a conception being altogether absent, the progress of animal zoology and botany was but loosely linked with that of human anatomy and physiology. Nevertheless they were progressing. The microscope was winning remarkable successes. The Dutchman Leeuwenhoek, one of the three or four great pioneers of microscopy, may be mentioned by name. He was an amateur, the holder of a modest official position, and he used his microscopes on a great variety of objects.[1] Whereas Harvey had only inferred that the blood circulated in the minute capillaries, Leeuwenhoek and others actually saw it there in circulation. His work was unsystematic and discursive, but some of his contemporaries in his own and other countries were turning out methodical and beautifully illustrated descriptions of the structure of animals, birds, fishes, and insects. On the whole, however, this zoological work must be described as preparatory. The great discoveries were yet to make, and the days were still remote in which biology would come to its full stature as a science. Similarly in botany, the active and able workers of this period must be regarded as precursors of the greater men of the eighteenth century. Still more is this true when we pass on to the other sciences which our modern point of view has brought into focus with biology. Only the barest beginning was made with palaeontology, the study of the ancient forms of life which are preserved in fossil remains. That fossils were relics of ancient living organisms had been guessed long before, but it was not universally admitted at the end of the century, and those who admitted it were uncertain how many kinds of stones to include in the class. Geology itself had, in fact, hardly reached the rank of a science. Rocks and strata were being industriously observed and described, and much shrewd guess-work was going on about their origin. Here again one of the ablest minds was that of the universal Leibniz, whose general ideas on the subject resemble those of modern geology except that he thought of past geological disturbances as catastrophic, and the strata as having been rapidly and tumultuously deposited. But he was conjecturing, not working as a scientist. He was not very far ahead of the English clergymen who about the same time were already speculating with greater or less intelligence about the relation of the strata to Noah's flood. They were doing less for the

[1] He knew no language but his own: see the account of Molyneux's visit to him in Birch, *History of the Royal Society*, iv. 366.

future of geology than the quieter men who were gathering specimens, classifying, and surveying.

There was, then, although some of the sciences were only beginning to respond to its touch, a general scientific movement. Great discoveries were being made, and they were more and more being brought into systematic relation with one another. The best minds in all countries were busy with scientific problems. Science had even become fashionable. Kings and princes, like Charles II and Prince Rupert, dabbled in it; the academies were equally filled with men of genius and men of quality. They were not more attracted by the possible utilitarian advantages of exact knowledge than by its intrinsic interest. The distinguishing quality of the western civilization of which we are the children had revealed itself: the union of the man of science with the man of action and affairs. We must look more closely at the spirit of this union, in the hope of finding in this early phase a clear indication of its meaning. First we must ask what were the leading intellectual characteristics of the movement. That one was the mathematical spirit we have amply seen. The greatest of the triumphs had been won by mathematical reasoning, and the lesser successes had all been aided more or less directly by weighing and measuring, and by the exactness of thought which is most perfectly exemplified in mathematics. This has led some eminent authors to describe the movement as rationalistic, but the name of rationalism has in this matter often been used very loosely. If rationalism means, as it ought to mean, the spirit which relies on the guidance of reason, of systematic thought, we cannot fail to identify rationalism as one of the components of this great movement of thought; but we must not remain blind to the presence of another component, altogether heterogeneous, which assisted it and set its tasks.

This was the spirit to which the name of empiricism is given. It is the search for truth not by the mere use of reason but by experience, in particular by observation and experiment. What distinguished Galileo, Boyle, the anatomists and the forerunners of geology from their predecessors was not merely their use of quantitative methods, but their use of these two means of providing themselves with materials for calculation. They not only weighed and measured, and reasoned about the figures they so obtained; before doing this they had collected or artificially created the objects which they wished to investigate. Even the astronomers had at their disposal a vast body of data, to which the telescope was making notable additions. This immediate contact with the facts of nature, this attention to what is perceived by the senses, is a characteristic of modern science as we have it in our own age, and is what most clearly distinguishes the science of the seventeenth century not only from remote earlier times, but even from the time immediately preceding. A clear token of the change is the fact that this century saw the first museums, the first botanical gardens, and if not the first collections of animals and plants, at least the first seriously scientific collections both of the physical creatures themselves and of careful records of them in drawings and engravings. In popular repute much, if not all, of the credit for this change is given to Francis Bacon. He is regarded as having once again brought philosophy down from heaven, and directed the attention of inquirers to the first-hand examination of nature. It is true that in his works he urged them in this direction. He himself made some actual experiments though without making discoveries. He had the further merits of great literary skill and influence, and a really comprehensive view of many branches of science, which he sought to bring together into a system. He had, however, serious limitations. Harvey said that he wrote about science like a lord chancellor, and Bacon's conclusions on scientific questions justify the jibe. He did not, for instance, accept the simple discoveries of his contemporaries about electricity and magnetism. What is even more important, he did not really grasp the way in which the direct knowledge of nature was to be of service. He thought that one set of men should collect facts and others reason about them. He was too hopeful about discoveries which were to be made according to a preconceived plan. The use which he wished to make of the facts when they were gathered was in principle the same which medieval science had made of the facts at its command. The philosophies on which medieval science was based regarded the universe as consisting of different classes of existents, and based their explanation on classifying. Bacon also regarded classification as the business of science: he did not exhort his contemporaries to the more fruitful method on which they were of their own accord setting out, that of measuring and calculation.[1]

The union of rationalism, particularly the confidence in mathematical reasoning, with empiricism, was not clearly foreseen by Bacon, and the two tendencies do not always harmonize together. Their harmony in this period was unusually complete, and it so happened that, while they cooperated in the work of building up new knowledge, they were also at unison in destroying old errors or imperfect beliefs. They were both at work in doing away with the old accepted opinions, the scholastic orthodoxy, in all scientific matters. The schoolmen had accepted what they understood in their Aristotle, and erected on that foundation an elaborate edifice of subtle reasoning. The scientists now knew more than Aristotle had known: in anatomy, in astronomy, in mechanics, and in chemistry they found that he was sometimes in error and sometimes in ignorance of the facts. At the same time the newer rationalism, measuring where the schoolmen had only classified, laid bare laws of nature, systematic relations between the facts, which had not been detected. It was no longer possible in these branches of science for the machinery of authority and censorship to sustain beliefs which had been definitely disproved. In 1633 the Inquisition passed a censure on Galileo for upholding the Copernican system. It was very surprising, for one pope had declared that the Copernican system was not heretical, and another had accepted the dedication of Galileo's book. Personal factors on both sides had something to do with this reversal of fortune. It cannot be denied that on the astro-

[1] This last point is brought out in various passages of Dr. A. N. Whitehead's provocative book, *Science and the Modern World* (1926).

nomical question the inquisitors were wrong and the condemned man was right, nor that before they obtained his submission they used a threat of torture. This incident therefore, along with the burning of Giordano Bruno, whose heresies were less purely scientific, in 1600, forms part of the long indictment against ecclesiastical obscurantism and persecution. Pleas in mitigation have been urged.[1] The sentence passed on Galileo was no more than to recite once a week for three years the seven penitential psalms: the imprisonment during pleasure, to which he was also sentenced, lasted no longer than three days. The threat of torture was never meant to be carried out. These comparatively mild proceedings were the culmination of a controversy which had lasted for many years, and they were the last of their kind. No other eminent scientist of the century was made by the Inquisition to recant his opinions. But there is no doubt about the indignation of the aged Galileo himself: nor can it seriously be doubted that the freedom of science was new and not easily won.

The overthrow of the scholastic systems on their scientific side had diminished the respect not only for their own exponents and for Aristotle, but for much else besides. It had delivered the first blow at the Greek and Latin classics in general. In the days of the Renaissance their authority had been enthusiastically accepted, the more so because they provided rods to beat the medieval idols. Now their turn had come: in natural science, at least, they were superseded. Ecclesiastical authority in the intellectual sphere was weakened in another way besides the brushing aside of the censures of the church in scientific matters. The advance of science, by revealing law where it had lain hidden, altered, as it must constantly alter, the notion of the miraculous. In the Middle Ages it was almost universally believed that miraculous interferences with the course of nature were literally everyday occurrences. They were and always had been produced by God and the saints, by devils, by prayer or by witchcraft, in a thousand ways and in every kind of material,

[1] For instance in Pastor, *History of the Papacy*, xxv. 286 ff., xxix. 42 ff.

from raising the dead and staying the wind to replenishing a broken cask of beer. At no time was there a complete lack of men who for various reasons regarded all this in a sceptical spirit, and from the sixteenth century this spirit was able with increasing frequency to peep out in conversation or even in print. Montaigne's *Essays*, which appeared in the year of the Spanish Armada, became the favourite book of the intellectual 'libertines', and they showed plainly enough the doubts of the man of the world. Before Queen Elizabeth was dead, Shakespeare read a translation of Montaigne and wrote a play in which one of the characters tells us plainly: 'They say miracles are past; and we have our philosophical persons, to make modern and familiar, things supernatural and causeless.' [1] By the end of the century these persons were far more numerous, far better equipped with arguments, far more widely heeded.

Many illustrations of this might be given. Astronomy alone supplies a number, amongst which the greatest in its effect on common ways of thinking was the triumph of the Copernican system, but the most striking was that of comets. Until late in the seventeenth century comets were believed not only to portend great calamities in human history but also to be without natural causes in the ordinary sense. Halley's calculation of the orbit of the comet of 1682 put an end to this. The critical spirit spread beyond the experimentalists and observers themselves, and there were two writers who addressed themselves to the great public on the question of comets, using this problem as a lever for what may be called propaganda against the blind acceptance of opinions which are vouched for by nothing except popular belief and irrelevant authority. One was Bayle, a man of books and not of telescopes, a scholar.[2] The other was Balthasar Bekker, a Dutch Calvinist minister, who was neither exactly a scholar nor exactly a scientist, but something more nearly resembling a philosopher. Bekker's works have been somewhat unfairly called unreadable, but as examples of well-directed thought they are at least worthy of comparison with

[1] *All's Well that Ends Well*, Act II, sc. iii.

[2] See above, p. 227, below, p. 334.

Bayle's.[1] In one of the great controversies where the new spirit met the old, Bayle did not definitely range himself on the right side, whereas Bekker struck stout blows in the front rank. This was the controversy about magic and witchcraft, one of the decisive encounters between science and authority.

Witch-hunting and the cruel punishment of witches had gone on all over Europe for centuries. In the later Middle Ages they had become more thorough and methodical, perhaps because there was an increase in the offences against which they were directed. Many innocent people perished; but there were many other victims, on both sides of the borderline of insanity, who had acted with criminal intent, although the crimes they tried to commit in league with the infernal powers were impossible and imaginary crimes. Most of the offenders were poor and ignorant, and so their acts and confessions were senseless and chaotic; but there seems to have been a widespread and traditional witch-cult, with its own ritual, practised in secret assemblies. It included blasphemous inversions of Christian ceremonial and also sexual elements which may be connected with ancient fertility rites; theologians could scarcely dismiss its demonology as absurd, and so it caused indignation and alarm. In the early seventeenth century both witchcraft and its repression grew worse, especially in countries where conditions were specially unfavourable to good sense and humanity. Such a country was Germany during the Thirty Years' War. In the first half of the century the French tribunals were active, and there were many prosecutions in England. In the Dutch republic, however, no witches were burnt in the seventeenth century: the Calvinist clergy were unable to stir up the civil authorities against them. The Protestant countries as a whole, however, had a worse record in this matter than the Catholic. The

[1] The English translation of part of his *Betoverde Weereld* (1691–3), with the title of *The World Turn'd Upside Down* (1700), unfortunately does not include the concluding part, an admirable criticism of the stories about ghosts and witchcraft collected by Joseph Glanvill (see below, p. 248); but this may be read in French.

Spanish Inquisition itself was more lenient in its punishments for sorcery than the secular courts; except for an outbreak of severity in Navarre in 1610 its prosecutions were few and were conducted without the use of torture. Italy also had a good record: many persons condemned by the Inquisition were not handed over to the secular arm, and from about 1620 the popes and inferior authorities set to work to remove the abuses of witch-trials. During the period of the most savage witch-hunting in both Catholic and Protestant Germany, no witches were burnt in Rome.

From about the middle of the century there was a general improvement. In 1672 Colbert directed that no more accusations of sorcery should be received in France, and he commuted many capital sentences to banishment. In the last twenty years of the century only seven sorcerers were burnt in France: the last or one of the last judicial executions was in 1718. The English laws against sorcery were not repealed until 1736, but in practice the process ran closely parallel to that in France: the executions came to an end in 1712. In the last decade of the seventeenth century, however, there was a savage persecution of witches in Massachusetts, which was applauded by the great English Puritan, Richard Baxter. In Scotland, where the record was even blacker than in England, and torture was freely used to obtain confessions, the last execution is generally held to have been in 1722. The last in any part of Europe seems to have occurred in Switzerland just sixty years later. The killing of witches died down everywhere *pari passu* with a decline of belief in their miraculous, diabolical powers; and this change of belief may be traced in the published controversial works. They began with a cautious and moderate work by a Protestant German doctor in 1563. Montaigne carried the discussion farther. The philosopher Malebranche mentions that in his time some of the French parlements had ceased to burn witches, and that in their jurisdiction the number of known witches had declined. In 1664, when two witches were hanged in Suffolk with Sir Matthew Hale as the judge and the celebrated author and physician Sir Thomas Browne as one of the witnesses for the prosecution, the better minds were already on the other side. In the same year as the last English execution for witchcraft there came the notorious trial of Jane Wenham in Hertfordshire. This woman was prosecuted by clergymen and was found guilty; but on the representations of the judge she was reprieved. The journalist Addison recommended the public to suspend its judgement, saying that he believed in witchcraft, though not in any particular instances of it;[1] but he was behind the times.

A view has been widely held about the relation between the paper controversy and the change in judicial practice which must be regarded as mistaken or misleading. Lecky, in his remarkable book *The History of the Rise and Progress of the Spirit of Rationalism*, maintained that the growth of what he called rationalism was due not to the persuasive effects of certain definite arguments, but to changes in the 'tone and habit of thought' or, in the phrase which he approvingly quotes from Joseph Glanvill, a seventeenth-century writer on these matters who had more style than judgement,[2] in 'climates of opinion'. The climate of opinion, according to Lecky, 'is created, not by the influences arising out of any one department of intellect, but by the combination of all the intellectual and even social tendencies of the age'. With this we can freely agree, though we must not make it an excuse for shirking the difficulties of the history of thought. We must not refuse to look for the antecedents of particular opinions and lightly refer them all to the spirit of the age. So in this instance we must not wholly accept the paradoxical view of Lecky that so long as the matter was controversial the weight of argument in published books remained on the side of the belief in witchcraft. More recent writers have put this in a more extreme form; but a careful examination of the original authorities shows that they are wrong. It is easy to enumerate men of great literary gifts or of high reputation

[1] *Spectator*, 14 July 1711.

[2] Glanvill's best-known book is the *Sadducismus Triumphatus*, first published under that title in 1681. It was from this Glanvill that Matthew Arnold took the story of the Scholar Gipsy.

in other spheres who believed in sorcery.[1] A number of eminent lawyers, both judges and advocates, held, with the conservatism of their profession, that cases of it were legally proved by evidence. There were even some amongst the great scientists who casually and incidentally gave their sanction to the belief, nor were its opponents all distinguished for their powers of reasoning. But no juggling with these facts can upset the real balance of the argument: whenever the belief was seriously and candidly examined in the light of the new standards of criticism, those who denied it had the better of the contest.

Witch-burning was ended by a change in the tone of thought, but one in which direct arguments against the possibility of witchcraft were a powerful ingredient. It had been upheld by the authority of churches, the citation of biblical texts, and that ecclesiastical interpretation of the universe according to which the intervention of spirits was constant and ubiquitous. Its defeat consequently assisted and was assisted by the other reverses of that spirit. Within the churches themselves, especially among the Protestants, there was much destructive criticism of the miracles of the church, and this led to the first sceptical inquiries into the miracles of the Bible itself. Descartes attempted to form a theory of the physical universe which should be self-contained, accounting for everything by natural law without interruption by spiritual agents. It was not long before theologians were venturing out to see how far the sphere of the miraculous should be restricted in the narratives of the Old and New Testaments. They did not as yet push very far, but nothing was needed except persistence to take them into the open sea of criticism. Spinoza, the most rigidly consistent thinker of his time, gave in his *Tractatus Theologico-Politicus* of 1670 one of the supreme examples of the interpretation of historical texts. He dealt mainly with the Old Testament, but by a method which could easily be extended

[1] As is done, for instance, in Miss Margaret A. Murray's book, *The Witch-Cult in Western Europe* (1921), pp. 10–11. The list of disbelievers there given is perfunctory: Hobbes, Spinoza, and others should have been named.

to the New. He guarded himself against the imputation of maintaining unlawful beliefs, and he did not bring to bear on the miracles any criteria of credibility drawn from natural science or profane history. To some extent he may have been actuated in this by motives of caution, for caution was needed even in Holland, where his speculations involved him in certain risks. But even with these self-imposed restrictions of method, he was able to prove, by strictly interpreting the Old Testament in the light of the knowledge which it by itself supplies, that the apparent miracles were manifestations of law. Within a few years before and after the publication of this penetrating work, various learned men working with more limited, usually linguistic, aims, and without challenging orthodox beliefs, whether Catholic or Protestant, began the tradition of moderate biblical criticism. Their work marks an extension of the spirit of science.

It marks also an interesting point in the prelude to the conflict between that spirit and the churches. These now had to answer new objections: much of their theology, Catholic and Protestant alike, seemed to require at least a restatement in terms of the new knowledge and new speculations. Conflict was not, however, for the present directly joined. The force of spiritual censures was weakening. There was no inherent incompatibility, though there was a long tradition of quarrels, between religious institutions and free inquiry. The scientists were countenanced and favoured by the powers that were. Some of them were too powerfully befriended to be attacked, and most were too busy with their own investigations to engage in disputes with the orthodox on theological matters. Newton, though not satisfied with the arguments for the doctrine of the Trinity, was unconscious of any discrepancy between science and religion. Within the sphere of science he claimed to be writing not speculations but certainties: he proudly wrote '*hypotheses non fingo*'. But, like Descartes, he explicitly, if coldly, asserted the existence of God: 'This most elegant structure of the sun, the planets, and the comets', he wrote, 'could not have come into being except by the design and the authority (*consilio et dominio*) of an intelligent and powerful being.' He encouraged the rather ludicrous efforts of his friend John Craig, a canon of Salisbury, who in his *Theologiae Christianae Principia Mathematica* of 1699, a title modelled on Newton's own, demonstrated by formal propositions the date of the second coming and the ratio between the highest attainable terrestrial happiness and the believer's happiness in paradise. The rent was beginning to open, but it still seemed capable of repair. It was for the eighteenth century to bring out the objections of historical science and for the nineteenth to add those of the natural sciences against the orthodox beliefs of Catholics and Protestants alike. We are not concerned with those disputes, nor with the efforts at reconciliation.

We must, however, notice an equally important division which the scientific revival of the seventeenth century widened. In the book we mentioned a moment ago, Spinoza, although he is scrupulous to offer no open affront to the beliefs prescribed by civil authority, scornfully sets himself against superstition. There ought to be no compromise between science and those errors which spring from ignorance and fear. When the fight between science and religion came on, the scientists fell into many errors from an inability to understand what it was that the believers were defending. They had perhaps some excuse for supposing that the churches were in alliance with superstition, for they clung to survivals of what once had been sciences and had become no better than the formless mass of prejudice and folk-lore. This mass of error has always existed, and to suppose that much was done in the seventeenth century to dispel it from the minds of the general population would be an utter mistake. On the contrary the scientific revolution affected only a small number of men, an aristocracy of intellect. The very fact that it made such profound changes in knowledge and beliefs restricted it to the few and made its percolation to the many inevitably very uncertain and very slow. It acted quickly on the outward organization of daily life because the aristocracy of intellect was closely in touch with the aristocracies of power and wealth. The public status of the academies, the knighthoods and the government offices granted to the men of thought are reminders of their alliance with worldly greatness, and they were new things in this age. But this rise of knowledge in the social and official scale meant a greater segregation of the educated class from the generality of mankind. The change in the status, the dress, the manners of the man of science or learning was symbolic of the gulf which now divided him from the labourer, the artisan, even the burgher. Not that the intellectual division in itself was altogether new. Educated men have always been a conscious minority. But now their distinctness was accentuated in two ways. On the one hand it was brought into relation with the divisions of social classes. On the other hand it became itself so extreme that communication between the educated and the uneducated was harder than it had ever been before. The ideas of the most learned Dominican of the fourteenth century were only a more profound and exact expression of the beliefs of the peasant or the craftsman. No one translated into tales and pictures the new creed which was expressed in the English motto of Huygens: 'The world is my country, to promote science my religion.' To this period belong, however, the feeble beginnings of the apparatus which was ultimately to try to re-establish the broken contact. There were writers of 'popular science', like Fontenelle, and journalistic intellectuals, like Addison. The crusaders of scientific education for the people were, however, still to come. As we shall see, it was only certain groups of men and women among the churches who tried to spread knowledge among the poor. Although they were no longer the leaders of thought, it was the adherents of the old theological ideas who kept alive the tradition of the medieval church in carrying, by such means as were appropriate, enlightenment to the masses. For long generations, however, it was to be one of the primary facts of European civilization that the educated man was not as other men were. Only by mighty revolutions in thought, in politics, in social organization could strength return to the ideal, not of an educated world, but of a world in which the highest education of the few should invigorate, instead of maiming, their fellowship and sympathy for men as men.

XVI
PHILOSOPHY [1]

THE name of 'philosophy' has been applied at different times to very different things. In the seventeenth century and long afterwards it was commonly used to mean what is now called science. The title of Newton's great book on mechanics and astronomy announced, as we have seen, that it dealt with natural philosophy. To take a more extreme example, one of the old writers on naval architecture says that it was in the reign of Charles II that British men-of-war were first constructed on philosophical principles. On the development of philosophy in that sense we have already touched: we must now turn to what is so called in our own time. This is much harder to define, but for our present purpose it will suffice to say that philosophy is the comprehensive and at the same time the most strictly critical study of the ultimate problems which are raised in the search for knowledge. These problems arise in many different ways. There are the problems of what Locke called 'the original, certainty, and extent of human knowledge'. When these are investigated, they are found to be intimately involved with problems about the nature of existence, reality, time and space, the universe, God. These in turn may be approached from quite other starting-points, from perplexities about the nature of man, about the real meaning of his moral principles or his sense of beauty, or his social institutions. Philosophy is thus usually divided into departments, such as logic, metaphysics, ethics, aesthetics, political philosophy; but it also forms a whole, and the history of philosophy, at least in this period, may be treated as one history.

The period does not, indeed, form a detachable chapter in that story any more than it does in economic history. It contains the beginning of a chapter, the most abrupt of

[1] Among the many histories of philosophy, that which will perhaps be found most useful as an introduction is Adamson, *The Development of Modern Philosophy* (1903). Among fuller works E. Cassirer, *Das Erkenntnisproblem in der Philosophie und Wissenschaft der neueren Zeit*, vols. i–ii, 3rd ed. (1922), should be named.

all the new beginnings since the rise of our philosophical tradition amongst the ancient Greeks; but the discussions of philosophers kept to the same general lines throughout the eighteenth century, and, in a sense, have kept to them until our own time, so that to sketch the development of philosophy in the seventeenth century is like reporting an unfinished debate. This is less true of political philosophy than of the other branches, because political thought must always be punctuated by changes corresponding with those of political fact; but even when it is concerned with politics, philosophical thought has a character of its own. The development of philosophy, once it had made its fresh start, was unlike that of the sciences. While they added one discovery to another and seemed to be perpetually advancing, it was concerned with establishing a stable foundation for its work of construction. One thinker laid down a principle, a second questioned its presuppositions, while a third and a fourth, examining its consequences, found that it was really ambiguous and might be developed in either of two contrary directions. Thus, the successive discoveries of the sciences made comparatively little difference to the philosophers. They were aware of what the scientists were doing and of what was going on in practical life. Indeed, all those whom we shall mention by name were remarkable for their versatility. Every one of them has been mentioned or will be mentioned for his eminence in at least one other pursuit besides philosophy in the strict sense. Not one of them was a professor of philosophy in a university. They were not narrow specialists, but men of wide interests, awake to the movements around them. Nevertheless as philosophers they had to return again and again upon their tracks. The events and discoveries of a decade or a century made little change in the data of their fundamental inquiries.

The way in which these data present themselves must indeed be altered by a really decisive change in the general ways of thought and life, and such great movements as the Renaissance, the Reformation and counter-Reformation, the scientific revolution, could not but lead to changes in philosophy. Medieval philosophy formed indeed a great body of discussion, incorporating much from the ancient world, and containing in germ a great deal of the philosophy which was to supersede it. Modern research has even detected in it anticipations of the central phrases and ideas of the succeeding age. It had been fashioned in four centuries of close reasoning, which left a permanent legacy, not least in the vocabulary of philosophy, the tools of thought, a legacy of which the value is more highly estimated at the present time than it was by the iconoclasts whom we are about to notice. The medieval systems were, however, closely bound up with certain habits of mind in which it was no longer possible for the pioneers of thought to persist. Those systems had been dogmatic. The philosophers had put their conclusions forward as certainties. It was not merely that they thought their own reasoning faultless: that was no peculiarity of theirs. Their certainties were confirmed by authority external to philosophy. Some beliefs were sanctioned and others were condemned by the church: dissent was heresy. Not only had the church an unquestionable authority, but something of the same subservience was paid to the writings of Aristotle and other classical authors, even when they wrote on questions of ascertainable fact. Truth in general was sought in the pronouncements of those who had authority. The methods of reasoning were studied and elaborated, especially in what is called syllogistic logic, but there was always a point where reasoning must stop, and submit to dogma. In another way the horizon of philosophy was narrow: attention was mainly directed to the problems of God and man, while nature was comparatively neglected. To be sure, the natural sciences were beginning to emerge. Alchemists, magicians, astrologers, physicians, authorities on herbs and hawks and hounds were often ingenious men, and their books prepared the way for modern science. They made, however, little permanent impression on the prevailing opinions about ultimate problems. There were sharp controversies over some of the fundamental questions about the nature of the universe, but, in general, all the parties to them worked and reworked certain time-honoured veins of thought.

All this now belonged to the past. The humanists had

derided the scholastic studies; the Protestants had flouted the authority of the church; the new rationalists like Montaigne had turned aside from the hope of certainties and declared themselves for scepticism, suspense of judgement, doubt. Above all there was the new activity in mathematics. A fresh start in philosophy had to be made, and it was made to such purpose that from this time the history of philosophy can be understood with very little knowledge of what went before. However much the philosophers of the seventeenth century carried along with them of the language, the methods, and the assumptions of their predecessors, they did not study the works of those predecessors as they had been studied before. Even in the most conservative intellectual circles much of the best medieval thought was soon neglected and forgotten. This was not the work of any one man. There may even be some dispute about exactly where to place the transition. It is sometimes traced to the Italian and French thinkers of the sixteenth century. In England, some time ago, it was usually traced to Bacon. Bacon was the herald of the scientific movement, but, as we have seen already, he was not a representative of its mature character, and it is also true that he did not ask the questions with which modern philosophy has chiefly been busied. That was done by a much younger contemporary of his, an equally conscious innovator, the mathematician Descartes, whom we have noticed as the inventor of co-ordinate geometry. René Descartes, a French gentleman of small independent means, was a pupil of the Jesuits and served as a volunteer in the early days of the Thirty Years' War. He spent most of his working life in the congenial atmosphere of Holland, and died in Sweden, whither he had been summoned by Queen Christina. Of his works the most important are the short French *Discours sur la méthode*, published in 1637, but written at an unknown earlier date, and the Latin *Meditationes*. In these he gave a systematic view of science and what it implied, but, with the detachment of the modern scientist, he let politics and the arts alone. He accepted scepticism as his starting-point, and from it set out to deduce his conclusions by a procedure as strict as that of mathematics. To him as to his contemporaries, mathematical knowledge was impressive because it appeared certain and exact, its truths orderly and connected, its presuppositions simple and self-evident. He hoped to unlock all the secrets of nature by keys like that of mathematics.

Such an attempt was due and even overdue, but it could not be made on Bacon's plan of amassing facts and trying to rise from them by induction to general laws. Bacon looked forward to the acquisition of new knowledge; but he dealt with all his problems in the same way as the schoolmen, by systematically arranging all that was known, and then arguing from it. Descartes started not from what was known but from the fact of knowing, from the operations of the individual mind. He admitted that it was legitimate to doubt everything, and then he asked whether there was not some truth which, by its very nature, did not admit of doubt. Such a truth he found in his famous proposition, 'Cogito, ergo sum', 'I think, therefore I exist'. What takes place within the individual mind so that it is directly aware of it, understanding, willing, perceiving, whatever it may be, proves beyond the possibility of doubt that that mind exists. Thus Descartes has got a certainty as a starting-point, and from it he goes on to infer other truths which necessarily follow from it. We cannot follow his arguments in detail, but must content ourselves with saying that he deduces the existence and attributes of God, and also the existence and nature of the external world. For him the existence of a thinking being implies that of an infinite and perfect being who is pure spirit, pure thought, as contrasted with the limited, imperfect individual. This being must be omnipotent, that is, absolutely free, and must be immortal and veracious.

An external world is also implied. Descartes asserts that the consciousness of the outside world cannot be due either to God or to our own minds, so that something else must exist outside ourselves and God. This external world is not, indeed, all that it appears to be. Distrust of the evidence of the senses is partly justified. A distinction may, however, be made between what is real in this world and what is illusory. Its real qualities are the mathematical qualities.

Its essence is to exist in space, that is, to have length, breadth, and depth.[1] Thus certain knowledge of the external world is mathematical. The whole account of it which Descartes gives is in terms of physics: it is deterministic and materialistic. He has distinguished mind, whether human or divine, sharply from all extended bodies. But in the spatial world there are animal and human bodies. In these mind and matter somehow act on one another, and Descartes has to explain their mutual relations. His view of their interaction is the least convincing part of his system. He cannot regard living bodies as exempt from the operation of physical laws. However the mind acts upon them, it must do so in conformity with the mathematical laws of existence in space. But it is necessary to explain how a mind, which is in its nature sharply distinguished from the external world, can act upon it. One of the least happy of his theories was that by which he tried to explain the action of the human mind on the body: he thought that in the pineal gland, in the centre of the brain, the mind and the 'vital spirits' met and communicated. He regarded animals as automata, and doubted whether they were sentient. Not only was he in a philosophical difficulty here, but he was out of touch with the contemporary knowledge of anatomy. Yet although it is easy nowadays to see that Descartes' speculations on 'psycho-physics' raised more questions than they answered, he had gone far beyond the crude view of mind and matter which is held in our own time by untutored common sense, the view that a human being is 'a ghost in a corpse', or that the mind is in the body like a boatman in his boat. By re-emphasizing the contrast of mind and matter, and rejecting the previous attempts to bridge the gap between them, he set a problem, and the setting it was far more important than his failure to find a solution.

The works of Descartes met with a mixed reception. He himself never broke with the Catholic church; but among

[1] This distinction between 'primary' and 'secondary' qualities is sometimes spoken of as characteristically new in science from the time of Galileo, but so far from being new it was known to the Greeks, and it is found in at least one of the Greek books of the Apocrypha, where we are told that God 'ordered all things by measure and number and weight' (The Wisdom of Solomon, xi. 20).

theologians and the authorities who controlled the professors in universities there was much opposition to the spread of his doctrines. Among the leaders of philosophical thought, however, their influence was profound. They became the point of departure for subsequent thought, and in equal degree for the thought of both the two opposing schools between which philosophy was divided until, at the end of the eighteenth century, another man of genius again summed them both up and left posterity again to renew the division in altered forms. The philosophy of Descartes mirrored the thought of his age in combining rationalism with empiricism. Each of these tendencies has something of its own to contribute to knowledge, but neither can subsist without the other, and it is one of the tasks of philosophy to reconcile the two without depriving either of anything that is due to it. Most of the attempts to do this have assigned greater importance to one tendency and minimized the other. Those among the followers of Descartes who took over so many of his doctrines as to be called 'Cartesians' insisted on the rationalist side of his teaching. They accepted the view, which was sometimes though not always his, that the infinite is prior to the finite, and they tried to smooth out the contradictions and difficulties which were detected in his system. Several of these Cartesians were men of considerable intellectual acuteness. They made ingenious attempts to find a satisfactory formula for the interaction of mind and matter, and these, although no one believes in them now, were of service to the progress of thought, because, when they in turn came to be examined, their rejection helped on the process of stating the problem better. Far different in character and strength was the influence exerted on posterity by another man who followed out the rationalist line of advance from Descartes. This was Baruch d'Espinoza, or in Latin Benedictus de Spinoza, a Jew who lived in Holland, but whose unorthodox speculations had led to his being expelled as a very young man from the Jewish community of Amsterdam. He had acquaintances among the most distinguished men of the age, but supported himself, at least partly and for a time, by the tranquil, if difficult, handicraft of grinding and polishing optical lenses. As we have already noticed, he wrote remarkable books on political theory and on the interpretation of the Old Testament, but it was perhaps in his purely philosophical works that his genius found its highest expression. The most important of these were the *Ethica* and the short treatise *De Intellectus Emendatione*, both published after his early death, which occurred in 1677. Their greatness was not appreciated until long afterwards, and by an absurd injustice their author's name became a byword for atheism, a description of his beliefs which only malice could have foisted on stupidity.

Spinoza was a follower of Descartes in his leading ideas of method,[1] so much so that he wrote two of his books in the form of propositions with as much mathematical notation as the subjects permitted, and the closest possible approximation to mathematical proofs. He had, however, to a far higher degree than Descartes, and indeed to a degree that has seldom been surpassed, the desire to make an absolutely coherent system. He regarded the whole universe as a unity. For him God alone was real and he regarded all finite, imperfect, and particular things, to use his most famous phrase, 'sub specie aeternitatis'.[2] The existence and attributes of God he demonstrates in much the same way as Descartes; but he adds elaborate, and it must be admitted obscure, speculations on the essence of existence or reality. For him the conditioned, the world of extension and finite consciousness, is only the sum of the modes of the unconditioned substance, the really existent, which is God. He does not succeed in explaining how the unity of God is connected with the diversity of the finite modes: but several of his leading principles enable him to make the contrast between them

[1] The question of Spinoza's other 'sources' is difficult. Meinsma's charming biography *Spinoza en zijn kring* (1896), which superseded all previous studies on that side, is now itself partly superseded, and is of little value for Spinoza's thought. Joachim, *A Study in the Ethics of Spinoza* (1901) is critical but not historical. Among recent works which attack the historical problem Dr. Leon Roth's essay, *Spinoza, Descartes and Maimonides* (1924), puts forward a view which seems to be refuted by T. de Boer in *Mededeelingen der Koninklijke Akademie*, Afd. Letterkunde, vol. lxiii.

[2] I prefer not to attempt here the delicate task of translating these words.

seem to be illusory. He identifies the laws of nature with the laws of the mind. He does not recognize two distinct systems of law in the universe; on the one hand, the physical laws regulating matter in accordance with the principle known to the sciences that causes must be quantitatively equal to their effects, and on the other hand, the laws of the mind which, in its freedom of choice, acts in accordance with what it thinks to be reasonable. He supplies an interpretation in which these two systems are identical. The physical laws are what we know of the operation of the divine mind: nature is God. At the same time the human mind acts according to the same divine law: man does not invent and pursue purposes any more than do the natural bodies. There are no final causes. The only causes of events are rational grounds for their occurrence. Thus mind is the idea of body, and the unity of the universe is revealed by a determinist theory of man and a spiritual theory of nature.

All this is hard to follow and harder still to epitomize. It is worked out in the original with great acuteness, force, and consistency; but it might well be supposed that the result would be an arid structure of abstractions. It is nothing of the kind. Even when he is engaged in his severest logical tasks, such as that of discussing the nature of error, Spinoza keeps close to life. In order to justify his view of the human mind he has to do away with the hard and fast distinction between truth and error, and reduce it to a difference of degree. One of the illustrations he uses is lifelike and even funny: 'My yard flew into my neighbour's hen.' His theories were meant to give solutions of the difficulties which occur in the course of actual thinking, and, more generally, his philosophy was meant to solve the supreme practical question, of how we ought to live. He called his great book 'Ethics'. His determinism did not render meaningless the distinction of good and bad. He believed, we may say, in self-determination in God by the intellect. The life of reason included the existence of a moral community and of the social contract. Although in a sense he eliminated the individual from the world, he favoured no ascetic self-denial, but taught, both in his books and in his own noble life, a reasonable virtue, for which the highest good was the intellectual love of God, a part of the infinite love of God Himself.

Six years after Spinoza died there arrived in the safety of the Dutch republic a distinguished political refugee from England, who, in the intermittent leisure of an active life, was already putting together the doctrines which were to make him, in his later period of prosperity in his own country, the founder of a distinctively British school of philosophic thought. This ran its more or less separate course until late in the nineteenth century. Great as the contrast was between its empirical attitude and the rationalism of the continental Cartesians, the British school also took its rise from Descartes. John Locke agreed with Descartes in his confidence in clear and distinct knowledge, and in the fundamental difference between thinking minds and extended matter. But, although he was as versatile as the other great philosophers of the century, and had as great an influence on political and general thought as on philosophy, there was one conspicuous difference between his outlook and that of Descartes or Spinoza or Leibniz. He was the one great philosopher of the seventeenth century who was not of any note as a mathematician. Hence he approached the problems of philosophy in a way of his own. The purpose of his *Essay concerning Human Understanding* of 1690 was practical or religious: he wished to refute the view of knowledge which underlay the opposition to reason and freedom. He wrote, with singularly little open allusion to the writings of his predecessors, in the character of the plain man, applying the methods of common sense. That was an assumed character, and in reality one of the greatest difficulties in understanding his doctrines is to disentangle the considerable amount of previous speculation which lies embedded in them; [1] but at the same time there was something radically new in his method. He said that it was 'plain historical', that is to say, descriptive. He intended to give not what the word would mean now, an account of the development of the mind in time, but a description of it: we should

[1] Gibson, *Locke's Theory of Knowledge* (1917) is a valuable contribution to this subject.

use the word in the same sense as his if we said that he aimed at giving a 'natural history' of the mind. His statement of his purpose is curiously like that given in his work on government. Just as he set out to define the extent of government, so one of the things he means to examine about knowledge is its extent. He follows the new way of ideas: that is, he takes the contents of the individual mind and examines them one by one, to see what they are. He too concludes that besides the individual mind there exist God and the external world, but he reaches this conclusion not by deducing what is implied in any knowledge, but by the psychological method of classifying the different kinds of ideas and finding how each of them is related to reality.

The mind, according to him, is, to begin with, entirely empty; it is a *tabula rasa*, a blank surface. Everything that it comes to contain must be impressed upon it by experience. It is in passive contact with reality. The senses and reflection furnish it with simple ideas, sights, sounds, and so forth, and also such simple ideas as perception, willing, remembrance, none of which in either class can be surpassed in clearness and distinctness. These are the data of knowledge, but they are not the only kind of knowledge. The mind does not merely receive them; it also works upon them. By combining them together it makes complex ideas, ideas like a dozen or beauty or theft. Besides sensation, therefore, there is another source of knowledge, reflection, and the two together make up experience. According to Locke they do not both correspond with the real in the same way. The simple ideas arise independently of the activity of the mind, and so they must correspond with real causes; but the complex ideas are made by ourselves. Thus, although all knowledge consists only of a collection or comparison of ideas, it is difficult for Locke to avoid the conclusion that everything that results from reflection, that is, the whole of our ordered knowledge, is further removed from reality than are the data of sense. He revives the 'nominalism' of one of the opposing schools of medieval philosophers, according to which all 'universals', all such terms as 'a dozen' or 'beauty' are merely names, which come into existence after the simple ideas, the units or the colour and figure which they group together. He has moved to the opposite point of view from that which led Descartes to say that the infinite was prior to the finite. Nor does he escape from the disparaging conclusions about human knowledge which this implies. It cannot go beyond our ideas, and these are imperfect and may be misleading; our knowledge is and must be less than our ignorance. If he had been rigidly consistent he would have had to admit that the knowledge built up by reflection is only hypothetical, and, since it is something more than the transient ideas which are its only materials, must all be precarious. He was not, however, by any means a rigorous or even a lucid thinker, and he loosely combined his empirical scepticism with a confidence in the general conclusions which had been certainties to the rationalistic method of Descartes.

This unstable union was bound to break down when criticism was applied to it, and that was the task of the later writers of the English school. Very soon after Locke's death they had begun to drive the empirical arguments to their logical conclusions, and, if we were following a merely chronological plan, we should have to say something about George Berkeley, bishop of Cloyne in Ireland, a great man who stands to Locke somewhat as Spinoza stands to Descartes. Berkeley had already disclosed some of his leading ideas in the early years of the reign of Queen Anne. It has been said of him that, of the three realities recognized by Descartes, the self, the external world, and God, he does away with one, the external world, and leaves only the other two. That is, at all events, a possible interpretation of what he stated in the memorable words: 'that all the choir of heaven and furniture of the earth, in a word all those bodies which compose the mighty frame of the world, have not any subsistence without a mind, that their *being* . . . is to be perceived or known.' It is easier to see whither Locke was tending from Berkeley's penetrating analysis than from his own cloudy arguments. But Berkeley too can best be understood by following the development of his ideas in the hands of David Hume, and even of the later thinkers down to our own time. There is thus no natural stopping-place, and

Locke is closer to the eighteenth century than to the seventeenth. He resembles the typical thinkers of the eighteenth century in being more concerned with political and human problems than with those which had been conjured up by the scientific revival. In comparison with those of his predecessors his works make easy reading. They have none of the difficulties of a mathematical form, the Latin language,[1] a hard vocabulary of technical terms. The ambiguity of his thought was no obstacle to its gaining a great influence over the educated classes of Europe generally, and, paradoxical as it may seem, it was Locke the empiricist who initiated the tendency which earned for the eighteenth century the name of the age of reason. The 'reason' of Voltaire and Diderot, the acid solvent which prepared the way for the French Revolution by discrediting the prejudices, the traditions, and the stability of an uncriticized social order, was not the rationalism of the physicists. It was merely common sense. Indifferent to the ultimate questions of philosophy, it rejected beliefs which could only be justified by far-fetched speculations, and institutions which inflicted visible and immediate injustice and inconvenience. In this combination of utilitarianism with shortness of theoretical reach, Locke was, if not its teacher, still its father. In knowledge he would admit no innate ideas, above the reach of criticism. In the state he would admit no arbitrary power. He defended Christianity as simple and reasonable, but he claimed in religion the same freedom of the individual mind which he had taken as the starting-point of his theory of knowledge.

Although he was fourteen years younger than Locke, the German philosopher, Gottfried Wilhelm Leibniz, in later life created a baron of the Holy Roman Empire, had more of the seventeenth century in him than of the eighteenth. He may, indeed, be called the typical figure of the age which preceded the age of reason. There is something of the baroque in his prodigious energy and versatility. Like Locke he was a politician, a pamphleteer, a philosopher, a theologian. He was also an eminent historian and a mathematician

[1] The *Letter on Toleration*, originally published in Latin, was quickly translated into modern languages.

of very high rank. He claimed to have made an independent discovery of the calculus, and he certainly supplied it with the notation which is still in use. He had read everything and knew everybody. In his youth he had been attracted by the works of Descartes; he conversed with Spinoza; he wrote a criticism of Locke's *Essay*, chapter by chapter. His own philosophy he never thoroughly worked out in a comprehensive treatise: it is to be found in a large number of partial and even occasional writings, and that which is most commonly read, the *Monadologie*, is a compendium which can be read in an hour and was written for the enlightenment of the famous soldier Prince Eugene of Savoy. The leading principles of Leibniz were reduced into a systematic form by others after his death, and thus became the reigning orthodoxy of the German universities during the greater part of the eighteenth century; but their influence was at that time restricted to the professed students of philosophy. Outside the universities French thought ruled in Germany. Only in recent years has the influence of Leibniz in foreign countries shown its full potentialities. New developments in mathematical physics have led to a renewed and closer study of his work, and many of the suggestions which he threw out in a more or less thoroughly considered shape have proved to be valuable guideposts.[1]

Leibniz, like Spinoza, tried to overcome the duality of mind and matter which Locke had taken over from Descartes. His way of doing so was, however, sharply opposed to that of Spinoza. Spinoza had found no room in his system for the conception of purposes, final causes, and in effect none for time and space. He had absorbed them into his conception of the divine substance; but Leibniz, although he too wished to arrive at a substance which should unite the two kinds of reality, sought for something capable of doing this and at the same time preserving those characteristics of matter and of human action which Spinoza had denied. This new doctrine of substance, at which he gradually arrived after many corrections of his arguments, was the central point of his system. It resembles the idea of quantity

[1] See Russell, *The Philosophy of Leibniz* (1909).

on which the calculus is based. A mathematician using the calculus regards any quantity as a function of something variable. Similarly Leibniz regarded the real not as an unchanging substance which underlies all apparent changes and differences, but as itself the principle of difference and change. For him substance was force. What constituted being was an activity, and activity he regarded in the light of the new mechanics. The Newtonian conception of mass had done away with the necessity to suppose an external compulsion which caused the movements of bodies, and had refuted the view of the Cartesians that although the total quantity of force in the world was constant, spirits could intervene to modify the direction of force. Accepting this new point of view, the philosophy of Leibniz represented the whole universe as consisting of self-moving units.

These units were the 'monads'. As a mathematical quantity is made up of an infinite number of small quantities, so the universe is made up of an infinite number of indivisible, simple substances. This is not, however, merely a resuscitation of the old theory of Democritus that it was made up of atoms. The monads are conceived in a way which would not have been possible at any earlier stage of the history of thought. They are neither material nor spiritual in the old senses of the words: each of them has a mind which has perception and appetition, but to each mind there belongs a body, or rather each is both mind and body, since its corporeal side is only the mechanism of the soul. Some of the monads have also memory, and these are the souls of living things, amongst which the highest are men, who have reason. All the monads together constitute the world or universe, and the way in which they are related to it and different from one another is that each reflects it from a different point of view. Thus the whole universe is represented in each of its constituent units; but, although each representation is different, what is represented is the same, and it is so because God has established a harmony according to which all the unceasing changes of the monads are regulated, and, in particular, bodies act as though there were no minds, and minds act as though there were no bodies, but each acts as if it were influenced by the other. The world owes to God not merely its coherence, but also its goodness. Not only is there nowhere in it any chaos or confusion except in appearance, but we also know of God, that, having an infinite number of possible worlds to choose from, he decided to create that one amongst them which was the best.

It was this last idea, the optimism of Leibniz, which became the most widely known of his doctrines, and was made familiar to thousands who had never heard of Leibniz by the inimitable caricature of Voltaire's *Candide.* To the modern philosopher, however, it is of little interest. Nor have subsequent thinkers followed Leibniz. What gives his system its value now is its closeness to the work of science. In constructing it Leibniz took into account not only the great mathematical discoveries, but also the work of the natural scientists. His notion of organism, for instance, which runs all through his work, was partly derived from the microscopists. He thus began with a far richer knowledge of the universe as science sees it than any of his predecessors, and he did not, like them, make the false simplification of separating mind from matter. As it turned out, however, he did not carry with him his successors either in philosophy or in science. For more than a century there was an estrangement between the two, and while philosophy paid little attention to the newer developments of science, science remained satisfied with a materialistic determinism. When science found this no longer an adequate framework for its acquisitions, the gap began to close, and very little knowledge of modern physics or psychology is needed to see how Leibniz supplies at many points hints for a new synthesis. Yet they are hints rather than solutions. Not only are there flaws and baseless assumptions in his own reasoning, but his ideas are also inapplicable to some of the modern problems because he did not anticipate the conception of development which was to enter into both philosophic and scientific thought. Although he says that the monads are always changing, and although he emphasizes the idea of organic unity, he does not work out the notion that the essence of anything is its history, the idea of evolution. The rise of that idea formed in this, as elsewhere, a watershed between his age and ours.

Nowhere has it produced, or rather, promised to produce, greater changes than in ethics, the theory of human conduct. Much was written about this in the seventeenth century, and we have seen that for some of the great philosophers it was no less important than the theory of knowledge. A number of other writers treated ethical problems either independently or in connexion with theological or other studies, and the groups into which they fall are similar to the groupings of the writers on the theory of knowledge.[1] The more rationalistic examined the distinction between right and wrong, showing what it implied about the nature of God and man, and how it fitted in with their view of the world. The more empirical tried to express the distinction, or to account for the moral obligation to act rightly, in terms of experience. That is to say they approached more or less closely to the utilitarian view of morality, according to which an act is made right or wrong by its good or evil consequences, not by some inherent rightness or sinfulness which cannot be explained. The utilitarian conception had emerged in a pretty mature state as early as the earlier days of the Italian Renaissance, and, in spite of the objections of the churches, it tended to recur whenever destructive criticism was applied to the current ideas of morals. In most of its forms, it identified the useful with the pleasant. Hobbes combined these notions with his deterministic psychology which was akin to, though not directly begotten by, the determinism of Descartes. Locke brought them out as results of his polemic against innate ideas. Both in England and in France, in spite of some confluents and side-branches, the general flow of ethical thought in the seventeenth century was in this direction, and utilitarianism in one form or another became the expression in ethics of the reasonableness of the eighteenth century.

As an ethical system it has the great merit of being definite

[1] For the English writers see Sidgwick, *Outlines of the History of Ethics*, of which the first edition was published in 1886.

and tangible. It gives an explanation of right and wrong, together with a criterion by which they may be discriminated in practice. It asserts that the advantages of doing right, whatever they may be, must in some way redound to the individual doer of right: that morality was made for man and not man for morality. Neither in the seventeenth nor in the eighteenth century, however, was utilitarianism ever formulated in such a way as to be immune against some obvious objections. In its cruder forms the theory that what makes conduct good is its utility or pleasureableness easily became a vindication of the pursuit of pleasure against the restrictions of morality. In the more considered forms in which it countenanced altruism and self-control, it usually assumed the validity of an ascertainable code of morality, and did not examine the way in which conformity with that code furthered the ultimate satisfaction of individuals. Neither of these lines of little resistance could have been followed if the historical data of ethics had been considered in their concrete richness and diversity. Codes of morality are relative to the other contemporary conditions of human life. Though the ends of right action are not subject to development, its demands on the individual must be studied as part of the general problems of his place in the world, and this must be studied as a problem of mutually related processes of growth. Hence the writers of the seventeenth century, to whom these conceptions were strange, are of little more than antiquarian interest to the modern student of ethics. They do not yield a crop of guiding principles like those which were made in their time for the theory of knowledge. It is chiefly on that side, in logic and metaphysics, that the seventeenth century, with a new method and a mass of new materials, inaugurated a new era in philosophy.

XVII

CLASSICAL AND HISTORICAL STUDIES

AT the opening of the seventeenth century two great men were still alive, both well on in middle age, with most of their work already behind them, who had been the leading figures in the classical studies of what has sometimes been called the second phase of the Renaissance, or at other times the reaction against the Renaissance. The conception of the Renaissance is indeed variable and liable to contradictory interpretations.[1] In the nineteenth century the great French historian Michelet crystallized in that name an idea that had been current among the humanists of the fifteenth and sixteenth centuries. They believed that by reviving the study of the arts and languages of the ancients they were breaking sharply away from the barbarism of the world into which they had been born. To more recent historians, however, the break has seemed less abrupt and less simple. We are accustomed now to think of the knowledge of the classics as having been gradually recovered, and of the wide changes in thought and art and government which accompanied the revolutionary phase of that recovery as having their origins in many historical processes, some of which had been in motion at least since the twelfth century. By the end of the sixteenth the classical revival had accomplished two great tasks. The bulk of the Greek and Latin classics, including all the greater authors, had been printed; and the two ancient languages had taken their place as the pillars of liberal education. In the chief place there was Latin as the Romans wrote it, and not as it was spoken in the Middle Ages, in the second place Greek. A beginning had been made in a third task which became relatively easier and relatively more absorbing as the other two were completed. The antiquities of Greece and Rome were explored: a systematic knowledge of their life was built up. It was in this, as well as in the prosecution of linguistic and literary

[1] The suggestive little book of Dr. K. Burdach, *Reformation, Renaissance, Humanismus*, 1926, should be read critically.

studies, that Lipsius and Scaliger became famous. Justus Lipsius, the younger of the two, was born in the Spanish Netherlands in 1547, and worked in the universities of Holland and Germany as well as in that of Louvain and in the great publishing house of the Plantins at Antwerp. In some ways he was not a strong character, for he changed his religion with his domicile; but he was an innovator in his work. He set a fashion in taking Tacitus and Seneca rather than the accepted Cicero as his models for writing Latin prose, and he added greatly to what was known of the life of the Romans, especially to what is now called archaeology and, as we have seen,[1] to military antiquities.

His older contemporary, Joseph Justus Scaliger, born in 1540, had done an even greater work. A Frenchman of Italian descent, he was an inflexible Protestant, and made his home in tolerant Holland. Amongst many other services to learning his greatest was this, that he first charted the formerly chaotic masses of ancient history by providing them with a scientific chronology. No kind of research requires greater exactitude than this, and the series of books by which Scaliger made it possible to work out the true temporal sequences of events in the ancient world marked an epoch. They belonged to the class of highly technical works which are useless except to specialists, but which to the specialists are indispensable.

We must pass quickly over the contribution of the rest of the century to classical studies, because in the main it consisted in continuing the branches of work already begun. More was done on the whole in Latin studies than in Greek, but in both there was a steady output of better texts of the authors and also of useful apparatus like improved grammars and dictionaries.[2] As the century went on the linguistic interest again resumed its predominance, but now with a difference. When it closed Richard Bentley, the special glory of England in classical scholarship, had recently published his most famous work, the *Dissertation on the Letters of Phalaris* (1699). This is an exposure of a forged classical text, remarkable

[1] See 112, 208, above. [2] See Sir J. E. Sandys, *History of Classical Scholarship*, 3rd ed., 3 vols., 1921, and works there mentioned.

not so much for its main conclusions, which did not need a tithe of the proofs advanced by Bentley, but for the wealth of learning brought in by the way, and for the homely energy of its style. In his other works, Bentley's main achievements lay in textual criticism; but it may be said of his work that, when every allowance is made for his individual genius, he could not have done it if his equipment had been merely linguistic. What he did was to bring to bear on textual problems all the accumulated mass of knowledge about the ancient world, and in the orderly shape which had been given to it by the synthetic labours of Lipsius, Scaliger, and their successors.

It was true in his day, as it has been increasingly true from that time to our own, that the thoroughness of the previous investigations in this field made it specially favourable for the display of certain great mental powers, verbal acuteness, realistic imagination, literary taste. At times the standard in these respects has been so high that classical studies have withered into scholastic pedantry; but there has never been a time since the late fifteenth century when they have not attracted some of the ablest men in Europe. This has strengthened their hold on education. In the period with which we are concerned their position in education was so central that we do not need at this point to attempt an estimate of their influence on thought in general. As we consider the different branches of thought, we find that in almost all of them and indeed also in the history of imaginative literature and art, each phase must be characterized by its relation to classical standards and models. Here it will be enough to say that the century saw a revolt against the ancients in some directions, as in physical science; but even in these the innovators learnt some of their methods from the ancient writers, and in others, such as the drama, the direction of progress was to submit to their rules. They conquered a new province for each that they surrendered.

If, on the one hand, classical learning is a part of the study of language, on another side it is a part of history, the study of the past of the world; and it influenced the developement of historical studies as it did that of other studies. The Italian Renaissance had given rise to a great school of historians. Their method had some things in common with that of the ancients: it was secular, not ecclesiastical, it was to some extent rationalistic. In its mannerisms it derived even more from the models it imitated. Imaginary speeches were sometimes inserted in the narrative. The language and arrangement of classical authors were imitated: the favourites in the sixteenth century were Livy and Suetonius. The historical writing of the Renaissance was not, of course, merely imitative. In the changed world that would not have been possible, and there were new forces, such as national feeling, which impressed themselves on it and gave it a character of its own, suited to the times. But the classical fashion was more than a mere disguise, and it survived, though constantly diminishing, throughout the seventeenth century and beyond it. There were changes similar to the changes in strictly classical studies. In place of the simpler masters formerly followed, the studied manner of Tacitus and Sallust became the admired model: Grotius, for instance, modelled his historical works on Tacitus, as did his great fellow countryman Hooft, although he wrote in Dutch. Even less desirable forms of imitation continued: tedious historical poems in Latin were still much esteemed, and many minor historical writers in various countries, especially those of the Counter-Reformation, carried to its dull consequences the Latin treatment of history as a branch of rhetoric. That so much imitation could be possible was a result of the poverty of the historical outlook of the time. It is scarcely an exaggeration to say that the sixteenth-century writers had no idea of change, no idea that one age was different from another. Just as Shakespeare's Romans wore the dress of his own day, so the Renaissance historians did not know that men and events are made what they are by the character of of the age to which they belong.

From a very early stage of the seventeenth century, however, new and living forces, the same forces which had worked through the brains of Lipsius and Scaliger, were transforming the study of history. Here as in natural science the empirical tendency found a welcome. Great exertions were made to collect and arrange, in particular to print, historical facts. The quantity of available historical information was immensely multiplied: in every western country the output of histories and of documentary materials for history went on with marked acceleration. Nor does the parallel with natural science end here: it is also true equally of both spheres that the growth of knowledge was accompanied and governed by a progress in critical method. The same union of empiricism with rationalism which recreated physics and astronomy was at work among the historians, and it is not a mere compliment but a sober statement of fact to say that the seventeenth century has to its credit the creation of the modern scientific study of history.

This meant in the first place a great improvement in the technique of the historian. Those 'auxiliary sciences' which enable him to estimate exactly the nature and value of his raw materials, his evidence, now first reached the stature of sciences. Chronology is the first of them. We have already seen that Scaliger gave ancient history its chronological groundwork. The chronology of the Middle Ages presented its own difficult problems. There had been in different times and places many different systems of reckoning time. The task of penetrating to the principles of each, of relating it to the others and to the fundamental basis of time-measurement in the movements of the earth, sun, and moon, still provides sufficient exercise in our own day for some of the most learned and subtle minds. It was in the seventeenth century that some of the chief clues to this labyrinth were made available for use. The power to co-ordinate a number of dates expressed in different terms was a great step towards exactness in history, and made it possible to trace the interrelation of events as to which it had been previously uncertain which preceded and which followed. But that was only one direction of advance. Several other kinds of systematic knowledge were needed in the study of historical materials. To know the date at which a book or document was composed is often essential if its value as evidence is to be rightly gauged. For this purpose the study of handwriting is needed, and the modern historian must be prepared to estimate the date of the handwriting before him.

If the point is difficult he must have the means of letting his reader understand how his conclusion is reached: the first printed facsimile of an ancient manuscript appeared in the early seventeenth century.[1] An old document may, however, be dated very precisely even if the handwriting is of uncertain age or if nothing exists except copies made long after the original. The manner in which documents have been drawn up has undergone its own historical evolution, and a legal formula may be as good a clue to date as any other. In the Middle Ages, when the forgery of documents, whether for interested reasons or for pious fraud, was very common, the people who had to deal professionally with charters and the like had a good deal of rough and ready knowledge of how to test their authenticity; but, here again, the modern historian does not need to rely on rules of thumb. He has at his disposal what is called the science of 'diplomatic'—from the word 'diploma'—and as a science or systematic body of knowledge this too is a creation of the seventeenth century. Its first classic, the treatise *De Re Diplomatica* of Jean Mabillon, was published in 1681, and is still often consulted. Another seventeenth-century book of reference may be mentioned which belongs to an allied field, and is not merely still consulted, but in modern editions which differ comparatively little from the first is still the standard work on its subject. This is the great dictionary of post-classical Latin, the *Glossarium ad Scriptores Mediae et Infimae Latinitatis* of Charles du Fresne, seigneur du Cange, which was published in 1688.

To these gigantic labours in providing the apparatus for handling texts there corresponded a copious output of the texts themselves. Since that time the standard of accuracy in transcribing and printing has been considerably raised, but a fair number of the large collections produced or projected at that time are still in use. Their mere size is important. Governments were beginning to regard it as useful to print extracts from their records: the great series of English official record publications may be said to begin with the *Foedera* for which Thomas Rymer was commissioned by King William III and Queen Anne. The huge task of the

[1] H. Delehaye, *The Work of the Bollandists* (1922), p. 103.

Bollandist fathers in the Southern Netherlands, the collecting and editing of all the materials for the lives of the saints, was begun in this century, a work which has expanded with the discovery of materials and the development of technique to such an extent that it is still unfinished and yet has produced a whole library of matter. For work on this scale some form of co-operation is necessary, and it was natural that both the older and the newer forms of associations of learned men should have lent themselves to it. The Bollandists were Jesuits. Theirs was, indeed, one of the newest religious orders; but the oldest, that of the Benedictines, was also able to accommodate itself to the requirements of historical work on the grand scale. Its monks had a long tradition of learning extending far back into the Middle Ages, and, if their works had now something of the limitation of the cloister in comparison with those of the more worldly-wise Jesuits, there were great pioneers among them, including Mabillon, who has already been named. The Congregation of St. Maur, to which he belonged, was founded in 1621, to revive the strictness of the monastic life among the Benedictine houses of France, most of which joined it. In 1632 the superior-general issued orders for the training of the young monks in research and organized work, and this was the beginning of a huge output of books and collections of documents. In the seventeenth century these were mainly editions of the Fathers of the Church, medieval documents and contributions to French and monastic history. The academies, the newest form of learned society, were later to have a great place in the regular production of learned works but as yet they were not strong enough to undertake great co-operative publications of documents. It may also be noted that in this as in so many other directions the universities were inactive. Their studies were not such as to contribute any notable proportion of the good historical editions and treatises of the time, and the jealous individualism characteristic of their controversies and quarrels was hostile to organized study or research.

As historical method improved, the field of historical inquiry was widened. In the age of the early Renaissance it had been actually narrower than in the Middle Ages. Historians had almost all been connected with some prince or republic, or if personally independent had fixed their attention on political or military events. Their most characteristic literary forms were biography and the kind of narrative which we call political history. The secular point of view of their time left out not only the miraculous, but also almost the whole of the human side of religion. When the Reformation and the Counter-Reformation brought religion and politics into such close relations that neither could be chronicled without the other, historians took their part in the confessional strife and every period of Christian history was written or rewritten by conflicting apologists. Yet it was in the political aspects of history that even these historians were most at home. Those who were openly partisans insisted most on the worldly intrigues and ambitions of their opponents in their own or earlier times, whether these were popes or heresiarchs. Impartiality was to be found only in those writers who neglected the religious motives of both sides alike. Thus there is a superficiality and a poverty of human sympathy in the best authors of the beginning of our period. Paolo Sarpi, a bold man, an industrious writer and himself a friar, was the spokesman of the Venetian Republic in a quarrel against the Holy See. His long history of the Council of Trent, first published in London in 1619,[1] was long held in high esteem for its insight and for its systematic use of original authorities. Yet it treats the council and the movement which led to it as nothing more than a series of moves and counter-moves in a game of domination: there is scarcely a hint in it that the council was the decisive phase in a great reformation of the Roman Church from within. And if historians were indifferent to the force of religion as a motive power in affairs, still less had they any interest in the more universal religious interpretation of history which had been, in a primitive form, part of the common stock of medieval ideas. The fall of man, the plan of salvation, the universal monarchy of Rome, the supposed historical foundation of

[1] The English translation published in 1629 was the work of Sir Nathaniel Brent, the Oxford opponent of Laud.

the papal claims, all had fitted into a scheme of history as a whole, a continuous story extending from the creation to the future end of the world. Now that many parts of that scheme, though not openly repudiated, were coolly ignored by half the world of learning, the separate periods and incidents of history came to be treated in an isolation like that of romances which have no set place in time. There was a gain in truth to fact, but it brought with it a danger of aridity and emptiness of meaning.

The scientific tendency carried within itself a corrective for this deficiency, and the reform of history was an integral part of the great programme for the advancement of knowledge which was drawn up by Bacon. Bacon himself as a historian, in his *History of Henry VII*, belonged to the school of Italian Renaissance and did not embrace any neglected departments of life: he wrote political history of the same type as the rest of his contemporaries. In his philosophical works, however, he discusses history with a breadth and clearness of vision which are amazing. He was not merely talking in the air: he gave a survey of the books already available on historical subjects. He classified the different kinds of history, natural, civil, ecclesiastical, and literary, and with prophetic truth he noted the last as deficient: 'for no man hath propounded to himself the general state of learning to be described and represented from age to age, as many have done the works of nature and the state civil and ecclesiastical'. It is remarkable that he noticed this want, still more remarkable that he gave as his reason for wishing to have it made good 'not so much . . . for curiosity or satisfaction of those that are the lovers of learning; but chiefly for a more serious and grave purpose, which is this in few words, that it will make learned men wise in the use and administration of learning. For it is not St. Augustine's nor St. Ambrose works that will make so wise a divine, as ecclesiastical history thoroughly read and observed; and the same reason is of learning.' [1] Besides this great gap in historical knowledge, he drew attention to many smaller tasks that needed to be done, and, in another of the passages in which he dealt with

[1] *Advancement of Learning*, Bk. II.

this matter, he drew out a programme for them all in the form of a 'Catalogue of Particular Histories by Titles'.[1] There are 130 titles altogether, of which ninety belong to human history. They are not all what we should call historical subjects, for they include the sciences of anatomy and physiology and other things which are not to be treated chronologically. Bacon, like Locke, and like ourselves when we talk about 'natural history', does not clearly distinguish the descriptive from the strictly historical treatment of a subject. His list, however, includes a great number of subjects in what we should now call economic and social history. It was not until long after Bacon's time that some of them, such as the history of pottery or of 'games of all kinds' were adequately written, some perhaps have not been written yet, such as the 'miscellaneous history of common experiments which have not grown into an art'. Most of them are being constantly improved and rewritten, but the list as it stands might well be mistaken for part of a subject-catalogue for a great modern historical library. The future of historical science was beginning to reveal itself to the thinker who saw the multifarious tasks of empirical research as parts of a whole.

There has always been a gulf between history as it has actually been written and history as theorists have expatiated upon it. We have seen that it separates Bacon's own work as an historian from his view of what history might become, and if his contemporaries had written history merely as he did, we might well have left his theories alone. But the century did see a notable advance in the direction he had pointed out. History became more various and more philosophical.[2] We have already seen that political thought became more scientific or historical: the reverse of this fact is the change by which political history became more critical

[1] *Parascue.*

[2] The excellent manual of Fueter, *Geschichte der neueren Historiographie*, 2nd ed., 1925, gives the titles of the principal guides to the historical literature of the period. Amongst later works Croce, *Teoria e storia della storiografia* (1917), is the most important. The English translation is not to be recommended.

and theoretical. A number of seventeenth-century writers approached, if they did not quite attain, to the writing of constitutional history of the true modern type. The constitutional struggles of Holland and England gave rise to much controversy on historical questions. Grotius and other Dutchmen [1] and the English antiquarian lawyers like Selden and Prynne wrote books in which, by examining the facts of past constitutional practice, they tried to establish conclusions as to the rights of the disputants of their own times. Their problems were closely akin to those of political theory. Their method, however, was still in the main antiquarian, and they were concerned to prove what had been the laws of their countries. Their appeal was to the authority of antiquity: they did not see that institutions grow and express the changes of the social life around them. That fact came to be appreciated only when there had been considerable changes in the general habits of thought. With these we shall be concerned in a moment; [2] for the present we shall be safe in saying that they did not become effective in the writing of history until some years after the opening of the eighteenth century.[3]

Something was done to prepare the way for this change of view by a school of writers who may seem very remote from it, the French writers of memoirs. Throughout the century, but in greater numbers from the time of the civil war of the Fronde, actors in French history wrote, soon after the events or much later, truthfully or mendaciously, their versions of what happened and of their own part in it. The greatest of them, Louis de Rouvroi, duc de Saint-Simon, is the acknowledged master in this kind of writing. A discontented courtier of Louis XIV and afterwards a leader in the unsuccessful political experiments of the regency, he was a close and penetrating observer of human nature, and his book, though very long and though clumsy in style, burns from end to end

[1] See Kampinga, *De opvattingen over onze oudere vaderlandsche geschiedenis bij de Hollandsche historici der XVIe en XVIIe eeuw* (1917).

[2] Below, p. 286.

[3] I am not qualified to say whether Giannone's history of the kingdom of Naples (1723) was the first real constitutional history, but several good writers say so; see Fueter, 2nd ed., p. 277; Croce, *Storia del regno di Napoli*, p. 33, indicates its European influence.

with the energy of his passions.[1] It is the product of a gregarious life, in which individual character seemed to be the decisive force in events. That life produced also a great school of letter-writing and it is characteristic of it that amongst the best writers of both memoirs and letters there were women. The directness of observation, the realism as we may call it, of all this writing was poles apart from the flat and conventional panegyric of the official historians of the time, and it was one of the elements which went to make a great school of English historians who, in the second half of the century, though wholly devoid of the spirit of Bacon, helped in their way to rescue history from its emptiness.

These were the party historians, of whom the greatest were Clarendon and Burnet, almost the only English historians of the time whose works can still be read by any except professed students. They had much in common with the writers of memoirs and learnt much from them; but their work is less personal. Their subject is their time as seen not by a single actor but by a member of a great body of men, taking one side in a national division. Thus, while they have all the faults of partiality, they saved for history the priceless possession of its seriousness. English historical writing is still not altogether free from their influence, and in its later course this tradition of partisanship has had unfortunate effects. Macaulay and other great writers who belonged to it had the fault of believing that the side they took in their own times was identical with the side they supported in a past century, and so they interpreted earlier ages unhistorically in terms of their own; but even so their error, great as it was, had its compensations. It never succumbed to the temptation of seeing in great movements nothing but petty and personal motives: it recognized that men are made great by the greatness of the causes they serve. Like Burke's defence of party, it touches something of what has been best in English life and thought.

This recovery of the earnestness of history was not yet universal, but it made itself felt in other departments and other countries. Something of it can be traced in the books

[1] The admirable edition of Boislisle (1881–1928) has 40 volumes.

on ecclesiastical history written at this time, and in those on the tremendous questions raised by the contact of Christianity and barbarism in America. On a smaller scale it shows itself in the rise of some of the minor branches of history. Local history may seem a trivial study, involving no large issues and solving no wide problems; but, small as its subjects are, they are real, they evoke the strong feeling for places, and, for the very reason that they are small, manageable, and close to the observer, they lend themselves well to scientific treatment. Useful books on the history of individual towns or districts were written in various countries, and one characteristic of some of those produced in England may be noted here as a link between practice and the theories of Bacon. Inspired directly or indirectly by his works, some of the local writers, notably Dr. Robert Plot who wrote on Oxfordshire and Staffordshire, treated human history and natural history as an inseparable whole. Looking directly at the life of the countryside, they saw that economic and even political facts cannot be explained unless soils and trees, minerals and watercourses have first been examined. In what they wrote about things they were preparing the way for new methods in writing about men. They groped towards prehistoric archaeology by trying to distinguish natural flints from artifacts. They threw out ideas to explain the local distribution of industries and the siting of roads and settlements. In the preparation for a synthesis of particular histories such as Bacon has foreseen, they have their modest place.

From the works of historians and of all other specialized writers there are distilled, by a process so complicated that it can seldom be followed, the opinions about the nature of man and of the universe which pass current among ordinary men, whether they are writers of books or merely readers and talkers. Two such opinions, which were common property in the seventeenth century and remained pretty widely accepted until our own time, belong specially to the historical sphere. The first is the division of history into the three compartments, ancient, medieval, and modern.[1] This

[1] This subject is admirably treated in Gordon, *Medium Aevum and the Middle Age* (S.P.E. Tract, no. xix. Oxford, 1925).

idea is so familiar, so much a part of our own way of thinking, that it requires no explanation. It has its roots in the period of the Renaissance: quite early in that movement the admirers of the ancient world began to think of themselves as standing at the threshold of a new age, emerging from an unhappy age of ignorance which separated them from the greatness of the 'exemplar states' and the arts of Greece and Rome. This was a new secular view of universal history, a substitute for the old Christian view. Before the first impulse of the Renaissance was spent, some influential historians had used it as the framework of their books, and Latin equivalents of the name 'Middle Ages' had been used here and there in learned works. The use of this term in the vernaculars began or became common in our period, and it is a sign of its growing prevalence that it now found its way into dictionaries and works of reference. There were, indeed, considerable variations in its application. The point at which the Middle Ages began did not appear the same by some centuries to the philologist who was thinking of the debasement of the Latin language as to the historian whose eyes were fixed on the breakdown of the old Roman empire. Nor could it be dated in the same generation by the Protestant who thought of them as the ages of Roman superstition and by the Catholic to whom the primitive Church appeared to be the same as his own. There were similar differences about the dating of the close of the period. None the less there was a general agreement, from which only exceptional theorists were excluded, that there had been a dark period from somewhere between the fifth and the ninth centuries to somewhere before the middle of the sixteenth. About many of its characteristics also there was agreement, as there always will be; and there was agreement that it must in general be regarded with contempt. Gothic art and monkish Latin were in disrepute; scholastic philosophy had its defenders, but they were becoming fewer; the age before gunpowder and printing and the discovery of America seemed barbarous to successors for whom it was as yet scarcely touched by the charm of distance. They took no interest in those aspects of it which most impress the modern student, its religious life and its intellectual progress. To a nearer observer these appeared so foreshortened as to be no progress at all but stationary ignorance. Although the new historical technique was preparing the way for a revision of these judgements, the judgements still held good. The method of Mabillon and his kind was not by itself enough to bring the Middle Ages back to life.

It was to find, in the still distant future, an ally in a second great historical generalization which came into being late in the century and ruled men's minds in the next age, a conception which is fundamentally irreconcilable with the threefold division of history but which succeeded for some generations in keeping an uneasy harmony with it. This was the belief in progress, the idea that human history forms a continuous movement from bad to good, from good to better, perhaps towards some ultimate and future best. This too is still alive in popular thought. Transformed by a series of intellectual revolutions, it still, in one form or another, satisfies the minds of many European men and women. In the seventeenth century it had not developed sufficiently to reach the point of explaining how the apparently dark ages constituted a necessary stage towards the later enlightenment. It was still in immature forms and it had not won general acceptance. Like all such pervading ideas, it drew from a number of different streams of thought.[1] It is not to be found in the works of Bacon, who at times writes of the world as passing through cycles of improvement and decline, and at other times regards his own period as that of the world's old age or maturity; but Bacon did much to lay one of the foundations of the idea. His insistence on the earthly purposes which were to be fulfilled by the advancement of learning points towards the notion of a perfected state of the world as the ultimate goal of human effort. It tends, although Bacon never professed to disbelieve in the intervention of Providence in human affairs, to eliminate the divine element from the general explanation of history, and to make it a self-contained process. The world which

[1] Bury, *The Idea of Progress*, 1920, surveys the subject admirably, though somewhat disguising its complexity.

interested the empirical scientists, if it was to have a general history, must have such a history as carried its explanation within itself. In many ways the other great tendency of seventeenth-century thought, the rationalistic tendency, was unfavourable to the fashioning of such an explanation, for the Cartesians conceived the universe as a mechanism, not as a growing, changing, and living organism; but even Descartes made his contribution to the idea of progress. The invariable laws which he believed to operate excluded the possibility of an intervening Providence, and his emphatic break with authority and repudiation of respect for the past struck the mortal blow at that reverence for antiquity which, until then, had amounted almost to a belief that the golden age of the world had ended with the fall of Rome. The step was shorter than might have been expected to the belief in a golden age in the future.

Outside the circles of systematic thinkers the idea of degeneration definitely made way for the idea of progress. In two famous controversies of the latter part of the century this idea more or less clearly emerged in the writings of some of the participants. One was an exchange of polemics between Bossuet [1] and others on the variations of Protestantism and kindred matters. It began with the assumption that their diversity, implying a failure to preserve the primitive purity of belief, was in itself an argument against the truth of Protestant tenets; but, before it had ended, the idea had been struck out that development, growth, change, variation may even be qualities of a true belief. A more definite landmark was a controversy which, on the whole, was conducted in a more frivolous but more brilliant manner, that on the relative merits of the ancients and the moderns. This fills a large space in the international literary history of the period, and it has left behind it at least one book which is still read for its learning, the masterpiece of Bentley, one which is read for its wit, the contribution of Swift,[2] and one, Fontenelle's *Digression sur les anciens et les modernes*, which has its place in popularizing the idea of progress. The most solid

[1] *Histoire des variations des églises protestantes*, 2 vols., 1688.

[2] *The Battle of the Books*, 1704.

ground Fontenelle had to go upon was the great advance in science, and it was this large, easily visible fact with its still more obtrusive consequences in material civilization which stamped the idea on popular thought for the next two centuries.

To it were owing during those centuries some of the best and some of the worst of the endeavours of men in thought and action, but it had not yet risen to a position of command. All that the seventeenth century did was to rough it out and to hand it over to posterity. Once again we must be on our guard against laying too much stress on anticipations; and this is true of all that has been said of historical studies at that time. Great as was their improvement, they yet fell far short of what they were to become when men of learning adopted in a later age what is sometimes called *par excellence* the historical method. One of the forerunners or beginners of this method was Montesquieu, who in a book published in 1734, *Considérations sur les causes de la grandeur des Romains et de leur décadence*, set himself not to narrate but to explain. His problem was to show how the Romans could do as they did while yet being themselves not 'd'autres hommes que nous'. He saw the relation of man to his social and political environment in a new way. At the same time, in an obscure corner of Europe, Giambattista Vico, a professor in Naples, was revolving in his mind the principles of a new science, *Principii di scienza nuova*,[1] as he called them in the title of a famous book which he published in 1725. It is a book about all kinds of things, religion, government, national character, jurisprudence, morals, everything which can be included in the 'natural course of nations'. Vico's new science was in fact nothing else than history as we understand it, and he put up a milestone in the road of thought when he wrote: 'Rebus ipsis dictantibus regna condita'. But we must not linger over his quaint, incompetent, and masterly works. They do not belong to the seventeenth century, for we can say without much exaggeration that they were not written until the eighteenth, not read until the nineteenth, and not

[1] The best edition is that of Nicolini (3 vols., Bari, 1911–16); the only satisfactory exposition, Croce, *La filosofia di Giambattista Vico*, 1911.

understood until the twentieth. For us they serve chiefly as an index of the immaturity and inadequacy of the historical thought of the age into which their author was born. That age did not know how deeply historical investigation can cut into the nature of things.

XVIII

EDUCATION[1]

THE educational institutions of western and central Europe at the beginning of the century were, in their main outlines, those which had been established in the Middle Ages. Like other medieval institutions, they showed an infinite irregularity of detail and a broad uniformity of type. There were schools and universities. The two classes were not so clearly distinguished as they are now; for the faculty of arts in the university, which gave a general training preparatory for the higher faculties of law, medicine, and theology, was like a higher school, and sometimes, as we shall see, schools attempted to do the work of universities. These, however, are merely instances of that irregularity which, as we have said, is infinite: the general distinction of schools and universities is clear enough. The university was a privileged corporation of teachers, in many ways resembling a guild. The position of its students was analogous to that of apprentices. It was often associated with residential colleges, which in their turn in many ways resembled the colleges of canons associated with churches. Most of the universities were small: fifteen or twenty professors and three or four hundred students made a moderately large university. The smallest had less than a hundred and none seems to have much exceeded, if any reached, a thousand.[2] As was natural in those days of bad communications, they were fairly thick on the ground.

[1] For this period in all countries much of the best work on the history of educational institutions and methods is to be sought in books on particular schools or universities. These cannot be enumerated here, though a number of them have been used for the purposes of the present chapter. Probably the best text-book for educational ideas and methods is T. Ziegler, *Geschichte der Pädagogik mit besonderer Rücksicht auf das höhere Unterrichtswesen* (1895), which has a good survey of the literature of the subject, but deals mainly with Germany. For England, Foster Watson, *English Grammar Schools to 1660* (1908) and other works by the same author are to be recommended.

[2] The minute investigation of F. Eulenberg, *Die Frequenz der deutschen Universitäten*, in the *Abhandlungen* of the Royal Saxon Academy, *Philologisch-historische Klasse*, 1904, does all that can be done for this prestatistical age, and has some facts about Dutch and Italian universities.

The number of students in Europe was large in proportion to the wealth and political development of the Continent.[1]

Schools were of many types, and it would be difficult to apply to them with any exactness the modern division into primary and secondary. Every town had, roughly speaking, by this time at least one school, and in the larger towns there were schools which carried the training of their pupils so far as to overlap with the more elementary work done in universities. There were day-schools and boarding-schools. Their finances and business management were, then as now, under a great variety of authorities, lay or ecclesiastical. In their internal organization the schools were framed either on the collegiate model, as associations of teachers, or on the simpler plan adopted, for instance, in the English grammar schools, where nothing was required except a building, a head master, and assistants. The provision of primary education was everywhere relatively the most insufficient. In a village there might chance to be a more or less useful school kept by the parson, or more likely by the parish clerk, or by some old man or woman with no qualification except inability to earn a livelihood in any other way. The elementary schools of the towns were more numerous, but everywhere they were in the main unsatisfactory in personnel, buildings, and methods: private enterprise had to provide them almost unaided and unguided. Consequently, just as the universities had to teach many of the students what they might have learnt at school, in the same way the higher schools often had to begin at the beginning of the education of the child.

The general aim of schools and universities was narrower than it has since become. It was the transmission of a given body of knowledge, a body of which the outlines were closed by the requirements of a rigid orthodoxy, and by the belief that authority in the past had established the main principles of what was useful and true. In this respect little change had been effected by the great intellectual revolutions of the fifteenth and sixteenth centuries. Humanism, with all its contempt for the scholastic philosophy, had not ousted it

[1] There are useful references in the general sketch of Stephan d'Irsay, *Histoire des universités françaises et étrangères*, 2 vols. (1933–5).

from education. It lasted on in the European universities in general throughout the seventeenth century. Only under the influence of Locke, who was himself trained in it, did it disappear from Oxford. Cartesianism took its place here and there on the Continent, but not everywhere, and when it had been abandoned in some countries it survived in others, for instance in the Spanish Netherlands, into the eighteenth century. Even in our own day it is not extinct: it is, for instance, still the basis of the great international educational system of the Jesuits. There had indeed grown up beside it, before the coming of the Reformation, the new humanistic teaching. A number of new universities had been founded under the influence of the movement. Greek studies had come in. Training in eloquence had become one of the principal aims of teaching, and the old philosophic attitude had formed a partnership with the new aesthetic and literary tendency. Thus humanism, not without encountering opposition, had reformed the universities, and a similar change had been accomplished more quietly in the schools; but these changes were made within the framework of the traditional system. The old shell of organization, especially the division of the universities into the four faculties of arts, theology, law, and medicine, remained. Not every university had all the faculties, but these were everywhere the departments between which studies were divided.

Neither was the old plan essentially altered by the Reformation and the Counter-Reformation. These too had led to the foundation of new universities. First there were a number of Protestant foundations, such as Königsberg in Prussia, one of the most easterly of the old European universities; and the last waves of this tide were still flowing in the earlier seventeenth century. With the exception of Strassburg, which became a university in 1621, and of Dorpat (1632), Äbo (1640), and Lund (1666) in the Swedish dominions, these seventeenth-century Protestant foundations were unimportant. One which may be mentioned for the circumstances of its origin is Giessen (1607): this was set up by the Lutherans because Marburg, near by, fell into the hands of the Calvinists. Religious opposition naturally stimulated such foundations on all hands: the foundation of Counter-Reformation universities in Germany went on, especially under Jesuit auspices, throughout the century. Of universities founded anywhere in Europe for any other reason there are very few. Nor did the new foundations on either side break with the tradition. There were of course minor changes. Among both Protestants and Catholics there was an increase of the theological [1] and law faculties: the education of the clergy improved and, on the other hand, the demand for laymen with legal training rose. In England it became common for gentlemen to get some training for affairs in the Inns of Court. The medical faculties remained small in proportion until the eighteenth and even the nineteenth century. The growth of the higher faculties combined with other causes to reduce the prevalence of 'living-in' for students. The age of students had risen since the Middle Ages: in the arts faculties they were now for the most part youths rather than boys. In the Protestant countries the abandonment of clerical celibacy weakened the hold of quasi-monastic discipline, and in Catholic countries other social changes among the students had a similar result. The college and the boarding-house kept by a teacher were thus ceasing to be the usual residences of students. In Oxford, Cambridge, Louvain, the Jesuit and some other universities the older systems still survived; but elsewhere the student freely chose his own lodging.

In the sphere of teaching, however, the religious changes did little to further freedom. A Protestant teacher could remove himself from the ecclesiastical censures of Calvinist superiors to take refuge in a Lutheran university, and so might take some risks with orthodoxy; but the fight against Cartesianism in the universities showed that there were limits which must be respected. In the earlier part of the century the liberty of teaching was probably greatest in the Dutch universities. These had been created as a direct

[1] S. Merkle, *Das Konzil von Trient und die Universitäten*, 1905, shows that the Tridentine seminaries were on the whole meant to supplement rather than to supersede the theological faculties of the universities. Rivalry became acute in the nineteenth century.

consequence of the political revolt, Leyden after the raising of the famous siege of that town, then, in order that the leading federated provinces might each have a university to itself, Harderwijk in 1600, Groningen in 1614, Utrecht in 1634. The diversity of provinces gave openings for individuality in the same way as the diversity of sects elsewhere, and this was one reason for the eminence of the Dutch universities during the century. During the Thirty Years' War many German students resorted to them. They partook in the general prosperity of the republic, and we have seen not only in dealing with science and medicine, but in such unexpected connexions as military matters, that they played an important part in the forward movements of the age.

These Dutch universities were, however, an exception, and only a partial exception at that, to the general fact that in the history of universities the seventeenth century was a period of decline. It was a decline to which many causes contributed. The first, no doubt, was religious strife. In England the successive purgings by Catholics, Protestants, Puritans, Anglicans divided and degraded the teaching body. In Paris years were wasted in barren theological controversy. In Germany the Thirty Years' War ruined the universities as it ruined everything else. Heidelberg, which had become, from the confluence of Calvinist refugees, the first internationally important university in Germany, was for a time extinguished and its library removed to Rome. Helmstädt, third among the German universities in numbers and specially noted as a resort for the sons of men of position, was temporarily starved out of existence. Everywhere the brutal indiscipline of the students reached an astonishing and shameful height.[1] Similar misfortunes came wherever the

[1] The essay on 'German Universities during and after the Thirty Years' War' in Sir Adolphus Ward's *Collected Papers*, i. 195 ff., fills the one important gap in the great work of Paulsen, *Geschichte des gelehrten Unterrichts*, 3rd ed., by R. Lehman, 2 vols., 1919– . Among older books on the German universities the most valuable is A. Tholuck, *Das akademische Leben des 17. Jahrhunderts*, 2 vols., 1853–4, which also sketches the conditions in the neighbouring Protestant countries. It deals especially with the Protestant theological faculties, and forms the first part of a *Vorgeschichte des Rationalismus*. The second part, *Das kirchliche Leben*, 2 vols., 1861–2, is also still useful.

universities were in or near the theatres of war. In the time of Louis XIV the numbers of the German students sank and the academic life of Louvain was almost extinguished. But there was decadence everywhere. In Spain the universities were touched by the general enfeeblement of the national life in the second half of the century. Both at aristocratic Alcalá and at the more popular Salamanca the numbers of students dwindled. In Italy no university held after 1650 the position which Padua, the university of the republic of Venice, took in the world of medical and physical science before that date. In France, as in Germany, degrees were sold for cash, studies were neglected, discipline vanished. The number of men who rose to real eminence as university teachers sank deplorably, and the great men of the century—Hobbes, Leibniz, Bayle—spoke of the professors and their work with contempt.

The careers of these three men and of their equals amply show how the life of philosophy and science had detached itself from the old educational institutions. The courts of princes afforded housing, society, and livelihood for Leibniz; noble patrons did the same for Hobbes; Bayle could support himself as the literary man of the present day supports himself, partly by writing for the public. But intellectual life always creates institutions to make itself a favourable environment, and when an old educational system loses touch with the needs of the time something new will arise to take its place. Thus there came a crop of new learned associations and new types of teaching bodies. Literature and science formed the academies. They marked the alliance of the courtly nobleman with the man of science which is one of the characteristic notes of the century. In education its counterpart was a new ideal, far apart from that of the medieval learned clerk, the ideal of the instructed man of the world. So inappropriate were the old discipline and the old curriculum for producing this new type that a new kind of institution began to appear which threatened to be a dangerous rival to the universities. In Spain, which in his time was still able to set the example in education, Philip IV set up in 1625 the Estudios Reales de San Isidro. This institution was especially meant to train the eldest sons of nobles for their position in life. It was conducted by the Jesuits, and to the old curriculum, which was naturally hemmed in by the process, it added political and economic subjects, military science, or generally speaking the subjects of general culture and liberal education, but not the professional studies of the old higher faculties. The modern studies, however, and schools in which they had the leading place, were destined to come into their own not under Spanish influence but under French.

They did not actually become so important in France as in other countries.[1] There was a tendency among the theorists and reformers of French education to introduce new studies, especially that of geography, and the direct teaching of the French language began to make headway; but circumstances held back the development of other 'subjects'. For modern foreign languages there was little demand, and that almost confined to Italian. History was as yet too lifeless and conventional to be of much use in education. The teaching of natural science to boys scarcely began before the eighteenth century. Yet, although the curriculum was still literary and classical, it was modified by the new spirit. The reading of classical authors took a more important place; composition and particularly verse composition took up less of the scholar's attention. Less time was spent on grammar, and the grammar-books used were written in French and were simplified. Pedantry was avoided. The old university methods lost their authority. Henry IV not only tried to reform the university of Paris: he also encouraged other and in a sense rival institutions such as the Collège de France or Collège des Trois Langues. When in the age of Louis XIV the French influence came to dominate the culture of continental Europe, this modernizing tendency in educational method was allied to the desire to study the French language and literature. It was thus even more

[1] A. Sicard, *Les études classiques avant la révolution*, 1887, has a wider scope than its title implies and gives a general sketch of French education from the time of the Renaissance. It is an historical defence of classical education.

modern abroad than in France. Among the strongholds of French influence were not only the palaces and the theatres, but also schools.

In Germany the first example of a courtly modern 'academy' for the noble class is to be found even before the Thirty Years' War. After the growth of French influence in the time of Richelieu and Mazarin and after the return of peace the 'Ritterakademien' became common. They were typical of the period: aristocratic and 'modern'. Enough of the classics was taught in them to satisfy the needs of public life, that is, something of the Latin language and literature; but the modern subjects predominated. Besides French and occasionally other modern languages there were history, geography, politics, genealogy, heraldry, law, with mathematics and the elements of fortification and some experimental science. There were ornamental subjects like architecture and painting, accomplishments like riding, fencing, music, and dancing. Above all there was the whole art of manners in all its branches, of conversation, etiquette, ceremonial, and conduct. In 1671 the governor of the Spanish Netherlands set up a military academy, or school of war or 'académie de cavalerie' in order to prevent the resort of young noblemen to Paris. It had the same kind of curriculum, and the head was an Italian who had held a similar post in Franche Comté. Many foreigners resorted to the academy, but after sixteen years it was superseded by a more technical military and naval training school for three hundred boarders, from the age of ten or upwards.[1]

In England, which was at war with France during much of the period when these schools grew up, it was not to be expected that they would be imitated; but by other channels the same educational ideal and influence made themselves to some extent visible.[2] Here too the education of the rich tended to become different from that of the majority. Here one of its agents was the private tutor. The position of

[1] *Correspondance de la cour d'Espagne sur les affaires des Pays-Bas*, ed. J. Cuvelier and J. Lefèvre, v (1935), nos. 236, 457, 1234, 1260.

[2] See the useful study of Miss K. Lambley, *The Teaching and Cultivation of the French Language in England in Tudor and Stuart Times*, 1920.

domestic or travelling tutor came, as the century went on, to attract more and more men of real ability, among them a number who became distinguished authors. In spite of its dependence and lack of dignity it gave a livelihood to many a young clergyman from the university, who, if all went well, might reasonably look forward to being presented to a fat benefice by his pupil or his pupil's father. The grand tour, which tutor and pupil made together, was already not uncommon at the beginning of the century, and, except for the difficulties of times of war, by the end it was customary for a large proportion of men of rank. It lasted from three to five years, and by far the longest stay was usually made in France. It meant visits to courts, to natural curiosities, to fencing masters, to language teachers. It meant, in fact, a smattering of what the Ritterakademien taught.

Another entirely independent stream brought the modern studies into a new and isolated branch of education in England. The English nonconformists, who were excluded by law from the main political and even educational institutions of the country, were permitted to start their own educational establishments so long as they were not grammar schools.[1] They wished to train their ministers, and they also opened schools for boys and girls. In neither were they fettered by any necessity of preparing for entrance to the universities, which were closed to them, and so by the end of the century they had made considerable headway in introducing a wider curriculum of modern subjects. Their curriculum had indeed the fault of being too wide and superficial, but in the eighteenth century it was to provide a training for some of the first scientists and philosophers in Europe.

At the bottom of the educational scale there was at work in England as elsewhere yet another tendency, utilitarian in aim, which began the building up of an education in which

[1] For a list of these see H. MacLachlan, *English Education under the Test Acts* (1931). The ruling in Cox's case of 1700 limited the ecclesiastical power of licensing schoolmasters, which had been often reaffirmed since the canons of Elizabeth. The statutory disabilities of the Clarendon Code had already become inoperative under William III and their renewal in 1713 was never effective. See J. E. G. de Montmorency, *State Intervention in English Education* (1902), pp. 105 ff., 170 ff.

the classics and the old learned studies generally had no part and were not contemplated as a further stage. Society now required that a much greater proportion of the people should not be absolutely illiterate. It could absorb and employ large numbers of persons who could read and write and do simple arithmetical sums; its conscience also caused it to spread religious instruction among the poor. Thus there was a large increase of elementary schools in England after 1670, and in 1698 the Society for Promoting Christian Knowledge, which still exists, inaugurated the first charity schools. In France the religious order of the Frères des Écoles Chrétiennes, nicknamed the Ignorantins, was founded in 1680, and did a great work in spreading elementary education in the countryside. So much did it achieve that there was soon raised against it the cry, still to be heard among reactionary critics of other educational movements, that it was taking away hands from agriculture and rendering the people unfit for manual work.

In Holland, where urban conditions were commoner, the general level of education was probably higher than in most parts of France and the British Isles. There too, however, the changes were not altogether dissimilar. The French influence made itself felt.[1] It was not quite the same as in Germany, for the Dutch feudal aristocracy was insignificant; but the burgher patriciate was also in its way an aristocracy and of a more modern cast of mind. The Latin schools were weakened at the end of the century and, in the smaller towns, fell into decay because French schools sprang up for those who were not intended for the learned professions, and because Latin was giving way to French as a 'universal' language. The French schools were frequented by boys of the more prosperous families, and these, besides those who

[1] See J. K. Riemens, *Esquisse historique de l'enseignement du français en Hollande du 16e au 19e siècle*, 1919. This author, pp. 148 ff., says that the influence of Huguenot refugees in teaching was slight, and even in the general dissemination of French culture was less than has been commonly held. As Miss Lambley's study ends with 1685, it is possible that the same may prove to be true of England. Though popular in form, G. D. J. Schotel, *Het oud-Hollandsch huisgezin der zeventiende eeuw* (ed. H. C. Rogge, *s.a.*) contains some particulars not to be found elsewhere.

had been to a university, often completed their studies by a journey in France. There seems to have been no teaching of High German in Dutch schools, but in a few of them English was taught for commercial reasons. In spite of ecclesiastical censures French immigrants into Holland set up dancing-schools. In elementary education for the poor Holland was well advanced; its municipal orphanages were famous.

These changes all pointed forward to great reforms which were not to be fulfilled until long after this period, and there were many writers on the theory of education who saw the weak points of the existing system and called for change. The two leading points on which most of them insisted were sound, and held promise for the future. The first was that punishments should be milder, the second that in all education greater attention should be paid to things as contrasted with words. Among the authors who urged these ideas, the most famous is John Amos Comenius or Komenski. He was a Czech by race, a bishop in the sect of the Bohemian brothers. As a young man he was driven from his native country by the calamities of the Thirty Years' War, to wander over Protestant Europe, teaching and writing. Of his works some were text-books, which came to be widely used in schools, others were attempts to systematize all knowledge in a way which was essentially barren and formal. What is now his best-known work belongs to neither of these classes, but is a treatise on educational method, the *Great Didactic*.[1] This was by no means the first such book, though it was perhaps the most comprehensive that had been written at that time. It is written in the pedantic manner of the first half of the century, formal, prolix, and laboured, with long, almost unreadable, similes and analogies which obscure instead of explaining its argument. It lays too much stress

[1] I have used the English translation by Dr. W. M. Keatinge. Some of the same ideas are presented more attractively in the ideal commonwealth *Christianopolis*, published in 1619 by Comenius's older contemporary and correspondent Johann Valentin Andreae, which also illustrates the merits and the limitations of German Lutheranism. The English translation by F. E. Held (1916) is not altogether satisfactory: I have not seen the original.

on uniformity and system. On the other hand, it has many true ideas on the nature of teaching, especially on the necessity of advancing systematically to new knowledge by the aid of what is already known. Above all, it has the teacher's optimism, a generous confidence in human nature which is far truer than the gloomy doctrine of the Calvinists. Protestants in the time of Comenius were especially interested in the theory of education, because they were conscious that in the arts of teaching they were the inferiors of their great opponents, the Jesuits; but their theorists had in fact singularly little influence over the development of schools and universities. Very different from Comenius is Locke. His *Thoughts on Education*, published in 1690, have the easy manner of the end of the century. To the merits of Comenius they add a deeper insight and a keener observation. They give what may be called an English and a Christian version of what was then the modern ideal. Although in some things they can now be seen to be mistaken, they are still among the best things of the kind.

When modern writers set about constructing a history of education they had to work with the materials that lay ready. The history of schools and universities was, as it still largely remains, dispersed in innumerable separate local and particular narratives and documents, and so it was inevitable that they should turn first to the comparatively solid and manageable body of theoretical writings. As the other scattered materials are brought together into a synthesis, these must necessarily sink into a relatively less prominent position. Even the best of them made little immediate impression on the workaday world of teaching and learning. That world as a whole was but slightly changed even by the powerful impulses towards a modern curriculum and a modern point of view which we have already noticed. In most of the schools and most of the universities, the old tradition in the aims and subject-matter and methods of teaching, though now obsolescent, held its own. The classics were still the mainstay of serious study. Though the bright enthusiasm of the Renaissance was gone, though it became increasingly evident that they were not the only key to knowledge, the old routine was little changed. The primary aim of learned schooling was still 'literata pietas'. Eloquence was still much in demand for the pulpit and the bar. Declamations and school play-acting, even in Calvinistic Holland, were not mere diversions for speech-days but an integral part of serious work. Hebrew was taught in many schools as a preparation for theological studies. Greek was losing ground almost everywhere and in Germany was ceasing to be taught to any except the prospective clergy: the subjects which gained at its expense were, however, not the specially modern studies, but theology and philosophy. The use of Latin as a medium of teaching, as the language in which lessons were given, still continued in many places, as did often the compulsory use of Latin in the conversation of schoolboys and students among themselves, a bad plan now that Latin was no longer in any sense a living language out of school. Not until the very end of the century do we find the beginnings of great changes in the spirit of university education. The scientific revival touched the universities. Anatomical schools from Italy to Holland were centres of it. Cambridge afforded at least a congenial home to Newton, as did Oxford to some of his great contemporaries. One faculty after another underwent the new influence. The foundation of the university of Halle in 1693–4 was a turning-point. It was a symptom of the new spirit that here for the first time a professor lectured in his native German. The full meaning of the new spirit was to become apparent a few years later when the professors there assumed the 'libertas docendi', the freedom to think for themselves and to teach as they thought, which in our day is the practice, or at least the boast, of university teachers, but until then had been their dread.[1]

The fulfilment of this new spirit belongs to the eighteenth and nineteenth centuries; as yet there was only the promise. The rambling medieval building, with its Renaissance furniture, was still inhabited; but the ground was being dug away from under it. The foundations were being undermined and underpinned: its survival had now to depend on the

[1] I leave this sentence as I wrote it in 1929.

strength of the props. The internal arrangements of the universities and the schools were much as they had been; but their place in the social whole was altered. That place had been defined first by their relation to the church. Medieval education had been created by the church: it was managed by churchmen under ecclesiastical control. Even the schools which grew up in the later Middle Ages under municipal supervision in various parts of Europe did not in any serious sense result from a secularizing tendency. They were no less subject than the rest to the authority of the church. In our own time, although there are few countries of which it can be said that the ecclesiastical influence dominates their education, it is still one of the distinctive features of European civilization that in many countries the churches are stronger in their control of education than in any other sphere. In the seventeenth century the ecclesiastical influence was not merely powerful, it was active and creative. In some Protestant countries it was, indeed, damped down by the fall in the social status of the clergy. Thus in the Lutheran states of Germany as in England, though the universities had their well-nourished divines, the clerical schoolmaster was commonly a needy and dissatisfied man on the look-out for a benefice. Where Calvinism prevailed, it naturally enclosed the schools in its grasp. In Holland the curators or governors of the town Latin schools were nominated partly by the municipality and partly by the assembly of the local ministers, one of whom acted as secretary. In the Dutch universities the theological faculties enjoyed the greatest consideration, and of them as of the Protestant universities generally it may be said that their principal function was to train the clergy.

In the Roman Catholic countries the religious impulse to teach was reinforced by the desire to combat the spread of Protestantism. Their superiors repeatedly spurred on the French parochial clergy to improve the schools in the villages, as a means of defence against heresy. Whether they had much success may be doubted; but there can be no question of the importance of another group of educational movements which were at least partly inspired by the same idea. The century saw, especially in France, a remarkable growth of new religious orders, and amongst these some of the most famous and the most influential were teaching orders. The foundation of new orders and the reform of those already existing had begun in the first days of the Counter-Reformation; but its full force was not felt in France until after the end of the Wars of Religion. In 1606 one great lady founded the Ursulines and four years later another founded the 'filles de Notre-Dame'. In the next year the congregation of the Oratory was formed for the instruction of priests, to which the teaching of boys was soon added: it soon adopted 'modern methods'. In 1624 Saint Vincent de Paul founded the Lazarists or 'prêtres de la mission' to evangelize the countryside and instruct the priesthood. The Eudistes, a congregation of teaching secular priests, was founded in 1643, two years after the Sulpicians, to whom Fénelon owed his career and Malebranche his education. The Ignorantins we have already noticed. These foundations were not all equally successful or important, but their total effect was very great, and, in a complete view of French education, there must be added the influence of other orders whose aims were primarily charitable or evangelistic, but which exerted a steady pressure on the conduct and beliefs of the young of every class.

The greatest educating body of Catholic Europe remains to be mentioned, the Society of Jesus. From the time of its rapid rise under St. Ignatius Loyola in the previous century, this body, one of the masterpieces of the Spanish spirit, had combined two great sources of strength. From its members it had exacted the utmost submission, imposing a discipline more than military in its severity; but to the world which it controlled in the interests of the church these relentless devotees had presented themselves not as hard censors, but as men skilled and useful in all practical affairs, exponents of the modern ideal, supple, accommodating, efficient. They were no less successful in their schools than in the princely courts. All Europe admitted at the beginning of the century that in educational practice they were supreme. In discipline, in teaching, in the care of their pupils' health, they were alike successful. Bacon's compliment is well known: 'As for the Pedagogical part, the shortest rule would be "Consult the schools of the Jesuits"; for nothing better has been put into practice.' The great college of Clermont numbered two thousand pupils in 1651 and nearly three thousand in 1675. The order gained almost a monopoly of education in provincial France; in Catholic Germany it had the greatest share in the education of the learned clergy and it controlled several universities; in Poland it had the university of Cracow and dominated the whole education of the country; from no Roman Catholic country was its influence absent. Both in the firmness of the impression which it made on the mind of the individual pupil, and in its effect on political and social life, the Jesuit education was unrivalled.

The Jesuits were thus the supreme example of the continuance of the ecclesiastical power over education, and yet their influence was unlike that of the medieval church. It was permeated by the modern spirit, and it was exerted in ways which were possible only because medieval society had ended, and the conditions had disappeared which had made medieval education a function of the church. The Jesuits, for all they were the standing army of the reformed papacy, made their conquests as auxiliaries of the state. We have seen how Philip IV called them to his aid in the Estudios Reales de San Isidro. It was the French monarchy which ultimately decided that the Jesuits were to exist alongside of the university of Paris, and Henry IV bequeathed his heart to one of their schools. In Germany the education which they gave was given gratuitously; yet it was not by the order that the expense was borne, but by the princes who invited its help. Its successes had everywhere been made possible by its skill in accepting what it could not alter, and it had to adapt its action to the great change of the century, the growing dominance of the state. In this it was only rendering a submission which was equally made by those who managed other educational institutions. The rise of state control over education was a necessary aspect of the rise of the modern state. In the Middle Ages kings had scarcely concerned themselves with schools and universities. They made foundations and granted charters, as they founded abbeys and chantries. They settled disputes as mere matters of police. They interfered to check teaching which seemed politically dangerous, as they checked the inordinate claims of prelates or burghers. But they did not make the aims and methods and daily conduct of teachers their own direct concern. These things they left to the teachers themselves or to the supervision of the church.

As the new monarchy arose, however, these relations were altered. Spain, as might have been expected, led the way; in the sixteenth century the Spanish universities differed from those of the rest of Europe in their intimate relations with the royal and municipal powers. In France the absolute monarchy took control in certain ways, though its interference was mainly negative and repressive and did nothing to end the decadence of the universities. The new Paris statutes of Henry IV, regulating the minutest details of teaching, failed to give it new life. Louis XIV made his own consent necessary before any teacher could become a candidate for the rectorate, or formal headship, of the university of Paris. The privileges of the university were curtailed, for instance, in 1672, its privilege of maintaining its own postal service, and, as early as Henry IV, its separate jurisdiction over offences committed by its members. The learned doctors, like the nobility, were tamed by being taught to aspire to royal honours and rewards.

In Protestant countries the state strengthened its hold over education as over everything else. The Tudors were amongst the strong monarchs of their time, and they prepared the way. They prescribed by law the Latin grammars that schools might use.[1] It is significant that in England King Henry VIII took the side of the advocates of Greek against the 'Trojans' of Oxford. The settlement of his daughter established the type of the English university clergy who, throughout the seventeenth century, never set themselves up against the state as such, but in their highest flights submitted to the Erastian yoke, and merely supported one party in the state against another, in order to obtain from political authority the defence or enforcement of their ecclesiastical views. The Puritans acted through parliament; the Laudians, the followers of the greatest English university

[1] As late as the reign of William and Mary there are, among the Privy Council Papers at the Public Record Office, applications from the heads of private schools for leave to use another Latin grammar instead of Lily's.

reformer of the century, were 'the least ecclesiastical of all ecclesiastical parties';[1] the colleges which braved the attack of James II were content with the parliamentary church of his brother and his daughters. In Holland the provincial estates kept a tight hold on the universities, as the municipalities did on the schools. There, as elsewhere, education had become national, or rather provincial, and territorial in its basis. The medieval universities had been international like the church. In the last days of the Thirty Years' War, when the vagabond Simplicissimus fell in with the resin-gatherers of the Black Forest and gave himself out to be a student, they cried: 'Thank God, there is peace, for the wandering scholars have come back.' But they did not come back to stay. They were vanishing with the old world: the wandering scholar of the new era was the travelling nobleman who wrote his name for a small fee in the matriculation book of Leyden or Padua, and ordered his horses to drive on next day to Amsterdam or Mestre. The business of universities now was to educate the youth of the territorial state. Philip II had given Louvain and Douai a monopoly of the right to teach the young men of the Spanish Netherlands.[2] In Louvain, a couple of generations later, financial embarrassments were relieved by a state subsidy, but at the price of state control. In the German Protestant states the princes paid out money from their treasuries for university scholarships and for the maintenance of schools; but they also drew up regulations and they appointed suitable professors to visit and inspect and see that the regulations were carried out. It was no longer a matter of indifference to the state what was taught, or how the teacher was appointed and paid. To the efforts of the state is due some part of the credit for the system of elementary education in Scotland which, gradually growing throughout the century, had by the end of it given that country the most enlightened peasantry in the world.[3] There was already a foretaste of the days in which the states, grown far richer and stronger, should become, for good and ill, the great promoters and directors of study and upbringing.

[1] Gardiner, *History of England*, vi (ed. of 1909), 204.

[2] See Pirenne, *Histoire de Belgique*, v. 450.

[3] P. Hume Brown, *History of Scotland*, ii. 282, 453, iii. 71.

XIX

RELIGION[1]

NOT long before the beginning of the century the division of western Christendom into mutually hostile and intolerant confessions had been completed. The Roman Catholic Church had defined its relation to Protestantism, and it had done so by rejecting the possibility of compromise or reconciliation. At the Council of Trent dogma, hitherto in some respects unsettled, had been formulated in such a way as to eliminate those doctrines which had been stepping-stones to the Protestant view of grace. While the Protestants held that the central reality of religion was the salvation of the individual believer by faith, and while their different sects built up on this foundation different systems of belief and church government, different ideals of practical life, the older church, diminished now in its geographical extent, preserved and reformed and strengthened the institutions in which salvation was offered through its own mediation. A celibate priesthood, for whose training special seminaries were now being established, directed consciences in the confessional. Monasticism endured. Ritual kept its traditional forms. Latin remained the language of worship. Belief was fixed and in the history of Roman Catholicism little space was now occupied by developments of thought. Such movements of criticism as have to be recorded failed to modify the accepted orthodoxy. The interest of that history from this time lay not in internal growth but in the contest with opposing forces. The process of reconstruction was soon completed. Thanks especially to the Jesuits and the other new religious orders, it was accompanied and followed by a process of conquest. The first enemy was

[1] Ranke's *History of the Popes*, 1st ed., 3 vols., 1834–6, though less full and continuous for this than for the previous period, is still important. Pastor, the Roman Catholic historian of the papacy, whose work has been translated into English, wrote on a much larger scale. There are a number of excellent manuals on the histories of the national churches; but few of them are free from controversial bias.

Protestantism. In the early years of the century the Roman Catholic Church in the Dutch republic was reorganized and strengthened. In Germany before the outbreak of the Thirty Years' War Protestant progress was stopped. The war, by extinguishing Protestantism in many parts of the Habsburg dominions, re-established an equilibrium between the two religious parties. In the later part of the century there was Catholic progress in many parts. England several times seemed to be on the verge of returning to the papal allegiance. Hungary was recovered not only from the Turks but from the Protestants. There were notable conversions among princes. Queen Christina of Sweden, like two of the English Stuarts, though after her abdication, made her peace with Rome. Saxony, once the leading Protestant state of Germany, saw its elector, Augustus the Strong, become a Catholic in order to compass the Polish crown. A number of minor German princes, without such reasons of interest, took the same step.

In Germany the aristocratic and French tendency of the century was on the side of the papacy, but in France itself the monarchy, with the support of national sentiment, at different times set up an opposition almost as menacing as that of Protestantism itself. Although they did not accept the full programme of the Council of Trent, Spain and the Catholic states of Germany and, with the exception of Venice, Italy, were in sympathy with the Counter-Reformation. The attitude of France was from the first less simple. In the wars of religion the unity of the kingdom had been almost overthrown, and when Henry IV restored it, although he became a Catholic, he could not make France a Catholic country. He had to allow the Calvinist minority, the Huguenots, such political privileges that they became, in their own fortified towns, an *imperium in imperio*, a separate kingdom under the same ruler. This position they retained from the Edict of Nantes in 1598 to the Edict of Nîmes in 1629. Furthermore, Catholic France itself was Catholic with a difference. Repeated resolutions of the clerical assemblies did not avail to make the crown accept the decrees of the Council of Trent. It refused to do so right down to the time of the French Revolution, maintaining its powers in relation to benefices, although these conflicted with the reforming policy of the church.[1] Thus the French higher clergy were still for the most part men of aristocratic families, and many of the richest preferments were used either to provide for younger sons or to reward political services.

Nevertheless, in France the greatest religious fact of the century was the Catholic revival. The Christian humanism of the Council of Trent found a perfect literary expression in the writings of St. Francis de Sales, whose personal work as a bishop and spiritual guide was on the same level as his writings. Catholic mysticism became a great force in France, and, if it failed to overcome the faults of Richelieu's favourite diplomatic agent Father Joseph, it was this mysticism which inspired the great reformer and organizer St. Vincent de Paul, who founded not only the work of the Sisters of Charity and other orders which have already been mentioned but, indirectly by example, much of the philanthropic activity even of Protestant countries. Not only were great new religious orders founded, but reform spread through the older orders. It was extravagant and inhuman in the hands of *l'abbé tempête*, de Rancé, the founder of the Trappists; but even he set himself against some of the evils of the time of Louis XIV, and the great scholar Mabillon upheld against him a wise and moderate interpretation of monachism which represented more truly the actual movement of reform. By their time the missionary work had passed through every stratum of French society. In the most fashionable and powerful and intellectually distinguished circles there were men and women who constantly reminded fashion and power and intellect that religion had standards of its own.

By successive steps during the century the Huguenots were deprived first of their political privileges and then of their toleration. The privileges enabled them to play a really dangerous part in the disturbances of the minority and reign of Louis XIII, and Richelieu therefore, after successfully

[1] In 1714 Louis XIV deprived the duc de Nevers of his right of patronage over the small see of Clamecy, and so abolished the last trace of 'mediate' bishoprics in France.

besieging the Huguenot stronghold of La Rochelle, terminated them. For the time being the Protestants were allowed to worship unmolested. Earlier in the century the Gallican liberties, the ancient rights of the French church and crown, had been systematically defined and justified in print. The Gallican system stood for a union of the interests of the king and the bishops against the papacy. Louis XIV in the earlier part of his reign maintained these rights with vigour. In 1682 the French clergy and crown agreed on the Four Gallican Articles, a firm though not an extreme statement of their position, but Pope Innocent XI annulled them and demanded their withdrawal. Louis further alienated the Holy See by provocatively asserting the rights of his ambassadors in Rome. In later life, however, under the influence of Jesuit confessors and of his morganatic wife, Mme de Maintenon, he became devout to the point of bigotry. His quarrels with the Holy See were settled, on the whole to his disadvantage. In the great question of Jansenism, which outlasted his time, he used his influence on the orthodox side. He brought France more into line with the general tendency of Catholicism, and to this end he contributed most of all by his signal achievement, the suppression of the Huguenots. After years of increasing disfavour and molestation they were deprived, by the revocation of the Edict of Nantes in 1685, of the right to worship in their own way. Thousands of them, in spite of legal prohibitions, fled the country, which thus lost many of its most industrious and intelligent inhabitants. The remnant who remained behind had no historical importance. A Protestant rebellion in the Cevennes during the war of the Spanish Succession was utterly put down. France became to all intents and purposes a country of one religion.

At the beginning of the century the Protestants were divided into irreconcilable 'confessions' and within each confession doctrine had become as rigid as that of Rome. In its first phase Lutheranism had been ambiguous or unsettled much as medieval theology had been, but the controversies of the second generation of Lutherans, ending in the Formula of Concord of 1577, had established an anti-Roman system of belief; and the successes of the German Catholics in the next period accentuated the demand for the definition of an orthodox Lutheranism. The theologians of the new century were hard and scholastic dogmatists. Their teachings, based on the Bible as the sole authoritative source of Christian belief, made a permanent impression on the popular mind in many parts of Germany, and the hymns by Paul Gerhardt in the period after the Thirty Years' War show that religious feeling was still alive;[1] but on the whole Lutheranism became sterile. It made no conquests. In its relations with the secular authorities it sank to a dull subjection. From the first it had been closely identified with the power of the princes. The first Lutheran churches had been organized as the state churches of particular countries, but in the spirit of a religious and theocratic view of the state. From this it was, however, an easy transition to the view in which the state's ecclesiastical supremacy is only a branch of its secular and territorial power. In the seventeenth century most of the nominally Lutheran princes in Germany, though not as yet in Denmark and Sweden, were indifferent to religion. Their state churches thus became mere teaching and preaching institutions, while religion, losing its influence on the life of emotion and conduct, became a thing apart, having no existence except on Sundays.

Calvinism, although originally inelastic, showed greater vitality than Lutheranism. Its strength lay in the fact that in every respect, in ritual, in organization, above all in dogma, it was the antithesis of Roman Catholicism. By a discipline for the laity as severe as any Christian body has ever imposed, it fostered a formidable self-sufficiency in the believers. In Geneva, Scotland, and Holland it had to submit to organization on the geographical basis of the territorial state, but it was not put under the state. In the two former states at least, and in France under the Edict of Nantes, it enjoyed what may not unjustly be called a separation of church and state. In Germany it prevailed, except on the Lower Rhine, in a mitigated form, less strict in both confession and constitution than the oldest Calvinist churches.

[1] Several of them may be found translated in *The English Hymnal.*

It was less rigid than Lutheranism became, and for this reason it gained the adherence of most of the Lutherans who were excluded by the Formula of Concord. It made notable progress. In 1613 the electoral house of Lutheran Brandenburg, having an interest in the Lower Rhine, turned Calvinist, a change with important results for the future. The Calvinistic Palatinate, to its cost, became the leading state in the politics of the Protestants. During the German campaigns of Gustavus Adolphus several German courts turned from Lutheranism to Calvinism. In England, during the rule of the Long Parliament and before the interference of the army in politics, Presbyterianism was the established religion. Few would then have guessed that this, transitory as it was, was the last conquest of Calvinism. Almost silently, almost unnoticed, the English Presbyterian Church sank into decadence. Calvinism was eradicated from France and oppressed in eastern Europe. It maintained its position only in Holland, Scotland, and Geneva.

It would, however, not be quite absurd to class the English Independents as a new type of Calvinists. They had their forerunners in the time of Queen Elizabeth and among the sects of Holland, but the main period of their rise is the later and more extreme stage of Puritanism under the Stuart kings. There grew up in different parts of the country groups of worshippers who for the most part accepted the Calvinistic dogma of predestination and the Calvinist discipline; but differed from one another in many other points of belief and practice, especially infant baptism. In their church government they were at the opposite pole from the old Calvinists. They abandoned the territorial system of organization altogether, and took the isolated congregation as the autonomous unit. There was in their theory an invisible church containing all the elect, but the visible church consisted only of these separate churches, each with Christ for its immediate head. Even for this doctrine a preparation may be found in earlier Presbyterian practice, for the congregation, under such names as 'kirk session' and 'colloquium', had been the lowest unit in the hierarchy of assemblies in which the Calvinistic churches had been organized; but the Independents, in eliminating all the regional and national superstructure, had taken a long step towards tolerating varieties of opinion and worship.[1] When they became the controlling section in the victorious New Model Army, they used their brief power in such a way that religious diversity took root and became a lasting feature of English life. Oliver Cromwell had that rare kind of greatness which combines intense conviction with a generous respect for some of the sincere beliefs of others. He saw that the confusion of sects was a sign of life. He understood the mind of George Fox, the founder of the Quakers. Fox, being both a prophet and an organizer, succeeded in combining an individualism even more extreme than that of the Independents with a closely knit system of discipline and mutual help. The immovable endurance of his followers in the face of persecution gave another defeat to the principle of uniformity, and after the Restoration, though all the fires of fanaticism were dying down, the English government had to set the example of permitting free churches to exist side by side with the state church. Never wholly suppressed under Charles II and James II, they were, if somewhat grudgingly, tolerated from the Revolution of 1688. Nonconformity was still a bar to full civil rights, but freedom of worship was granted once and for all.

Every one of these transactions in every country of Europe was the occasion of acrimonious controversy. The prevailing note of the theological writings of the century is ferocity. There were not wanting men of sufficient breadth to deplore the hardening and multiplication of religious divisions; but their efforts came to nothing. Some of them, like Grotius or Comenius, were respected as theorists, but lacked the power to influence events. Some were oddities like Marc Antonio de Dominis who, after being bishop of Spalato in Dalmatia, became an Anglican clergyman and died in the prison of the inquisition at Rome. One tragic figure was Cyril Loukaris,

[1] It must also be remembered that some of the earlier sects which were among their forerunners, such as the Mennonites, rejected the characteristic tenets of Calvin. The English Baptists, though holding in general the Independent view of the nature and government of the church, had a complex ancestry on the side of belief.

Orthodox patriarch of Alexandria and afterwards of Constantinople, whose sympathy and correspondence with the Protestants ended in his murder. There were others in the highest positions. In the spheres of both doctrine and diplomacy, King James I of England cast about for pathways to reunion. Oliver Cromwell dreamed of a militant Protestant alliance, and tried to avert persecution from the Vaudois of the Piedmontese valleys. But even these were only dreams. It may be doubted whether the century affords a single instance of the reconciliation of two divided religious bodies. The only quarter in which there can in any sense be said to have been progress towards reunion was in eastern Europe, and there the progress was made by way of extending the frontiers of Roman Catholicism. Between the Roman Catholics and the Greek Orthodox Church there were interposed the Uniats, the Churches of the Greek rite and the Roman obedience. The Synod of Brest-Litovsk, Brest in Lithuania, in 1596 had inaugurated an eastward movement of such Roman Catholicism on a more northerly front than that of its earlier advances. It began the absorption of the churches of Lithuania, and after bitter disputes this was completed by the submission of the dioceses of Lemberg in 1700 and Lutsk in 1702. This, however, marked no better understanding between the eastern and the western churches, but only the extension of papal authority over the whole of the politically western states. So far from being a progress towards real reunion, this advance is merely another illustration of ecclesiastical divisions and their close conformity to those of the territorial states.

Within the churches, as in their relations with one another, intolerance and exclusiveness prevailed whenever a serious division of opinion arose. Among the Roman Catholics the leading example was that of the Jansenist controversy. Cornelius Jansen, a learned Flemish theologian, was rewarded for his services to the Spanish authorities in the Netherlands with the bishopric of Ypres. Desiring to bring back Christianity from the divergent dangers of scholasticism, formal 'devotions', and mere ethical natural religion, to an evangelical directness, he wrote a study of St. Augustine, that one amongst the Latin fathers whose ideas had been most drawn upon by the Protestant founders. As was to be expected, he produced a system which had a good deal in common with Protestant beliefs, such as that of predestination. During his own lifetime the consequences were not serious; but when his ideas were popularized in France, the Jesuits took alarm. Their great power had been built up on the belief in free will, with its corollary of obedience to the confessor. In 1649 the university of Paris condemned certain propositions which were alleged to occur in Jansen's works, and in 1653 Pope Innocent X added his censure to that of the theologians. The Jansenists, however, were in earnest and were ably led. They embarked on a long struggle for the recognition of their ideas. The French government became one of the parties to the dispute. A preliminary repression was followed by a lull; but at last, in the period when the more moderate advisers about him had died or lost their influence, King Louis XIV turned against Jansenism with fanatical severity. He procured bull after bull condemning this and that in the Jansenist teachings, going so far that many orthodox Catholics, including the archbishop of Paris, were driven into opposition. Louis died in the middle of the contest, which dragged on all through the remaining days of the old régime, the papal condemnations being then opposed by the Gallicanism of the law courts as ultramontane encroachments.

This wearisome history has its noble episodes, and the Jansenists have a high place in religious and literary history. One of their centres was the Cistercian nunnery of Port Royal, which had its original home a few miles from Paris and a second house in the city. These became places of resort for many of the best men and women in France. In the school attached to the Paris house Racine had his education. With all the wastefulness of intolerance the nuns were dispersed by the police, their buildings pulled down and even their cemetery destroyed. From the whole controversy one book has remained ever since a classic, the *Lettres Provinciales* published serially by Pascal in 1656–7. This refutation of the anti-Jansenist positions is equally great for three things, an exemplary prose style, a relentless logic, and a moral earnestness. It has made the calculated indulgence of a certain school of casuists a byword ever since; and though Jansenism has as good as vanished now, it did this service to the churches. Nor ought we to regret without qualification that it was worsted. The sufferings of the Jansenists and their unquestionable sincerity easily blind a modern student to the narrowness and harshness of their opinions. Like the Calvinists, they derived their vivid sense of right and wrong from the sharp separation in their minds of the things which belonged to salvation and those which belonged to reprobation. If, instead of being persecuted, they had been able to rule, we can hardly doubt that they would have been as hard masters as the elect have been at other times.

Another controversy of the seventeenth century shows the behaviour of believers in predestination when they won the upper hand. Deplorable as the Jansenist affair showed the state of the Roman Church to be, the Protestants could not regard it with the complacency of men free from the same evils. Each of the great Protestant confessions has an equally painful recollection. There is almost a parallelism between Jansenism and the quarrel among the Calvinists over Arminianism. Jacobus Arminius was a peace-loving professor of theology at Leyden who was influenced by his reading of the Jesuit theologians. His speculations led him to abandon the hard-and-fast doctrine of predestination. He was also an Erastian. He died in the year when the Dutch republic made its truce with Spain, and the controversy which arose from his opinions became the axis of Dutch politics in the ensuing period of peace. The orthodox Calvinists furiously attacked a doctrine which seemed to them little short of popery, but some of the leading politicians, broad-minded men of affairs, tried to shelter the 'remonstrant' ministers from the onslaught. Unhappily they were led on from an assertion of lay rights against the ministers to resisting the ministers' protectors, the states-general. They took steps which threatened the political unity of the republic, and their temerity brought down a *coup d'état* and an ecclesiastical persecution. It was as political victims that Oldenbarnevelt died on the block and Grotius went to prison and exile; but the attempt to moderate Calvinist fanaticism was also stamped out. The Synod of Dort, which did the work in 1618–19, was no more than national in its authority, but it was attended by advisory deputies from Switzerland, the Palatinate, Nassau, Hesse, East Friesland, Bremen, and England.[1] It was the nearest approach that was ever made to a universal meeting of the Calvinistic churches, and it is significant that its result was to narrow and not to widen their formulae of belief.[2]

No less than Calvinism, Lutheranism persisted in exclusiveness throughout the greater part of the century. It had its theologians of wider outlook, but they too met with stubborn hostility. The most important of these was Georg Calixtus, who had travelled in Holland and England, and became the leader in North Germany of a more liberal theology which was called 'syncretism'. This provided a basis for harmonizing Lutheran with Calvinistic beliefs, and it had the support of the Great Elector of Brandenburg, a Calvinist ruler whose dominions, including both confessions, succeeded to the primacy among German Protestant states after the ruin of the Palatinate. But Calixtus, like so many peace-makers, was hated by both sides, and the disputes over his teaching settled nothing. They raged until a new set of innovators came forward in the later years of the century, the Pietists. With these we do reach a religious revival which drew upon several sources beyond the boundaries of Lutheranism, and established itself in defiance of the attempts of the orthodox to suppress it. On the one hand, it was an influx of the Calvinist spirit of discipline, moral precision, and personal salvation; on the other, since it came in partly under English influences, it tended to Congregationalism, and this, except in Württemberg where a compromise was effected, was disapproved by the church authorities. Its father was Philipp Jakob Spener, an Alsatian whose activity extended from Frankfort to Berlin; but he himself did not show the fully developed characteristics of the move-

[1] Curiously enough, not Scotland: Walter Balcanqual, though a Scot by birth, was a clergyman of the Church of England. On the other hand the decrees of the synod had great influence in Scotland: see G. D. Henderson, *Religious Life in Seventeenth-Century Scotland* (1937).

[2] A. W. Harrison, *The Beginnings of Arminianism* (1924), gives the most recent English account.

ment. After his death in 1705 it entered on its great work in the university of Halle and in foreign missions. It is thus to the eighteenth century that it really belongs, and it has qualities so typical of that age as to become one of the sources of English Methodism. There is emotionalism, other-worldliness, a contempt of learning, an unhealthy probing of the believer's experience. That these should be the defects of spiritual revival when it did come was, as we shall see, the inevitable result of the course the churches had followed in the seventeenth century.

Paradoxical as it may sound after this summary of fissions and heresy-hunts, there was much in common between the histories of the different churches and sects. Although there was so little communication or mutual understanding between them, there are striking resemblances. Even the tendency to define and persecute was, as we have seen, common to almost all of them. It was not merely a negative tendency. In setting a high value on true belief it had a positive side which was genuinely a part of the religious mind of Europe. Other similarities in the religious experience of men or women divided by the hostilities of creeds are not far to seek.[1] Molière's *Tartuffe*, a satire on the lay confessors who worked among the French Quietists,[2] as well as on all hypocrites, served almost equally well, with a few alterations by the translator, as a satire on the English Puritans. A hundred more serious instances might be given to prove that, for all their differences, there was a solid nucleus of common doctrine which all Christians accepted. If we are disposed to think that even so there were elemental differences between their creeds, we may find a corrective in the history of the Church of England. The special distinction of that church is that it was linked with the territorial state, but with a state which never consistently and for long together attempted to enforce more than a minimum of uniformity in belief and ritual. In the first half of the century it gave up the

[1] I am not competent to discuss how far contemporary western Judaism was influenced by the same currents of opinion, but the reader of Graetz, *Geschichte der Juden*, vols. ix and x, will be struck, for instance in the tragedy of Uriel da Costa, by many points of similarity.

[2] See below, p. 321.

ideal of comprehension, but the theology prevalent among its leading 'high churchmen' was that very Arminianism which had been too little one-sided to survive on the Continent. Anglican apologists were free to assimilate materials from foreigners of many persuasions, and the rise of toleration was facilitated not only by the growth of sects but by the traditional intermediacy of the established church itself. It is a mistake to regard this merely as the crowning example of the English aptitude for muddling through. What it really illustrates is the underlying unity of western Christianity, which the failures of ecclesiastical statesmanship and especially the political alliances of churches had disastrously interrupted.

It is possible, then, to make abstraction of all the divisions and controversies, to ignore them, and trace some common religious life in Europe. To do so will not indeed be to turn from the evils of false religion to a comforting picture of saints and martyrs who were untouched by the outward proceedings of the churches. Far from that, it will be to a great extent tracing the repercussions of intolerance and authoritarianism on the spiritual life itself. The first and most striking fact about the religion of the period, as distinguished from its ecclesiastical affairs, is its loss of effective contact with the great world of action and thought. Philosophy, science, and literature followed a well-marked path towards utilitarian ethics and a 'natural religion' which contained nothing of the miraculous or of revelation. The late seventeenth century handed on to the eighteenth the reasonable and colourless belief of deism, 'a constitutional monarchy in heaven'. The movement towards this was reflected in the decline of religious enthusiasm, in the change, for instance, from the Quakerism of George Fox to that of William Penn; but there was little mutual intellectual fertilization between scientists or philosophers and theologians. Theology contributed nothing to the scientific revival. In the countries where that revival was most active there was no lack of theologians who were willing to embody its results in their speculations. There was a considerable number of works of 'natural theology' written both by ecclesiastics and by laymen such as Locke. These authors were by no means devoid of religious feeling, and there is much more in their works than mere arguments to prove that current scientific knowledge was compatible with Christian belief. The attempt to demonstrate this led, however, inevitably to a less sharp insistence on dogma. The scientists, as we have seen, threw out no challenge; but theologians who were affected by their spirit were necessarily sceptical of some articles and unable to accept others in their old literal meanings. The tendency to soften and generalize had the advantage of offering a way out from the old unprofitable polemics. In the English Latitudinarians of the end of the century the spirit of charity joined with a good measure of the spirit of science; but they failed to convince the churches, and in the course of the eighteenth century 'reason' and Christianity drifted wide apart.

In this way it came about that only one man gained a place both in the front rank of the scientific revival and amongst the classical defenders of Christianity. Blaise Pascal was the son of a Frenchman of the legal and official caste. He was born in 1623, proved to be a remarkably precocious child and, after long ill health, died before he was forty. We have come across his name as a mathematician, as a master of French prose, as the defender of Jansenism. His *Pensées*, published after his death, are for the most part fragments of a defence of Christianity which he had planned, and of which some of the main arguments had been given as addresses at Port Royal. He states his own view in relation to what he took to be the principal intellectual currents of his own time, and also in relation to the chief doctrines which had been rivals to Christianity throughout history. What he has to say against the Jews and the Stoics is of less interest than what he has to say against Montaigne and Descartes, and it may be remarked that he is surprisingly untouched by the tendency towards historical criticism of the Bible which, during his lifetime, was already awake. He sees that scepticism, 'Pyrrhonism' as he calls it, must not be merely denounced as unorthodox. He sees that there is much truth in Montaigne's arguments for it, but he turns it round to serve the cause of orthodoxy by making it prove the helplessness of the unaided human mind. With the same result he makes light of the metaphysical arguments for the existence of God and the immortality of the soul. 'I cannot forgive Descartes;' he writes, 'he would have liked to be able to dispense with God in the whole of his philosophy; but he could not avoid bringing him in to set the world in motion by a twist of his finger and thumb; after that he has no further use for God.' To Pascal, on the other hand, there are two great truths, the misery of man and the greatness of God. He draws the contrast between the uncertainties of human life and the infinite promises of religion; and he insists that man is like a player in a game in which he must bet, staking his future either on belief or unbelief, and in which the only way to win is to bet on the existence of God. His God, however, is not the God of deism, which seems to him almost as hostile to Christianity as atheism, but the crucified Christ. The misery of man, and all the arguments of scepticism and cynicism are for him proofs of man's fallen state, and he accepts the whole system of prophecies, revelations, and miracles by which Christianity supported its claim to be the sole foundation for morality, for the hope of immortality, and for happiness in this life. He advocates at once absolute submission to the church and a self-renunciation so severe that it censured all personal affection, and regarded sickness, with its suffering, privations, loss of all desire, and expectation of death, as the natural state of Christians and as exemplifying the way in which they ought to pass their lives.

Pascal's genius has been widely applauded; but it had no influence of any importance on the history of thought in the century after his time. Many of those who were able to appreciate his arguments were steadily drifting into rationalism, whether of the deistic or some other type, and ceasing to regard faith as co-ordinate with reason, let alone superior to it. In contrast with the unemotional rigidity of theologians and scientists, there were, on the other hand, ardent mystical movements. They were not limited to any one part of Europe nor were any of the churches untouched by them. They were the expression of a tendency which, however differently it fared in different places, was general. In former ages mystics had sometimes been troublesome to the authorities, but the Counter-Reformation knew how to value its mystics, like St. Theresa, whose visions and raptures were untainted by doctrinal speculation. The tradition then begun is still alive, and its character needs no explanation now because it is a contemporary fact to be observed without difficulty in any part of our present world. Such devotion, suited to the atmosphere of the seventeenth century, has been made familiar by the artists of the period. In them, indeed, it is possible to see more clearly than in the great mystics themselves the dangers which lie in wait for an undisciplined surrender to these great forces of anguish and illumination. Bernini's wonderful statue of St. Theresa translates spiritual rapture, within the rules of propriety, into something very near a purely physical expression. At the end of the century the rise of the cult of the Sacred Heart and the visions of Marie Alacoque were examples of what may be called erotic mysticism. Late in the seventeenth century mysticism threw off a shoot which seemed to the watchful theologians likely to develop the subversive individualism or even anarchism to which exaggerated mysticism is always liable.

Miguel de Molinos, a Spaniard, was a fashionable priest in Rome. The 'Quietism' which he preached aimed at giving, through a certain mode of life and certain ways of devotion, direct access to the deity, not only without such outward aid as that of rosaries, but altogether without the mediation of the church. This was a negative mysticism of which the ideal was the quiet of personal non-existence. It does not seem that Molinos at all understood how far a consistent pursuit of his principles would have taken him. He may have been one of the many men who have suffered less for what they meant to say than for what they were understood to mean. Many erroneous statements about him are current: it is certain that he fell from his high position and, after a trial in 1685–7, he died in the prison of the Inquisition in 1696. In France controversy over Quietism was one of the disturbing factors in the last phase of Louis XIV.

There were Protestant *illuminés* who ended as miserably as Molinos, for the cruelty of that age reached its heights when it was reinforced by outraged righteousness. The greatest among the Protestant mystics was Jakob Boehme, a German who had lived into the earlier period of the Thirty Years' War, and whose writings, little liked by official Lutheranism while he was alive, have never ceased to find a response in one country or another. In the general ferment of ideas which English Puritanism aroused there were many extravagant mystical sects. The 'Behmenists' were regularly organized followers of Boehme. This was one of the confluent streams from which Quakerism flowed, and some of the early Quakers passed in their fervour beyond the borderlines of law and sanity. James Nayler's admirers hailed him as the Messiah, and the savage punishment inflicted on him is a stain on the history of the Puritan rule in England. Lodowicke Muggleton, another prophet, founded a sect of which some remnant still lingers. Little as we may respect them as thinkers, we must not forget that these and their likes were merely the extremists of a movement which had also its moderate and even its intellectually distinguished representatives. The mystic's protest against the aridity of outward religion and philosophy was a characteristic note of the time. It is found among divines of the Church of England in the Caroline devotional verse which is still a living part of the English religious tradition. Towards the end of the century again it was exemplified by the half-philosophical, half-spiritualistic school of academic writers who are known by the somewhat misleading name of the Cambridge Platonists. With Plato they were only remotely connected, through the Neoplatonic writers who have attracted mystics in many ages. Several of them were men of great intellectual acuteness, with that credulity which is sometimes the nemesis of an overstrained scepticism.

When we touch upon mysticism, however, and even when we consider some of the other varieties of religious experience to which that name cannot be given, we reach the confines of civilization in the sense in which we are examining it. These things have, it is true, their history. They have their own continuity: attachment to old books like that of the English seventeenth-century Benedictine, Dom Augustine Baker, is one of the constant traits of the mystical mind. They have also their connexion with the changes of the outer world. They receive, although it is through an incalculable refractive medium, the lights of contemporary thought. The mysticism of each age carries the marks of that age upon it, and in that sense it belongs to the history of the age. But in another sense it is outside history. More than any other experience, it seems to those who have it to transcend time and place and circumstance, bringing direct contact with absolute reality. It repudiates any dependence on the real as it is apprehended in other ways. It often despises or contradicts the ascertained results of science or philosophy, and so it has no explicable place in the 'dialectic' of the visible and intelligible world. It is an end in itself, which can never be swallowed up in the ends of knowledge or action. What it contributes to the structure of civilization, in so far as there is such a coherent structure, is not of its own essence, but a derivative, an ectype, the religion which enters into daily life.

Of the part which that secondary religion played in the seventeenth century two further observations may be made. The first is familiar. Life was then coloured to an uncommon degree by certain religious modes of expression and behaviour. Much was said in religious language which would now be expressed without any such allusion. A good cause was the cause of God; morality was a matter of sin and salvation; injustice and wrong were Satanic. In Protestant countries the Bible was almost universally known with immense though unintelligent exactitude. John Richard Green, in a memorable passage of his *Short History of the English People*,[1] showed how the English became the people of a book, and that book the Bible, how the Old and New Testaments were their whole popular literature. It was equally so in the Protestant countries of the Continent. In the Roman Catholic countries it was less Bible-reading than the varied histories and legends of the church which supplied the materials, but the result, though not quite the same, was comparable.[2] There is thus always a difficulty in estimating the degree to which what we call religion enters into any-

[1] Cap. viii, sec. 1.

[2] See the delightful account of the lives of the saints written for popular reading in France in H. Bremond, *Histoire littéraire du sentiment religieux en France*, i (1916), 239 ff.

thing which was said in the seventeenth century in religious language. It is not solved by discounting all theological terms and treating them merely as common form. On the contrary, it is more often necessary to remind ourselves that these words were then seldom used without their accompaniment of meaning, and that their use did generally imply a heightened intensity of feeling. This sense of the closeness of God and the Devil to every act and fact of daily life is an integral part of the character of the century.

It must, however, be added that it was receding from many regions where once it had been prevalent. One thing after another which had been spiritual was becoming secular. The churches were losing their hold on politics. Science and philosophy became completely detached from theology. Side by side with sacred art and music there grew up purely secular schools of painting and forms of musical composition. In education the process was less simple, but if the churches kept much, they also lost ground. They had little part in the aristocratic ideal of conduct and accomplishment which mastered literature and social life. The Jesuits, who were not strangers to that ideal, roused up for that very reason many opponents. All the tendencies to enthusiasm and puritanism were out of sympathy with it. Thus religion wore increasingly an appearance which has since, at some times and places, been habitual to it. It was the treasure of the humble. Some of the religious classics of the seventeenth century, like the *Pilgrim's Progress*, are books of the people. Some of the religious movements were touched, like German Pietism, with the contempt of worldly learning which comes easily to the ignorant. In all walks of life there were thousands of men and women whose simple goodness was far removed from the acrimony of theological polemics and of the contests for ecclesiastical rights. The constituted leaders of the churches and sects did not succeed in disengaging themselves from these disputes, even when they had visibly lost their central and unifying place in the European thought. By the end of the century philosophy and statecraft, though they generally maintained relations of politeness with official religion, were almost estranged from the Christian ethical and devotional inheritance.

XX

LITERATURE[1]

If the question were asked what the seventeenth century did for the permanent enrichment of human life, it would be answered differently according to the scales of values which were applied, but, whatever disagreement there might be about some of its other legacies, all would concur in setting a very high price on its great works of poetry and imaginative prose. It is true that the list of those which are now admired does not coincide at all closely with any list that would have been drawn up at the time when they were written. We often deceive ourselves when we suppose that we can read an old book as it was read by contemporaries. Even very learned and very sympathetic students of old literature cannot help being creatures of their own age. In our houses we have seventeenth-century furniture. Some of it has come down to us almost unnoticed and stays in its old uses; some we have acquired because it is beautiful and was meant by its makers to be beautiful; there is yet more which we find picturesque but which to them was commonplace; some again, like their common household gear, once useful and necessary, is now useless, so that we do not trouble to preserve it. Not one of these 'antiques' is exactly the same to us as it was to its first owners. Even when we sit in their oak arm-chairs we are not doing as they did, for we have sofas and soft chairs, and sitting upright is not the same to us as it was to them. What is true of furniture, which satisfies simple and comparatively unchanging purposes, is far more true of literature, the sensitive and perpetually responsive apparatus

[1] Taste has changed so much that Hallam's *Introduction to the Literature of Europe*, first ed., 1837–9, which is still useful for other subjects, is now out of date in its treatment of imaginative literature. The whole great field is covered by two text-books, which give further references, in the series 'A History of European Literature': *The First Half of the Seventeenth Century*, by Professor H. J. C. Grierson, 1906, and *The Augustan Ages*, by Professor Oliver Elton, 1899. Among works subsequently published one of considerable importance is Benedetto Croce, *Studi sulla letteratura italiana del seicento*, 1924.

by which the world of imagination is adjusted to the most complex and most personal requirements of the human soul. A few great masterpieces of seventeenth-century literature, though they have meant different things to different generations, have been continuously prized. Others have been forgotten and revived, some of them to be forgotten again. Still others are attractive to students who want them as expressions of the civilization which made them. The whole mass is only a selection, and a selection made for changing needs, but it is sufficient to set the seventeenth century among the great creative periods.

This is true especially of three among the national literatures which have ranked highest in their influence on the world, and of two among those of the next lower level. In England the Elizabethan glory was at its brightest when the century opened. The whole life of Milton fell within it. When it ended the 'Restoration' drama had almost run its course; the prose and verse of the Augustan age were nearing their best. In France, with much else, it produced in both comedy and tragedy all the greatest works of that classical drama which is still the highest and typical embodiment of the French genius. In Spain, as in England, its earlier years fell within a time, already begun, of many-sided splendour. It gave to the Spaniards the most famous of their dramatists, and to all the world Don Quixote. The language of Spain's neighbour, Portugal, is now little read by foreigners, but the Portuguese account some of their seventeenth-century writers among their greatest. In the same way the Dutch, although they are deprived by accident of the confirmation of foreign opinion, regard Vondel as their greatest poet and his time as the best in their literary annals.[1]

When we pass to the other countries of Europe, we do not find any of which the same can be said. In Sweden it was a good period, but, on the whole, a period of promise rather than of maturity. In Germany there was decline: foreign influences and false standards overcame all but a few writers of powerful individuality. Poland and Hungary look back

[1] A. J. Barnouw, *Vondel* (1925 in English, 1926 in Dutch), gives a general account of the period.

on this as a time of decadence.[1] Even in Italy, but lately the source of inspiration for the whole of Europe, although there was much literary activity about the princely courts, its results were feeble. There was no prose of any importance except in treatises or sermons. In poetry nothing remained alive except intellectual ingenuity and a prettified sensualism. The lyrics of the period are, for the most part, slight in content, strained and artificial in form.

The good health of literature was in fact dependent on political vigour. Where the life of the state was robust, even when, as in England, it was turbulent, men found better things to write than in the misery of Germany or the stagnant passivity of the Italians. There is never a complete divorce between letters and politics. The literary languages of Europe, as they have been formed from the multitude of dialects, have crystallized round political centres, separating when these have divided, coalescing as they unite. A language cannot be defined except as the speech of an organized people, and a literature cannot arise except in the medium of a common life. Battles and the enforcement of justice, civil strife and the fortunes of kings, make a large part of the common stock of imaginative experience: they colour even the most personal affections and ideals. In the seventeenth century this was true to an exceptional degree. It was the age of the political ode and the political satire. The drama, free from the tutelage of the church, had entered the service of the other great institution of ceremonial and pageantry, the royal court. The minds of the spectators were reflected in its choice of subjects. Even where political discussion was prohibited the dramatists had their minds full of state affairs. It was by making them monarchs or state conspirators that Shakespeare and Racine alike raised their heroes to the tragic scale of grandeur. Among the human types which the dramatists, the writers of 'characters', or the novelists portrayed, none were more shrewdly observed than the counsellors, the place-hunters, the sycophants and adventurers who clustered round the kings. Constitutional history and

[1] As elsewhere in this book, I rely entirely on the statements of others in anything that I say about Scandinavian, Polish, or Magyar literature.

political theory fall into a wrong perspective if they take the point of view merely of obligation and utility, forgetting that the state, as the focus of the most unquestioning loyalties and the arena of the keenest of all contests for power, is, like love and war, one of the themes of the literary artists.

In bringing about this result the force of political passions was seconded by the social conditions of authorship. The royal protection accorded to the drama was not so much a part of the diversions of kings as of their work as rulers. The more enlightened European rulers well understood how much they could do by judiciously distributing favours among the literary men, and teaching them, as they taught the nobles, to look to royal bounty for the fulfilment of their ambitions. It was the age of patronage in every walk of life, but in none more than in literature. Noblemen and other writers who needed no protectors were less prominent among the writers than they had been in the sixteenth century. Authorship was less often an incident in a life of action and adventure, more often a means of livelihood. It was coming to be normally a professional pursuit. The amateur was less to the fore than he had been in the days of Sidney and Montaigne. Cervantes, early in the period, belonged to the old heroic line, but most of the great writers were comparatively sedentary men. They could earn something from the sale of their books or from the box-offices of the theatres, but these were seldom sufficient rewards, and even these could scarcely be earned without the good offices of some nobleman who would accept a dedication or gave his livery to a company of players. A patron might provide a minor office at court, a tutorship, a pension in cash, an ecclesiastical benefice, at the very least hospitality and a passport to fashionable society. His requirements might vary as much as his benefactions. He might be content with a flattering dedicatory epistle and with the friendship and gratitude of his client, or he might demand some more direct literary service such as a defence of his policy or a panegyric on his family. But whatever he demanded and whatever he gave in return, he was almost indispensable to the author. Authors sought after the most powerful patrons they could get. In London, where the aristocracy was never overshadowed by the crown, the Stuart kings merely played their part as the first among equals; but in the absolutist countries the kings were as much the masters in literary patronage as they were in politics or society.

The dependence of letters on worldly power moulded not only the relation of the individual writer to his own patron or patrons, but also the relations of authors among themselves. The men of words, especially perhaps those of less than the highest merit, are gregarious. Vanity and jealousy are among their besetting faults, but even these lamentable qualities, so far from discouraging intercourse, find their most nourishing pasture in a social circle. From the dawn of the Italian renaissance, and indeed from even earlier times, there had been academies, some more freely formed and others under princely auspices. In the course of time they had become specialized, and we have noticed the considerable services of those devoted to science and learning. For pure literature this form of association is less certainly beneficial than where the object is co-operation in acquiring knowledge. Its influence is almost sure to be in the direction of setting up and enforcing rigid standards, and, although this may be a useful service to the correction and improvement of language, it is dangerous to apply it to the substance of literature, to sentiments and even to matters of style and to the forms of expression in verse and prose. Thus the French academy has undeniably done much good by its dictionary, which was begun in 1639 and first published in 1694;[1] but by its distribution of praise and blame in higher matters, although it has been one of the formative influences of French literature, it has probably at times exalted mediocrity and depressed true genius. If that is in some measure true of the greatest of all modern academies, it is far more so with the numerous fantastically named societies which in Italy, Germany, and elsewhere carried on the tradition of those of the Renaissance. The mutual admiration of poetasters who met to exchange verses in the characters of shepherds could only result in a deterioration of taste. The exceptions

[1] It did not at once gain recognition as the supreme authority.

are those where the academies were strengthened from without. In France the connexion with the monarchy, in Holland the solidity of the national culture, outweighed the tendency to frivolous ingenuity.

In many ways like the academies, but much more favourable to real individuality, were those other characteristic resorts of the authors of the time, the *salons*. In the history of French literature a great place must be assigned to the Hôtel de Rambouillet, which has been called, with pardonable exaggeration, the first society on this side of the Alps which united the aristocracies of rank and of genius in one circle. There, under the eyes of a gifted hostess, Richelieu used to meet the great dramatist Corneille. A *salon* is less formal than an academy, more purely a social gathering, less pleased with erudition and more given to wit. Its conversation revolves round the women, and the literature of the second half of the seventeenth century bears many signs that its writers met ladies of fashion on terms of social equality. 'The town' became one of the favourite settings for verse, and when the country was described, it was the country as it is seen by the guests in a château or mansion. The literary class was growing more numerous and more compact. Like the learned class it was taking its tone and manners from the aristocracy. It helped in the formation of the standards and social consciousness of the upper classes. At the time when the old feudal aristocracy was silently assimilating recruits from the *bourgeoisie* of every country from Ireland to Naples, men and women were specially self-conscious in matters of deportment. When Molière satirized the *Bourgeois Gentilhomme* and the rich peasant who married above his station, his audiences were crowded with newcomers to high life who laughed the more because they were separated from Monsieur Jourdain and Georges Dandin only by the thin partition of conformity to accepted usage. Even Molière, who saw through pretentious shams as well as any man who ever lived, could flatter the complacency of the 'best people', and from about his time it became the general rule that the pen was a modest auxiliary of the purse.

For the causes of another great change in the purposes of

writing we must look also to the improvement in the methods of communication. Together with the spread of education, the rise of postal systems and the other changes connected with it were making a deep impression on the habits of the general population. Letter-writing was ceasing to be a luxury confined to the rich and learned. More and more as time went on it was becoming an everyday incident for commonplace people. That meant not only a widening of the common man's horizon; it also meant that it became less and less easy for governments to control the exchanging of news. They had, of course, their very skilful experts for opening and reading letters; but now they could open only a small proportion of those that were sent, and their chances of damming up a broad stream of information or opinion were diminishing. An increasing number of people had regular confidential correspondents who sent them political or commercial reports from a capital to the provinces, or even from one country to another. The trade in news was facilitated and grew. Professional writers of newsletters had existed in all countries for a long time and were still to go on for some time to come. In Queen Anne's reign, for instance, Abel Boyer, the historian, used to send a newsletter to the ambassador, Lord Strafford, at The Hague by every post for a guinea a week.[1] But it was not by this old-fashioned system that Boyer made his living. He published an excellent monthly magazine.[2] In much the same way Oldenburg, the first secretary of the Royal Society, gave up his plan of sending monthly reports of scientific progress to individuals,[3] and started, as a private venture, the society's *Philosophical Transactions*. It had become safe to sell the news broadcast, and it paid better to make it common property than to dole it out furtively to a limited clientele.

Journalism was born and grew to maturity in the seventeenth century. A string of dates will show that plainly. In 1609 comes the first printed periodical, the *Strassburger Zeitung*. In 1621 come the first English newspapers (printed

[1] *Wentworth Papers*, pp. 393, 410, 420.

[2] *The Political State of Great Britain*.

[3] See his letter of August 1664 to Boyle quoted by Meinsma, p. 244: Oldenburg's tariff was to be £10, £8, or £6 a year.

in Holland for British soldiers there). In 1631 Richelieu started the first official newspaper, the *Gazette de France*. Its English counterpart was started in 1665 and became the *London Gazette* in 1666. In 1665 was the first review, the *Journal des Scavans*. In 1702 began the first daily newspaper, the *Daily Courant*. Each of these was imitated rapidly in many parts of the world: 'the press' was beginning to be one of the main institutions of Europe. In several ways, it is true, its later developments were as yet only dimly foreshadowed. The purveyance of news was at first in other hands than those which wrote to influence opinion. The earliest newspapers were like their forerunners the news-letters, collections of information from correspondents, facts about war and politics or signs and wonders. They did not meddle with literature, and the literary or scientific journals also kept to their own bounds. One-sided news was common enough: the Protestant correspondent in the Thirty Years' War has his way of telling the story, and the Catholic his own. But the leader-writer came late: it was not for some time that argumentative articles began to be combined with the news in the same sheet, and not until much later that the newspaper leader became the principal vehicle for forming political opinion. The seventeenth and eighteenth centuries, or more exactly the period from the Reformation to the French Revolution, constituted the golden age of the political pamphlet. Special circumstances made this phase begin and end at rather different times in different countries. For England Macaulay, in his essay on Addison, defined its height as the time from the end of the licensing of the press to the beginning of the regular reporting of parliamentary debates. In France the great days of the pamphleteers began somewhat earlier; but everywhere, though their character and influence varied with the social and political conditions, the later seventeenth century saw them in full cry.

Another thing which distinguishes the journalism of the seventeenth century from that of the modern world is that it was less commercial. Every one knows that advertisements, open or concealed, are the basis of the finance of modern newspapers, and that they often have something to do with their policy. That state of things has been brought about by the fusion of several distinct elements which had then met but not combined. There were advertisements, handbills, and placards pasted to walls, very soon after printing was invented and long before there were newspapers. Quite early they were printed in newspapers themselves, and beside the regular newspaper press there grew up in the seventeenth century some of the special kinds of commercial periodicals, 'advertisers' and lists of current prices of various commodities or of stocks and shares. But at first there was comparatively little money in advertising, because it was slow to take its place in the business world. The early newspaper advertisements are not predominantly commercial; there is a larger proportion of lost dogs, lodgings to let, and miscellaneous trivialities than now, and those items which are commercial relate more to special types of business like auction sales or lotteries or patent medicines or luxuries than to 'staple articles'. Thus it was not until the reign of George III in England that the fateful discovery was made of making the advertisements pay for the news. Nor was there as yet any indication that literature would become the distinguished poor relation of journalism. The success of Steele's *Tatler* was the first hint that a periodical might arouse literary interests in a large and very remunerative public. It may also be said that the *Tatler* and *Spectator*, coming at the time when such a public was first available, gave the first hint of that dilution of literary quality which is necessary for the purposes of mass consumption. A witty essayist, Mr. Bonamy Dobrée, has called Addison 'the first Victorian'.[1] His almost commercial decency and respectability do indeed give a foretaste of the age of broadcloth.

The changes in the outward condition of the literary life could not fail to be mirrored in what was written. The contrast between the literature of the beginning and that of the end of the period may be expressed in many ways, but it is remarkable that, whatever point of view is taken, its general effect is much the same. The student of pure literature observes that there prevailed at first in each of the vernacular

[1] *Essays in Biography*, 1925.

literatures, especially when the rush of inspiration from the Renaissance began to fail, a taste for the difficult, the obscure, even the pedantic. Spontaneity was lost, but violence remained, and under different names at different times and places poetry and prose were clothed in verbal inversions, thought was deliberately contorted, allusions were made which had to be hunted out, sentences which had to be reread backwards. Ben Jonson in England, full of real life as he was, had something of these faults. They were at their extreme in the verse of his Spanish and Italian contemporaries, and not far from it in the metaphysical poetry of John Donne and his school. They were not universal. The desire to persuade is inimical to obscurity, and there were always propagandist writers who respected their readers sufficiently to write clearly. St. Francis de Sales is lucid; so were the English radicals like the Levellers. Then again there is the lucidity of the exact thinker: Calvin was a master of it. There is the easy familiarity of French and English letter-writers. But the desire to impress by a difficult style was characteristic of the early seventeenth century. It resembles the tricks of the baroque in painting and architecture, which pursued the grand to the borderline of the grotesque. In the course of the century it was ousted from one stronghold after another by a perfectly opposite spirit, that of neatness, lucidity, the intelligible and the simple. The economic historian relates this change to the change from an aristocratic to a bourgeois public. He sees how utility and instructiveness become the aims of English writers in the days of Pope and Addison and Defoe, and how they were to spread southwards over the literature of Europe. His explanation is, however, only partial. Another side of the truth is seen by the historian of thought, to whom the new tendency is only another expression of what he has seen working in the history of science and learning.[1]

[1] See above, pp. 125, 298, on Grotius and Comenius. The one great exception among the writers of the later period is Bayle who, in spite of his critical sense, prefers the display of erudition to relevance. He rightly calls his *Pensées diverses sur la comète* (best ed. by E. Prat, 2 vols., 1911–12) an 'étrange amas de pensées'. His *Dictionary* (1697, first Eng.

It may even be called without much injustice a scientific tendency. For the new methods which they applied to thought the scientists demanded improvements in language. The old rambling complexities of sixteenth-century prose would not serve their turn. In France Montaigne was one of the promoters of 'rationalism', but as a writer, quite apart from his preference for suspense of judgement, he was more concerned to take a roundabout road and see many curious prospects on the way than to make the shortest journey to a conclusion. All this was altered for the men who thought mathematics the type of all good reasoning. Pascal, himself a mathematician, wrote about the deepest problems of the universe with an insistent will to prove the truth. So doing, he created that prose of exactness and economy of means which has been ever since the vehicle of what we call the Gallic logic, and the Gallic irony. He knew and explained what he was doing. The other scientists were working in the same way; the adequacy of the French language as an instrument of expression was being carefully examined. The dictionary of the Academy belongs to the same movement, and if Fontenelle exaggerated when he attributed 'l'ordre, la netteté, la précision, l'exactitude qui règnent dans les bons livres depuis un certain temps' to 'l'esprit géométrique', there can be no doubt that the two tendencies were closely allied.[1]

Even the *salons* helped in the same direction. In them the purifying of language was one aspect of the growing refinement of manners. They were the scenes of endless and often very acute discussions on subtle points of grammar or the exact sense of words. Their influence can be clearly traced, for instance, in 'the versification of good sense and select diction'[2] of Malherbe. In Holland the social circle called the 'Muiderkring' had its share in the movement for purifying the language. In England it was as in France. The older prose had its great masters. Milton was one and Sir Thomas

tr., 5 vols., 1710), a rich mine of facts and ideas, has the entries in alphabetical order but is one of the least orderly of all great books.

[1] 'Sur l'utilité des mathématiques', in *Œuvres* (1818), i. 34.

[2] Hallam, Pt. III, cap. v, sec. 3.

Browne was another. What they wrote was sonorous and impressive and full of marvellous images, but it was not clear. Sir Thomas Browne, who when he wrote on scientific subjects discussed the most patently absurd of popular fallacies with a caressing indulgence, never became a member of the Royal Society. He was not in sympathy with its spirit, and it showed little patience with the old-fashioned use of language of which he was one of the last and most skilful adepts. Dr. Wilkins, the brother-in-law of Oliver Cromwell, one of the earliest members of the society, studied minutely the relation of words to thought. Like some of his contemporaries in other countries he tried to work towards a symbolic language which should be as precise and as free from irrelevant atmospheres and associations as the notation of mathematics.[1] The society as a whole, as we are told by its first historian, exacted from its members 'a close, naked, natural, way of speaking; positive expressions; clear senses; a native easiness; bringing all things as near the Mathematical plainness as they can'. They were to write without 'amplifications, digressions, and swellings of style: to return back to the primitive purity, and shortness, when men delivered so many *things* almost in an equal number of *words*'.[2] This spirit spread outwards into the language of polite literature generally. Even the historian Bishop Burnet, whose style is natural and vigorous but incorrect, believed himself to have caught it, and in contrast with Clarendon he did truly belong to the new school. The homely virility of Richard Bentley was his own creation, but neither he nor Swift could at any earlier period have written as they did. Addison, who became the recognized model for imitation, stood for 'the essential and inherent perfection of simplicity of thought above that which I call the Gothic manner in writing'.[3]

The scientific revival might seem by itself to account sufficiently for this change in the armoury of thought, but in reality another tendency equally assisted it which we have

[1] *An Essay towards a Real Character and a Philosophical Language*, 1668.

[2] Sprat, *History of the Royal Society*, 1667, p. 113.

[3] *Spectator*, No. 70.

hitherto seen as the opponent of science. While science was emancipating itself from the authority of the classics, that same authority was being invoked in other regions to destroy the grandeurs which science was expelling from prose. Even in prose it was not only the mathematical clearness that set the example, but also the directness and terseness of the classical, especially the Latin, writers. Bentley, Swift, and Addison were influenced by these. In poetry, it was the classical writers who set the standard: Pope in England, following Boileau in France, revived the maxims of Horace's *Ars Poetica*, and one of their principles was that

> Words are like leaves; and where they most abound
> Much fruit of sense beneath is rarely found.[1]

In poetry as in prose the change of style was wedded to a change of content. The classical tendency meant harmony, dignity, and purity, not only in words but in sentiments and construction. It meant indeed something much more classical than the classics. To us at the present day the value of the great Greek authors lies in their nearness to realities. We have eyes for their colour and concreteness, and for the warfare in their bosoms between reason and the manifold irrationalities of human nature. In the seventeenth century it was not this that was observed in them. They were valued for their remoteness from the Gothic and the barbarous, and just as their statuary survived as white marble, stripped of its pigments, so their literature, partly because it was seen through the clarifying medium of Latin taste, seemed to embody an abstract and superhuman regularity. Classical forms had been adopted by some of the dramatists all through the time of the Renaissance. After 1650 they were in general use, and the Gothic was discredited. Dryden rewrote Shakespeare smoothly and according to rule. Milton's *Samson Agonistes* was the last imitation of Greek dramatic form for a long time in which there was anything of the volcanic heat of thought which smouldered under the religious ritual drama of the Greeks. The new classical

[1] *Essay on Criticism*, lines 311–12.

manner was to Aeschylus and Euripides what Canova was to be to Pheidias.

In this lay its strength. It must be judged not by its resemblance to the archetypes from which, in fact, it selected rather than copied, but by its services in its own time. The French classical drama, the greatest literary creation of the second half of the century, is still the typical product of the French mind and one of the living literatures of the world. To appreciate it requires from the modern Englishman the deliberate acquisition of a foreign point of view. Its purpose cannot be stated without referring to standards which seem to us external to the work of the artist. The first of these standards may seem to operate in a merely negative and limiting way. It is the observance of certain rules which were found in authoritative ancient texts, chief among them the unities of time, place, and action. The second also appears to be restrictive, though it too has the positive result of heightening the effect of unity and simplicity: it is the use of faultless diction in a carefully polished style. Corneille bowed to the linguistic criticisms of the Academy. Racine departs from this correctness sometimes, though only very slightly, in the attempt to make a play more lifelike, but verisimilitude is less his aim than appropriateness, a consistency in the representation of character, which again seems to be external, decided by a process of reasoning more akin to the working of a critic's mind than to the spontaneous, irregular, first-hand creation of a Shakespeare. Racine indeed was, like all his contemporaries, his own critic: his prefaces are vindications of his plays against the aspersions of his fellow poets that he was falling short of the standards. What is more, in all his work he was upholding a system of morality, and this was a reasoned system, well ordered, simplified, even conventional; and it, too, was an external standard which was present to the poet's mind before he began to write, and by which the characters were measured as virtuous or evil. The structure of the plays fits in with these purposes. Each person and each situation may be explained in a short formula. The conflicts are joined and resolved with a neatness which may be called geometrical.

This is generalized art, from which the local, the temporary, the particular, are almost excluded. The palaces and temples which form the scenes of its masterpieces are merely a lightly indicated framework for the action. What we need to know about the circumstances of the characters, their occupations, or their environment in time and place is scarcely more than we can grasp in a moment as the curtain rises. But instead of making them into empty types or abstractions, this merely relieves them from the incrustation of what is irrelevant to the central interest of the artist. What is delineated is not a crowd of men and women, with their clothes and their mannerisms and the confusion of their daily lives, but the interplay of the great human passions. Jean Racine was the man who carried this method to its culmination: a long line of earlier dramatists had prepared the way. Educated at Port Royal, he wrote his best works during the period of the greatest political power of Louis XIV, and his great successes nearly coincide in time with those of Molière, the most eminent French writer of comedy. Comedy cannot reach the same austere simplification as tragedy, but so far as may be, the characteristics of Molière resemble those of Racine. He, too, passed over the complexities of human nature, and, though he gives us much of their social environment, each of his leading characters is the embodiment of one simple ruling passion, the miser, the hypocrite, the misanthrope, the jealous husband.

There never existed a man who was a jealous husband or a misanthrope, or a miser or a hypocrite without having some other qualities at the same time, but if this is a weakness in generalized art, it has its compensating advantage in the fact that jealousy, misanthropy, meanness, and hypocrisy have always and everywhere existed, and can be recognized by the playgoers of the most distant times and places, to whom the subtleties of Hamlet or the idiom of Falstaff may mean nothing. The abstract and the general can be translated and transplanted. There never was a literature better suited for export than the drama, the poetry, and the prose of the age of Louis XIV. In the original or in translations, or in imitated or adapted forms, it became the standard literature of Europe. We know how it furnished the English stage in the reigns of Charles II and his successors. In much the same way, more in one country and less in another, it overran Europe. It was one of the most effective instruments of French influence, and it was in literature, even more than in politics and education and manners, that the age which began with Louis XIV was the age of French ascendancy. The French tongue rose gradually during the century to the position of an international language. At the beginning, with the decline of the universities and with the growing isolation of the national churches, Latin was losing ground as the language of learning. It was in the course of the century almost altogether ousted from the imaginative *genres*. Milton, Grotius, and a score of others were famous for their Latin poetry, but that artificial literature, which is now almost completely unread, was dwindling in quantity and fast losing its vigour. When it had ceased to be used in verse except for prize-exercises and inscriptions, Latin remained predominant in academic treatises, except in England; but even for these serious subjects, the vernaculars made headway. It was less so, from their own nature, in mathematics than in scientific and sociological subjects. It was less so in eastern than in western Europe. But the seventeenth century prepared the way for the general abandonment of Latin in the eighteenth. Descartes struck one blow at it when he wrote the *Discours de la méthode* in French. The conjunction of all these changes within a few years, the diminishing use of Latin for scientific purposes with the rise of a great intellectual movement which expressed itself in French, the decadence of Latin poetry, with the prestige of French poetry, helped French to spread beyond the frontiers of France. The Dutchman Huygens chose it as the language of some of his scientific treatises. Between the time of Richelieu and that of Racine it became the language of diplomacy for most of the western and northern states.[1] It began to be a second language for polite

[1] See F. Brunot, *Histoire de la langue française*, vols. v and viii. It became the language for negotiations with the Empire not, as used to be said, from the Treaty of Nijmegen but from that of Rastadt in 1715.

society, and even the conversational language of aristocratic homes, wherever, as in Poland or Gelderland, the native speech was such as to isolate its users from the world. Where periwigs were the fashion, there French was understood.

If the literary history of the century is to be summed up, it may then be said that the first half, roughly speaking, saw the working out of the rich mines of the Renaissance, and the second the opening up of the resources of the age of reason, with its easy, polished accomplishment, and its cosmopolitanism under French auspices. But a glance still further ahead, beyond the age of reason into the romantic period when men turned back to the earlier seventeenth century and behind it for their inspiration, will remind us that these tendencies were superficial. The literatures of Europe had reached a greater uniformity of standards and practices than at any other time, and this was of incalculable value for the world's education, but like the uniformity which is inculcated by the schoolmaster it often drove individuality underground. It could be attained only by excluding certain subjects from literature and by treating the rest only in a prescribed manner. Not only vulgarity and violence, but soon grandeur and strength disappeared from the author's range, and the abstract emotions which had been first distilled from materials of real life were soon compounded by a mere fusion of intellectual elements. For all their cultivated airs, the inhabitants of Europe had barbarian blood in them, and the time was to come when, tired of simulating the sentiments they approved, they were to give way to those they had been taught to repress. The serenity and logic of the poets and critics and essayists were on the surface. Instead of really assimilating all human nature into their interpretation, they had merely used what could be treated by their methods, and forgotten that the alliance between literature and reason had been drawn unnaturally close.

Imaginative literature is nearer akin to religion than to science. In those regions where science has nothing to say, one or other of these two less systematic interpretations of the world must make up for its silences. When science takes a great subject out of the realm of mystery and miracle into that of law, it seems to be lost to literature and religion, so that these appear to possess only a constantly diminishing residuum of the universe. Either or both of them may, therefore, at times dispute the advances of science and try to keep for itself some part of its inheritance to which science asserts a title. An example may be taken from Milton, and it is the more apposite because it shows him doing this both as an artist and as a man of religion. In his Italian travels he had 'found and visited' the great Galileo, and in *Paradise Lost* he twice refers to the 'Tuscan artist's' observations of the moon. There is, however, in one of these places a note of hesitation. The astronomer's vision is 'less assured' than God's. Milton might have accepted Galileo's astronomical conclusions and made them part of his own cosmology. We find, however, that when his Adam interrogates the archangel on 'celestial motions', Raphael doubtfully answers:

> This to attain, whether heav'n move or Earth,
> Imports not, if thou reck'n right; the rest
> From man or angel the great Architect
> Did wisely to conceal, and not divulge
> His secrets to be scann'd by them who ought
> Rather admire.[1]

It was not that Milton could not understand the arguments, or that he had objections to lodge against them. What moved him was the need for wonder, and the need therefore to retain the inscrutability of the universe. These were needs which his contemporaries were content to neglect. When he wrote the men of letters were already losing interest in the vague, the vast, and the irrational whether in nature or in man.

Not that they were ever completely expelled from poetry and fiction. Even Pope's *Essay on Man* is more than an essay: it is somewhat like a poem. And, around and below the best accepted literature, there still lived the unsophisticated writing which chose and handled its subjects without regard to the rules. While the 'noble savage' was becoming one of the stock figures of conventional and sentimental literature, travellers and historians were drawing their clumsy portraits

[1] *Paradise Lost*, Bk. VIII, lines 65 ff.

of slave-hunters and cannibals. While the academies were perfecting the rules of occasional verse, scholars were getting to work on the *Heimskringla Saga* and making ready the revival of the barbarous epics of the dark ages of Iceland, of Germany, of France, and of England. All over Europe there were chap-books and children's tales. We all know the *Contes* of Charles Perrault—Puss in Boots, the Sleeping Beauty, Cinderella—even if we have never heard the title or the author's name. They wear the dress of the *grand siècle*, but belong to every age and none. It was in the seventeenth century that the Punch and Judy show emerged from its undiscovered origins and travelled from Italy to England. Popular art and national feeling, religious prejudice, and rough humour were not extinct. Although the garden of literature presented, as it has never done before or since, a prospect of smooth lawns and symmetrical avenues, the winds were bringing back the seeds of wild flowers and strong growths of the forest.

XXI

PAINTING AND ARCHITECTURE[1]

It is not difficult to see that seventeenth-century painting is an expression of the general life of the time. The painters were men of their age, for the most part, as was natural in that smaller world, much less cut off from men of other occupations than painters have been in subsequent times, when they were more conscious of their peculiarity as artists. They thought as their neighbours thought; their social life was lived in close contact with the rest of the community. Their work was influenced by the tastes and demands of their patrons, and, as the painter tended to become more an individual working by himself than a member of an organized craft, while, at the same time, there came to be a greater number of laymen trained in critical appreciation, the patron's influence over the artist came to grow. Thus there is a general correspondence between the history of painting and the history of civilization. The use of classical subjects and of the apparatus of classical antiquarianism by painters follows the course of Greek and Latin studies among the picture-buying classes. It was not for nothing that Rubens lived in the city where Lipsius, whose portrait he painted, worked for the printing-house of the Plantins. His humanized and psychological treatment of themes from classical mythology owes much to the humanism of the second stage of the classical renaissance. So, later in the century, Nicolas Poussin is very near akin to Racine. Both express with simplicity and refinement an interpretation of the antique which is at the same time a vehicle for presenting what is permanent and common both to antiquity and their own time, for Racine the great human passions, for Poussin the elegances of formal arrangement and rhythm. Just as the classical influences were reflected in painting, so was the history of religion and of the churches. Rubens is

[1] A useful, though not invariably trustworthy, general guide, with short lists of books, is the *Histoire de l'Art*, ed. A. Michel, vol. vi, 2 parts, 1921–2.

of the reformed Catholic church which made the pompous marble pulpits of the Spanish Netherlands and the pretentious eloquence of Bossuet. Rembrandt was touched by the biblical and oriental learning of his own Leyden and Amsterdam. Even the scientific and mathematical discoveries of the age had their reactions on pictorial art. The technical mastery of optical problems matched with a determined realism, an almost universal effort to paint what was seen. Although many of the great show-pictures of the century have an exuberance which piles up figures and draperies without regard for the possibilities of nature, yet it is all rigorously and skilfully composed, keenly observed. Its extravagance is not that of fantasy but of intentional building. The poetry and sentiment which this art engenders are created from corporeal elements.

The history of painting cannot, of course, be exhausted by enumerating the different tendencies from outside which meet in it and make it part of life in general. A school of painters lives by a tradition which affects at most a few hundreds of workers, and, although they may be scattered over several cities and a succession of generations, they are, none the less, bound together by this tradition as closely as the members of one college or one regiment. They see and know one another's pieces. They imitate and surpass. However dispersed, they are still united by the strong bond of a common work. And in the history of a close, intense tradition of this kind, personality plays a part far other than it can ever play in the history of senates and camps and courts. The story of painting is a collection of human lives, not capable of being summed up in formulae and general causes.

Another aspect of this fact may be expressed by saying that national and local differences are much more evident in painting than in intellectual or even in practical things. Art was, indeed, then, as always, international. The stock of technical accomplishment with which the seventeenth century began was what was passed on to it from the Italian schools of the sixteenth, and they in turn had gathered it from widely different local sources. The Italian influence on the painters of other countries was not merely something from which they started, but also something which was constantly renewed by new connexions such as the visits of Velasquez to Italy, the buying and sketching of Italian paintings by Rembrandt, and the resorting of northern students to the Bolognese and other Italian academies. It was in Italy that the Poussins and Claude Lorrain did their work. Throughout the seventeenth century a succession of southern influences can be seen to affect the development of transalpine painting.

The Dutch and Spanish painters of the century did indeed derive less from their contemporaries in Italy than from the masters of the sixteenth century. Italian art changed its character and exerted a new kind of influence in new directions. Significantly it ceased to respond to influences from outside: there was a good market in Rome and Florence for Dutch pictures, but it was to the galleries of princely collectors that they went, and little resulted from their coming except, after an interval, something in the manner of minor masters like the Venetians, Canaletto, the painter of architectural landscapes, and Longhi, the genre-painter. The great creation of seventeenth-century Italy, and above all of Rome, was the baroque. Long before then there had been traceable, side by side with the classicism which found its themes and its designs in the remains of ancient Greece and Rome this different tendency, or rather a number of tendencies towards adventure and away from restraint. There was a romantic tendency, for instance in the landscapes of the Neapolitan Salvator Rosa, 'wild Salvator', with their grottoes and groups of bandits. There was a tendency to the gigantic and the grand. In Rome in the aftermath of the Counter-Reformation they grew stronger and were fused together. Rome grew in size; by 1600 it was twice as large as it had been in the high Renaissance; by 1700 it was nearly half as large again, and it was radiating its influence over Catholic Europe. Its splendid new buildings, its entertainments and religious festivals, the concourse of scientists and ecclesiastics in the brilliant society of its salons, gave it power. This power was the greater, and at the same time restricted to narrower spheres of operation, because it was controlled by the Catholic reform. Censorship and patronage in close alliance eliminated the pagan strain of the Renaissance; but the new age of draperies and fig-leaves was also the age of emotionalism. The Jesuits were now the greatest patrons of the arts in Italy and under their auspices religious painting came to be as relentlessly material as photography, but unrestrained in its dramatic handling of ecstasy or horror. The anguished saints of Guido Reni were the work of a great painter, but of one who belonged only to the world that the Counter-Reformation had mastered.

In three countries art was independently alive: the Dutch republic, the Spanish Netherlands, and Spain.[1]

That a great school of painting should have grown up in the Northern Netherlands might at first sight seem astonishing, the more so since it had its birth and adolescence in the time of the political troubles of the late sixteenth century. When Karel van Mander, who deserves to be called the Dutch Vasari, laboriously collected and wrote the lives of his compatriot painters, a work which he finished in 1604,[2] although many of them were still alive, he may well have thought that he was dealing with a completed series. In the Netherlands the conditions might well seem adverse to the arts. Long before, in the days of the primitives who were merely legendary figures to Karel van Mander, there had been feudal splendours to which the painters had contributed and from which they had drawn a livelihood. The brothers van Eyck and their sister were favoured by the 'good' Duke Philip of Burgundy. Jean Mabuse was a court-painter to the count of Veere, and, at a critical moment in his career, won

[1] The most convenient book of reference for the art of both the Northern and the Southern Netherlands is Wurzbach, *Niederländisches Künstlerlexikon*, 3 vols., 1906–11. Since it was published some valuable sources for the outward history of Dutch painting have been printed. For Spanish painting A. L. Mayer, *Geschichte der spanischen Malerei*, 2 vols., 1913, may be recommended. Among critical works K. Voll, *Entwicklungsgeschichte der Malerei*, vol. iii, 1917, is valuable, as are many of the monographs on particular painters.

[2] *Het schilder-boek*: I have not seen the English translation by C. van de Wall (1936). A. Houbraken, *De groote schouwburg der nederlandsche konstschilders*, 3 vols., 1753, is a continuation.

the praises of the emperor, Charles V. But Charles was dead more than a generation ago. No more painters were wanted to put up triumphal arches for him, nor for any one else, in Mechlin and Brussels. The names of some of the young noblemen who had revelled and joked with the artists had passed into a sterner history. Frans Floris, a wealthy, ostentatious, and bibulous painter, had associated on familiar terms with the young prince of Orange and the counts of Egmont and Hoorn: those names by themselves, without any commentary, tell of the dark days which came down, dark not only with civil strife but also with the Calvinistic hatred of the arts. Time and again the biographer has to say that this or that masterpiece of a sixteenth-century painter was destroyed in the iconoclastic outbreaks of the mob. One good painter fell into despair at the destruction of the work by which he had hoped to be remembered in after times, and even incurred some risk by talking freely about it to a powerful man of the new opinions. Another, a glass-designer, thrown entirely out of work, had to change his craft and work at etchings of Aesop's fables. A third was burnt as a heretic; a fourth who turned Anabaptist and died in exile was not even allowed to lie quiet in his grave; a fifth survived in the surprising character of a Protestant divine. Besides these great ills, Karel van Mander complains of other conditions of the times, some of which are the things which modern sentimentalists choose to admire. Painting was not regarded as an art, but as an 'ambacht', a base word which meant both a craft and a trade. Painters were cramped by the system of guilds, and in some towns there were not only vexatious difficulties about getting into the guild, especially for strangers, but when they got into it, they had to share it with low people like the makers of kettles and harness and such-like.

Yet Dutch painting lived and did not die. The lives which Karel wrote turned out to be those only of forerunners, and the greatest masters were still to come. Rembrandt was born two years after the book was published, and a few weeks before its author died. That fact is a challenge to the historian. It is easy to see what was against the Dutch school at that moment; is it difficult to find what was in its favour? What was there left, when religion and peace and courtly delights had all turned their faces away? The answer is that there were some old conditions and some new. The demand for the painters' products was never wholly interrupted: the tradition of interest in them was old and strong. Most of the towns where Dutch (or Flemish, which is the same thing) was spoken had painters' shops. The Walloons had little knowledge of the art, but even in Tournay and Courtray, which were bad enough places in that way, it was possible to pick up odd jobs at painting pairs of bellows. In other places there was much more to do. When the churches ceased to ask for pictures, the market for portraits was still good. A bakers' guild might want to decorate its hall with an appropriate picture of Shadrach, Meshach, and Abednego 'in the glowing oven'. The 'doelen' and 'regent' pictures, groups of the officers of train-bands in the towns, or of the various corporations and charitable or social institutions, had been in request since the first half of the sixteenth century. With the rise of the wealth and self-confidence of the Dutch burgher oligarchy in the seventeenth century more of them were wanted, and bigger and better pictures. So it was that a number of good painters immortalized in these great portrait-groups the dignified splendour of the Dutch golden age, and that such work provided the subjects for the most daring achievements of Frans Hals and for the *Stalmeesters* or 'Syndics', one of the supreme masterpieces of Rembrandt himself.

It is indeed true that the ending of religious art in the Protestant Netherlands was the very change which released the great movement of private art for which they became famous. So long as they were Catholic and feudal, they had the same sort of Catholic and courtly art, though with a difference, that the Italians taught them. The difference was that their painting tapped a deep spring of common popular life, a homely northern humour and a pleasure in familiar things which belong partly to their race and habits, partly to the great commercial middle-class which had already made Bruges and Antwerp and was making Amsterdam when Protestantism began. Protestantism was strong enough to turn art out of the churches, but not strong enough to turn it out of the country altogether; so that it was still wanted, but now it had to do no longer with Madonnas and Crucifixions, forbidden things, nor with classical allegories, suitable for the princes and cardinals, who were now enemies on the other side of a newly created frontier, but with men and women in their ordinary clothes, with ships and bourgeois houses, with cattle and meadows, with windmills and inns. From the time of the political separation of the northern and southern Netherlands, but not before, in style as in the choice of subjects a definite North Netherlands school, not itself seriously divided by local differences, can be sharply distinguished.

English travellers, coming from a country where painting was still for the rich and cultivated class, were surprised to find that in Holland it was appreciated by every rank.[1] John Evelyn tried to give an economic explanation of the fact. Evelyn was only twenty when he went to Holland in 1641, but he may have touched up long afterwards the curious entry in his diary for 13 August in that year.

'We arrived late at Rotterdam, where was their annual mart or fair, so furnished with pictures, especially landscapes and drolleries (as they call those clownish representations), that I was amazed. Some of these I bought and sent into England. The reason of this store of pictures, and their cheapness, proceeds from their want of land to employ their stock, so that it is an ordinary thing to find a common farmer lay out two or three thousand pounds in this commodity. Their houses are full of them, and they vend them at their fairs to very great gains.'

Whether the shortage of land had anything to do with it or not, which appears very unlikely, it is certain that this democratic appeal of Dutch art was one of the greater facts of the century. It was not confined to painting. Delft tiles, of which many thousands survive in Holland and the countries to which they were exported, are specially interesting from

[1] Peter Mundy, *Travels* (Hakluyt Society), iv. 70, says that 'many times blacksmithes, Coblers, etts., will have some picture or other by their Forge and in their stalle'. This was in 1640.

this point of view. For the most part they were quite humble accessories of the decoration of houses, but they never sank below a creditable level of taste and execution, were never without a touch of real craftsmanship, and yet they were turned out, so far as was then possible, by what is now called 'mass-production'. The prosperity of Holland was accompanied by a marvellous rise in the common man's appreciation of visible beauty. Nowhere is this better seen than in the close relation of painting to daily life. The Dutch painters added new provinces to the realm of the imagination. There arose new *genres* of painting. If the painting of sea pieces, which was one of them, did not produce any work of the highest rank, in another, the painting of views of towns, there were, besides many of a more ordinary excellence, the paintings of Delft by Jan Vermeer. Both these classes of paintings, like the interiors and peasant-scenes and still-life and other characteristic specimens of the school, stood in that relation to life which is attained when an art, instead of being exotic and aloof, intimately belongs to a whole community of men and women. The painters, even some of the greatest among them, merely expressed clearly and skilfully realities of which their neighbours were indistinctly aware.

This is the relation of the school as a whole to its public, and consequently to the permanent public of posterity which shares the vision and the limitations of that intensely living and yet matter-of-fact Dutch bourgeoisie. The one great man whom all agree to place highest among the Dutch painters has this local quality too: in his paintings and etchings Rembrandt often enough handled the landscape and portrait-subjects which were familiar to his contemporaries; even in his historical or Biblical or legendary themes he is a man of his country and of his time. As he advanced, however, through his lifetime of close application and uninterrupted technical improvement, he lifted himself into the highest rank of all, that of the few artists whose work speaks to the many and yet can never be adequately comprehended by the most educated eye nor imitated by the nimblest hand. He made of shadow and light the means for producing over and over again the miracle of the artist, which gives the conviction, or it may be the illusion, that it has displayed the inmost secrets of the universe. What little we know of his biography, an outline blurred by too much conjecture, seems to show the greatness of character which may sometimes accompany this endowment. He lived, in prosperity and in adversity, first for his work. He cared nothing for the praises of his inferiors; he had no vulgar social ambitions. 'A picture is finished', he said, 'when it satisfies the master.'

In spite of its wide popularity Dutch painting was as much an exception to the general course of seventeenth-century art as was the Dutch republic to seventeenth-century government. Not all the Dutch painters were equally national, but some of the national qualities, especially the homeliness which we have noted, were common to many or most of them. Rembrandt and some of those who stand close to him, like Vermeer, have another special quality, hard to describe, which is seldom found even in the greatest works of visual art. They achieve entire freedom from affectation. Rembrandt, in some of his early pieces like the 'Night Watch', has the pomp and display which generally please in a commissioned painting. In some of his later portraits he discards almost all adventitious detail and gives a direct rendering of a man or a woman and nothing else; but he can reach the same sincerity even when he retains much detail, and even when, in the manner of his time, he keeps costumes and trappings which, in the work of others, would be theatrical. The picture of a man in armour, now in the gallery at Glasgow, is one of these masterpieces. The armour is the armour of no particular time and place. The man is only the artist's son in fancy dress. But the picture is a picture of something more real than any human man-at-arms. In this inner simplicity, as in many other things, Rembrandt rose above his time. To his contemporaries the pomp and costume were ends in themselves: save among the Dutch, exceptions can scarcely be found. So, too, in the treatment of the human body, the Dutch stand apart from their contemporaries. They take it as they find it, without refining elegance; they can be coarse; but they are neither squeamish nor voluptuous. The general life of the time is better represented by the fleshly and upholstered art of the neighbouring Southern Netherlands.

In personal character or in the circumstances of their careers no two men of their calling ever presented a more abrupt contrast than Rembrandt and the older Flemish master who must be named with him as one of the most famous painters of the world. Rembrandt was born in 1606, Rubens in 1577: they died in 1669 and 1640 respectively, their lives being thus almost of equal length. While Rembrandt's was outwardly almost uneventful except in its personal relations, that of Rubens was full of movement and adventure. His father was an exile for religion who fled from Antwerp before the approach of Alva, to become the lover of the drunken and unfaithful wife of William the Silent. Rubens himself, brought up by the Jesuits, had the characteristic ideas and beliefs of the Flemish counter-reformation. He would have stood out in any age or any profession. His energy can only be called superhuman. Understanding and writing seven languages, rich, ostentatious, and intellectually able, he was a diplomatist as well as a painter, and as a painter he dominated the activity of his numerous pupils and assistants, indeed of the whole Flemish school. His work, as different from Rembrandt's as his life, mirrors one side of the century. Not light and shade but colour is his instrument. Magnificence, force, and enjoyment are his results. His crowded canvases and opulent nudes express ambition and its triumphs.

For the school of which he was the head, the historical preparation had differed from that of the Northern Netherlands exactly as might have been expected from the difference in the political fortunes of the two groups of provinces. In the sixteenth century, painting had reached a high development in the great Flemish towns, and had absorbed much of the Italian influence. Some of the best of the painters who grew to maturity during the troubled period at the end of the century carried on its tradition unimpaired far into the seventeenth. The two sons of 'Old' Brueghel, themselves the fathers of distinguished painters, carried on the work of their wonderful family in Antwerp during the time when the armies of Maurice and Spinola were deciding the fate of the country. The colour, the humour, and the sense of landscape in their pictures, as in their father's, belong to the Netherlands and carry something from their medieval art forward into the new world. In the south as in the north, the demand for painting survived the troubles of the revolt and war, but there was no religious change except the change which had taken place within Catholicism itself. The buying of religious paintings not only continued, but was even accelerated by the need for making good the havoc done by Calvinist fanatics. The archduke Albert, who with his consort Isabella of Spain became the ruler of the Southern Netherlands in 1598, was a patron of the arts. Although anxiously intolerant of heresy in his provinces, he extended a special toleration to the painter Michael Mierevelt, who was not merely a Protestant but a member of one of the most hated sects. During the absence of Rubens in Italy, where as a young man he was for eight years court painter to the Duke of Mantua, Albert tried to procure his return to his own country. The painter's genius had by then hardly manifested itself, but when he returned in 1609 he almost immediately took his place as the greatest painter of Flanders. The activity of the school may be judged from the fact that in 1610 the Antwerp guild of painters had 398 members, in 1614 no fewer than 465. The days of pageantry returned, to reach their height in 1635 with the entry of the Cardinal Infant Ferdinand as governor, when Rubens had charge of the gorgeous display. He and his followers filled the churches of Flanders, the palaces of Paris and London, and the rich men's houses of western Europe generally with such works as could delight the wealthy and great. No name among them can be set beside that of their master. Sir Antony van Dijck, the best of the followers, will always be remembered as the interpreter of the England of Charles I, and, like Teniers, a pleasant *genre* painter, has his place in the transition from the full strength of the baroque to the capricious lightness and daintiness of the rococo.

That transition, which we have already noticed in literature, will occupy our attention in a moment, but first it is necessary to say something of the third great national school of the time, that of Spain. There is indeed less similarity among the Spanish painters of the time than among those of Flanders, or even of Holland, and this is natural enough in a country so much divided by physical barriers. Yet in some respects, in spite of this and of their wholly different political histories, the three schools may be said to stand in much the same relation to the example and influence of Italy. This may possibly seem strange to the modern Englishman, who thinks of the Italians and the Spaniards as two southern peoples, Latin in speech, alike in their Roman Catholic religion and both living on the shores of the Mediterranean. It is well to remember that it is farther in a straight line from Madrid to Rome than from Rome to Brussels or from Brussels to Madrid. That does not prove that in intercourse and civilization Rome and Madrid were not the most closely linked of the three capitals, but it does at least show that to expect Spaniards to be simply the imitators of Italian art would be as mistaken as thinking the political connexion of Spain and the Netherlands geographically appropriate. The communications of the Spanish artists with their masters were not much easier than those of the kings with their Flemish subjects. Spain was the remote western outpost of the mainland, and its cities, walled in by plateau and mountain, were the homes of intensely separate national and local traditions. Hence it is interesting to notice how the greatness of the Spanish school coincided in time with that of the northern schools. It was under the influence of the Italian renaissance in the sixteenth century, and its steady course was not interrupted by political upheavals, but favoured by continuity in church and state.

A painter of amazing depth and power was El Greco, a Cretan by birth and a pupil of Titian in Venice, but a painter of Spanish men and women, with something in him that could not be of any other country. He was original to the point almost of eccentricity, certainly of mannerism; his twisted figures and unnatural colouring appeal to our own tormented age. El Greco was in middle life when the century began; but the painter whose place at the head of the

Spanish school is settled not by fashion or the taste of a passing moment, but by the full consensus of centuries, came later. Both the birth and the death of Velasquez fall intermediately between those of Rubens and Rembrandt; he was forty-one when Rubens died. His origin was Portuguese, and his art in its maturity owed much to his Italian journeys, but he too is as Spanish as Cervantes. Not only has he the Spanish realism, but he has given, with a technical skill which has never been surpassed, a record of that which was central in the life of his country. The only seventeenth-century king who is still alive is Philip IV of Spain, whom Velasquez painted. The clearest statement of the dignity and chivalry in which Spaniards still set the world an example is in his picture of the surrender of Breda to Spinola. In all respects he is one of the great men of the century, belonging to the courtly old world that lasted better in unhappy Spain than in the striving countries of the north.

The other interests of the period had also their painters in Spain, and among the religious artists of the second half of the century Murillo has long been one of the most popular, because he has, with sufficient skill in colour and composition, that emotionalism, or perhaps rather that sentimentalism, which serve with the great public as substitutes for religious and aesthetic experience. There is no need here to say more of him, or of many other painters of the century, because these were not originators, especially not originators in their way of looking at the world. As painters they did what they had been taught to do, either by their predecessors or by contemporary examples in the three living schools; in their wider task they followed the tendencies of the times, where literature or the circumstances of their lives pointed out the way. So far from being innovators, they built up the organization which has done more than anything else to prevent artists from innovating, and has, at times, even gone far to deprive them of their first necessity, the power to see for themselves. In painting, as in literature, it was the age of academies. The guild organization in the northern countries was, as we have seen, dying out in painting as it was in industry, at the beginning of the period, and in

Italy also the place where the painter learnt his work was ceasing to be the workshop of the master. That perfect method of vocational training fitted ill with the princely or aristocratic patronage which made the painter an appendage of the life of leisure and distinction. The more he became a fashionable and superior figure, the less he had in common with the makers and sellers of things. In Bologna in 1585 the Caracci family had started their academy. This was a well-organized school of art in which the pupils learnt from professors. It became the model for the new method of training, which has continued in the orthodox schools of art to the present day. In 1648 there was set up in France the Académie de Peinture et de Sculpture, which completed the separation of the artist and the craftsman. It was imitated before the end of the century in more than one continental centre, leaving England and some other countries to adopt the same plan later. The earlier academies were great resorts for foreign students, and even before they were numerous they had great influence over the aims and methods of painters all over the world.

The academic virtue of correctness may be exacted by painters of very various ideals. In that century it was applied by practitioners of the tumultuous baroque; but the union was unstable, and, as it turned out, the new attitude had a share in putting an end to the rule of that style. In the latter part of the century, when painting was not merely conservative or eclectic, it underwent the same change which we have already traced in poetry, in prose style, and in the general complexion of thought. During the reign of Louis XIV the painting of France, assimilated to the French accomplishment in other directions, took a more prominent position. As it advanced in comparison with the declining or stationary arts of the neighbouring countries, all alike relinquished the grand and the grandiose, to content themselves with a more limited and more intelligible perfection. But as this change went forward, painting ceased to be so important a part of life. None of the painters who were working at the end of Louis's reign, not even the enchanting Watteau, are among the artists who can be said to have, in the wider sense, historical significance. In Holland, Flanders, and Italy, there was not a painter even of the second rank. An interval of exhaustion had succeeded the great productive period. When the masters had climbed to the summits of achievement, the schools, as they always seem to do, lost ground and trod a low, roundabout path, awaiting new guides to heights unknown.

Thus ended one of the periods in which painting was at its highest importance in comparison with the other arts. Of its relation to literature enough has been said already, and this is not the place for a survey of the minor graphic arts such as engraving, nor of the minor applied arts which make articles of utility or ornament. A word, however, may be said about architecture and its attendant sculpture. In the Middle Ages, architecture had been the mistress of the arts, and every other, including painting, was subordinated to it. With the Renaissance painting emancipated itself and became more and more a direct and independent mode of creation: that process was now complete, and the typical picture was now an easel picture, painted not for a given position in a building, nor with special reference to what were to be its surroundings, but for itself alone, its limits being its own frame. In size and subject and manner, no doubt, it was made for a parlour or a dining-hall or a cathedral as the case might be; but, once there, it was meant to be looked at alone, and to the exclusion of its context. In this sense, painting had put itself on a level with architecture; and the baroque brought architecture under the influence of painting.

The central figure of the baroque was the Cavalliere Bernini, who lived from 1598 to 1680. He was a man of unlimited personal and artistic ambition, painter, architect, and sculptor, the friend of a pope, the transformer of Rome. When he visited France national jealousy stood in the way of his executing anything larger than a statue of Louis XIV, but he travelled like a prince. The most famous of all his works, the colonnade in front of St. Peter's, is plain and massive, but it has a theatrical vastness, and baroque building generally confounded structure with ornament. It worked with spaces and masses, concealing outlines and making them disappear to give an illusion of infinity. It paid the minimum of attention to the intractable nature of its materials. Bernini delighted in coloured marbles, in bas-reliefs with gilded clouds, in portrait-busts with brilliantly executed marble periwigs, in painted ceilings with swirling, gigantic figures. In detail 'naturalness' was carried to the point of absurdity. The architect of a church in Venice ornamented the bases of his pilasters with the ground-plans of fortresses. But 'natural' detail was framed in an immense *décor*, in which story was piled upon story with a freedom like that of the painter whose only limit is the stretch of his imagination.

This tendency to sweep and flourish was carried farthest in the southern countries of strong sunlight, but it suited the mood of South Germany and Poland, and it competed with the classical tradition throughout Catholic Europe. In the prosperous and practical countries of economic and political success, it was held in check both by a conservatism of taste and by a sense of utilitarian convenience. In England, France, the Netherlands, and Germany, at the beginning of the century, the Renaissance had not completely overlaid the Gothic art. It had provided first ornaments, then new modes of design on the greater scale. As the century wore on, this often charming combination of two alien elements gradually gave way before the increasing strictness of classical standards, as they had been formulated by the Italian Renaissance. Inigo Jones came back to England from Italy, taking Denmark on his way, and set up buildings which might have been in Vicenza. In France Versailles was built, the monument of the material greatness and the spiritual limitations of Louis XIV, and it became the model for the palaces and public buildings of the world. The last part of the century was the time of the greatest uniformity that has ever been known in the architecture of western Europe as a whole since the Roman empire fell. In part this was due to the dominance of French example, in part to the admiration for Italy and the ancient world.

Yet this uniformity was never absolutely completed. The

Cotswold cottage and the Westphalian *Bauernhof* escaped it. In England there were never ten consecutive years in which, in some obscure town or another, there was not made some substantial building of which the manner preserved strong traces of the medieval arch or tracery. Sir Christopher Wren himself, the greatest of the English architects in the new manner, typical of the learned designers who followed the old designing builders, was also one of those who fanned the sinking flame of the Gothic style. From his time onwards a movement went on with gradual acceleration which was to preserve and to revive the older type of building. In this, to be sure, as in so much else, England was insular and exceptional, but the development is an index to the nature of the classical tendency which it interrupted. Elsewhere, as in England, that tendency was not merely artificial, though art is everywhere made and does not grow. It was the product of social conditions which favoured the classical, the cosmopolitan, and the pretentious. Only a royal and aristocratic age could have brought it about, and only an age in which kings and aristocrats were the patrons of artists and men of learning. It furnishes one more example of the tendencies which we have encountered in every department of the century, the increase of wealth, the growing power of the state and the intellectual revolution.

The painters and sculptors and architects worked for their great and powerful masters; but they brought with them skill and aptitudes acquired here, there, and everywhere, often far away from grandeur and politeness. Some of them, like the engraver Callot, *gentilhomme Franche-Comtois*, chose squalid and repulsive subjects, the horrors of war and the picturesqueness, such as it was, of gypsies and wandering beggars. Some, like the innkeeper of genius Jan Steen, amused and attracted the well-to-do with the unsophisticated gambollings of a simpler kind of human animals. An artist's model from a sordid Roman alley might become immortal in an altar-piece, and the awkward posturing of a village dance might provide the pattern for a statuary group. The schemes and rhythms of art, like its subjects, came from below as well as from above, and so, though sometimes it seems that inspiration moved downwards from the great artists through the schools to the people, from another point of view it seems that standardized, cosmopolitan, consciously polished accomplishment must have withered away if it had not been constantly refreshed from the earth of direct and unembarrassed feeling. Everywhere, beneath the coherent arts, was the unschooled energy of swarming life.

In this book we have examined some of the ordered and organized activities of the seventeenth century, but we have never been far away from the world in which reason, purpose, and standards of perfection play no such part. Superstition jostled against religion; languages contended with dialects; physicians competed with quacks; the rabble murdered statesmen. While Italy was the teacher of Europe in so many refinements, her brigands and bravoes plied their trades all through the century. Francesco Cenci stood his trial in 1595, and the loathsome record of his family was not relieved, as it is in Shelley's drama, by the noble character of the villain's daughter. Almost a hundred years later the same underworld was revealed by the crimes which Browning transmuted into the poetry of *The Ring and the Book*. To see the seventeenth century as it really was we must include all this evil, and also the endless variety of the second-rate, the ordinary, and the trivial. Wherever we look there is the same duality, and everywhere it occasions two opposite historical explanations. On the one hand there is the view which was accepted at that time, that whatever is valuable in common life has been disciplined or ennobled from above. Historians have identified the highly artificial origins of popular customs which seem fresh and spontaneous. The morris-dance originated not on the village green but in the stately hall. The mummers' play may derive from a dim antiquity but its text as we have it, owes much, directly or indirectly, to Richard Johnson's *Famous Historie of the Seaven Champions of Christendom*, which was printed in 1596–7.[1] The herbs and simples of popular medicine were scraps of superseded science. There were folk-songs, fairy-tales, and legends which had come down from the literary masters of distant times and places. In

[1] Sir Edmund K. Chambers, *The English Folk-Play* (1933).

contrast with all this is the romantic theory, which was to irrigate every field of thought in the eighteenth century, from literary criticism to political theory, that all life grows organically from the people, and that civilization is empty unless it is enriched from the inexhaustible resources of human nature. Woodrow Wilson summed up one side of this view of history: 'I see this written on every page: that the nations are renewed from the bottom, not from the top; that the genius which springs up from the ranks of unknown men is the genius which renews the youth and energy of the people.'

This doctrine has been expressed in an analogy which is more than an analogy. In a flower-garden there are rare and perfect specimens which could only have been produced by patient cultivation, by taste and scientific knowledge, but every one of them, however much it depends on shelter and care, is lineally descended from some plant which once grew wild in the open. Yet this analogy has been used to illustrate the opposite principle. If once the gardener's attention is relaxed, if his glass-houses are broken and his tools lie idle, the garden will be choked by weeds and his choice plants will degenerate. The analogy is ambiguous because it is more than an analogy; it is an example taken from the double process of civilization itself. The institutions and endeavours, old and new, which embodied the organized thought and will may seem to have belonged only to the exceptional higher strata of mankind: the old educational routine of the classics, the new scientific movement with its growing command over matter, the inherited feudal usages, the capitalist innovations in the multiplication of wealth, the new devices in government and administration may all be analysed without any reference to the common man except to regard him as the underling; but such an analysis stops short before it is finished. In their daily operation these institutions and endeavours all included renewal from below. We have seen how the flexible structure of classes allowed the lucky and the ambitious to step into the shoes of highborn failures. However many men of equal powers were denied a fair field for their exercise, it was at least possible for men of genius like Jean Bart and Newton to rise from modest stations. The schoolmaster, the clergyman, the employer, if they knew their business, looked out for promising boys who might earn promotion. Society had not yet invented safeguards for equality of opportunity; but neither was it rigid enough or confident enough of its own security to allot functions to individuals altogether without regard to their capacities. There were great chances even for impostors and adventurers. In a bungling and disjointed way the custodians of civilization accepted something of what was offered them from the throbbing obscurity of popular life, enough to make it one of the great ages of the world.

APPENDIX

RACES AND LANGUAGES

It is not uncommon to see attempts to build up a picture of Europe from its primary elements, and, when this is done, the starting-point is usually physical geography, after which human geography is considered. About physical geography we have said nothing because in the main it does not change: we have noticed only the puny attempts of man to modify it by making roads by land and water or by blocking natural roads with forts and booms. In the ordinary modern atlas there are maps which appear to give the anatomy of human geography in much the same way as geological maps give the anatomy of physical geography, namely, the maps which show the distribution of races. They are there partly because many historians believe in 'race' as one of the master-keys to history, and partly for a more practical reason.

Much use is made in our time of ethnographical statistics, figures which show the distribution of the 'races' or nationalities. They are wanted mainly because for about a century past frontiers have often been drawn according to the boundaries or supposed boundaries between these groups of men. In the seventeenth century we shall not expect to find them, for that principle had not been invented. Modern scholars have brought into prominence one or two phrases, beginning as early as an utterance of King Louis XI to the Walloons and including one of Henry IV to Savoy, in which it seems to be anticipated.[1] Louis says: 'Vous autres Wallons, vous parlez françois, il vous faut un prince de France, non pas un Allemand.' Henry's alleged words are: 'Il étoit raisonnable que puisque vous parlez naturellement françois, vous fussiez suiects à un roy de France. Je veux bien que la langue espagnole demeure à l'Espagnol, l'allemand à l'Allemand, mais toute la françoise doit estre à moy.' But both these kings are on much firmer scientific ground than

[1] Guizot, *Hist. de France*, ii. 432; Mathieu, *Hist. de Henri IV* (1631), quoted by Sorel, *L'Europe et la révolution française*, i. 257, 271.

modern writers who have theories about nationality and race. They put forward a clean, simple, and matter-of-fact, if rather disingenuous, practical argument that it is convenient to have all the people of one speech under one prince. They did not bring in the idea of race, and philologists now rightly refuse to bring it in when they are discussing the distribution of languages. The distribution of languages is a definite matter about which much is known, both in the way of facts and in the way of scientific conjectures about causes. The distribution of races is at present in a very different stage of exploration. If a race means a body of men united by physical consanguinity, little is known about what races there are now or have been at any given point of time. If it means a body of men having in common certain physical characteristics, a good deal of information is being collected and provisionally arranged about what races there are now, but next to nothing is known about their continuity with similar groups in the seventeenth century. In neither case has any connexion been discovered or formulated with precision between race and language, nor, *a fortiori*, between race and national character.[1] National character must be assumed, in the absence of any reasonably critical attempt to connect it with some physical *primum mobile*, to be partly moulded by social environment. It must be assumed to be not only a cause but also a result of the whole history of the nation concerned. But, since language-groups coincide pretty closely with groups of the same customs and social organization, the linguistic map is as interesting to the historian as any ethnic map ever could be.

The first thing to notice about the distribution of languages is its stability. Of all the maps which can be drawn to illustrate the human geography of Europe in the last three hundred years, the map of the languages shows least change. While the political frontiers have almost all moved far and often, the linguistic frontiers have remained comparatively steady. Of such changes as took place in the seventeenth century few affected large numbers of people. None the less

[1] See the conclusive discussion by Professor G. C. Field, in *Hibbert Journal*, vol. xxi (1923), pp. 287 ff.

they sprang from causes which are worth examination. The map was, as it is now, extremely confused, but such changes as were then going on, or as have come since, may be classified, very roughly, in two sets. On the one hand, in various ways, the map was growing simpler, on the other, fresh complications were being added to it. In the seventeenth century the former tendency was, on the whole, the stronger. Several languages were then spoken in Europe which have since died out, and these were then visibly declining. In the duchy of Hanover, on the lower Elbe, there was Polabic, an island of Slavonic speech which vanished in the eighteenth century. In the British Isles there was Cornish, which was already declining. The vanishing of these languages was only the most striking manifestation of a tendency which had other results. In a number of different ways some of the languages, roughly speaking the languages of the strong and prospering political units, were making headway at the expense of their neighbours. Perhaps the most important side of this movement was one which had been going on since the invention of printing or even before it, the establishment of the great 'standard' languages, like New High German or, later, literary Dutch, which were more or less intentionally formed by a selection from the confusion of dialects and then spread by schools, universities, churches, official departments, all the institutions whose purposes were served by uniformity or by maintaining a definite standard of correctness. That tendency would, in any age, be hard to measure or to show on a map. It would be almost impossible at the present day and quite out of the question for the seventeenth century to form an idea of the proportion of 'correct' speakers of any language in different social classes and different localities. We may, however, venture to say that generally dialects were weakened in proportion to the growth of political unity. In France the literary language made progress, though it was slow progress, at the expense of Provençal and other local patois. In disunited Italy dialect literature was still important, and the best-known European writer of the eighteenth century who wrote not in a standard language but in a dialect was the

Venetian Goldoni. With certain reservations the principle may also be applied to the other regions of Europe.

Where the frontiers divided not dialects but distinct languages, their movements are easier to trace. As a consequence of the French conquests from the Spanish Netherlands, French made some slight advances at the expense of Flemish.[1] Here there is no evidence of deliberate pressure. Louis XIV and his ministers made little effort to encourage French in the annexed provinces where it was not spoken. In Alsace, to take one instance, they did not enforce the laws for its official use. Language was not thought of as a means of assimilation; religious conversion was then the method preferred. The English followed the same line in Ireland. The Irish language lost ground in the seventeenth century through civil war, famine, and the forcible displacement of those who spoke it. At the end of the century it was still receding somewhat, but it was spoken by the population of most of the country. There was opposition to the printing of Irish books and the use of Irish as a vehicle for Protestant propaganda by Robert Boyle and his friends; but there was no attempt to promote education in English. When a country was governed by a limited ruling class it did not matter what language the masses spoke, so long as they kept their place.

There were, however, places where language was already a symbol of independence. From the time of Dante this attitude to language had been spreading over Europe, and it may well have a primitive fitness that goes back far beyond Dante. The king of England was 'lord of this langage' to Chaucer,[2] and the French kings whose sayings we have quoted may have been aware of a community of political sentiment among those who spoke the same vernacular, or at least may have wished to evoke it. In Geneva in the time of Scaliger the Savoyard dialect was spoken in the senate and anyone who used French had to pay a fine. In Béarn also all legal proceedings were in Béarnais 'pour montrer

[1] G. Kurth, *La frontière linguistique en Belgique et dans le nord de la France*, ii. 78–9. This work is a model well deserving imitation elsewhere.

[2] *Astrolabe*, Prologue.

qu'ils sont libre et à eux'.[1] So, conversely, there were some governments which deliberately tried to put down exceptional languages. The electors of Brandenburg-Prussia, from 1678 to 1708, tried and failed to extinguish the small Slavonic patch of Wendish speech south of Berlin.[2] Their motives may have had no reference to nationality: it may have been administratively inconvenient to deal with a few thousand people who could not understand German, and there may have been no question of keeping them apart from the Czechs and Poles. But the history of Bohemia, where Czech and German had long existed side by side, affords a clear instance of a national language-question. After the Habsburg victory at the White Mountain the Jesuits conducted a deliberate and largely successful campaign against the language, destroying books. In no modern language are so many books known to have disappeared.

These cases where the spread of a major language had a political aspect were still highly exceptional. Generally only social and intellectual forces were at work. The decline of Welsh was as marked as that of Irish; but there was no trace of a political ground for the weakening of this language. John Aubrey wrote: 'It wears out more and more in South Wales, especially since the Civil Warres.'[3] The increase of intercourse with England was the main reason and its effect was the more marked because, in consequence of the censorship laws, there were no printing-presses in Wales or nearer to Wales than Oxford. Elsewhere the improvement of communications had a like effect. In the Alps some of the isolated patches of German among the Romance languages and contrariwise were dwindling as they are dwindling still.

Thus in many parts of Europe there was, for several reasons, a smoothing and levelling of linguistic contrasts of all kinds. The opposite process, the introduction of new

[1] *Scaligerana*, s.v. 'langue'.

[2] C. Anderson, *Memorial on Behalf of the Native Irish* (1815), and *Historical Sketches of the Ancient Native Irish* (1828), Appendix.

[3] *Brief Lives*, ii. 329. The decline of Cornish is mentioned in the same place. It was in the same century and for the same reason that the old Scots language sank to the status of a dialect.

irregularities, new patchiness, in the linguistic map was also going on, but it is safe to say that it was less common and that, where it happened, it sprang from special, exceptional, local causes. The most striking example, and the most important for subsequent history, of a more uniform map in the seventeenth century with a very multiform map now is in Hungary. Here the change seems to have been almost entirely due to the policy of the Habsburg rulers of the eighteenth century. After the recovery of central Hungary from the Turks and the reunion of Transylvania with the rest of Hungary at the end of the seventeenth century, the Habsburgs pursued a deliberate policy of weakening Magyar power, or at least the power of the Magyar landowner. This had many sides—the creation of large German estates, the introduction of German and Slovak colonists, the permitting of Serb and Roumanian immigration—and, although modern Magyar writers have an interest in magnifying what happened at this time, as compared with earlier times, to increase racial diversity, there can be little doubt that large numbers of people were affected. It is thought that the proportion of Magyar-speakers was halved (80 per cent. to 39 per cent.). This mainly happened after the seventeenth century, though it is not denied that most of the different kinds of immigration had been known in earlier times and that considerable numbers of Serbs and Roumanians came in during all the second half of the seventeenth century; but from the point of view of the seventeenth century, what is interesting is to notice the reason why the late 'denationalizing' of Hungary was so different from that of Bohemia, which also the Habsburgs attempted. The reason is that in Hungary there was a void to be filled up, the emptiness caused by the Turkish invasion and the subsequent wars.

This might appear to be a suitable point for discussing the other movements of emigration which went on in the seventeenth century. The writers of that time said a good deal about them when they were discussing population, and writers of the present time are apt to dwell on them when they discuss questions of 'racial' distribution. In reality, however, they are not of much significance in either of these respects. There is indeed some reason to think that, with the general improvement in the means of communication, the whole population of Europe was becoming more mobile, but this is uncertain, and in our own day we know that some of the greatest waves of emigration, like the eastward drift of Russians, have owed nothing to railways and little even to roads, so that in old days better means of movement need not necessarily have meant more movement. What movement there was tended, for several reasons, to be more clearly recorded as time went on and so perhaps to appear unduly large in comparison with the vaguer events of earlier times. But even the greatest of these recorded migrations can have had little effect on 'demography'. In the early part of the century the Moriscoes, the descendants of the Moors, were ruthlessly expelled from southern Spain, but the survivors of this exodus were lost to Europe. France lost probably a quarter of a million or more of Huguenots through the persecution of Louis XIV; but in the countries which received them they are more a subject for the genealogist and the local historian than for the scientific analyst of 'races'.[1]

[1] For a brief survey of languages see A. Meillet and W. Prinz, *Einführung in die vergleichende Grammatik der indogermanischen Sprachen*, 1909, pp. 24 ff.; for races W. Z. Ripley, *The Races of Europe*, 1900.

INDEX

FRONTIERS OF WESTERN AND CENTRAL EUROPE IN 1715

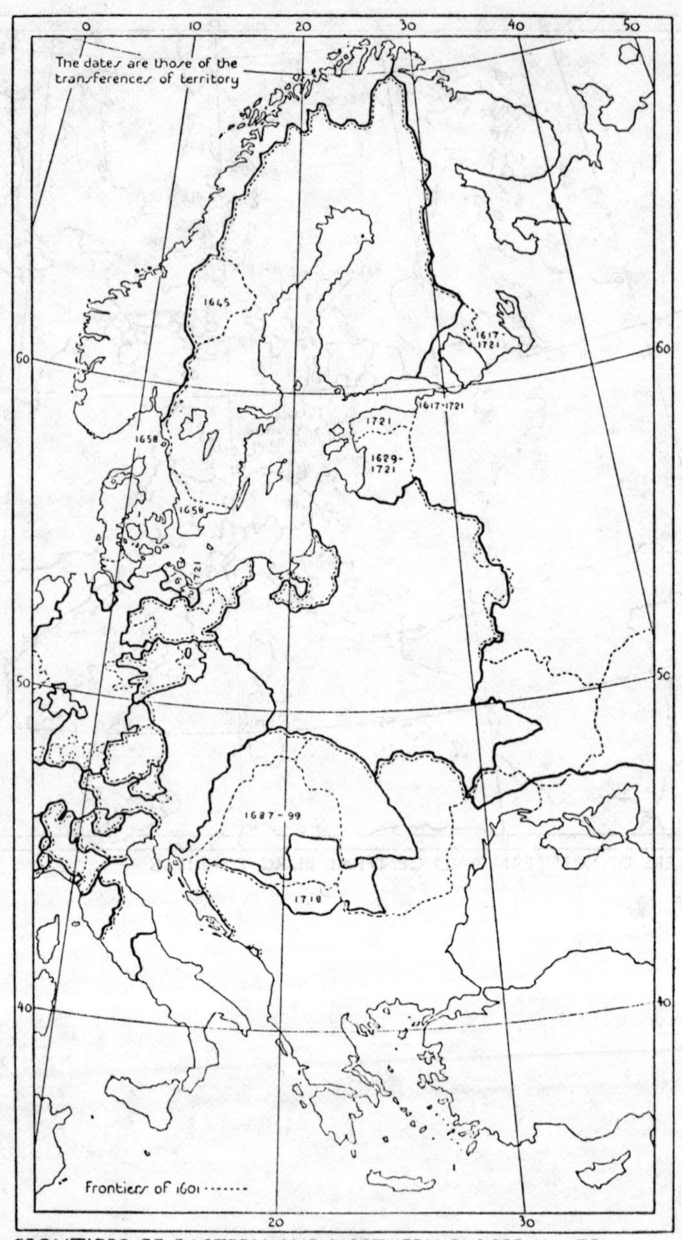

FRONTIERS OF EASTERN AND NORTHERN EUROPE IN 1721

UNIVERSITIES OF EUROPE

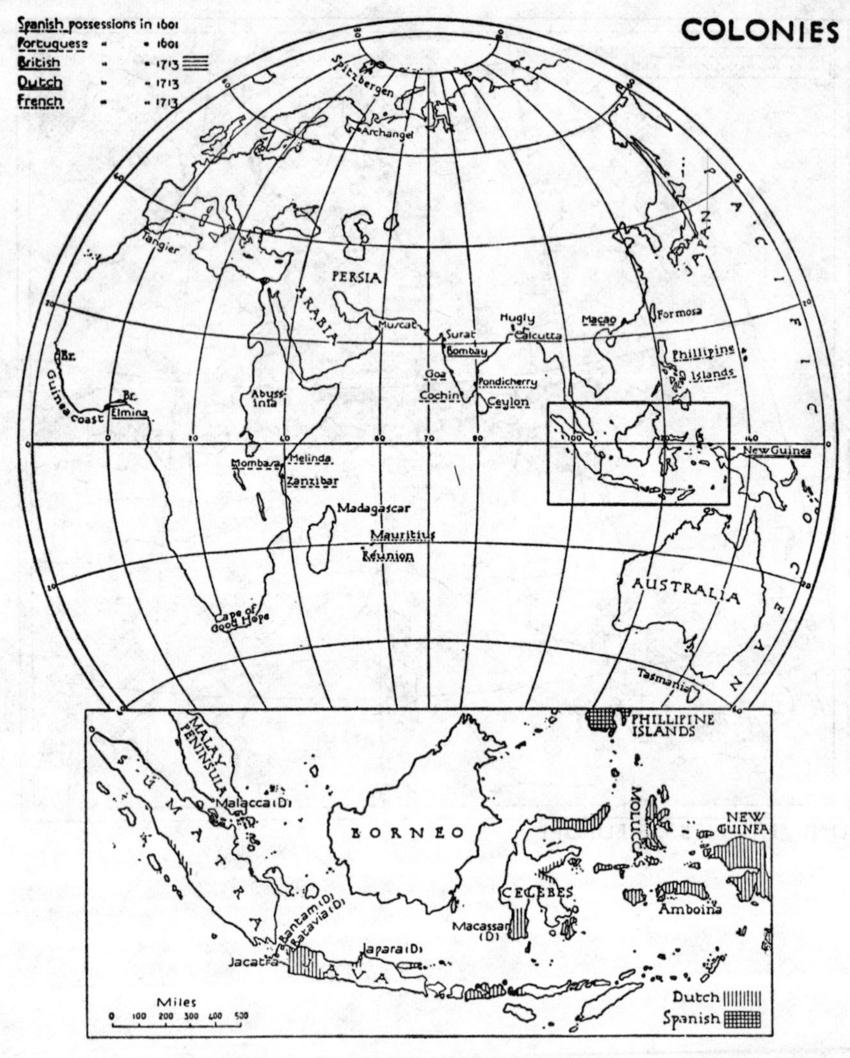
COLONIES
Spanish possessions in 1601
Portuguese " " 1601
British " " 1713
Dutch " " 1713
French " " 1713
Spitzbergen
Archangel
Tangier
PERSIA
ARABIA
Muscat
Surat
Bombay
Hugly
Calcutta
Macao
Formosa
JAPAN
PACIFIC OCEAN
Phillipine Islands
Goa
Cochin
Pondicherry
Ceylon
Br.
Guinea coast
Br.
Elmina
Abyssinia
Mombasa
Melinda
Zanzibar
New Guinea
Madagascar
Mauritius
Réunion
AUSTRALIA
Cape of Good Hope
Tasmania
MALAY PENINSULA
SUMATRA
Malacca (D)
BORNEO
PHILLIPINE ISLANDS
MOLUCCAS
NEW GUINEA
CELEBES
Amboina
Macassar (D)
Bantam (D)
Batavia (D)
Japara (D)
Jacatra
JAVA
Miles
0 100 200 300 400 500
Dutch
Spanish